SAVING BUFFALO BASEBALL
1956 BUFFALO BISONS

Howard W. Henry Jr.

NFB Publishing
Buffalo, New York

Saving Buffalo Baseball:1956 Buffalo Bisons/ Henry Jr. — 1st Edition

ISBN: 978-1-953610-22-5
        1. Title.
        2. Sports>Baseball>Buffalo Bisons
        3. History>Sports>Basebal>1956 Buffalo Bisons
        4. History>Buffalo New York
        5. Baseball>History of
        6. Regional>Buffalo New York>Athletics>Baseball

NFB
NFB Publishing/Amelia Press
119 Dorchester Road
Buffalo, New York 14213

For more information visit Nfbpublishing.com

This book is dedicated to my dad, Howard William Henry, who took me to the 1956 home opener, and to my mom, Catherine (Ahlheim) Henry, who gave my Rawlings three-finger Stan Musial glove to a kid in the neighborhood who didn't have one—and you have two, she said (oh, Mom!), and to my wife, Lee Ann Grace, who has educated me about opera and tolerated my manias for baseball and ballparks.

CONTENTS

FOREWORD

IT WAS THE fall of 1954. I was nearing 13 years of age, and the Cleveland Indians were setting an American League pennant-winning record of 111 victories. Growing up in Western New York, all of my friends were Yankee fans. I was the different one, having been born in Ohio. The Indians were my team. Finally, they were going to win a pennant!

And then came the end of September and the end of youthful dreams. Teenage puberty raised its pimply heads and the Indians got … squished! It was a story of two fly balls. Both took place on the same day in the same ballpark: September 29, 1954, the Polo Grounds in New York City. The home run hit by Vic Wertz in the eighth inning traveled some 440 feet or so and was turned into just a very long out by a miraculous Willie Mays, whose throw kept the Indians from scoring on what would have been a world-class sacrifice fly. The pop out struck by Dusty Rhodes two innings later, in the tenth, traveled all of 256 feet and just out of the grasp of a desperately leaping Dave Pope. It went into the right-field stands for a three-run home run that both won the ballgame for the Giants and demoralized the Clevelanders. The Indians got swept, four games to none.

A year of personal mourning followed, to be replaced by a new hope.

My dad grew up in Buffalo, New York, where each opening day of the baseball season he and his classmates got out of school at midday in order to go see the Bisons play ball. The school board officially closed the schools so the children could enjoy themselves. What a community-minded idea! When the team was purchased by the community in 1955 to save baseball for the city, my dad bought 12 shares and eight tickets to aid the cause. Twenty dollars.

Dad and mom raised our family in the nearby southern suburb of the Township of Hamburg, and, beginning with the spring of 1956, Dad initiated an annual routine that took me out of school every morning of every home opening game in order to have my eyes examined. I truly did have terrible eyesight. I loved the game and tried diligently, but I couldn't hit or catch what I couldn't see.

Of course, the optometrist my family went to was located in Buffalo on lower Main Street, about two miles south of the ballpark. My appointment was always set for noon. What could we do after I had had my vision checked but go to the baseball opener? It was much too late to drive me back out to school.

Those are still wonderful memories of times spent with my father. At the ballpark, the sun was always shining and the temperature was warm and inviting. (Real Buffalonians know what early April weather can truly be like, but memories create a life of their own.) The grass was always a deep green, the scoreboard a looming black, the outfield walls splashed with colorful ads and the home plate, the bases and the home uniforms a brilliant white. We ate "steamers" (hot dogs) with bright yellow mustard and bags of peanuts. Concessions were passed down the rows of fans, hand to hand, while the money flowed in the opposite direction to the vendor in the aisle. Open paper cups of beer went that same way, hand to hand.

Cracking bats, long balls belted into the left field screen or over it, or into Woodlawn Avenue beyond the right-field fence, doubles whisked down the lines, crisp double plays, and exciting catches in the outfield. How simple and good was life, even if the experience only lasted for a couple of hours.

Perhaps I have written this account of the 1956 season in an attempt to keep that simple world alive, a world of hopes and heroes and a boy's enchantment with a dream that he would not himself realize. Perhaps it is something of an escape, although escaping every now and then is a useful, maybe even a very necessary thing to do. And it was a time with my father.

In the course of the research and the writing of this book, the reality of the exceeding effort of the front office, the ballplayers and the community to keep baseball alive in Buffalo in the face of multitudinous hardships encountered throughout the long season presented itself to me. It is a long season. It wore me out just reading about it, researching it, reliving it and trying to put it into the right words to describe it. You may experience a similar reaction in your own reading. "What will go wrong next?" I found myself shaking my head and asking that question as I read of yet another injury, of yet another financial challenge to be faced and overcome, another treacherous betrayal by a supposed ally.

This was a hard life, this baseball season that I read about in the 1956 game accounts from the distance of many decades later. This was a game these men were playing as their job, a way to pay the rent and put food on the table. This was not the simple life it seemed from the vantage point of the seats where we sat, or from the box scores I pored over at home in the newspapers. In the stadium, the only obstacle we fans encountered was sitting behind a post that blocked part of your view of the field if you got there late.

My dad made these memories possible to me, but others associated with the team helped, too, and not just the players. They were in the front office and on the playing field, behind the scenes and behind the microphone (thank you, Bill Mazer and those White Owl Wallops). My thanks go to those associated with that long-ago Bison club, but also to the other professional baseball people here in Buffalo and elsewhere who were kind enough to meet with me or correspond with me and answer my questions about the game. My thanks go to the ballplayers from 1956 through 1961 who responded to me to share some of their experience of the city, the stadium and the games during their time spent in Buffalo.

My thanks particularly go to Louis Peter Ortiz, the second baseman for the Buffalo Bison squads from 1956 through 1958, and to his family for befriending me and assisting me in learning something about the life of a professional ballplayer. I was fortunate to meet Lou in 2002, tracking him down through an internet search.

Lou's career fascinated me. He came to Buffalo at age 33 and tied for second place in the league in home runs in 1956. Luke Easter slugged 35 as the International League home run leader. Lou and Montreal's John Roseboro each counted 25. Lou hit 22 more in 1957. In 1958, his final season in pro ball, he hit 19. I believe he may still hold the record for most home runs hit by a Buffalo second baseman. Of the 66 total he struck in a Bison uniform, 64 came while he was playing the second base position. When I initiated this research as an adult, I looked for his major league statistics, but he has none. A second baseman who could hit like this? I couldn't believe it. Reality starts to dawn upon the unaware.

Lou Ortiz's baseball life parallels the story of many men who labored in the minors in the 1940s and 1950s, when teams and players were many but opportunities for advancement were few. The major leagues had only 16 teams (with room for only 400 players) and the owners held all the cards. There was no such thing as free agency in those days. Lou Ortiz was an outstanding fielder at the Triple A level, but he was not fast nor possessed of a very strong arm. The St. Louis Cardinals, who owned his contract, had tried him at both shortstop (he looked like Marty Marion, tall and lean) and third base, but the experiments did not pan out. Lou himself finally decided that if he was going to make it to the big time, he would have to do it at second base.

Despite his size (6 feet, 3 inches tall), Lou Ortiz was not a significant home run hitter. Long fly balls to left center were simply long fly outs. It wasn't until Wally Moses taught him to turn his hips into his swing at age 32 that the home runs started to come. Lou smacked 19 that year (1955), eight more than his previous best. Had the offensive ability come even a year earlier, Lou might yet have had his major league career. As it was, he had to settle for being an All Star second baseman in the International League in 1953 and 1954, being featured in that same capacity in Life Magazine in each of those seasons. No one faulted his defensive abilities. He led the International League five times in double plays, four times in assists, three times in put outs and three times in fielding percentage in six years as a full-time second baseman. In 2007 he was inducted into the Rochester Red Wings Hall of Fame.

Lou had signed with the wrong team, he told me. Back in 1946, after mustering out of the service, he had tryouts with both the St. Louis Browns and the St. Louis Cardinals. Only the Cards could offer him the $1000 signing bonus he needed to start a family, plus Cardinal starting second baseman Lou Klein had just jumped to the Mexican League and a super-confident young Lou Ortiz believed the major league St. Louis Cardinal second-base position would soon be his for the taking. Nobody figured that Red Schoendienst, pegged as the Cardinal shortstop of the future, would injure his right shoulder in military service in 1944 and again in 1945 in a fall as the Cardinal left fielder. (The Cardinals had him in the lineup in left while waiting for 1944's National League Most Valuable Player, Marty Marion, to finish his career at short.) The arm problem meant a shift to second base for the future Hall of Famer and the end of the road for any second-base challengers in the St. Louis Cardinal farm system for a long, long time. Having Lou Ortiz down on the farm was good insurance for the Cards in case they needed it, and after he had served a nine-year Reserve Clause sentence and newer talent was in the pipeline, the big-league operation was content to let him go.

Buffalo badly needed a second baseman for its 1956 squad, a veteran who could bring defense to the infield and a newfound potency at the plate. Lou Ortiz was available, and he and the Bisons both got the best of the deal. As with Luke Easter, Ortiz became a fan favorite in his three years in the city from 1956 to 1958, helping to lead the club to the 1957 Junior World Series. He was a skilled performer who rose to the challenge, although the games where he was stationed in left field in 1958 gave him fits. The club wanted to keep his bat in the lineup and install a set of younger legs at the keystone position. The experiment didn't work. Lou finished out the year back at second.

I am grateful to have been able to know him and to talk about those years with him.

Baseball is a hard game and a long season, as Lou passed on to me. One of my major challenges was deciphering some of the newspaper accounts and the box scores I was reading. I am grateful for having had microfilm access to the sports pages and the game accounts of the sports writers of the Buffalo Courier-Express (Bill Coughlin) and the Buffalo Evening News (Cy Kritzer). Most of the time, matters were very clear. On a number of occasions, however, I found myself scratching my head trying to figure out what was going on, and were the writers actually watching the same game, and why did some of the box scores not agree with the game accounts. Was it because of laxness on the part of the sportswriters? Was it because the writers at the out-of-town games didn't pass on accurate accounts? Was it due to the editors or the typesetters? Did the newspaper page run out of space and so game accounts and statistics were truncated? Was it too late at night and someone got sleepy? Did somebody have to run out to the men's room?

I went to other newspapers, especially The Sporting News, for additional sources to see what they might have to offer about the games in question. I sought to recreate some games—I had to recreate some games, inning by inning—in an attempt to make sense of what was going on in the conflicting accounts and box scores in front of me. I probably succeeded for the most part. The game summaries and the box scores I have written in these pages are my best effort at reconciling the confusion I sometimes encountered.

ACKNOWLEDGMENTS

THANKS GO TO many, many people for the production of this book, which I have been thinking about or working on in fits and starts for many years. It is time to finish the book and get on to other things.

Of course, I want to thank Lou Ortiz and his family for allowing me to meet them and for trusting me with his story, his scrapbooks and his memorabilia. I flew from Buffalo to Milwaukee in 2002 to meet him. He had driven in from San Diego to visit his brother, Vince, who lived in Wisconsin. The two men and their wives treated me to lunch as I overcame their suspicions that I was trying to take advantage of an old ballplayer and, amazingly, sent me home to Buffalo with a box of Lou's scrapbooks and loose clippings. I hadn't planned to do this, but I wound up archiving Lou's baseball history from 1950 to 1958, picking up where his wife Lois had left off after the three children started to come along.

Over the years, I met with Lou on a number of occasions, flying out to San Diego and also meeting with him and the family in Rochester during his 2007 induction into the Rochester Red Wings Hall of Fame. I returned the scrapbooks to him. I also returned his baseball glove. He had sent it to me in the mail as a gift, but I thought something that valuable needed to remain with the family. For the grandchildren, at least. I spoke with his sister Rosemary, a couple of his brothers and his daughter Lorraine. Lou and I kept in touch via mail and the occasional telephone call. "Hungry Lou," his baseball moniker, was a persistent man on the ballfield and a quiet man in his private life. He painted for a hobby, although he was embarrassed to be found out when Lorraine brought it up. He usually referred to himself as a "cowboy" (born in Albuquerque, New Mexico), a tough guy, a means of shrugging off both injury and emotional sensitivity, hardening himself for the combat of the ballfield.

Lou Ortiz died on October 3, 2010. I flew out to Lake San Marcos, north of San Diego, to attend the funeral and burial. A good friend of Lou's, Christine Simpson, loaned me a car so I could get to the church and the family gathering after the burial.

Other ballplayers from the 1956 through 1961 squads who were kind enough to write to me about their time in Buffalo were: Ruben Amaro, Babe Birrer, John Blatnik*, Bob Borkowski, Pete Castiglione*, Billy DeMars*, Carolyn Donovan (wife of Larry Donovan)*, Don Erickson, Bernadette Graff (wife of Milt Graff), Dallas Green, Ray Herbert, Ken Johnson, Lou Kretlow, Don Landrum, Joe Lonnett, Dave Melton, Bob Miller, Bobby Morgan, Ron Mrozinski*, Steve Nagy*, Cal Neeman, Al Neiger, William Taylor Phillips, Ted Savage, Norm Sherry*, Russ Sullivan, Dick Teed, Pat Tomkinson*, Bubs Weiss (widow of John Weiss)* and Bobby Wine. (*Denotes Bisons from 1956 team.)

Frank Offermann, Jr., son of the former club owner, met and corresponded with me and provided research materials. Dan Carnevale invited me to a Bisons game and treated me to lunch when I reached out to him. Vic Baron, a member of the 1966 Bisons, and Karen, Vic's wife, provided me with material for much of the background for the high-school players mentioned in the last chapter.

The folks at SUNY Buffalo State (State University of New York College at Buffalo) and the E.H. Butler Library were amazingly helpful to me in all of my research. Provost Dennis Ponton, Dean Gary Jones and Library Director Maryruth Glogowski made it possible for me to have special access to the library. Dan DiLandro, the Buffalo State Archivist, and Peggy Hatfield gave me much of their time and interest and even independently searched through various archival materials on my behalf to help me track down information I was seeking. I was also wonderfully helped toward the end of my research by Linda Wagner, Jane Richardson and Hope Dunbar. Chuck Newman and Al Reiss were early readers of other works I authored and gave me encouragement that helped me continue my writing efforts.

Cynthia Van Ness, Director of Library and Archives at the Buffalo History Museum (BHM), has been equally gracious in her assistance with my research, helping me track down material and offering suggestions to find corroborating detail. She both encouraged my research efforts and fixed the microfilm machines for me when they broke down. Amy Miller was an excellent source of assistance in the BHM library, as were other BHM personnel in the past.

The research librarians at the Buffalo and Erie County Library Central Branch were most helpful when I turned to the microfilm collection there.

I am a member of the Society for American Baseball Research (SABR). Members of this organization have helped me over the years with various aspects of research. Specific to this book: Ryan Brecker and Joe Territo, members of the Luke Easter Chapter, helped me research Rochester Democrat and Chronical accounts; Tom Grace, a local friend, encouraged me to join SABR many years back and has encouraged my writing; Ron Selter is the SABR baseball stadium guru and offered methodology for my analysis of Offermann Stadium; Stew Thornley offered advice on creating box scores.

And then there are friends with whom I have discussed the book and who have also helped in the process. Bill Krellner is a friend with whom I attend Bison baseball games as we discuss the teams and the players of the past. Bill has been a helpful resource for photos and program books. Playwright Darryl Schneider offered a way of expressing my writing. Photographer Rick Steinberg helped me figure out how to acknowledge the photographs Lou Ortiz and others had given me, as did his friend William Altrueter.

My niece, Robin Henry, added her editorial expertise to the final stages of the process, helping me to decide upon format and structure and printing of the book.

Most importantly, I am extremely grateful to my wife, Dr. Lee Ann Grace, who read through and edited this work, and tolerated my many "golly, this is interesting and let me tell you about it" discoveries. I am grateful for her encouragement of my manias.

I hope you find this history interesting and informative. If you are a Buffalonian or have Buffalo roots, you might find the name of someone from your family or friendship circle mentioned in this book, someone who was an active community member in 1955 and 1956 and helped in the effort to save the baseball club, or someone who attended the home opener in 1956 or another game during that year, whether in spring training or the regular season. Bill Coughlin of the Courier-Express was diligent in naming the fans who came out to the games. I have included those names in this book in the index, thinking that it might be fun for the reader to see if he or she or someone they knew or somebody in the family was mentioned.

When it comes to reading about the season itself, you may choose to take it one day at a time, the way the season was played. This could give you a feel for the length of the season and also the highs and lows experienced by the players and the fans as and when the events happened. You, too, may find yourself saying as you read, "Oh, no, what else can go wrong?" or "Well, finally we're getting somewhere," only to have those hopes dashed the next day. Persevere! The Bisons did!

I hope you enjoy the book. All the errors in it are mine, all mine!

Howard W. Henry, Jr.

CHAPTER 1: ABSENTEE OWNERSHIP

BUFFALO, NEW YORK, was booming in 1955. The city's population had surged to 580,132 according to the 1950 census, making it the 15th-largest municipality in the country. Good-paying jobs in manufacturing and trades were plentiful and more were on the way. The city of Lackawanna, immediately to the south of Buffalo and home to the Bethlehem Steel Plant, had learned of a $60 million plant expansion on the horizon.

February brought the news of Bell Aircraft Company's successful new vertical takeoff plane, as well as an improvement in helicopter rotors that would enable the craft to fly as fast as conventional planes. In May it was learned that the Buffalo Water Department would introduce fluoride into the city's water supply to enhance dental health.

The Buffalo Harbor was due for $2 million in improvements, thanks to the efforts of the region's congressional committee in securing federal funds for the task. And, to speed the influx of vehicle traffic from the southtowns into the city and back home again, the new elevated Skyway opened for business in October. This last improvement would do away with the bottlenecks caused at the Michigan Street and Ohio Street bridges when the bridges had to be raised for Great Lakes shipping vessels to navigate the Buffalo River.

Still, there were some setbacks. On March 1, a total of 2.5 inches of rain fell in parts of Western New York and created massive flooding. March 23 brought winds in excess of 60 miles per hour, which created an ice dam at the mouth of the Niagara River of a size never before seen. Homes, boathouses and docks were destroyed on Grand Island and on both the U.S. and Canadian sides of the river as far as Lake Ontario. Many families had to be evacuated along the shoreline, and even the flow of water over Niagara Falls diminished.

April witnessed the destruction of both Maid of the Mist boats at Niagara Falls as they succumbed to a fire. A more minor, yet still nagging, aggravation was the raising of fares on the Niagara Frontier Transit buses to 20 cents a trip. Of minor league note, but of major importance to the city and the region, was the question of what was to become of the city's professional Triple A baseball club, the Buffalo Bisons.

The team had been under absentee ownership by the major league Detroit Tigers since 1951. What decisions would now be made concerning the ball club's fate following the recent death of the man at the head of the operation, Tigers owner Walter O. Briggs, Sr.? Although the city and region had been on the upswing in recent years, the same could not be said for the baseball club.

Back in 1949, the third year of manager Paul Rapier Richards' tenacious leadership, the Buffalo Bisons had won their first International League pennant in 13 years. The club finished with a 90-64 record, drawing 393,483 fans to cozy Offermann Stadium. This was the highest attendance in team history. Five pitchers won in double figures, led by Bob Hooper with an outstanding 19-3 record. Saul Rogovin and Clem Hausmann won 16 and 15 games, respectively. Seven men clubbed double figures in home runs, Gene Markland topping the list with 25. Three players had more than 100 RBIs. Ray Coleman led with 113. Despite this powerhouse team and Richards' incisive direction, the team lost to the Montreal Royals in the second round of the Governor's Cup playoffs and would not advance to that year's Little World Series.

Postseason losses continued to mount when manager Richards, also serving as the club's general manager, announced his resignation in October. He was heading for the Seattle club of the Pacific

Coast League. Word was that this leave-taking may have been spurred by the midseason action of Bisons' president John Gehm, who had assigned Richards a "front-office assistant" to help manage the team's affairs. For the next six years the Bisons continued in the tailspin that had begun with the playoff defeat by the Royals.

As good as the 1949 team was, the 1950 edition was just the opposite, so much so that the Bisons dropped from first to eighth place and fan attendance fell nearly 300,000 to the club's lowest turnout ever (96,237). Offensive production plummeted. Coaker Triplett hit .337, but his aging legs reduced him to part-time status and only three men hit more than 10 home runs. Hank Biasetti had 18. The RBI leader was Fred Hancock with 69. Only one pitcher on the staff won as many as 10 games. Ernie Silverman, a 12-game winner the year before, fell to 10-14, and led the team with an ERA of 4.13. The next year could not help but be better, and so the 1951 squad rebounded to fourth place and featured the league's MVP, left fielder Archie Wilson, a .316 hitter with 28 home runs and 112 RBIs. There was also significantly improved pitching. Ernie Silverman recorded a 12-11 mark; Rudy Minarcin led the club in wins with 16 against 12 losses; Moe Savranski won 11 and lost 11 but had a sparkling 2.92 ERA. Back in the playoffs once more, the team again lost to Montreal, but this time they went out in the first round.

Fans continued to stay away, and the money-losing ball club was finally sold to the out-of-town Detroit interests on November 15, 1951. The local Jacobs Brothers, owners of the international concession business bearing that family name (later to become Sportservice Corporation), sold the team with a contract stipulation that Buffalo interests would have the first opportunity to repurchase the club if it was later resold by the Tigers. The Jacobs Brothers wisely retained ownership of Offermann Stadium through their Ferry-Woodlawn Realty Corporation.

There were highlights following the sale. The 1952 season saw another Bison left fielder, Frank Carswell, lead the league in hitting (.344) and home runs (30). His 101 RBIs fell short of the triple crown by a dozen. The Bisons took team league home run honors with 115, and hurler Dick Marlowe pitched a nine-inning perfect game against Baltimore on August 15. This was only the second time this feat had been accomplished in league history. (The earlier perfecto was also authored by a Bison, Chet Carmichael, who had thrown the first one back on August 10, 1910.) Unfortunately, by the end of the season the club had dropped back to fifth place in the standings and the attendance was a disappointing 152,173. The accountants' figures were even worse—much worse. At the time of the sale to Detroit, financial records showed that the club had debts of $326,000 and was close to bankruptcy.

There was an effort to rebound in 1953. Spurred on by Tiger farmhands, fan attendance jumped by over 100,000 and was now up to 268,086, while the ball club climbed two spots to third place. Nevertheless, they lost once again in the first round of the playoffs, and once more it was to Montreal. Jack Wallaesa, obtained in an early-season trade, had the most productive year of his career, leading the league with 36 home runs and driving home 111. Frank Carswell continued his hot hitting, finishing at .323 and adding 25 home runs and 75 RBIs in only 105 games. The team boasted two soon-to-be major league pitchers in Paul Foytack (13 wins) and Frank Lary (17 victories), while Ken Johnson and Milt Jordan each notched 12 in the win column.

The attendance yo-yo bounced down again in 1954 as the club fell to sixth place. Fan turnout tumbled to 120,621. Carswell contributed a third straight season of offensive leadership, batting .318 and driving home 87 runs. Fellow outfielder Ron Northey hit .308 and a team-leading 25 home runs and sent 85 runners across the plate. Center fielder Chick King was heard from with 16 home runs and 61 RBIs. First baseman Dick Gernert swatted 13 homers in only 74 games. Frank Lary had another stellar year (15 wins) and missed hurling a perfect game with two outs to go in the ninth against Toronto. Ken Johnson had 14 victories. Of these men, only Chick King would return for the following year.

The Bisons wound up in sixth place again in 1955 but dropped six more games than the 1954 version. Attendance climbed by almost 15,000, but still the club lost $75,000 after all the bills were tallied. No Bison hit .300. The squad ended up last in the league in batting. The team leader in home runs (17) and RBIs (79) was 20-year-old third baseman Steve Demeter, a .285 hitter who was voted the team's MVP. No Bison team leader had hit fewer home runs since 1922. Most popular player Chuck Kress, splitting his time between first base and the outfield, had 16 home runs and 76 RBIs for the 140 games in which he appeared. First baseman Wayne Belardi was the only other Bison in home run double figures. He had 10 in half a season but had only 29 runners driven home and a lowly .229 average.

An excellent pitching year by Ben Flowers (12-9 and 2.24 ERA) went for naught. Even the leadership of manager Danny Carnevale, a Buffalo native and former Bison shortstop (he had suited up for the club in both 1938 and 1940) and a proven winning manager in the lower minor leagues, could not overcome the distressing problems at the plate. Even more distressing were the growing rumors that the Tigers were looking to end their relationship with the ball club.

What was to be the future of baseball in Buffalo? What could the locals do to make sure the Bisons stayed here and played here? Minor league cities were losing their ball clubs to disaffiliation and relocation. Even the major league Boston Braves had picked up and moved to Milwaukee, Wisconsin, in 1953, the first such move for a major league franchise in more than 50 years.

CHAPTER 2: COMMUNITY PURCHASE

THE AUGUST 26, 1955, edition of the Buffalo Evening News offered the report that many had been dreading to read: "Inheritance tax problems likely will force the sale of the Detroit Tigers and the Tigers' farm system." The article added that Walter O. (Spike) Briggs, Jr., son of the deceased Walter O. Briggs, Sr., would try to form a new syndicate to purchase the Tigers and their farm teams. What would this mean for the Bisons?

Buffalo had been a proud professional baseball town since 1877, starting as a member of the International Association in 1878. Playing at a new ball grounds in the block formed by West and Fargo Avenues and Rhode Island (home plate) and Vermont Streets, that year's edition of the Bisons captured first place in the Association with a winning percentage of .750, a record of 24 wins and 8 losses. The club went 81-32 in all games played, not counting three ties. It was a strong case for a jump to a higher level of competition. Mound stalwart James (Pud) Galvin fashioned an amazing record of 72-25. He was even the pitcher of record for the three tie ballgames.

The Bisons achieved major league status the very next year, in 1879, by joining the National League. They would play ball in that esteemed circuit through 1885. Taking the field in a new location in 1884, now in the northeast quadrant where Richmond Avenue met Summer Street (referred to as Olympic Park I), that year's club achieved its highest major league ranking ever, finishing the season in third place. Although finishing up 19 1/2 games back of the pennant-winning Providence Grays, and 10 games behind the Boston Beaneaters, the team finished 2 1/2 games in front of the New York Giants. But in 1885 calamity struck!

The franchise and all of its players were sold, late season, to the National League rival Detroit Wolverines. This transaction occurred so that the Wolverines could acquire the services of the Bisons' "Big Four" players—Dan Brouthers, Deacon White, Jack Rowe and Hardy Richardson—all of whom donned Detroit regalia before the season was out. Galvin, with a subpar 13-19 record, had been sold to Pittsburgh in July, and thus a rag-tag assemblage of players finished out the year for the Bisons, tumbling the team into seventh place. Buffalo wound up 49 games behind the league-leading Chicago White Sox. In 1886 the Herd was out of the major leagues altogether.

Reverting to minor league status, Buffalo joined up with the International League. From that season (1886) to the 1956 club, the team remained in that organization through a series of league name changes. The International League became the International Association, then the Eastern League, then the Eastern Association, and finally the International League once more.

By 1899, Buffalo had again moved to a new playing field. International League Park (or Olympic Park II) was sandwiched into the block bounded by Michigan and Woodlawn Avenues and East Ferry and Masten Streets. The grandstand and home plate were nestled behind Covenant Presbyterian Church in the northwest corner at Michigan and East Ferry. The right-field fence gave immediately onto Woodlawn Avenue. Backyard boundaries of the homes on Masten limited the depth of the ballpark's left-field wall.

The 1899 season also saw the Bisons sign on with Ban Johnson's Western Association. Johnson renamed his organization the American League in 1900. In 1901, Johnson declared his American League to be a new major league to rival the National, but in the process the Buffalo ball club was abandoned. The Queen City franchise was shifted to Boston, and the Bisons had no choice but to revert to minor league status, once again with the Eastern League. That assemblage itself reverted to a previous name for 1912: the Bisons were International Leaguers yet again. It was certain that 1956 would not bring a new league name change, but less clear was the question of whether Buffalo would continue its participation in any league at all.

Following the debacle of 1885, the city had twice more flirted with major league membership. The Players League began operation in 1890, and Buffalo was a founding member. Connie Mack, born Cornelius McGillicuddy, took the field as the team's catcher and part owner. (Mr. Mack would later become the longtime owner and manager of the Philadelphia Athletics and a Baseball Hall of Fame inductee.) The Players League lasted only one season. The Buffalo entry finished in last place. The Buffalo Bisons, the minor league squad, was squeezed out of their home grounds at Michigan and East Ferry and barely survived at a tiny ballpark on the city's east side at Barthel and Fougeron.

A third major league again made its presence felt in 1914 and 1915 as a challenge to the National and American League monopolies. Buffalo was once more a founding member of the new Federal League, and the club built their own new ballpark at the southeast quadrant formed by Northland Avenue and Lonsdale Road. Only a few blocks northeast of the Bisons' home grounds, the 1914 Buf-Feds finished in fourth position. Renamed the Buffalo Blues, the squad dropped to sixth place in 1915.

At the close of 1915, National and American League magnates and their Federal League counterparts made peace. Some Federal League clubs would join the two older organizations, but Buffalo would not be among them. The minor league Bisons, who had struggled to stay alive back in 1890, remained staunchly active during the 1914 and 1915 seasons and would continue to represent the city in the International League.

Buffalo baseball had proved its worth over the years, and the Bisons were a symbol of community pride and entertainment. The 1904 Eastern League Buffalo squad had finished in first place under manager George Stallings and went on to defeat the American Association St. Paul Saints in a weather-shortened postseason playoff, two games to one. It was the very first Little World Series, later to be known also as the Junior World Series. In fact, it was the only baseball World Series of any nature to be played that year.

John McGraw's 1904 National League pennant-winning New York Giants refused to take on the champions of the American League, the Boston Americans. There was to be no major league World Series played in 1904. Perhaps the National League was still stinging from the five games-to-three defeat of its 1903 pennant victors, the Pittsburgh Pirates, at the hands of this same American League Boston nine.

In 1906 the Bisons emerged as Eastern League champions once again, and again under Stallings. This time they took on the Columbus American Association ball team. Again, weather prevented a full series from being played, but Buffalo also prevailed in this confrontation, this time by three games to two.

The minor league Buffalo squad took the crown as International League champions in 1915 and 1916, both times under manager Patsy Donovan. Alas, there was no postseason rival. The interleague series with the American Association pennant winners had been suspended following the 1907 clash won by the Toronto Maple Leafs. After an 11-year hiatus from the winners' circle, the 1927 Bisons emerged once more as International League pennant victors. In the now revived postseason set-to against the American Association, the Buffalo club fell to the Toledo Mud Hens by an embarrassing five games-to-one margin.

That same Little World Series fate befell the 1933 Buffalo team, which had actually finished in fourth position at the close of the International League pennant race. However, this Bison squad also became the very first victors of the International League's newly inaugurated Shaughnessy Playoffs system, wherein the top four finishers played off against one another for the right to represent the league in the postseason series against their American Association rivals. The powerful Newark Bears had won 102 games and captured the pennant. The Bisons had won the playoffs. The American Association's Columbus ball club avenged its defeat by Buffalo back in 1906 by winning five of the eight games played.

Three years later, the 1936 Buffalo club won both the pennant and the Shaughnessy Playoffs, but in the Junior World Series it was the same old story. Despite the presence of the Bisons' first league MVP, center fielder Frank (Beauty) McGowan, the Milwaukee Brewers prevailed by four games to one.

The most recent Buffalo club to take home the International League pennant was the 1949 edition, overseen by manager Paul Richards. When Richards left at the end of the year, after his club lost in the International League playoffs, the Bisons' good fortunes went with him. The 1950 team ended up in the cellar. The club finished in fourth place in 1951 and began operation under a new ownership by the Detroit Tigers late in that year. Detroit's oversight led to mixed success through the next several campaigns.

With a history of pennant and playoff winners, although frequently frustrated in postseason contests with American Association opponents, Buffalo was a city used to watching top-quality ball. Famous men who had donned Bison uniforms included Connie Mack (player-owner), Hoss Radbourne, Jimmy Collins, Jim O'Rourke, Dan Brouthers, Joe Tinker (coach), Herb Pennock, Gabby Hartnett (manager) and Ray Schalk (player-manager). Each of these men had since been inducted into the National Baseball Hall of Fame in Cooperstown, New York. It was now rumored that a light-hitting second baseman from the 1914 and 1915 Bisons could soon be joining them, a man named Joseph McCarthy. He had since gone on to greater fame in both Chicago and New York City in a managerial role. A baseball legacy of this nature could not be ignored. A National League Detroit ball club had ruined the Bisons back in 1885. What would this current management of the American League Detroit Tigers do now, 70 years later?

Writing in his "Sport Comment" column in the August 29 edition of the Buffalo Evening News, Bob Stedler attempted to allay concerns. He championed the efforts that Spike Briggs was making and called for a continuation of the working relationship between Detroit and the Buffalo club, saying, "We believe that with the encouraging reports we've been receiving from the Detroit farm system, better days are ahead for both Detroit and its affiliates in the higher minors, of which Buffalo is at the top."

The Bison players did what they could to respond to fan uncertainty. On that same night of August 29, they played and beat the Columbus Jets to take over sole possession of sixth place in the standings. On Danny Carnevale Night at Offermann Stadium, the Bisons, playing for pride if not for the playoffs, rallied behind Ben Flowers' complete game effort. Despite a muggy night when his knuckler wasn't working, Flowers kept the Herd in the lead until the Jets threatened to tie the game in the top of the ninth. With two outs, a line single to left sent the Columbus baserunner on second on a dash for home plate, only to be nailed at the dish on a fine throw from outfielder J.W. Porter. It was the final out of the game and sealed the 4-3 Buffalo victory. It was the fourth win in a row for the Herd, who would go on to stretch their unbeaten streak to six, their longest such feat of the season.

SEPTEMBER 1955

THE Bisons held onto sixth place to finish out the year, but the heady six-game winning streak was followed by a season ending run of six straight losses. Would this sad close to the year affect the efforts that were now under way to keep the team here in Buffalo? Who would provide the leadership, and how would the fans respond?

Two Buffalo representatives of an "emergency committee" to save baseball in the Queen City, John C. Stiglmeier and Harry Bisgeier, sat down with Detroit front office personnel on September 7, 1955, in the Motor City to see what could be worked out. Tigers president Spike Briggs; Jimmy Campbell, business manager of the Tigers; John McHale, director of the Tigers' minor league system; and Harold (Muddy) Ruel, the Tigers' general manager, met with them.

Charley Young, Buffalo Evening News sports editor, was also present at the discussions. Young reported that the two Buffalo men "negotiated a 30-day option to buy the club from the Detroit Tigers and, as Stiglmeier put it: 'Now the work begins.'" As a condition of the sale, Buffalo would receive the International League franchise, equipment and a nucleus of Detroit players to be named later. The Bisons were to become a community-owned operation, but that would necessitate the creation of a local organization to raise more than $150,000 within a month's time. At that, according to Young, the Bisons had been given exceptionally generous terms. The recent selling price for the Pacific Coast League San Diego Padres had been $250,000.

According to McHale, the Tigers wanted to "realign" their farm system to benefit the major league club without "burdening" the Tigers with "the problems of ownership." The News quoted him as saying, "A community-owned club, capably run by men like John Stiglmeier and Harry Bisgeier, can be a great thing for the city." President Spike Briggs officially commented, "We of the Detroit club are sorry that our relationship with Buffalo is not going to be as close as it has been in the past. We are happy, however, to step aside in order to make it possible for the Buffalo team to be owned by the fans who support it." Muddy Ruel added, "I personally feel that the community ownership plan as proposed for the Buffalo club can be very successful because Buffalo is the type of close-knit city that can adequately support a team of its own... Community ownership of baseball teams has been successful. It will be interesting to watch the developments of the Buffalo undertaking." He added that the "whole nation" would be watching what Buffalo did in this "step that may set minor league history."

Stiglmeier and Bisgeier responded with their own assurances: "We feel that a community-owned club, with vigorous, intelligent local leadership, can produce a contending team and regenerate baseball interest in Buffalo." The two men added later, "We fully realize that we are undertaking a gigantic task in securing this option to buy and re-organize the Buffalo Baseball club. We do not pretend to be miracle men. This is a task that must be undertaken with the support and effort of all the baseball fans of Buffalo and Western New York...[The club would be] operated not by a few select persons, but owned by thousands of fans who have an active interest in their own ball club. We have every confidence in the Buffalo fans, otherwise we wouldn't have undertaken this step to save professional baseball in Buffalo." The faith of these men would not be in vain, but it would take a late-innings entry of some deep-pocketed relief to make this dream come true. It was to the credit of men like Stiglmeier and Bisgeier that these sources eventually did step up to the plate.

Upon their return to Buffalo from Detroit, Stiglmeier and Bisgeier began the arrangements that would complete the purchase of the Bisons and establish a corporation that would operate the club, according to Charley Young's account in the September 9 issue of the Buffalo Evening News. The money—more than $150,000—would need to be raised by October 8.

PROFILE: JOHN C. STIGLMEIER

John C. Stiglmeier, born in 1889, had started out as a blacksmith's apprentice at age 12, continuing his education in night school. A big-muscled, iron-jawed, straight-talking man, "Stiggy" found his rightful place on the gridiron as a football fullback, starting his own youth team before graduating to the semipro ranks in 1906. His passion placed him in the top-rated local clubs and took him to Ohio in 1915 to play against the legendary Jim Thorpe of the Canton Bulldogs, then to suit up with Thorpe as a member of the 1916 Toledo Maroons. Buffalo's own Tommy Hughitt (All-American quarterback for the University of Michigan, 1913), was his 1917 teammate on the local Niagaras.

Stiglmeier had joined the Buffalo Bisons as a club director in 1924 and was prevailed upon to take over as general manager in 1941. In that role, he was instrumental in bringing baseball's winter meetings to Buffalo in December 1944. The Association of Professional Baseball Clubs met at the Buffalo Hotel Statler, December 6–8, to plan the ongoing survival of minor and major operations during World War II. For his efforts, Stiglmeier won the accolade of "Mr. Baseball" even as he finished second in the voting for Minor League Executive of the Year. He resigned his position with the Bisons the following year—under protest—after disagreement with another member of the board of directors.

A man of Stiglmeier's personality would not be immune to the call of politics. Stiglmeier served 16 years as Mayor of Depew starting in 1917. Also elected town supervisor in Cheektowaga in 1919, he was reelected four times to that post. He had served as treasurer of the Cheektowaga Union Free School District 9 from 1918 to 1927; was Erie County deputy county clerk in the charge of the Auto License Bureau from 1934 through 1940 and again in 1949; and was Erie County Democratic Committee chairman in 1930 and 1931.

Even a 1934 auto accident could not stop the man. Initially feared to have suffered a broken back (later x-rays revealed a "bruised sciatic nerve"), Stiglmeier was up and walking 10 days later. He was later voted president of the Buffalo Bowling Association. A man with this sort of background obviously would not allow Buffalo to say no to this new community-owned baseball opportunity. Given his experience and contacts in the baseball world, half the battle was won with John C. Stiglmeier on your side.

With only a month to achieve their goal, Stiglmeier and Bisgeier met with a "select group of advisors," "civic minded men" who would be asked to serve on a steering committee to lead the "crusade to save Buffalo baseball." Stiglmeier also met with attorneys to arrange to hold fan investments in trust (to ensure that all investors would get their money back if the drive failed), and Bisgeier moved into Offermann Stadium to begin meeting with the Bisons' general manager Hillman Lyons and business manager Bob Steinhelper to work out the details of the inventory of club property.

Bisgeier arranged to move into the stadium offices on Monday, September 12, likening the effort to D-Day in Normandy, when the allied forces "just couldn't fail. Only this is B-Day—for baseball—and we can't fail, either," he said. Commenting on their activities thus far, Bisgeier added that he and Stiglmeier and the others, in keeping with the flavor of a crusade, "prayed a little, too."

Six new faces joined the public effort on September 12. Herbert J. Vogelsang, vice president of Manufacturers & Traders Trust Company; Thomas W. Ryan, former New York State commissioner of public safety; Ralph Saft, attorney; J. Eugene McMahon, attorney; Mike Ellis, advertising executive; and George J. Trimper, president of the American Power Boat Association, agreed to help Stiglmeier and Bisgeier in the quest to complete the purchase. An incorporation figure of $275,000 was set, but only $150,000 was to be needed by B-Day. Stock was set at $1 per share, but fans would be asked to purchase five game tickets for the season for an additional $8. A call for volunteers to help with the marketing was issued. Stiglmeier and Bisgeier were volunteers, too; neither man was being paid for his efforts.

Among the first purchasers of Bisons stock and seats were the mayor of the City of Buffalo, Steven Pankow, and his secretary, John Kane. "Where do we get in line to buy this stock in the Buffalo Bisons?" Pankow asked at the stadium window. Pankow explained his reasoning for the investment: "Sports is just as important to the City of Buffalo as business and industry. I want to be sure this campaign to keep the Bisons in Buffalo goes over." Charley Young reported in the News on September 15 that the mayor had purchased 100 shares of stock and tickets while secretary Kane had ponied up his own capital investment.

Other buyers this day included 80-year-old Frank Szatkowski, a fan who remembered the Bisons playing in Franklin Park on Buffalo's East Side in the 1890s, and his son Edward, each purchasing 10 shares. A.T. O'Neill, a retired chairman of the board of Niagara-Mohawk Power Corporation, was also a first-day purchaser of 100 shares. Chairman of the civic drive that raised $300,000 in an unsuccessful attempt to save professional football for the city—the Buffalo Bills of the old American Association—O'Neill encouraged every citizen to share in the responsibility to make the drive successful. "For something like this to fail would set the city back to the status of a village," he commented. Niagara Frontier Transit bus driver Ted O'Shea, manager of his son's Midget League baseball team, also showed up to buy 100 shares, knowing how important it was to the children of the area.

PROFILE: HARRY BISGEIER

Harry Bisgeier also brought an experienced baseball resume to the cause, plus a showman's promotional touch. Born in Hell's Kitchen, New York City, in 1898, Bisgeier was working in a movie theater by age 11 and wound up doing just about everything in sight but perform. He moved to Buffalo in 1915, where he began his sports promotion and ownership career. In partnership with Sam Siegel, Bisgeier was part owner of the Buffalo Bisons basketball team in the National League. The two men helped create the professional basketball Midwest Conference. Bisgeier also initiated basketball doubleheaders in Buffalo in the 1930s.

New York State Senator Arthur L. Schwartz and Bisgeier later joined forces to stage the Semi-Pro Congress of Baseball in Niagara Falls, New York, and were then instrumental in the formation of baseball's PONY (Pennsylvania–Ontario–New York) League in 1939. The two men jointly owned the Niagara Falls entry until Schwartz's death, whereupon Bisgeier assumed full ownership and moved the team to Jamestown, New York, in 1940. Bisgeier then formed a working relationship with the Buffalo Bisons that continued until he sold the Jamestown club in 1945. Now, 10 years later, it was time to return to the Buffalo baseball world and to offer his talents for this new undertaking.

Representing the East Side, tavern owner John Krysinski made a 100-share investment. The Bisons were to be a fan-owned team where all investors were equal and no one was to predominate.

Among those "equal investors" on day two of the drive were Mike Martinek, a veteran pro baseball player living in Riverside, still looking fit enough to play, and Patrick J. Black, a painter and decorator who purchased shares and tickets for his five children—Maurice, 16; Patrick Jr., 15; Margaret, 12; Noreen, 10; and Kathleen, 8. Robert B. Devine also made an investment in teenagers (his five godsons), and Buffalonian Mary Cierlicki bought shares for herself and her two sisters in Rochester, Frances Cierlicki and Dodie Sams. Another East Side tavern owner, Ed Warzel, took 500 shares, saying that "everybody in my place is talking about the Bisons. They can't see how this drive can miss." Stan Barron, radio station WKBW sports director, announced that he would be holding a "marathon" broadcast from the stadium, encouraging fans to come in to purchase stock and go on the air with him to be interviewed, going through the night if necessary.

OCTOBER 1955

By October 1, the Buffalo Evening News reported that the drive had reached $90,000 pledged in subscriptions but only about $75,000 in hand. The drive had only a week until B-Day to raise another amount equal to that already received, an average of $10,000 per day to cap the effort. Stiglmeier and Bisgeier continued to be optimistic. Sales were now being offered not only at the stadium but at all Manufacturers & Traders Trust Company offices and at many business establishments in the city and the suburbs. Meetings to stimulate sales were planned for the Montefiore Club, the Western New York Retail Liquor Dealers and the Buffalo Ad Club.

In addition, Stiglmeier had just returned from the World Series in New York City and, while there, had talked to a number of Buffalo residents, lining up commitments in the process. To help the endeavor reach its goal, Stiglmeier and Bisgeier would turn to a newly formed 28-member "steering committee" composed of investors who had already pledged a total of $40,000 to the cause. Still, the goal remained the same. "The little guy—Mr. Average Fan—is the fellow we need most to make sure we have a team in Buffalo. Without his active support this drive will fail," Stiglmeier said. Mayor Pankow renewed his appeal to the public, encouraging close friends to participate, and a newly created 400 Member Citizens' Committee headed by Ray Nabor and Frank Cannon began making personal contacts.

The tension mounted. With five days to go, the campaign was still well short of the required figure. Stanley A. Pack's Kensington Kiwanis Club made a commitment of $50. Bob Stedler's Buffalo Evening News "Sport Comment" on October 4 urged on the fans by saying, "There's no time to delay. The simple question is: Do you want professional baseball in Buffalo? Coming forth with stock subscriptions is the only possible way to have it." The Buffalo Evening News and the Buffalo Courier-Express ran coupons that read: "Public-Spirited Citizens! Save the Buffalo Bisons—Invest in a community-owned baseball team." Readers could clip the coupon and send in money for shares of stock at $1 apiece and an additional $8 for five reserved seat tickets (not good for opening day, Sundays or holidays).

Campaign leaders pulled every string they could reach, including those supporting a freckled, red-headed Buffalo institution—Howdy Doody. Speaking on behalf of the television star, Buffalo Bob Smith sent a check for $100 from New York City and called upon "all my Howdy Doody fans in

Buffalo to help me see that the city doesn't lose baseball." Buffalo Bob revealed that he had been a peanut and popcorn vendor in Offermann during his school days and eventually graduated to the gigantic wooden scoreboard in center field, helping scorekeeper Sal Amico, before going on to fame with his smaller wooden co-star.

The effort became international when Jack Kent Cooke, millionaire owner of the Toronto Maple Leafs of the International League, offered his encouragement with only two days to go. Cy Kritzer's column in the News of October 6 quoted Cooke as saying, "'I'm rooting for the drive in Buffalo to go over the top. If I were permitted, I'd buy some stock for myself. But that's against baseball law. If the International League moves out of Buffalo, we lose a natural rival.'"

On October 6, the Common Council of the city of Buffalo passed a resolution calling upon all citizens to "subscribe to the stock of the company [i.e., the Bisons] as offered and to purchase five tickets each for the 1956 season." The resolution was immediately signed by Mayor Pankow. The following day, the Common Council called for a special meeting that evening at 7:00, urging all city employees to attend and join in the effort to save the ball club. Niagara District Councilman Anthony F. Tauriello addressed the city's need for the team for its public image. Masten District Councilman Joseph S. Swartz called upon his district's residents to support the drive.

Stormy weather that night limited the turnout to approximately 30 hardy souls, but Patrick J. McGroder, chairman of the Board of Civic Stadium and Memorial Auditorium, was there and addressed the "status of the drive to date and the need for baseball for the youth of Buffalo," reported the News on October 8. Police Captain Frank N. Felicetta was also present and strongly supported the argument for preserving baseball on behalf of the youth. "If all pitch in and help, there will be an opening day for baseball in Buffalo next year...," said City Assessor Alfonso V. Bellanca, likening the effort to a "moral responsibility." At the meeting, City Comptroller Chester Kowal illustrated what those words meant; he presented a check for $250 that had been raised from concerned members of the powerful Easter Brands semipro team of the 1930s that had toured about the Buffalo area. Harry Bisgeier gave the up-to-date figures for the drive, and sports retailer Dick Fischer lauded Stiglmeier and Bisgeier for "records in local sports that speak for themselves." He pointed out that the Bisons had never been in the red during Stiglmeier's five years as general manager of the club (1941–1945). He noted that Bisgeier had taken over the PONY League's Jamestown club and raised its attendance from 18,000 to 150,000 in the short space of four years.

Anthony R. Lombardo, the Republican minority leader of the Common Council, announced that the council was fully united in support of the effort. His remarks were echoed by Ellicott District Councilman Leeland N. Jones, Jr., South District Councilman Vincent P. Masterson, Walden District Councilman Thaddeus J. Dulski, Masten District Councilman Joseph S. Swartz and Niagara District Councilman Anthony F. Tauriello.

Now the Buffalo Chamber of Commerce stepped forward. Wade Stevenson, chairman of the group's executive committee, weighed in on October 6, saying, "We all certainly feel that Buffalo must have baseball next season. However, we'll need a little time." A luncheon meeting at the Buffalo Club to address the matter included Clayton G. Maxwell, Leston P. Faneuf, George E. O'Neill, Duncan A. MacLeod, Council President Elmer F. Lux, Roy W. Doolittle, P.O. Rial, Walter A. Yates, Dick Fischer, Peter T. Allen and the aforementioned Stevenson. The group planned to meet again October 10.

Stevenson launched into personal requests to influential friends. Dick Fischer contacted a list of donors, seeking to convert their promises into hard cash. Ray Nabor and Frank Cannon redoubled their efforts with the 400 Member Citizens Committee, personally requesting purchases from those who had not yet committed to the cause. The Offermann Stadium box office was to stay open into the evening hours. Doomsday—not B-Day—would be ushered in at 12:01 a.m. on Wednesday, October 8, if the goal was not met. Responding to the announcement of this new business and private backing, Tigers' farm director John McHale let it be known that additional days beyond the 8th could be granted "to tabulate the results."

On Thursday, October 7, responding to the crisis, Howard Henry, resident of Hamburg, New York, bought 12 shares of Bison stock and five game tickets to share with his 14-year-old son and namesake, Howard Jr.

On Friday, October 8, "B-Day" arrived, and so, too, did a last-minute reprieve for the campaign's final accounting. Much like the downpour the night before, a flood of late Friday stock and ticket requests prevented accurate tabulation of these new demands for stock shares. So busy was the action that the Lackawanna branch of the Manufacturers & Traders Trust Company ran out of applications. The piles of mail at Offermann could not be accurately tabulated within the time allotted. So the newspapers said.

Much as a deluge of this nature on the field would occasion a rain delay in a game already in progress, so the Tigers graciously suspended the deadline until Tuesday, October 11, "to get an accurate accounting," wrote Charley Young in his column on the 8th. However, this was not to be considered a formal extension and would be the movement's last chance. No further grace period would be possible. By the laws governing professional baseball, the Tigers had to assign their players to a club roster by October 15. If Buffalo had no team to offer, the players would have to go elsewhere. The Offermann Stadium ticket office opened for Saturday and Sunday sales.

"Loan of $70,000 Saves the Baseball Bisons for Buffalo" screamed the secondary headline on page one of the October 11 edition of the Buffalo Evening News. "Baseball has been saved in Buffalo," wrote Charley Young. "A Buffalo team is assured in the International League next season. A group of civic-minded citizens, called together by Wade Stevenson, Buffalo's No. 1 fan, today met and agreed to loan the local baseball club $70,000. This amount will insure the fielding and operation of an International League team for the 1956 season. [...] This money is a loan, Mr. Stevenson emphasized. The men who put up the money do not become owners of the baseball club. To them, it is an investment in their community. They want a community-owned ball club. The sale of the stock in the club will continue until the loan is repaid. The small investor still is the important power behind this team." The men behind the loan would buy small amounts of shares in the team, but they insisted that this was to remain a "community project."

Local business leaders who assisted with the team-saving loan, in addition to Wade Stevenson and Reginald B. Taylor, were Edward A. Atwill, Peter T. Allen, Howard W. Clother, Roy W. Doolittle, Charles R. Diefendorf, Paul E. Fitzpatrick, James Kennedy, Dick Fischer, Cy King, Joe McCarthy, Robert L. Millonzi, William I. Marcy, Albert H. Meyer, Patrick J. McGroder, Tony Naples, Leston P. Faneuf, George O'Neill, Ralph F. Peo, Dexter P. Rumsey, P.O. Rial, Leonard Simon, Charles Turner, Dan Roblin, Walter A Yates and C. Taylor Wettlaufer.

Tigers representatives John McHale and Jimmy Campbell flew to Buffalo for a noon meeting with the group on October 11. A revised price of $75,000 was negotiated for the International League franchise, equipment and the contracts of 10 players. Several additional players would be later optioned to the Buffalo team to support the on-field performance. Thus, the team that had been sold to the Tigers in 1951 for $100,000 was repurchased for $25,000 less, and with $50,000 worth of equipment and 10 player contracts included. A pretty good deal! The last-minute loan would provide funding for the team to field a squad for the 1956 season.

At Stevenson's instigation, a nominating committee was formed to propose temporary officers and directors of the Buffalo Baseball Club, Inc., until the loan was repaid. A.T. O'Neill was selected chairman of the committee, which would also include Lewis G. Harriman and John C. Montana. Attorneys Edwin F. Jaeckle and J. Eugene McMahon would manage incorporation of the club on Friday, October 14, and attend to other legal matters. Stevenson suggested the name of Reginald B. Taylor, former New York State parole commissioner ("Commish" to friends and family alike), as temporary president of the club.

Stiglmeier swung into gear in his general manager duties, contacting major league clubs and seeking a working arrangement that would bring their players to the Buffalo team for 1956. He also spoke with International League president Frank Shaughnessy in Montreal and arranged for a league meeting in Buffalo in November. The new Bisons would be officially recognized as a member of the league at that time. Harry Bisgeier was busy, too. He took on business manager duties designed to enhance ticket selling, with a goal of 250,000 attendance for the 1956 season.

An additional $5000 in stock purchases from small investors was received on October 13. Outgoing Bisons general manager Hillman Lyons helped to raise $3000 of this amount. The mail on October 14 brought in orders for another $1000 in purchases. It was hoped the drive would reach the $150,000 mark by December 15, the date of the final payment to Detroit, and the club set the goal of having 10,000 shareholders by that time. As of the middle of October, shareholders numbered only 1600.

A stock certificate of incorporation for the Buffalo Bisons Baseball Club, Inc., was filed in Albany on October 14, 1955. As incorporators it listed Thomas W. Ryan, John C. Stiglmeier, Harry Bisgeier and J. Eugene McMahon. Named associates were Edwin F. Jaeckle, Dick Fischer, Frank H. Cannon, John Krysinski, Reginald B. Taylor, John C. Montante, Wade Stevenson and Herbert J. Vogelsang.

This was followed by a meeting of the club's major stockholders, which took place on Monday, October 17, to select the "temporary" officers. They would surrender their seats as more shares were sold to increase the stockholder base to the desired 10,000. During the meeting in the law offices of Edwin F. Jaeckle in the Rand Building, Reginald B. Taylor was chosen as the man who would become the club's first president. John C. Stiglmeier was selected as first vice president and would assume the duties of general manager. Harry Bisgeier was named second vice president and would act as business manager. J. Eugene McMahon was elected to the secretary position with the responsibility of providing attorney services for the corporation. Herbert J. Vogelsang was chosen as treasurer. All of these men would serve without pay.

"We have a big job to do with the Bisons," president Taylor told Charley Young in the October 21 edition of the Buffalo Evening News. There were many details to arrange, not the least of them putting a team on the field, scheduling for spring training and establishing a working agreement with a major league club, but he and the board of directors were looking forward to the challenge.

Meanwhile, another business executive, Jack Kent Cooke of Toronto, had finished his visit to the city and had reported favorably on the Buffalo organization to International League president Shaughnessy. One more step towards official acceptance of the team into the league had been completed. Now the question was: who would play on the team, where would the players come from, when would they arrive and who would manage them?

PROFILE: REGINALD B. TAYLOR

"Temporary president" nominee Reginald B. Taylor was born in 1898, a patrician's son who didn't act the part. Following his brother, Moses, who died in action in France in 1918 as a member of the American Expeditionary Force, Taylor joined the American Field Service and was attached to the British 8th Army as an ambulance driver prior to the entrance of the United States into World War I. Taylor suffered a 13-inch head wound when his ambulance hit a mine. He convalesced until the United States joined the fray, then quickly made sergeant in the 76th Massachusetts Cavalry, served a brief time in the trenches in France with the 301st Machine Gun Company and was finally sent to officers' training school after catching the flu and nearly dying. He saw later duty as a French interpreter for President Woodrow Wilson's Peace Mission.

Back home, Taylor spent a year at Yale and then ditched his studies to come to Buffalo in 1920. He signed on as a "general roustabout sailor" on a coal and ore lake carrier while his father was board chairman of the Delaware, Lackawanna & Western Railroad, and later worked as a laborer at Lackawanna Steel when his father took over the chairmanship of that industrial giant. Taylor became an aide to the general manager at the steel plant before being sent off to the Western Pennsylvania coal mines. There he joined the United Mine Workers of America and was eventually made a foreman.

Taylor's service on the front lines served him well in the front office. As executive vice president and treasurer of the Sterling Engine Company, a firm that made engines for the war effort, Taylor was made a lifetime member of his workers' union when he again went off for further service on the Italian Front in World War II. He was a 47-year-old private and ambulance driver. His service activities continued beyond the war with his appointment by Governor Dewey as a New York State Parole Board Commissioner for nine years.

A National City Bank executive at the time of the Bisons purchase, and formerly a director at one time or another of four railroads and four banks, Taylor had a drive for competition, leadership and sports (a steeplechase rider, a 4-goal rated polo player, and the first president of the Buffalo Hockey Club when it played at the Peace Bridge Arena). Taylor was also a man with a reputation for many a civic committee and fundraising drive. What better, more experienced man to serve his community yet again, now as the temporary president of the new community-owned Buffalo Bisons?

Buffalo fans buy stock and tickets

President Reginald
Taylor conducts a
stockholder meeting

Certification of fan support

Pat McGroder and Albert
T. O'Neill watch as Mayor
Steven Pankow pledges
5000 tickets

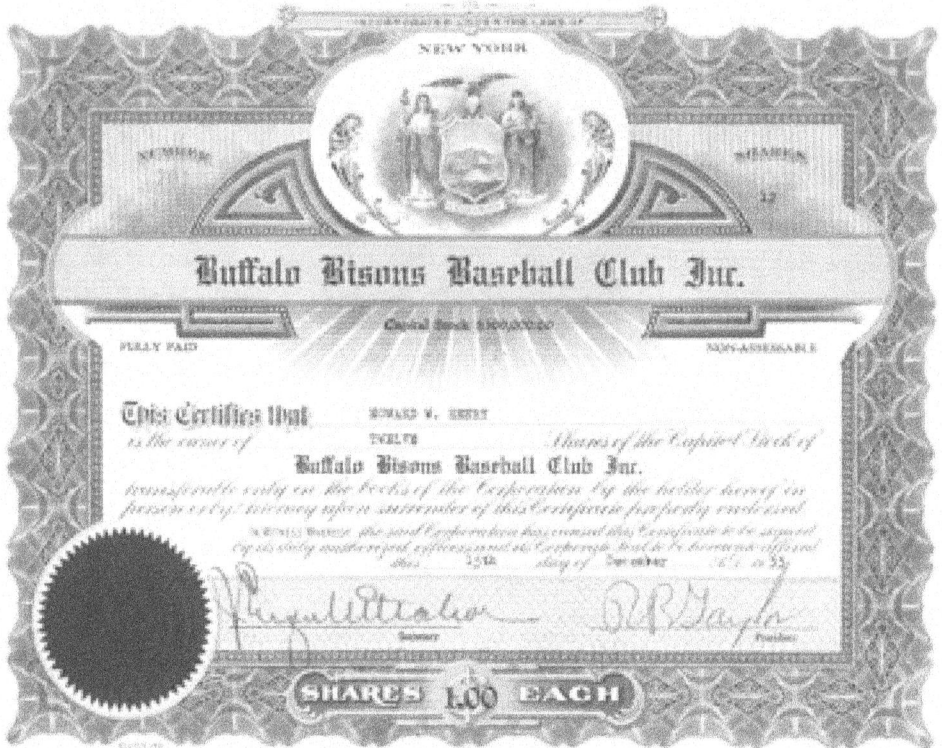

Buffalo Bisons Baseball Club Inc. stock certificate

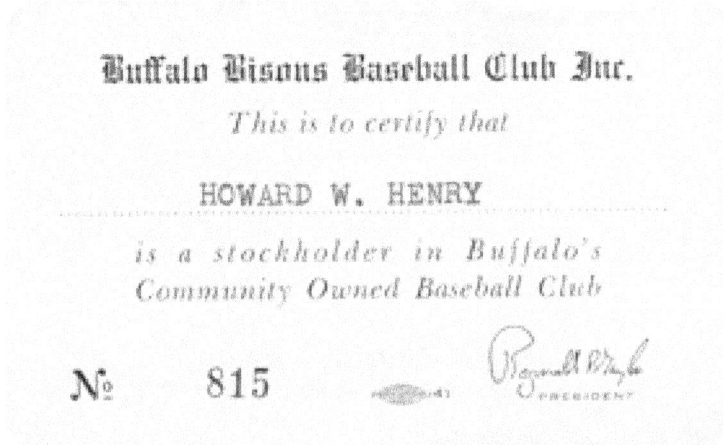

Stockholder certification

Chapter 3: Assembling the Team

Stiglmeier, with complete authority to arrange player deals and working agreements with major league clubs, noted that the Bisons had purchased 10 player contracts from the Tigers as part of the sale price. He was already working on a major league tie-up to acquire players on loan from a big-league organization. Additionally, he, Taylor and Bisgeier would represent the club at the annual baseball draft meetings to be held in Columbus, Ohio, from November 28-30. This was an opportunity for the higher leagues (including the majors) to select players from lower classifications for an established draft price. The Bisons were hoping to find available player talent to fill out the roster with a competitive edge.

OCTOBER 1955

The first acquisition, made but two days after the stockholder meeting of October 17, was a blockbuster of a deal that would change the face of Buffalo baseball for all time. The Bisons had procured a major league talent with a major league personality: Luscious "Luke" Easter would play ball in Buffalo in 1956.

Listed at 34 years of age (but perhaps closer to 40, or more?), 6 feet, 4 inches tall, and 240 pounds, Luke Easter became the Bisons' first African-American player in 67 years. (Frank Grant, "often regarded as the greatest black ballplayer of the 19th century," according to his National Baseball Hall of Fame plaque, had played second base for the Bisons from 1886 to 1888, batting .344, .366 and .331, and leading the International League in home runs in 1887 with 11. Racism and abusive on-field physical treatment had driven him from the league and integrated baseball. He was elected to the Baseball Hall of Fame as a member of the Class of 2006.)

Easter had enjoyed an outstanding power career in the Negro Leagues, and then with San Diego of the Pacific Coast League and the American League Cleveland Indians following Jackie Robinson's integration of baseball in 1946. From 1950 to 1952, Easter averaged more than 28 home runs and more than 102 RBIs in each of his three major league seasons. A serious knee injury curtailed his Cleveland career in 1953, but returning to Triple A baseball in 1954 and 1955 saw a resurgence of his power numbers. He hit a combined 28 home runs with 90 RBIs and a .315 average for San Diego (Pacific Coast League) and Ottawa (International League) in 1954. He bettered those numbers with Charleston (American Association) in 1955 (30, 102, .283) and became available at the end of the season only because of a dispute with the team's owner. It was said that Luke had taken to giving baseballs away to youngsters behind first base at the end of those games where he had snagged the final out. He was suspended for five games but did not lose any pay, according to the Charleston owner Danny Menendez, because of the great effort he had put into the team's success.

From their vantage point, Stiglmeier and Taylor saw that there was no disputing Big Luke's power and commitment to baseball. They jumped on the opportunity. The deal would have to await the December 1 trading deadline before it could become official, but the Bisons front office had demonstrated to all that it, too, knew how to hit a home run.

President Taylor, general manager Stiglmeier and business manager Bisgeier strategized how to acquire the players they would need to put the team they wanted on the field. Bisgeier then set off to meet with former Cleveland Indians owner Bill Veeck, seeking information on available baseball talent, how to access it and how to promote the club, making the cash registers ring so as to afford the new purchases. Bisgeier reported that chances of a major league tie-up were slim this late in the year, but he hoped some kind of arrangements still might be possible, and after talking with Veeck, why not dream a little?

And dream they did. How about former Yankee greats Vic Raschi and Eddie Lopat on the mound? Ex-Clevelander Wally Westlake and former Cub Harry (Peanuts) Lowrey in the outfield? All it would take was money and the agreement of such big-league stalwarts to set up shop in the Queen City. Lopat (36) and Raschi (35) probably felt they could still make the grade in the majors, the committee decided. It would take a lot of money to convince them to suit up with Buffalo. (Lopat had gone 7-12 with the Yankees and Baltimore in 1955. He would not pitch again in the majors, nor would Raschi, a combined 4-7 that same season with St. Louis and Kansas City.) Westlake, 34 years of age, had seen time the previous season with Cleveland and Baltimore in the American League before catching on with two Pacific Coast League clubs. He undoubtedly felt he had more major league time in him. Lowrey, at 36, had just finished an off year with the Phillies, struggling to hit .189. His availability would be much more promising.

As the hunt for players went on, so did the search for community investors. Over $4000 in stock and ticket sales was taken in during the third week of October. As of October 25, the club could count 1852 fans who had purchased 66,073 shares of stock and tickets, resulting in a cash total of $85,019.80. There was an addition to the front office, as well. Veteran office manager Joseph V. McShane, formerly of the major league St. Louis Browns and most recently of the same Charleston club Luke Easter had played for in 1955, was signed on to assist.

The October 26 mail brought a $50 stock request from Franklin Dilger of recently flood-ravaged Westbury, Connecticut. He wanted to help keep the Bisons afloat. A second out-of-town contact received that same day validated Dilger's faith as well as that of all of those who had been working toward the Bisons' survival: International League president Frank Shaughnessy had telephoned president Taylor to advise that the community-owned Buffalo Bisons would be formally admitted into the International League at a meeting to be held on November 5 at the Buffalo Hotel Lafayette. George (Red) Trautman, commissioner of minor league baseball, was heard from a week later. In town to address the MUNY League (Buffalo Municipal Baseball League) Honor Banquet on November 1, Trautman pledged himself to "do everything in my power to assist the Buffalo situation," according to Charley Young's News article of November 2.

Meanwhile, reckoning that recent major leaguers might not be so available as hoped for, nor the funds to persuade them, president Taylor offered a different tack. "We'd like to get a backbone of proved Triple A minor league players for our team," he commented on October 27 in the News. "And around these men we'll be able to fill in with the talent we get on loan from the major leagues." Detroit was promising four to five more players, he added, while John Stiglmeier was seeking commitments from other teams and Harry Bisgeier was continuing his scouting forays into both minor and major league cities.

NOVEMBER 1955

Back in town on November 1, the business manager reported that the Chicago White Sox, the Baltimore Orioles, the Milwaukee Braves, the Chicago Cubs and the Kansas City A's had all promised to either sell or loan players to the team.

Early November, prior to the Columbus meetings, brought speculation in the newspapers about the Bison manager selection. Was manager Danny Carnevale, skipper of the 1955 squad, to return? Other names mentioned were former major leaguers Rollie Hemsley, a pennant-winning manager for the Columbus American Association team several years prior; Phil Cavarretta, former Chicago Cub player and manager; and Dick Bartell, a former New York Giant infielder and Cincinnati coach. On November 8, former Bison catcher and big-leaguer Clyde McCullough was added to the candidate list. With now over 2000 stockholders, club president Taylor suggested the fans might write in to the stadium and offer their suggestions. He added that any decision would need to wait until the draft meetings were held later in the month.

Mid-November brought a new wrinkle to the stock and ticket effort. The promotion was led by Burt P. Flickinger, Jr., Buffalo branch manager of the S. M. Flickinger Co., Inc, assisted by Richard W. Jasper and S. M. Flickinger of the same firm; Chester Borowicz and Mike Gigante of the Peter Schmitt Co.; and Howard Schmitt and Harry Neureiter of the Hasselbeck Cheese Division of the Borden Company. These men would see to it that special sales booths were set up in an estimated 1500 food stores in Western New York, to be staffed by students from eight local colleges. Student body presidents from Canisius (William Holcomb), the University of Buffalo (Sal Carallo), State Teachers (Dan Idzik), Erie County Tech (Dan Bernicki), St. Bonaventure (William Schrouth), Niagara (Charles Kelly), Rosary Hill (Maureen Castine) and D'Youville (Barbara Meyers) pledged their support. The R&W Supermarkets, Red & White Food Stores, Sattler's, Bell Markets, Shop-Rite Stores, New Era Markets, P.S. Stores, Bishop Stores and Bis-Co Stores all agreed to create space for the Bison booths. Offermann Stadium reported a new total of 2100 stock subscribers and close to $95,000 on hand.

The baseball winter meetings got under way in Columbus, Ohio, on November 28, and on this date the Detroit Tigers released the names of the players who would be coming to the Bisons as part of the franchise deal: pitchers Milt Jordan, John Weiss, Bob Schultz, Joe Tully and Dick Rozek; outfielders George Bullard and Clyde Vollmer; catcher Pierce McWhorter; and infielder Mel Hoderlein. It was to be nine men, not 10 as had been initially anticipated.

Righthander Jordan, 28 years old, had had two good seasons with the Bisons in 1952 and 1953, going 12-9 and 12-1, respectively. He had appeared in eight games with Detroit in 1953, compiling a record of 0-1. In 1954 he was demoted from Buffalo to Double A Little Rock. He won 7 games and lost 6 for the Travelers in 1955. John Weiss, aged 30, also righthanded, had failed to stick with the Bisons in 1952, went 5-5 with the club in 1953 and had put together back-to-back 7-15 records with Little Rock in 1954 and 1955. Lefthander Bob Schultz (31), had seen limited duty with the Chicago Cubs and Pittsburgh Pirates from 1951 through 1953. After two successful years at Double A New Orleans, he had been acquired by the Tigers. In 1955, in a little more than one inning for Detroit, he had surrendered three earned runs. He finished the year with Buffalo, winning 10 and losing 14, second only to staff ace Ben Flowers in the win column.

Joe Tully (27), righthanded, had been an effective pitcher in the low minors in the Boston chain but had never made a good showing in Triple A after posting a 15-8 record with Class A Albany of the Eastern League. He was 0-1 with Syracuse in 1955. Lefty Dick Rozek had appeared in 33 games for Cleveland and the Philadelphia Phillies over five straight seasons, 1950 through 1954. His major league record was 1-0 with a 4.55 ERA. The 28-year-old's 1955 mark with Little Rock was 5-14.

Five-foot, nine-inch speedster George Bullard, signed for a $20,000 bonus as a shortstop and now a center fielder, had appeared in four games with the Tigers in 1954 as a pinch-runner and late-inning defensive shortstop. He had gone hitless in his only plate appearance. A broken hand after being hit by a pitch on September 25 of that year ended his season. The 26-year-old righthanded batter had played 70 games for Little Rock in 1955, hitting .275. In 52 games with Buffalo that season he had hit .249. Clyde Vollmer, 33, was a bona-fide 10-year veteran major leaguer with Cincinnati, Washington and the Boston Red Sox. In 1951, thanks to the short left-field fence at Fenway Park, the righthanded slugger had belted 22 home runs. He had split 1955 between Charleston and Buffalo, batting .278 with seven home runs for the Herd in 69 games.

Hamilton Pierce McWhorter was a career minor league catcher whose first appearance at the Triple A level was in 1955 with the Bisons. The 26-year-old part timer got into 21 games, hitting .231 in 52 at-bats. Mel Hoderlein had played parts of four seasons with Boston and Washington in the American League, hitting .269 in 72 contests with the 1952 Senators. He had spent 1954 and 1955 with the Bisons, filling in at second, short and third base as needed. A .257 average in his first year had dropped to .229 in 1955. He was now 32 years old.

On November 29, Stiglmeier and Bisgeier continued their pursuit of players and a vital working arrangement, even partial, with a major league club. Baseball Commissioner Ford C. Frick added his plea to the clubs that they give the Bisons all possible aid. Cy Kritzer quoted Frick in the News on November 29: "Community-ownership is one of the solutions to the problems of minor-league baseball." To Stiglmeier, he added, "I have followed your operation closely and I feel you have the right plan."

In good news, Buffalo learned that they had won the right to a first deal with Toronto if that organization decided to sell its veteran outfielders Sam Jethroe and Lew Morton or infielder Billy DeMars. The Syracuse Chiefs would be approached to see if outfielder Johnny Blatnik, a formidable hitter in Offermann Stadium, was available. But the most important news of the day was the confirmation of Luke Easter's spot on the Bison roster. Purchased conditionally from Charleston, Big Luke had been passed over in the major league draft and was to officially become a Bison.

Mixed news greeted the Herd's front office on November 30 in Columbus. Manager candidate Rollie Hemsley took himself out of the running by signing to manage the Charlotte, North Carolina, club in the South Atlantic League. Detroit notified the Bisons that third baseman Tom Sarna, a .315 hitter at Augusta, would be coming their way. Congenial talks were held with the Philadelphia Phillies (manager Mayo Smith was a former Bison), but no players were forthcoming, nor was an affiliation with the team. The Phillies system was bound to its working agreement with Syracuse.

Toronto owner Jack Kent Cooke suggested that the Bisons might be better off without a major league connection, but Stiglmeier remained doubtful. Contemplating several offers for the newly assigned pitcher Bob Schultz, Stiglmeier responded that Buffalo did not have Cooke's deep pockets to buy and sell as needed. Efforts to land catcher Nelson Burbrink, infielder Stan Jok and outfielder Tom Burgess from the St. Louis Cardinals went nowhere.

DECEMBER 1955

On December 2, Buffalo fans learned that their new player-manager would be Phil Cavarretta, a no-nonsense veteran of 22 big-league seasons and a no-nonsense manager as well. As an 18-year-old rookie with the National League Chicago Cubs, Cavarretta had homered in his first major league starting assignment, leading his team to a 1-0 victory over the Cincinnati Reds on September 25, 1934. Cavarretta helped spur the Cubs to National League pennants in 1935, 1938 and 1945, hitting .317 in all postseason play. He was chosen the National League's MVP in 1945 while winning the batting crown that year with a .355 average. In three All-Star game appearances he had hit an even .500. As manager of the Cubs, he had made no bones about his club's chances in 1954 spring training, predicting a second-division finish. Following that pronouncement, he was then summarily dismissed by the team's owner, Philip Wrigley. Cavarretta returned to a player role for the 1954 and 1955 seasons, now with the south side Chicago White Sox, but by 1956 he was itching to get back to the managerial reins.

Cy Kritzer's News column of December 2 reminded his readers that "veteran teams, stocked with a strong bench, have been the successful clubs" in Offermann Stadium. Cavarretta's goal, the new manager stated, was to "open the season with veterans, an aggressive team that makes few mistakes. It's the younger teams that make the defensive miscues that hurt in the early part of the race. Then, as the season wears along and our veterans show signs of getting tired, we can fill in with the youngsters that the Buffalo club has been promised from five different major league clubs." Kritzer summed it up with the assessment that Cavarretta had "big-league written all over him."

Bison president Taylor confided to News columnist Bob Stedler on December 12 that there were three factors in Cavarretta's presentation that had impressed him the most. Confidence was number one. Cavarretta, Taylor commented, had turned down several other offers because he felt he would have input into the building of the new Bison ball club. Secondly, he was in great physical condition. Taylor described him as a "young 38" (Cavarretta was actually 39), only two pounds over his rookie playing weight in 1934 and likely to be able to play 75 games at first base during the 1956 season if that was necessary. Lastly, Taylor credited Cavarretta's poise and his approach to managing veteran players.

It was a certainty that Cavarretta would have a veteran club to direct. His background would give him the knowledge and approach necessary to get winning results from those men. It was less certain that the major league clubs would fulfill their promises of sending winning ballplayers Buffalo's way when the season was preparing to open.

December 2 also brought news of more player acquisitions. Harry Nicholas, aged 25 with a 9-6 record and a 5.08 ERA with Little World Series victors Minneapolis of the American Association, was one of the new purchases. Nicholas had been named the New York State Most Valuable High School Player by the New York World Telegram in 1947, finishing a high-school career for Central High of Valley Stream with only two losses. In his senior year he struck out 146 batters in 90 innings of work, allowing but 27 hits and walking 34. He followed two consecutive no-hitters with a one-hitter. Nicholas, signed originally by the Yankees for a $35,000 bonus, had been released from that contract by Baseball Commissioner Happy Chandler due to questionable tactics by the New York club. The pitcher had then taken his talents across the river and signed a second bonus contract with the New York Giants. No slouch mentally, Nicholas had graduated in June 1955 from Wake Forest Law School, probably with his tuition fully paid.

Also from the Minneapolis club, but purchased from the Philadelphia Phillies who owned his contract, came 32-year-old second baseman Lou Ortiz, "one of the top double play pivots in baseball." Ortiz, 6 feet, 3 inches and 195 pounds, a Triple A player since 1950, had helped both Rochester and Minneapolis to Junior World Series titles in 1952 and 1955, respectively. As would be said of many of the new men, he hit well in Offermann Stadium. In the year just past, he had struck a career-high 19 home runs, crediting Wally Moses with teaching him the previous season how to finally get his hips into his swing to maximize his power.

Ortiz was used to playing in top-flight competition even as a youth. Back in 1940 he was a starter for the famed American Legion Post 6 squad from San Diego, California, that went to the Legion World Series in Albemarle, South Carolina. Jim Crow decided the outcome of the series when Legion authorities barred two black players on the Post 6 squad from performing on the same field with white teammates. Third baseman Nelson Manuel and catcher John Ritchey had to look on from a segregated bleacher section as their club dropped the series, three games to two. (A distinguished World War II veteran and Negro Leagues batting champion, Richey would integrate the Pacific Coast League in 1948 with the San Diego Padres.) In California sports, a man's performance was more important than the color of his skin. In Buffalo, New York, in 1956, Ortiz would be teammates with another black slugger, and both men together would help lead their club to success.

An International League All-Star keystone sacker in 1953 and 1954 with Rochester and a loop leader in double plays on four occasions, it seemed unthinkable that Ortiz had not yet seen duty as a major league ballplayer. Although military service in World War II delayed his entrance into organized baseball, the real answer to this conundrum might be summed up in four words: "Red Schoendienst" and "Reserve Clause." While Ortiz remained St. Louis Cardinal property, he was a valuable backup to perennial major league All-Star Schoendienst. And, held captive by baseball's reserve clause, he had no opportunity to concoct a deal that would allow him to play for any other club. An uncredited movie appearance, standing in for Jimmy Stewart's character on a baseball diamond long shot in Strategic Air Command, offered no consolation.

Johnny Blatnik (34) had a .260 year with the Phillies in 1948 and brief looks the following two seasons. In the high minors he could be counted on annually for 15 home runs and a .280 average. A broken collarbone had held him to 37 games for Syracuse in 1955, but he had hit .308 when he was on the field. A righty swinger, he was already known for putting dents in Offermann's high left-field barrier.

New pitchers added to the roster were Karl Drews (35) and Duane Pillette (31), both from the Pacific Coast League. Six feet, four inches tall, Drews had been a part time starter for the Yankees and St. Louis Browns from 1946 through 1949. He had been a member of the 1947 World Series-winning New York squad and had pitched three innings in two games against the losing Brooklyn Dodgers. The Yankees took the series, four games to three. Sent down to Baltimore (then in the International League), Drews suffered a fractured skull that ended his 1950 season, but a record of 17-13 in 1951 propelled him back to the majors with the Philadelphia Phillies. He went 14-15 in 1952 and finished up his major league career with Cincinnati in 1954. He had won 9 and lost 13 for Triple A Oakland in the season just concluded.

Similar to Drews in height and baseball service, Pillette stood 6 feet, 3 inches, and had hurled from 1946 to 1953 for the Yankees and Browns. When the Browns relocated to become the major league Baltimore Orioles in 1954, Pillette accompanied them. He was the pitcher of record in the first game won by the modern-day Baltimore major leaguers. He compiled a 10-14 record that campaign but dropped his only three decisions to start 1955. He was then sent down to Oakland midseason and finished the year at 2-3 with the Oaks, pitching alongside Drews.

Perhaps the biggest name in signings, as well as the tallest of all signees, was 6-foot, 5-inch Clint Hartung. Signed following high school in Hondo, Texas, the tall youngster had been unfairly ballyhooed as the next Babe Ruth or Christy Mathewson—or both. In 1942, the 19-year-old had hit .339 with Class C Eau Clair in his first professional season, slugging 12 home runs in 66 games and adding a won-three, lost-one record on the mound. Entering the military, he then played with the powerful Army Air Force Hickham Field Bombers in Hawaii, winning 25 consecutive games and punishing the ball at a .567 clip. Life magazine called him a "One-Man Ball Club." The New York Giants brought him up to the National League in 1947 where he won nine and lost seven, hitting .309 in 34 games. But this was his high-water mark. Hartung finished his big-league career in 1950, having won 29 games and losing the same number. His major league batting average wound up at .238. He had managed 14 home runs in six seasons. In the minor leagues, his numbers had slumped from .334 and 27 home runs in 1952 to .228 and 8 home runs in 61 games in 1955. The Bisons were hoping for a comeback from the struggling 32-year-old.

One new arm for the mound was added on December 3, as was a double-play partner for Lou Ortiz, both purchased from Toronto. Mario Picone, 29, had pitched in 13 games with the Giants and Cincinnati over three different call-ups between 1947 and 1954. His major league record was 0-2. In 1955, for last-place Richmond of the International League, he had gone 4-13. Traded to Toronto late in the season, he rang up a 3-3 mark with the Maple Leafs and crafted an outstanding 2.57 ERA. Picone had been signed by the New York Giants in 1944 as a sandlot player and had struck out 28 batters in a 19-inning game in his first year of organized baseball, pitching for Class D Bristol. He made his major league debut with the Giants in September 1947. He had gone 14-8 with Triple A Minnesota as recently as 1953, so perhaps the showing late last year with the Maple Leafs indicated a return to form.

Meanwhile, Billy DeMars (30) was no stranger to the Buffalo club. After a brief look with the Philadelphia Athletics in 1948, he had taken over as shortstop for Paul Richards' International League pennant-winning 1949 Bisons. The St. Louis Browns acquired him for the 1950 season, where he managed .247 in 61 games. He got into one game with the Browns in 1951, picked up a single in four at-bats, and was farmed out to San Antonio in the Texas League. Jack Kent Cooke picked up his contract the following year, and DeMars anchored the infield as the regular Toronto shortstop for 1952 and 1953. When the Leafs latched onto former International League Rookie of the Year (1951) Hector Rodriguez to play the position, DeMars was pushed into a utility role. He served in that capacity for 1954 and 1955, batting .299 and .283 as a part-timer. The Bisons were getting a good glove and a decent hitter to solidify the middle.

The Buffalo Evening News on December 5 informed its readership that the Bisons' front office was now in Chicago at the major league meetings with an inside track on a power-hitting catcher who could "pound the left field wall for up to 25 homers." Stiglmeier was also seeking a center fielder and two lefthanded hurlers. Citing pitching as the team's "main problem," the Bisons' general manager added that he was entertaining no offers for lefty Bob Schultz. In the meantime, what the club needed most from its fans was cash for player purchases. The club had already laid out almost $40,000 and more was needed. Buffalonians were encouraged to step forward and take advantage of a newly devised $10 "Christmas Package"—two shares of stock and five reserved seat tickets. The local supermarkets would put them on sale this week.

(In baseball news elsewhere on December 6, 1955, 81-year-old Honus Wagner, baseball's greatest shortstop and an original member of the Baseball Hall of Fame, died in his sleep in Carnegie, Pennsylvania.)

Good will engendered at the minor league convention in Columbus paid off with the purchase of infielder Bob Reed from the Milwaukee Braves on December 14. Milwaukee general manager John Quinn had wanted to move the Triple A Toledo, Ohio, farm club to Miami, Florida, but his efforts were blocked by the American Association. A potential working relationship with Buffalo had then been discussed with Stiglmeier and Bisgeier, and the two Bison executives agreed to hold off on any commitments to any other ball clubs until they heard from Quinn. Milwaukee eventually renewed the Toledo linkage, but Quinn was now rewarding the Bisons for the front office's willingness to help.

Reed had played in 15 games with the then Boston Braves in 1952, batting only .250, but he was a 10-year minor league veteran with a solid .314 average. Able to play both second and third base, the 32-year-old had started for Toledo for the past three seasons, making the American Association All-Star teams in 1953 and 1954. Skilled at hit and run, he was considered by Stiglmeier as an excellent backup for Ortiz at second and Mel Hoderlein at third.

On December 17, Bison president Reginald B. Taylor reported that the final $25,000 payment had been made to Detroit for the ball club's purchase. The Buffalo Bisons were now owned by 2300 local stockholders. A new member of that group, a season ticket holder for 10 years, a local automobile dealer who had not believed that an independent, fan-owned club could succeed, had turned up at the Offermann Stadium ticket booth several days before and plunked down $1000 for stock and tickets. A grateful Taylor reiterated the club's need for the ongoing influx of cash for player purchases.

Cy Kritzer reported in the News that the Bisons had now accumulated $125,000 in stock and $21,000 in ticket sales. Of that total, $75,000 had been used to purchase the ball club. Another $50,000 had been set aside to buy ballplayers. The remainder was reserved for operating expenses, salaries, spring training and administrative costs. The player purchase pool of $50,000 was nearly exhausted, team president Taylor reported. The club needed an additional $60,000 in order to solidify the pitching and sign the kind of quality center fielder that was required. To achieve that amount, the Bison front office was hoping to triple the stockholder ranks.

That Buffalo had been fortunate to hold onto its ball club was made evident in Buffalo Evening News articles on December 20. The fiscally ailing Syracuse, New York, franchise, one of the Bisons' natural rivals, had been sold for $100,000 and was being moved to Miami, Florida. This, in spite of the fact that Syracuse fans had raised $54,000 to buy the team. The brains behind the new operation would be none other than Bill Veeck, the baseball showman who knew how to win (his Cleveland Indians had won the 1948 World Series), to innovate and to bring in the fans wherever he was. Not only would he make the Miami club succeed, but he would also fatten the wallets of the visiting opposition through the anticipated increased gate receipts.

Syracuse was now the sixth International League ball club to have been relocated since the decade began. Springfield, Massachusetts, had replaced Newark, New Jersey, in the International League lineup in 1950. The Jersey City, New Jersey, club had been relocated to Ottawa, Ontario, Canada, in 1951. The Springfield entry had lasted only until 1953 and had been replaced by the Havana, Cuba, Sugar Kings in 1954. That same 1954 saw the International League Baltimore Orioles booted out of town by the new American League Baltimore Orioles. Richmond, Virginia, replaced Baltimore in the International League lineup. The following year, 1955, saw Ottawa cede its franchise to Columbus, Ohio. Stiglmeier and Bisgeier had not been understating the perilous nature of saving the Bisons for Buffalo.

While sad to lose the rivalry with Syracuse, Buffalo's leadership also had to look at the bottom line. Buffalo would petition to open the 1956 season in Miami instead of Montreal. This would reduce travel costs following spring training. The team would follow up with a series in Havana and then seek to play Richmond before heading back north. Miami's entry into the league meant that travel costs would be ameliorated, since the northern clubs could play games in those three southern cities mentioned before returning to their home stadia. Travel costs could be partly offset by the visiting team's share of the gate receipts.

December 22 brought the news that the sons of the highly regarded Detroit Tiger scout Cy Williams, a Buffalo native, were investing in the ball club. Williams, as an employee of another baseball organization, was barred from any such purchase in his own name. What he could contribute was an assessment of the team that might spur on other subscribers. That was a Christmas present in itself. "We think you have made a grand start towards building the Bisons," Williams commented. The News quoted him as follows: "Lou Ortiz at second base is the best double play maker in Triple A baseball and Luke Easter should thrive in Offermann Stadium. If he hit 31 home runs in Charleston, he could lead the International League for the Bisons. Billy DeMars is steady and capable and look for Mel Hoderlein to make a comeback at third base. At one stage of the 1955 season, he was the best third baseman in the league."

Evaluating the outfield, Williams suggested that George Bullard in center could be a "real surprise." He advocated giving the youngster a good opportunity before looking elsewhere. "He has the ability," Williams added, "and it's just a question of meeting the right manager who can bring it out." As for Clint Hartung, "[t]he [ball]park is made for him."

Behind the scenes, the Bisons had signed veteran baseball and hockey conditioner Jimmy Mack as the club's trainer. Mack, who was a "well-known bantamweight boxer in his youth," had previously served as the Bisons trainer before leaving to spend 17 seasons with the International League's Newark Bears. His 1954 duties had included serving as trainer for Portsmouth in the Piedmont League. He had also been a trainer for the Buffalo, Springfield, Syracuse and Hershey professional hockey teams in the American Hockey League. Mack could identify with the needs of a veteran team; he was 63.

"Why does the Buffalo baseball club need at least $60,000 more to insure a successful operation in its first season as a community owned team?" Bob Stedler posed this question in his Buffalo Evening News December 27 "Sport Comment." He then gave the floor to general manager John C. Stiglmeier to respond. Stiglmeier advised that the Buffalo club, without a major league working agreement, would have to spend from $15,000 to $20,000 more than last year on spring training expenses, including travel. Secondly, there would be no major league team to pay a percentage of each player's salary. As an example, the general manager pointed out, a player optioned to Buffalo who was earning $1350 per month would have $750 of that figure covered by the major league ball team. That player would cost the Bisons only $600 for his services. Thirdly, the Bisons had purchased some established Triple A stars with salaries of better than $8000 per year, at least $2000 above the current major league minimum. Those men would not be content to sign for less money.

President Reginald B. Taylor added his thoughts. "Being an independent club is a far more costly operation, but in the long run I'm sure it will be worth it to the fans of Buffalo. The team will be draftproof against major league raids. It will be our own ball club and that should mean a lot." That was a strong argument to anyone who could remember the 1939 season. Buffalo was fighting for the pennant that year, sparked by the exciting double-play combination of shortstop Lou Boudreau and second baseman Ray Mack, whizzes in the field and potent at the plate. In 115 games, Boudreau had slugged .331 with 17 home runs. Mack had chipped in with 15 roundtrippers and a .293 mark in the same number of contests. And there it had ended. The Cleveland Indians, on their way to a woeful third place finish—20 1/2 games behind the New York Yankees—recalled the two men and Buffalo stumbled to third place and a quick exit from the playoffs. To have ballplayers safe from major league raids spoke volumes in Buffalo.

Still, with stock subscriptions falling behind the hoped-for expectations, would the fans truly get behind the club? The rest of the baseball world was watching, Buffalo fans were advised. If the Buffalo venture could succeed, it might prove the pattern for all of the minor leagues to follow. According to Stiglmeier, "We are building and stretching every resource to produce a winner, and we think we can...but if we fail, will the fans stick with us?" Frank (Trader) Lane, formerly general manager of the Chicago White Sox and now of the St. Louis Cardinals, encouraged the Buffalo fan base to see baseball as entertainment, noting that "a losing ball club can be as interesting and as colorful as a winner that scores few runs and stays on top with defense and pitching." Tom McCaffery, owner of the independent Albany Senators in the Eastern League, had finished in last place in 1955 but had provided the fans with an interesting club that could "rack the fences" and stay in almost every game to the end. It was "the kind of team you enjoyed," McCaffery commented to the Bison executives. Were the Bisons sending a similar kind of message to their followers?

On December 28, Bisons president Taylor received a message from International League president Frank Shaughnessy inviting him to attend the upcoming league meetings where the new Miami club—last year's Syracuse Chiefs—was to be inducted into the league. Also to be discussed was the new playing schedule for 1956, where Buffalo could raise its request for series in Havana and Richmond to follow the season-opening games against the Florida club. This would help immeasurably with travel expenses while allowing the weather to warm up in the Queen City for the anticipated May 2 home opener.

On this same December 28, general manager Stiglmeier sent out a message of his own. He was pleased to inform his fellow Bisons directors (Taylor, Bisgeier, secretary Eugene J. McMahon, Thomas W. Ryan, Herbert J. Vogelsang, Dick Fischer, John C. Montana, Edwin F. Jaeckle, Wade Stevenson, John Krysinski and Frank Cannon) that a reception was to be held for the new Buffalo manager, Phil Cavarretta, who would be arriving in town on January 6. With both Cavarretta and the New Year fast approaching, and with the new experiment in community-owned Buffalo baseball capably under way, all involved felt that they and the fans were already winners for the season to come, regardless of where the club finished in the standings.

Baseball, after all, was staying in Buffalo.

Luke Easter signs contract with General Manager John Stiglmeier while William Comstock and Don Labruzzo look on

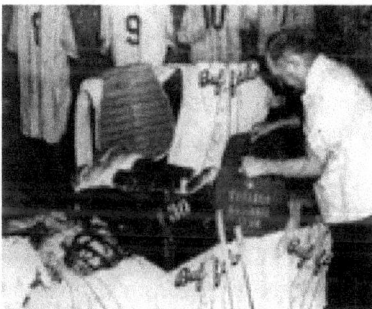

Trainer Jimmy Mack packs the bags for spring training

Stadium superintendent Max Felerski instructs John Stiglmeier at Offermann Stadium

All photos courtesy of SUNY Buffalo State Courier-Express Collection

Chapter 4: Preseason, 1956

JANUARY

New manager Phil Cavarretta's plane arrived an hour late at the Buffalo airport on his January 6 flight from Dallas, Texas, but they kept the reception warm for him at the Bison offices at Offermann Stadium. Here he met with team executives, the local press, and radio and television representatives. Following the official signing of the one-year managerial contract agreed to at the winter meetings in Columbus, Ohio, he told the welcoming party that he wanted to avoid any rash predictions about the team this early in the process. While he believed that a first-division finish was certainly possible with the players already on the roster (the Bisons had finished in sixth place in 1955, trailing the fourth-place Rochester Red Wings by 11 1/2 games and the pennant-winning Montreal Royals by a distant 30), he needed to take a personal look at his team's talent in spring training before he spoke further. Based on his years as a major league manager, Cavarretta knew that there was a chance for more pitching and position help to be found before opening day. Furthermore, he had to see what the seven other International League clubs might look like come the end of the exhibition season. "It would not be fair to management, players or public," he told the Courier's Bill Coughlin, "to do any popping off on my first day in town or in the immediate future."

Even so, the new manager was not hesitant to answer questions about the Buffalo boy on the roster, Pat Tomkinson, a catcher out of Seneca Vocational High School who had made the Buffalo Evening News High School 1944 All-Star team as an honorable mention in his senior year. "I saw Tomkinson play a series with Oklahoma City against Dallas in Texas League action last season and he looks all over the 'take charge' type of catcher so important in handling a pitching staff." Cavarretta added that the club would enjoy a significant display of power from the bat of former Cleveland Indian Luke Easter. He told the assemblage that the big first baseman was pounding the ball at a .310 clip at Hermosillo in the Mexican winter league, having already driven out 15 home runs "in the big ballparks down that way." President Reginald B. Taylor added to the positive outlook for the squad thus far assembled. Referring to the two-time International League All-Star second baseman Lou Ortiz, Taylor revealed that the team had already been offered four players in trade for Ortiz's services. "Maybe we got a bargain there," he told the News for its January 9 edition.

Cavarretta's plans called for him to make an inspection of the ballpark, remain in Buffalo for the January 8 sports writers and sportscasters' March of Dimes Dinner at the Hotel Statler and meet with the newly appointed team trainer, Jimmy (Doc) Mack.

Earlier in the day of the meeting with Cavarretta, the team's board of directors had met in formal session to take official action on the business already transacted by president Taylor, general manager Stiglmeier and business manager Bisgeier. A vote of confidence was issued for the previously enacted player deals, player purchases and related expenses totaling nearly $60,000 that had been undertaken at the Columbus winter meetings. President Taylor announced that he had closed a contract for spring training in Bartow, Florida, a site where the Bisons had gotten into shape for the season back in 1947 and again in 1952. For the past several years the Bisons had been at Detroit's spring headquarters, in Lakeland, Florida, under their arrangement as a Tiger farm club.

Taylor advised that the training season would be cut to four weeks, with the players scheduled to report on March 22. Cavarretta agreed to this plan, stating that for the veteran players the team was fielding, a four-week spring training period should be sufficient. As pros, these men would know they needed to be in shape before reporting to Florida. Stiglmeier announced that 11 spring training contests had been scheduled starting April 1. Opponents would include the Richmond, Miami, Denver, Charleston and Augusta clubs.

On January 4, Buffalo Evening News readers learned that the Bisons would indeed open the 1956 season on April 18 against the Miami Marlins. The new Florida entry, relocated from Syracuse, had been embroiled in a stadium controversy between the Miami club's owner, Sid Salomon, Jr., and the Miami City Commission. To resolve the conflict, the city finally proposed purchasing the stadium from its present owner and guaranteeing Salomon and his partners a 10-year lease, with an option for 10 years more. Bill Veeck, one of the advisors for the Syracuse club's purchase and past owner of the major league Cleveland Indians and the St. Louis Browns, was instrumental in helping all parties come to a satisfactory solution. Veeck said he was there only to help Salomon and another partner, Elliott Stein, get the ball club up and running. He would bow out after the new franchise had set up their front office, picked a manager and secured some additional players.

With Veeck in the picture and with the goal to eventually bring major league ball to Miami, the parties were able to resolve their differences. Thus, the International League's board of directors voted unanimously to endorse the transfer of the Syracuse franchise to Miami. The Chiefs of 1955 would take the field as the Marlins of 1956, but the Buffalo Bisons would stay the Bisons and remain in Buffalo.

Bartow, Florida, was located in mid-state Polk County, a dry town with no nightlife but plenty of other recreation. The Bisons could avail themselves of a community golf course, a large outdoor swimming pool (usually not opened until May, after the team would have left camp) and plenty of nearby lakes for fishing. More fishing was available on the state's West Coast, only 60 miles distant. Cypress Gardens was nearby and for those who really wanted to swim, Winter Haven was only nine miles away. Visitors were welcomed to that city's publicly owned bathhouse and beach.

An old town of approximately 9500 residents, with a plethora of oak and jacaranda trees shading the sidewalks, Bartow found itself surrounded by a wealth of cattle ranches, timber production, citrus and pimiento canning plants, a sawmill and a crate factory nearby. Bartow also boasted the largest phosphate deposits and mines in the world. An airport and two major railroads served a large shipping business in fruits and vegetables, while the cattle ranching industry had resulted in the largest rodeo in the South being held each spring in Bartow. Two motels and the Gilbert Oaks Hotel—the Bisons would stay at the latter—hosted out-of-town visitors.

This was music to the ears of the Bisons' faithful. With 2300 people now signed up as stockholders, January 6 total assets amounted to $166,994.80, of which $149,399 had been subscribed as stock and the remaining $23,545.80 for tickets. However, as president Taylor pointed out, the team had had to purchase the Bisons franchise from Detroit—a outlay of $75,000—and nearly $50,000 more had been expended purchasing additional players. Taylor announced that there would be a general stockholders' meeting in February at which an official slate of club directors and officers would be chosen. Also to be undertaken was the matter of a salary for business manager Harry Bisgeier, now taking on additional tasks as the club's assistant general manager. While the other officers would remain unsalaried, Bisgeier would have to devote full time to his duties and could not go the year unremunerated.

True to Cavarretta's predictions, the Bisons picked up another hurler on January 12. Lefty Roger Bowman was purchased from the Hollywood Stars of the Pacific Coast League. Harry Bisgeier, speaking to Kritzer of the News on January 12, had this to say about the purchase: "When he was with one club an entire season Bowman was a winning pitcher. We are hoping he can return to his 1954 form and give us a 20-victory season." Bisgeier added that Bowman's poor 1955 showing had made him available, but Stiglmeier noted that Stars manager Bobby Bragan was loath to part with the pitcher and the only reason he was obtained was because of a promise to the Bisons made by Pirates general manager, Joe Brown, later approved by Branch Rickey.

Bowman's presence now gave the Bisons three lefthanders: Bowman, Dick Rozek and Bob Schultz. From the right side, the team could count on Milt Jordan, Johnny Weiss, Karl Drews, Duane Pillette, Harry Nicholas and Mario Picone. At Cavarretta's request, pitchers and catchers would report to spring training on March 18. The catchers would be Pat Tomkinson and Pierce McWhorter.

Lefthander Roger Bowman, now 28, had been a standout high school hurler in Amsterdam, New York. In 1945, pitching in the All-American Amateur Baseball Association Tournament held in Johnstown, Pennsylvania, he had fanned an incredible 71 batters in 27⅓ innings. Signed the following year by the New York Giants, Bowman had hurled in 50 games for the Giants and the Pittsburgh Pirates since 1949 (overall record 2-11 with a 5.81 ERA). Although he could not get untracked in the National League, Bowman was a proven performer at the Triple A level. With the 1949 International League Jersey City Giants, he had notched 15 victories. He improved to 16 wins in 1950 as well as leading the league in strikeouts. For the 1952 Pacific Coast League Oakland Oaks, he had no-hit the Hollywood Stars.

Pitching for Hollywood in 1954, Bowman had led the Pacific Coast League with 22 wins, losing 13 and crafting a 2.51 ERA. On the last day of the season he threw a seven-inning perfect game against the Portland Beavers, pulling his team into a tie for the pennant. Bowman's heroics had earned him another shot at the majors. On the mound for the Pittsburgh Pirates in 1955, the 6-foot, 180-pound Colgate graduate lost his only three decisions before being sent down to Hollywood in the Pacific Coast League. Hurling for the Stars, Bowman slumped to a 5-10 record while his ERA jumped more than a run to 3.70.

Maybe Cavarretta's request for the earlier reporting date had come at the suggestion of Myrtle Power, photographed whispering in his ear at the March of Dimes dinner. Mrs. Power had recently won $32,000 as a baseball expert on the television game show "$64,000 Question," having correctly named the six men since 1900 who had collected 3000 hits in their major league careers—Ty Cobb, Tris Speaker, Honus Wagner, Eddie Collins, Napoleon Lajoie and Paul Waner. The 70-year-old Power had become a celebrity, hired by the Hearst newspapers to cover the 1955 World Series and also signed by CBS to provide sports commentary for one week. As such, she became the first woman on television in that type of role. At the Buffalo March of Dimes dinner Cavarretta was an agreeable listener. An extra week for pitchers and catchers made a lot of sense to a man in the know.

Position players would adhere to the previously announced March 22 date. Among the infielders, Cavarretta would call upon himself and Luke Easter at first base. Lou Ortiz would cover second base and Billy DeMars, shortstop. Mel Hoderlein and Bill Reed were going to compete for third. Cavarretta could count on George Bullard, Clyde Vollmer, Johnny Blatnik, Clint Hartung and Bill Killinger in the outfield.

Hard at work, Stiglmeier now updated the spring exhibition schedule. The first of 16 games would take place on March 31. The Bisons would face off against American Association franchises Charleston and Denver, International League rivals Miami and Richmond and the three Detroit

Tiger farm clubs representing Augusta, Georgia; Terre Haute, Indiana; and Durham, North Carolina.

Along with encouragement for more fans to join the ranks of stockholders, the newspapers continued to update the roster developments. Outfielder Eric Rodin was optioned to the Bisons from the New York Giants on January 26. At 6 feet, 2 inches tall, the 210-pound native of Whitehouse, New Jersey, wrote to the Bisons to express his gratitude for being able to play ball in the east, close to his home. He added that Offermann's small dimensions well suited his game. President Taylor announced that Giants owner Horace Stoneham was fulfilling his promise to help the Bison squad.

Rodin had spent 1955 shuttling between Columbus, Ohio, and Minneapolis, Minnesota, in the American Association, eventually winding up the year with the Oakland Oaks in the Pacific Coast League. His batting suffered as a result: he hit .227 in Columbus and .247 at Minneapolis, but he finished strong with a .362 mark for the Oaks in 18 games. Only the year before he had slugged .336 and 18 home runs at Double A Nashville and had even been called up to the Giants in September for pinch-hitting duties. He remained with the big club through their World Series victory over the Cleveland Indians, but his major league numbers revealed that he had failed to get a hit in six plate appearances. Rodin was showing his appreciation for the opportunity to get a fair chance to play in Buffalo by offering to report early with the pitchers and catchers and assist in warming up the moundsmen.

On January 26, Cy Kritzer of the News reported that pitcher Karl Drews had become the first Bison to ink a contract. Off the field, Max Felerski's services were retained as the new Offermann Stadium superintendent. He would live on the premises. John Boersma, who had been a stadium staff member for a dozen years, was named the new groundskeeper. And to close out the month with additional welcome information, the News' Bob Stedler revealed in his January 30 "Sport Comment" that Al Schacht, the "Clown Prince of Baseball," had gotten in touch with the team saying, "I want to do my part in helping your new ball club."

Schacht, a righthanded winner of 19 games with the 1919 Jersey City Skeeters (International League) and victor of 14 games with the Washington Senators from 1919 to 1921, had seen his promising career come to a stop following a sore arm. Reluctant to leave the baseball world, he had transformed himself into a world-class on-field entertainer, a clown who performed for the fans in the seats and for the GIs overseas on World War II tours to Africa, Europe and the Pacific. To the Bisons he had written, "I am now arranging my own schedule. So let's get together on a date for Buffalo, as soon as possible. I'll do my show for free in Offermann Stadium and pay all my expenses."

News of that nature led Harry Bisgeier to comment, "It makes us feel that Buffalo has staunch friends everywhere in baseball." John Stiglmeier planned to call on Schacht during the International League meeting in New York City on Saturday, February 4. Stedler once again urged the Buffalo' fandom to pick up a dozen or more shares in the ball club as a "matter of pride."

FEBRUARY

When Bob Stedler talked, people apparently listened. Or was it fraternal arm-twisting at the Buffalo Athletic Club? Or maybe a combination of civic pride and good business sense? On February 1, Arthur L. Chapman, vice president in charge of operations at the Radio and Television Division of Sylvania Electric Products Inc. at 254 Rano Street, Buffalo, presented Bison president Reginald B. Taylor with a $5000 check to support the stock purchase campaign.

Over lunch at the Buffalo Athletic Club, Chapman lauded Taylor's efforts on behalf of the Bisons. "Now it is our turn to help," he offered to the News, explaining that the stock would be distributed to Sylvania dealers, who would pass it on to their customers. Carl G. Luhman, president of Cladco Distributors Inc., said that there were more than 400 dealers served by his organization. "Thus," Chapman continued, "many of us will share in the ownership of the team. We fervently hope that other industries in the area—others with a large stake in Buffalo and Western New York—will see fit to follow this example." He finished by saying, "We want the Bisons to stay. And [we want them to] become a championship team."

The International League meetings held in New York City on Saturday, February 4, at first took something away from the Bisons and then granted them a concession that would more than make up for the loss. With Miami now an International League city, league officials granted Bob Maduro, owner of the Havana Baseball Club, a reprieve from having to pay part of the travel expenses of the other ball clubs when they traveled to Cuba to play the Sugar Kings. The Bison brass protested this decision until they were given the right to play the Havana club on Cuban Day, August 13, a contest which usually resulted in a turnout of up to 25,000 paying customers and a very healthy road reimbursement to the visitors.

In other league news, a new All-Star format was planned for the 1956 season. An All-Star cast from the league would be pitted against "the best major league team available." League president Frank J. Shaughnessy reported that the game would be played in a "northern city." Here was another chance for a big payday for the fledgling community-owned Bisons, if they could beat out the competition. Rochester, Toronto and Montreal also wanted to host the event. The players for the International League All-Star team would be chosen by the fans and the circuit's sports writers.

Attending their own concurrent meeting in New York City, the league's sports writers finally admitted Marse Joe McCarthy into the International League Hall of Fame. McCarthy, now a Lockport, New York, resident, had won eight pennants and seven World Series titles with the New York Yankees, but he had played only two seasons in the International League—both as a Buffalo Bison second baseman. His numbers were not impressive. He hit only .266 in both 1914 and 1915. His lifetime average for 15 minor league campaigns was only .261. His strengths as a baseball man obviously lay elsewhere.

The writers also elected George Earnshaw, a dominant pitcher for the Philadelphia Athletics from 1929 through 1932 (86 victories in that span) and a 29-game winner for the International League's Baltimore Orioles in 1925. Jimmy Ripple was the third selection for the Hall, a 10-year outfielder in the International League, batting .333 for the 1935 Montreal Royals, and a seven-year National League veteran with the New York Giants, Brooklyn Dodgers and Cincinnati Reds.

Speaking of the major leagues, club owners on this date refused to raise the major league minimum salary from $6000 to $7200. They also affirmed that players would have no influence over World Series television and radio sales. That was to remain the sole province of the Baseball Commissioner. Owners did agree to meet to discuss the pension system. John Galbreath of Pittsburgh and Joe Cronin of the Red Sox would represent the owners. They would confer with pitchers Bob Feller (Cleveland Indians) and Robin Roberts (Philadelphia Athletics), who would speak for the players.

Spring training would not get under way for the majors until March 1 (and for Buffalo's pitchers and catchers, it was not to begin until March 18), but this did not prevent Buffalo's native professional ballplayers from loosening up beforehand. The Lanigan Fieldhouse at 150 Fulton Street had become a gathering spot for at least one major leaguer with Buffalo roots and for a number of others aspiring to those heights. Werner (Babe) Birrer, Detroit hurler who had won 4, lost 3 and saved 6 in 1955, was photographed by the News on February 10 throwing to new Bison receiver Pat Tomkinson. Other local talent on hand were Jimmy Lumadue, a shortstop headed for Durham, North Carolina; Nick Koleff, a pitcher assigned to Augusta, Georgia; Bobby Williams, a rookie due to report to Terre Haute, Indiana; and Al Henningham, on the roster for Idaho Falls, Idaho.

South Buffalo star Tommy Van Remmen was also throwing to Tiger scout Cy Williams. Williams was very high on Van Remmen's chances after an outstanding 16-5 at Jamestown in 1954 and a solid 11-9 last year in higher classification. Two Yankee farmhands were also taking part in the workouts, shortstop Jimmy Ludka and pitcher Art Buczkowski. Allen Chester, toiling in the Kansas City farm system, rounded out the group.

Birrer thought he had a chance to make the Detroit staff despite the presence of such veteran hurlers as Virgil Trucks (13-8 with the 1955 Chicago White Sox), Steve Gromek (13-10 with the Tigers) and Ned Garver (12-16 with Detroit). "That's why I wanted to do some throwing and conditioning before reporting March 1 at Lakeland, Florida," he added. The younger players wanted to know how Birrer had pitched to both Mickey Mantle and Ted Williams. Mantle, Birrer said, had homered off him in New York, but Birrer had had later success getting him out on low breaking pitches. Williams was another story. In a game in which Birrer had emerged the victor, Williams had reached him for a home run, a double that just missed flying out of the park, and a single.

The news on February 15 was that the Bisons had added veteran minor league righthander Vic Stryska to the mound corps. A Navy veteran, Stryska had won 90 games and lost 54 in the lower minors, but had struggled at several attempts at Class Double A, going 1 and 5 overall. Here he was being considered for Triple A ball. Perhaps he was a long shot, or perhaps he was showing something with the Carta Vieja club in this winter's Panama Canal Zone league. Cavarretta would be the one to make the call once spring training got under way.

On February 19, the Courier-Express reported that 32-year-old major league veteran Bill Serena was going to be the new candidate for the Herd's third-base position. It was Cavarretta, Serena's Cubs manager from 1951 to 1953, who insisted to the Bison brass that they reach out to acquire the third baseman. President Taylor told the Buffalo Evening News that Cavarretta felt Serena was good for 30 home runs at Offermann Stadium if he could get off to a good start. General manager John Stiglmeier opined that Serena and Luke Easter could both contend for the league home run crown.

In other news, team shareholders were informed of a March 10 meeting to be held at the Lafayette Hotel to elect directors of the Buffalo Bisons Baseball Club, Inc. The directors, in turn, would designate the officers of the organization. Also to be considered was a proposal to enlarge the board of directors from 12 to as many as 21 persons. The preseason was getting under way with signings for the field and elections for the board.

On February 22, the News alerted Bisons fans that the Cavarretta connection was continuing to pay off: Harry L. (Peanuts) Lowrey, Cavarretta's old Cubs roommate, had been signed as a coach and utility outfielder. General manager Stiglmeier reported that Lowrey had turned down two major league opportunities to be able to work as Cavarretta's coach, being promised that he would accompany the skipper in the same capacity if Cavarretta returned to managing in the majors.

In a monster year in 1947 with Class C Lubbock, Texas, third baseman Bill Serena had collected 57 home runs in 137 games and a .374 batting average, 183 runs scored and 190 driven home. He then added 13 more home runs in 15 season-ending playoff games, a total of 70 homers in 152 games.

Serena had already seen service as a Bison third baseman for half a season when he was a member of Paul Richards' 1948 pennant-winning ball club. He had slammed 13 homers and driven home 32 runs in 63 games, adding a .258 average. At the time a Detroit signee, Serena, along with several others, had then been declared a free agent by Baseball Commissioner Happy Chandler, who accused the Tigers of covering up the ballplayers after the Tigers' working relationship with the Dallas club had ended. Detroit was apparently trying to hide Serena in Buffalo in 1948.

Suddenly freed from his Detroit contract, Serena signed back with the Dallas club to play out the remainder of 1948. Dallas was able to offer him more money than the Bisons could. He belted nine more home runs with Dallas to finish out the year, fashioned a solid 1949 season with the Texas League club and was sold to the Chicago Cubs. In spring training he won a starting spot in the 1950 Cubs lineup.

Serena thus became a Chicago teammate of Phil Cavarretta that year and put together a rookie season of 17 home runs, 61 RBIs and a .239 average. A fractured wrist suffered in a game on May 6 ended his 1951 season before it had a chance to get started, but he rebounded in 1952 with 15 more homers, 61 RBIs and his best major league average of .274. Reduced playing time in the next two years led to his sale to the Chicago White Sox and assignment to the Pacific Coast League for the 1955 season. Splitting the season with Oakland and San Francisco, Serena hit 18 home runs, knocked 71 runners across the plate and batted .269.

Harry "Peanuts" Lowrey, at 37, had filled in for the injured Philadelphia Phillie center fielder Richie Ashburn in 1955, hitting only .189 but "doing a great job for us," according to Phillies manager Mayo Smith. The 13-year major league veteran "is still fast," Smith told the Bisons, and could also fill in at second base and third. He owned a lifetime major league average of .273.

Lowrey's nickname may have come from his grandfather, who allegedly remarked that he was "no bigger than a peanut" at birth. Perhaps it was his size that got him roles in Hollywood Our Gang movies, but as a ballplayer he went from stealing scenes to stealing signs. He was ranked among the best in baseball in reading pitchers, a talent expected to serve the Bisons well. Among his credits, Lowrey owned the major league mark for seven consecutive pinch hits, which he set in 1952. His World Series batting average of .310 was crafted in the Cubs' 1945 loss to the Detroit Tigers. He also collected a single in two at-bats in the 1946 All-Star Game.

February 24 brought more news of pitching additions and subtractions. Twenty-eight-year-old Dick Rozek, a lefthander with a 5-14 mark with Double A Little Rock in 1955, announced his retirement from the game to go into executive training with a refrigeration company. Thirty-year-old Ed March (Edward Marchefsky), 1-0 with an 8.10 ERA with the 1949 Bisons and subsequently unable to stick in 1955, was back for a third try. For the 1954 pennant-winning Eastern League (Single A) Wilkes-Barre Barons, he had won 8, lost 9 and saved 15 games.

New to the scene but not to the city (he was born in Buffalo in 1928) was Dan Lewandowski. Dan had lost one game with the 1951 St. Louis Cardinals, surrendering a winning run in one inning pitched. A standout in the lower minors—he had gone 24 and 6 at Allentown, Pennsylvania, in 1951—Dan was a sub .500 pitcher at A ball and above. He had retired in 1955 but kept his hand in the game by pitching semipro ball in Galt, Ontario. It was worth a try for a hometown boy to see what might happen.

The newspapers reported on further late February ballplayer signings. Pat Tomkinson, now living in Kenmore, and Billy DeMars had come to terms with the team, as had Luke Easter and George Bullard. Second baseman Lou Ortiz's contract was received on Leap Day, February 29. The number of Bisons now under contract was an even dozen. Trainer Jimmy Mack had begun full-time activity at the ballpark, readying the equipment for shipment to Florida by the end of the first week in March.

MARCH

Buffalo's "First on Your Dial," your "FIRST Sports Station," WGR Radio 55 proudly announced that all of the Bisons' games, home and away, would be broadcast by the experienced team of Roger Baker and Bill Mazer. Fans could look forward to a "vivid word picture of the exciting play." In a March 4 Courier-Express advertisement, the station called out to their listeners, saying, "with a new 'fighting' team, you won't want to miss a game."

The first complete team roster was published in the newspapers on March 6. It listed 12 pitchers, two catchers, seven infielders and seven outfielders. The average age was just over 30, including 39-year-old player-manager Cavarretta and 37-year-old player-coach Lowrey. Only one pitcher had won as many as 10 games in 1955—Bob Schultz, with the Bisons, going 10-14 with a 5.75 ERA. The fate of two other hurler positions was unclear. Dick Rozek had announced his retirement, although Detroit promised they would provide the Herd with another moundsman if Rozek made good on his notification. Also, although Duane Pillette was listed on the roster, he was being considered for a pitching role by the Cleveland Indians. All of the other men, as pointed out by the News' Bob Stedler, were owned outright by the Bisons and thus not liable to recall by any major league operation. The team would have a stable roster for the season.

Only two men had hit over .300 in 1955. John Blatnik had registered a .308 mark with Syracuse prior to his injury, and third baseman Bill Reed had hit the ball at a .307 clip in 75 games with Toledo. Luke Easter at first base had accounted for 30 home runs. Second baseman Lou Ortiz had rung up 19. Bill Serena at third had sent 17 balls over the fences. As for runs batted in, Easter led the roster with last season's 101. Serena had knocked in 67. Ortiz had managed 48.

Cavarretta was optimistic about a first-division finish for his club but was still looking for more front-line pitching, another catcher and help in the outfield. The Courier-Express quoted him as adding that he was "looking forward to our opening day of training [March 18 in Bartow, Florida] with high hopes. I know one thing. All of us will work hard at camp, and we'll be in good shape when the season opens." Bob Schultz inked his contract the next day.

Charley Young, Buffalo Evening News sports editor, gave the fans an inside look at the club's efforts to run an "economical" but not "cheap" training program. On March 8, he reminded his readers that the Bison directors had chosen Bartow for the spring training site in part because of its location in the middle of the state. That meant that the longest trip for an exhibition game would be only 30 miles. Additionally, the Bartow Chamber of Commerce had agreed to pick up the tab for transportation for those away contests. The ballfield was good, and the Gilbert Oaks Hotel food was satisfactory. President Taylor had ordered the complete menus from the hotel over the previous three weeks to ensure that the food would be adequate. The key point, general manager Stiglmeier emphasized, was that the officers were the "custodians of the money of nearly 3000 little stockholders. We want to run this camp as economically as possible…and still not be cheap with the players."

A $300 expense was saved when the Bisons were able to borrow a rudimentary batting cage from nearby Haines City, Florida. It could be fixed up with little outlay to be more serviceable. With a mostly veteran team, the players were also expected to come into camp already in shape.

Shortening the training period to four and a half weeks from five or six would save $7 per man per day for room and board. This would cut nearly $21,000 from the spring expenses. Thus, with equipment already shipped and trainer Jimmy Mack set to leave on Saturday, March 10, all was primed for the pitchers and catchers' arrival on the 18th. Cavarretta anticipated a brief workout on day one of camp, followed by a routine of running, running, running to bring ancient legs back into shape. The team would focus on fundamentals such as pickoff plays, backing up and pitcher covering first base situations.

On Saturday, March 10, the Hotel Lafayette witnessed the first general meeting of the stockholders of the newly created and community-owned Buffalo baseball club. Approximately 300 people attended, including 10-year-old David Milch of 44 Hallam Road, the proud owner of one share of stock, and his 11-year-old friend, Michael Fineberg of 80 Traymore. The original slate of directors and officers was elected to continue their responsibilities until November, but an additional vote by acclamation added three "little fellow" shareholders: Edward F. Kelly, Helen Berny and Roxie Gian.

Mrs. Berny, describing herself as "an avid baseball fan" who hadn't missed a Bison home opener for 10 years, became the first woman on the board in nearly 20 years. The last had been Mrs. Frank J. Offermann, who had held such a position until the late 1930s following the death of her husband, the team's previous owner. Mrs. Berny admitted that it was her husband Stanley and her son Stanley Jr. who had encouraged her interest in the game, but she now found it to be a way of relaxing and forgetting business. She was a bookkeeper for a heating concern partly owned by her husband. She had also gotten close to a number of the Bison players over this stretch, even to the point of becoming the godmother for Verla Bea Hausmann, daughter of Clem Hausmann, who had pitched for the Bisons from 1947 through 1951. (Hausmann had posted a Buffalo record of 45 wins, 40 losses.)

Kelly, a graduate of the Park School (he earned two varsity letters in baseball), Hamilton College and the graduate school of Georgetown, was the president of Kelly Letter Services. He saw armed service as a sergeant in the Armed Forces Radio Service in the Panama Canal Dept. and was a member of the Saturn Club, a past director of the Junior Chamber of Commerce and an occasional thespian at the Studio Arena Theater.

Roxie Gian began his general contracting business in 1945 with a $95 junked truck. He parlayed that investment along with hard work and dedication into building 11 Loblaws grocery stores in Western New York, plus two more near Utica. In World War II he served as a salvage inspector for the Bell Aircraft Corporation. The membership also passed a motion that an incorporation amendment be prepared to raise the directorate number to 21 at the May meeting.

Stiglmeier told the crowd that the current officers—president Reginald B. Taylor, himself as general manager, treasurer Herbert J. Vogelsang and secretary J. Eugene McMahon—still intended to serve for the year without compensation. In doing so, however, and to break even financially, Stiglmeier forecast that a total attendance of 250,000 at the ballpark would be required. Only the day before, Bob Stedler's News column had reported that season box and reserved seat purchases were well below expectations. The club was in possession of less than half of its anticipated resources and already facing a shortfall of $66,686. Stedler added, "It's now or never...and the time is immediate. Never let it be said that Buffalo failed in this community project." Vogelsang announced the good news to the membership that the WGR purchase of the rights to air the Bison games had brought in $18,000.

Just before the meeting began, attendees were treated to the news that another Buffalo boy was to be heading south to Bartow, Florida. Twenty-four-year-old Don McAndrews of South Buffalo, formerly in the Philadelphia Phillies farm system, would make it an all-Buffalo catching cast in spring training, joining Pat Tomkinson. McAndrews had hit .249 in two seasons at the Class D and B levels and then went into military service for two years. Last season he had been employed with the Nickel Plate railroad and had starred for the Ebenezer club in the Buffalo MUNY League. Now that catcher Pierce McWhorter had announced his retirement from the game, the Bisons were left with only Tomkinson and McAndrews behind the plate.

The ides of March was a notoriously bad date for Julius Caesar, and the middle of March 1956 looked like it wouldn't bode particularly well for International League pitchers. The Bisons announced the March 14 purchase of lefty swinging Joe Brovia, a 1955 Pacific Coast League All-Star with the Oakland Oaks. Here was the outfield help that manager Phil Cavarretta had alluded to, a deal that the Bisons had had in the making since the minor league baseball meetings in Columbus, Ohio.

It was Roger Bowman, a 22-game winner with the Pacific Coast League's Hollywood Stars in 1954, who tipped the balance. "He was one of the toughest batters I ever pitched against," the pitcher was quoted in the March 14 News, putting Brovia in the same league with "Stan Musial and Jackie Robinson...the hardest guys for me to get out." Brovia was a proven .300 hitter who would give the Bisons a second dangerous lefthanded bat in the lineup to go with Luke Easter. The two men would likely battle for the cleanup slot.

On the 15th of the month, it was announced that Dr. Leonard Berman, a Detroit native who had been in Buffalo since 1949, was to become the ball club's team physician. On the 16th, the signings of Milt Jordan and Roger Bowman were announced. Little by little the pieces of the new organization were falling into place.

In major league news, the March 1956 edition of Television Age magazine revealed that 1956 would be a good year financially for major league ball clubs. Thirteen teams, with the exception of Milwaukee, would split $5,200,000 in sponsor fees for the right to televise baseball games during the season. An additional $1,000,000 would be coming their way for carrying the All-Star game and the World Series. It was an announcement that John C. Stiglmeier would take keen interest in later on during the season.

Joe Brovia had averaged 26 home runs and over 100 RBIs for his past six seasons in Triple A ball. The only blot on this Pacific Coast League All-Star's career was his 1955 experience with the Cincinnati Reds. The purchase from the Oakland Oaks by Cincinnati to fill the major league club's pinch-hitting need turned out to be a bust for both the player and the club. Brovia found himself platooned by the Reds and struggled to hit .111 in 18 at-bats, with six strikeouts. He was now back in Triple A and eager to demonstrate that Cincinnati had misused his talents. Additional testimony to the worth of the Bisons' new acquisition was seen in the newspapers on the following day. Even while announcing his retirement after a decade of major league and minor league ball, Buffalo's own Stan Rojek testified that Brovia "wore out Coast League pitchers with his power."

Signed 1956 and 1957 Buffalo Bisons baseballs

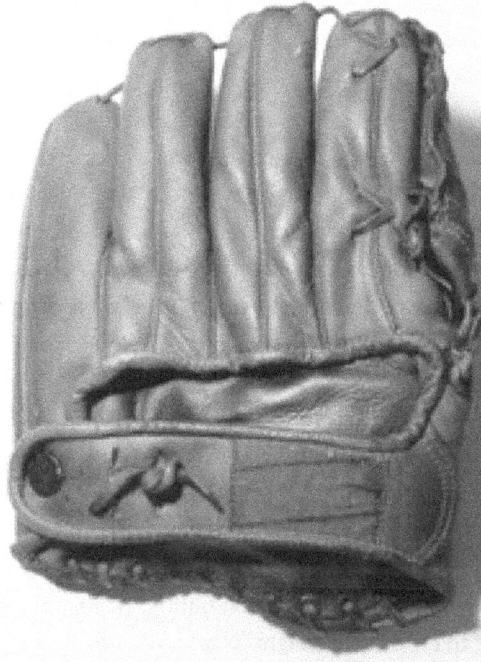

Lou Ortiz "Mort Cooper" Glove

1956 Buffalo Bisons Team Cufflinks and Tie Tack

Chapter 5: Spring Training, 1956

PITCHERS AND CATCHERS reported to the Bisons' spring training complex in Bartow, Florida, as planned. The men began with a two-hour session organized by manager Cavarretta and player-coach Lowrey to start conditioning the legs and building endurance. Pitchers reporting were Bob Schultz, Harry Nicholas, Mario Picone, Vic Stryska, Milt Jordan, John Weiss, Eddie (Jigger) March and Dan Lewandowski. Karl Drews was a late arrival and missed this opening workout. Catchers on hand were the Buffalo boys Phil Tomkinson, newly signed Don McAndrews and outfielder-catcher Eric Rodin, who surprised everyone by announcing that he was seeking the first-string catcher's job. Billy DeMars was the only position player in camp, having asked special permission to log in with this early group.

Cavarretta and Lowrey stayed on for a third-hour workout for themselves after dismissing their charges. Lowrey let all on hand know that he was planning to stress the "player" role in his double-duty assignment. Tired of filling in as a utility man or pinch-hitting, as he had been used over the past several seasons, Lowrey felt he still had good enough skills to win a regular job. He would be quite capable of playing third base or second, he stated, or center field or left.

McAndrews was the only casualty of this initial outing. Having played only MUNY ball for the past two years and needing to drop some weight to get back into shape, he became ill after the first hour and had to retreat to the clubhouse to seek assistance from trainer Jimmy Mack. Schultz, on the other hand, had come to camp in such trim shape that Cavarretta was particularly pleased. He was sure to be a winner if he kept at this weight, Cavarretta offered, noting that he had managed Schultz back in 1952 when the righthander had won six and lost three for the Cubs.

General manager Stiglmeier showed up in camp to report that he had signed both Picone and Nicholas to contracts. He also confirmed that outfielder Clint Hartung, catcher Pierce McWhorter and pitcher Dick Rozek had all retired from baseball. He was not certain about the status of third baseman Bill Reed or outfielder Johnny Blatnik. Reed had requested another week to make up his mind. Blatnik had notified the club that his decision would be forthcoming after he had learned the results of a civil service test he had taken back in his hometown in Ohio.

The day also brought the news of the signing of veteran outfielder Clyde Vollmer, .278 with seven home runs in 69 games for the 1955 Bisons. Twenty-six-year-old righthanded hurler Milt Jordan, winner of nine games and loser of six for the previous season's Minneapolis Millers, was also signed, and the team received the news that two Detroit pitchers were being optioned, names still to be revealed.

The first Buffalonians to drop in to see the team in camp also arrived this same day. Noted eye surgeon Dr. Joseph A. Schultz and friend Clarence Loomis and their wives were given a hearty welcome by Stiglmeier. They planned to spend the night en route to a visit with a pair of notable Buffalo residents now in Clearwater: Philadelphia Phillies manager Mayo Smith and nationally known television personality Buffalo Bob Smith of the Howdy Doody Show.

March 19, Monday

Bill Froats arrived from the Tigers. The lefthander had won seven games and lost five for the 1954 Bisons but had had a difficult year in 1955. Following a two-inning scoreless stint with the parent club against Cleveland early in the year (no hits, but two walks), he was sent to Buffalo, where he lost all five decisions. He had come across as disgruntled, being "farmed out without a chance to pitch." He was eventually demoted to the Sally League, where he struggled with a record of 5-7 for the Augusta club.

Signed out of the University of Notre Dame in 1951 by Detroit, Froats was one of the fastest throwers on the Tiger roster but also one of the wildest. It was hoped that Cavarretta's guidance might help him manage his control, although the hurler believed he was already beginning to make progress on that front. He credited Tiger teammate lefthander Bob Miller with showing him how to bend his back more on the follow-through to help master his curveball. The same technique had worked for lefty pitcher Billy Hoeft just two years earlier, Froats noted.

March 20, Tuesday

"You'll see a different Froats out there [on the mound] this season," the player opened up to the News' Cy Kritzer. Eager to talk with the newspaperman, Froats revealed that the Tigers had wanted to assign him to Charleston in the American Association, but that he had requested a return to the Bisons. "Now I'm ready," he said. "This has to be my big year, and no one has to tell me that. I must make good now or think of another career. I never did get going last season; maybe some of my trouble came from a bad attitude. I got what I thought was a bad deal and didn't shake it off."

General manager Stiglmeier welcomed Froats back to the fold, and the pitcher expressed his gratitude for being given another chance with the team. After all, he was now a Buffalo resident, having married Buffalo native Dorothy Steivater during the 1954 season. Residing at 923 Humboldt Parkway, the delighted couple had just become the proud parents of three-week-old son Michael, whom Froats had not yet even seen. He had had to leave his off-season Buffalo insurance job five weeks earlier to report to the Tigers' spring training camp.

Coming over with him from Detroit's Lakeland camp was 6-foot, 3-inch Larry (Red) Donovan. A standout high-school ballplayer at Ionia High School, Michigan, the 22-year-old righthander was also back for his second try with the Bisons, having grown half an inch and filled out to 210 pounds. In 1955 he had lost one game with the Herd and was sent down to last-place Little Rock in the Southern Association. There he picked up seven victories and lost 13, but back in 1954 he had won 12 and lost nine for Danny Carnevale's pennant-winning Eastern League Wilkes-Barre Barons. He contended that that was a far more accurate reflection of his ability. He and Froats, with already five weeks of fitness under their belts, immediately donned uniforms and joined the club work-outs. Cavarretta was impressed with the two men's physical condition, but equally so with the foot speed that Donovan displayed. "Now I know where to look when I need a pinch runner," Cavarretta told the press.

Cavarretta was also pleased with the performance that Karl Drews displayed, popping the ball into catcher Phil Tomkinson's glove like it was the "Fourth of July," the skipper said. Cavarretta allowed as how he had thought the big righthander had lost his fastball but was "glad to discover he still has it." Drews, an off-season employee with the City Recreation Department in Hollywood, Florida, remarked that he had never had a sore arm in his life and still had plenty of victories left in his wing.

Also suiting up this day was Herb Fleischer, arriving from the Washington Senators' training complex at Orlando. The youngster was fresh out of the armed services and claimed a brief pitching stint with Beaumont in the Texas League before stepping into fatigues. Cavarretta was willing to see what he could produce. A man who had served his country deserved a look-see, however remote his chances might be, and the Bisons needed to avoid overlooking anyone who might possibly be of help to them.

Fleischer was one of the batting practice hurlers on a day that had turned cool and windy, leading Cavarretta to call a halt to the workout after 2 1/2 hours. He added that he might delay tomorrow's session until 11 a.m. if the weather continued in the same vein. Buffalo boy Pat Tomkinson was notable at the plate, stinging line drives all over the outfield. Not so fortunate was the other Buffalo catcher Don McAndrews, who was now sporting a sore arm. This ailment was also a complaint of the team's third catching candidate, Eric Rodin.

More Buffalo fans showed up for the day's proceedings. Sloan police captain Henry Herman and football great Tommy Hughitt and their wives looked in on the athletes. The Hermans had stopped by on their way home from a Hollywood, Florida, vacation. The Hughitts drove over from their quarters in Winter Haven. (Hughitt, an All-American quarterback for the University of Michigan in 1913, had been "Mr. Everything" as a player-coach for the professional Buffalo All-Americans of the National Football League, being selected to the First Team All-NFL squad in 1922. He later served one term on the Buffalo Common Council.) Detroit scout Cy Williams and his son, Bobby, now a Tiger minor league pitcher-infielder signee, also stopped in on their way to the Tigers' Lakeland camp.

Following the workout, Stiglmeier, Cavarretta and Lowrey headed off to Tampa for the annual dinner hosted by Florida Governor Leroy Collins for upwards of 300 baseball men. At the gathering of baseball officials, managers, coaches, sports writers and sportscasters, Stiglmeier was called upon to comment on the Bisons' organizational effort. The assemblage, noting that the number of minor leagues in existence had fallen to 28 from a high of 59, with a concomitant loss of baseball cities, centered its discussion on the likelihood that independent teams such as the Buffalo operation were the wave of the future in keeping minor league ball alive. Bob Finch, the promotional director of the National Association of Professional Baseball Leagues, offered hope with his report that season ticket sales were up in many of the cities and towns where play was continuing.

March 21, Wednesday

Long balls were featured at today's practice. Manager Cavarretta was the first Bison to crash one out of the park over the right-field wall. He then declared himself capable of two more seasons of playing time, albeit not as a regular. After three days in camp he advised that his legs, his arm and his batting eye were all in good shape. And he discounted the age factor as a handicap. At 38, he told the newspapermen, conveniently shaving a year off his true age, he was the same age as Ted Williams and Mickey Vernon, starters for this year's pennant-contending Boston Red Sox. He then ticked off an All-Star cast of men who were still in the major leagues and counted on to lead their squads to victory: Pee Wee Reese (37) and Jackie Robinson (38) of the Brooklyn Dodgers, Phil Rizzuto (37) of the Yankees, and Cleveland's Bob Lemon (37) and Early Wynn (39), adding the names of players in their mid-30s such as Roy Campanella, Andy Seminick and Hank Bauer.

"Age is overemphasized in baseball," he commented to Kritzer. "It's strictly a question of legs and reflexes. If they're okay, a ballplayer can go on indefinitely." He added that Ty Cobb was 44 when he chose to retire and still could have played had he wanted to do so. As if to emphasize Cavarretta's point, big Luke Easter, at a reported age of 34—though who could really say—had signed in at camp this morning and immediately sent seven drives over the outfield fences during his turn at the plate. Shaking hands all around at the time of his arrival, Easter commented, "I'm happy to join this ball club...lots of power on this club...we'll make a lot of runs. Have we got any pitching?"

Unawed by Easter's performance, catcher-outfielder Eric Rodin clouted one to the clubhouse door, 460 feet away, and also sent a ball that carried out to John Stiglmeier's car—parked safely, he had thought, in deep left field. Pat Tomkinson's bat continued to impress with stinging line drives. Later in the day, general manager Stiglmeier took on the role of master carpenter and spent several hours refurbishing the antiquated batting cage the team had obtained. Assisted by Milt Jordan, Stiglmeier added wings to the backstop with 2 × 4s and some free fishing nets he had acquired from several shrimp boats during the Tampa dinner visit. He did not need to worry about the outfield fences, not yet anyway, since the ballplayers were sending their drives over the walls and not up against them.

Throwing batting practice, Milt Jordan looked particularly sharp. The Clearfield, Pennsylvania, product, going 12-1 with the 1953 Bisons before a sore arm ended his season, offered that the 1954 and 1955 campaigns he had spent at Little Rock, Arkansas, had provided the warm-weather setting needed to heal the ailment. The remainder of batting practice was hurled by Froats, Donovan and Drews as the men most ready to go. Pitcher Mario Picone had injured his leg running into an outfield fence while shagging flies. Harry Nicholas was limited in duty after being struck in the head by a thrown ball in a pepper drill. Cavarretta indicated he might forego batting practice the next day, not willing to overtax his limited group of sound pitchers.

Clyde Vollmer arrived in Bartow in the late afternoon. He would suit up the following day. Not so for infielder Mel Hoderlein. The bad back that had taken him out of the Bison lineup the previous season was again acting up, and Stiglmeier thought that the third baseman was likely to retire. The remainder of the roster was expected to report on Thursday.

Back in the clubhouse, the chatter was about Easter's monumental blasts from the past, highlights to whet the enthusiasm of Buffalo fandom while awaiting the May 2 season home opener. DeMars asked the big man if a ball he had hit over the pavilion in Sportsman's Park in St. Louis was the longest of his career. Roger Bowman brought up a ball that Easter was said to have driven over the center-field trees in the Hollywood, California, ballpark. Drews referred to yet another soaring blow that sailed over the parking lot outside Seals Stadium in San Francisco. Easter responded that the drive he remembered the best had happened in Offermann Stadium, in Buffalo, in a 1947 game between the Homestead Grays and Atlanta. In the seventh inning with the bases loaded, he said, he had hit a ball straight over the center-field scoreboard.

It was a fond memory. No one, he had been told, not even Babe Ruth, had been able to accomplish that feat. Unfortunately for the fans, this occurrence, as was the case with most Negro League baseball events, went unreported in the mainstream press.

March 22, Thursday

Back home in Buffalo, diligent work continued on ticket sales. Vice president and business manager Harry Bisgeier reached out to the press to spread the word that the team still needed to sell 225 more season box seats and 225 more season reserved seats to meet the preseason budget for financial stability. The Buffalo Bisons Women's Volunteer Workers were on that job already, headed by Helen Berny, newly elected club director, and Elizabeth Horvath. Lucy Strzelczyk was also a member of this leadership committee. Not to be outdone, the Junior Chamber of Commerce had put together a sales promotion committee, reaching out to businesses and allied organizations to take advantage of all the good seats still available.

In Bartow, the Bisons' double-play combination was now in camp. Two-time International League All-Star second baseman Lou Ortiz (1953, 1954) had arrived to join Billy DeMars. Ortiz had helped set a modern-day International League record for double plays with Rochester in 1953—187 twin killings, although the mark was broken just last year, led by second-sacker Spook Jacobs and the Columbus Jets. Ortiz let on he'd like the record back.

"You're the best double-play pivot I've ever seen," DeMars was overheard telling his towering, 6-foot, 3-inch teammate. (In fact, the St. Louis Cardinals organization had made a movie of Ortiz's pivot maneuver and had been teaching it throughout their system.) "I've always wanted to play alongside you," he added. To help meld the combination, Cavarretta assigned the two as room-mates, adding "they're both real pros...and I'm sure I can't tell them much about improving on the double play." DeMars suggested to newspaperman Kritzer that the pair might collaborate for 165 double plays this season, more if both men stayed sound and "our pitching can keep the ball on the ground with low breaking stuff."

Ortiz, fresh from winter ball in the Mexican League, looked sharp at the plate. Easter sent another three drives over the fences. However, the pitching staff, reinforced by Roger Bowman, Buster Nicholas, Bob Schultz and Mario Picone, all of whom took the mound for the first time this spring, clamped down on the recent distance hitting that had been taking place. Outside of throwing bat-ting practice, the pitchers put in serious work on their bunt fielding skills.

Third baseman Bill Serena arrived early Thursday evening to round out the anticipated infield of Easter, Ortiz, DeMars and Serena, but third base could still be in play, it was rumored. The Tigers might be loaning the team a young power hitter named Tom Sarna. Stiglmeier was also talking with the Yankees about extra infield help. As for the outfield, slugger Joe Brovia, in the playoffs with Hermosillo in the Mexican League, would not be reporting until the following Tuesday. His numbers for winter ball were 14 home runs and a .352 average in 56 games, plus another five roundtrippers in nine playoff contests. Outfielder Emil Restaino, 27, had joined the team to work out. He had hit .253 in 95 games for the Bisons in 1953 but left the Detroit organization in 1955 rather than be farmed out to Albany in the Eastern League. Playing semipro ball for the rest of the year, the Lakeland, Florida, resident had decided to give organized ball yet another go. With Vollmer and catcher-outfielder Eric Rodin already in camp, and Johnny Blatnik scheduled to report later today, only outfielder George Bullard was an unexplained absence.

Cavarretta's major concern was his receiving corps and now Pat Tomkinson's big toe. Struck on the digit by a pitch in the dirt from Bob Schultz during warmups on Wednesday, Tomkinson had been unable to put on a shoe for the morning's workout. X-rays had initially indicated no break, but a bone specialist was scheduled to look at the pictures on Friday. In the interim, the player was under the care of trainer Jimmy Mack while manager Cavarretta and general manager Stiglmei-er conferred on the depleted catching staff. Stiglmeier contacted Chuck Comiskey of the Chicago White Sox and secured the promise of a catcher on option, but no cuts were scheduled before the coming Monday or Tuesday. The White Sox had the luxury of choosing among five receivers.

More Buffalonians dropped in for a look at the team. Bud Crimi had called in on Wednesday to give encouragement to Pat Tomkinson. Now it was Mr. and Mrs. William Hull, residents of Wana-kah, who stopped by on their way back home from vacation.

In other news related to Buffalo and baseball, two Tiger prospects, Lackawanna High's Nick Koleff and Buffalonian Tommy Van Remman, were reported to be heading in opposite directions. Koleff had been moved to the Triple A Charleston squad, while Van Remmen, troubled by wildness, was working with the Class A Augusta team. Froats and Donovan had earlier reported on Babe Birrer's struggles with a back ailment at the Tiger camp.

March 23, Friday

Continued overcast weather led Cavarretta to cancel batting practice, but he kept the pitchers busy with an hourlong drill of fielding bunts and getting their legs in shape. Easter and Cavarretta alternated covering first base. The anticipated starting infield unit of Easter, Ortiz, DeMars and Serena also worked together for the first time, handling hot drives from Cavarretta and Lowrey. Again, the skipper took some turns at first base, getting himself ready for a backup role when Easter's legs might require some time out.

Serena commented how pleased he was to be in Buffalo and back with Cavarretta, his former roommate and then manager with the Cubs. Serena reminded all that he had been with the Bisons for the first half of the pennant-winning 1948 season. Of the 13 home runs he'd struck, the first had come in his very first time at bat. It was a pinch home run against Toronto. He was looking forward to sending even more long balls over Offermann's short left-field dimensions. Cavarretta expressed his pleasure at seeing Serena in such good shape, obviously a benefit of his play in the winter Mexican League, but the skipper also told him he could face some competition for his position. Serena accepted the challenge, noting that the Herd was likely to meet a lot of lefthanded pitching to counter the presence of Easter and Brovia and even Cavarretta in the lineup. This would play into Serena's righthanded strength.

March 24, Saturday

The best news of the day was Pat Tomkinson's return behind the plate. Wearing an oversized shoe, Tomkinson made it through a full day's workout. Nevertheless, Stiglmeier pursued his conversations with Chuck Comiskey. The Bisons needed a catcher on option, or even for purchase if that was required. Stiglmeier had his eyes on Carl Sawatski, receiver for last season's Junior World Series victors, the Minneapolis Millers. A squat 5-foot, 10-inch, 210-pounder, Sawatski had a potent bat that had produced 27 home runs in 1955. He would add yet another dangerous lefthanded power hitter to the Bisons' lineup.

The team's size and slugging prowess were immediately noted by outfielder Johnny Blatnik, who had by now made it into camp. "One thing about this squad rings a bell for sure," Blatnik told Bill Coughlin of the Courier-Express. "We'll scare a lot of clubs in the case trouble brews, if we don't do anything else." Still, it was the pitchers who again dominated batting practice. Only Easter and Cavarretta could find the empty spaces behind the fences against the hurling of Karl Drews, Bill Froats, Larry Donovan, Milt Jordan, Bob Schultz and John Weiss.

Two more new faces joined Blatnik in reporting: George Bullard, delayed by storms in his Boston, Massachusetts, area, and Buffalo native and infielder Hank Nasternak. Nasternak, now 33, had joined the Chicago Cubs organization in 1947 after a year of MUNY ball with the Kicks A.C. Before his stint in MUNY ball, he had put in three more demanding years in the Marines, seeing combat duty on Okinawa. A seven-year minor league veteran who had posted a sparkling .338 for Rock Hill in the Tri-State League back in 1951, he had most recently hit .237 at Pacific Coast League Los Angeles in 1954. He had left baseball after that season but now had been encouraged by former MUNY League president Lou DePoe and friend Torchy Reimann to try out for the Bisons. The shortstop signed a free agent contract with the Herd to see what he might do.

March 25, Sunday

Batting practice was the order of the day, a rotation of Dan Lewandowski, Vic Stryska, Mario Picone, Digger March and Harry Nicholas pitching 15-minute sessions over the three-hour program. Easter's bat was again noteworthy, sending a number of pitches over the outfield walls, and John Blatnik also joined him with one of his drives. It looked to most observers that the former Syracuse slugger had recovered nicely from the previous season's injury.

Cavarretta then surprised everyone by calling for an intra-squad game for the next day. The Peanut Lowreys would square off against the Billy DeMars contingent. Lowrey's lineup would feature Hank Nasternak at short, Emil Restaino in center, Lowrey at second, Easter at first, John Blatnik in right, Pat Tomkinson covering third, Don McAndrews catching, Digger March in left and Karl Drews, Larry Donovan and Milt Jordan on the mound. Billy DeMars' lineup had George Bullard in center, DeMars at short, Cavarretta at first, Bill Serena at third, Lou Ortiz at second, Eric Rodin catching, Clyde Vollmer in left, Dan Lewandowski in right and pitchers Bill Froats, Bob Schultz and John Weiss.

In player news, general manager Stiglmeier announced the retirement of three of the men assigned to Buffalo in the purchase of the club from the Tigers: outfielder Bill Killinger, pitcher Dick Rozek and catcher Pierce McWhorter. Mel Hoderlein, 1955's Bison third baseman, was not going to be able to report due to his ailing back. In negotiations with Detroit farm club director John McHale, Stiglmeier had nixed the offer of outfielder Fred Fleming, a lefthanded swinger who had hit only .167 in 25 games with the Herd in 1955. He had finished that season batting .288 for the Class Double A Little Rock Travelers. But Stiglmeier did welcome the assignment of pitcher Fred Hahn to replace the retiring Rozek. The 27-year-old Hahn had won five and lost four for last year's Bisons, registering an ERA of 4.43.

The 1956 season would be Hahn's 10th in organized baseball. The 6-foot, 3-inch lefty had jumped to Triple A Rochester after an All-Star appearance with Class C Fresno in 1949 and a sparkling 12-8 record and astonishing 1.65 ERA with Class B Lynchburg the following season. A record of 7-8 with the Red Wings in 1951 had given him an opportunity to show his stuff to the parent St. Louis Cardinals club. Making his major league debut on April 19, 1952. Hahn pitched two innings, surrendered two base hits, gave up a walk and was sent back to Rochester. A .500 hurler splitting his time in starting and relief roles, Hahn had toiled mainly in relief with Toronto and Buffalo over the past two seasons and had won a total of nine ballgames while dropping five.

Visitors to camp on this day included Cavarretta's family: his wife, four daughters and mother in law, en route to a Pompano Beach three-week vacation. They were able to stay the night and have dinner with the manager. Cy Williams, the Tiger scout, also dropped over to chew the fat with friends in the Bison retinue. His son Bobby had signed a Class D contract and was working out with the Durham team, he reported. Lastly, team president Taylor telephoned Stiglmeier to let him know that he would be able to arrive on April 2, following the conclusion of his other business responsibilities.

March 26, Monday

The morning's six-inning intra-squad contest between the Lowreys and the DeMars nine ended in a 2-2 draw. The hurlers showed that they were ahead of the hitters. The Lowreys could manage only five safeties; the DeMars contingent was held to three. DeMars had two of those himself, including a Texas League double behind third in the final frame, and scored the tying run.

Pitchers were limited to two innings apiece. Karl Drews looked certain to nail down the victory for the Lowreys until his catcher, Don McAndrews, dropped a popup from Mario Picone to put a runner on first. DeMars then came through with his double, putting men on second and third. Digger March, a pitcher but playing out in left field for the Lowreys, dropped a fly ball from Cavarretta that allowed two unearned runs to score and tie the game. The manager called a halt to the proceedings at the end of six.

McAndrews, he of the dropped pop fly, had been the offensive weapon for the Lowreys. He collected the only solid hit of the game, driving in Johnny Blatnik (double) and Pat Tomkinson (single) with a long double to right center in the top of the second inning. Bill Froats was the victim of these three bunched blows. Lowrey got a hit himself and so did Vic Stryska, pinch-hitting for Milt Jordan. Eric Rodin picked up the only other safety for the DeMars team. Milt Jordan (Lowreys) and Bob Schultz (DeMars) each set down six men in order. John Weiss fanned four of the men to face him. Luke Easter was caught on a knuckler for a third strike in the top of the sixth, which led to a double play when catcher Eric Rodin threw out baserunner Eric Restaino at third on the attempted steal.

Cavarretta had watched George Bullard at the plate in the previous day's batting practice and again today in the intra-squad affair and identified the two batting flaws that had led to the outfielder's demotion to Little Rock midway through the 1955 season after he had fallen to a .249 batting mark with the Bisons. Bullard was failing to stay in the crouch from which he batted. Rising up as he swung was causing him to mis-hit the ball. Secondly, the outfielder needed to learn the strike zone. If he could master those two weaknesses, the manager told him, he was going to be the ball club's starting center fielder "until you prove to me you can't hit .275." The team needed Bullard's speed in center, Cavarretta said, and he would settle for an average offensive output from the player, but he also stated that a mark close to .300 could be in Bullard's future if he could correct those two faults.

The game gave Cavarretta a chance to evaluate his pitching staff, and he was not pleased with several of the performances. He identified Drews, Froats and Donovan as likely starters for the five-man rotation he anticipated using during the season, and he offered some words of praise for both Milt Jordan and John Weiss, but he warned that it was time for the others to "cut loose" with their efforts. Men would be judged on what they showed in camp, not on past records. Witness to this philosophy was the signing of Buffalo boy Hank Nasternak to a free agent contract. His workouts and his play in the intra-squad game had demonstrated that he deserved a chance to prove himself further. Catcher candidate Rodin was certainly putting forth such an effort. He had weighed in before the game down six pounds after catching the previous day's batting practice. In the intra-squad contest, he had made a tough catch of a foul ball near the grandstand.

Bartow dignitaries mayor Pete Lawrence and Chamber of Commerce president John E. Davis presented the keys of the city to the Bison officials at an afternoon open-air chicken barbecue. John C. Stiglmeier spoke on behalf of the Bisons. He was accompanied to the gathering by former Cheektowaga judge Thomas E. Delahunt, who had driven up from his winter vacation sojourn at DeLand.

Later in the day, more Buffalonians dropped in to pay a visit to the club. John Del Negro and his wife stopped by on their way north from Ft. Lauderdale, as did Mr. and Mrs. Frank Schimmer, new shareholders in the ball club. Tiny Parker, a former International League umpire now making a living with the Florida State Highway Department, rounded out the list of visitors.

March 27, Tuesday

With Stiglmeier still on the horn to such as Joe Cronin of the Red Sox and John Quinn of the Milwaukee Braves and visiting nearby major league camps to talk with the White Sox, the Yankees, the Dodgers and Detroit, Cavarretta expounded on the team's need for two additional starting pitchers, a center fielder, a shortstop and a lefthanded hitting catcher. He expressed faith in both Billy DeMars and George Bullard but spoke of the critical need for players who could back up those middle positions and provide a strong bench, a must for a serious contender. He also wanted another lefthanded bat to provide offense against righthanded hurlers. Catcher Carl Sawatski in the White Sox chain would fit that bill perfectly, but chances were now looking slim that he would be available. Cavarretta had said no to the purchases of catcher Ebba St. Clair from Rochester (poor defense) and struggling pitcher Gene Bearden from the Braves.

March 28, Wednesday

A short workout on fundamentals was the order of the day, as Cavarretta wanted to save his pitchers for the upcoming 16-game exhibition schedule. Batting practice was dispensed with to allow sore muscles some time to rest. The news photographers, television cameras and movie men were given the green light to get in some of their media work with the players under a hot sun that beat down at 81 degrees.

The manager announced his lineup for Saturday's opening of the exhibition schedule against the Class A Augusta Tigers of the South Atlantic League. George Bullard would lead off in center field, followed by Billy DeMars at shortstop, John Blatnik in right field, Luke Easter at first base and Bill Serena at third. Clyde Vollmer would patrol left, Lou Ortiz would cover second and Pat Tomkinson behind the plate would round out the starters. Vic Stryska, Ed March and Dan Lewandowski were scheduled to pitch.

Concerning the latter, a product of St. John Kanty School in Buffalo, Cavarretta had several words of praise. Lewandowski was showing a quickly developing fastball that came in low and alive to the plate, and the manager was designating him for special tutoring on his curve. He would be turned over to Karl Drews and Roger Bowman, the curve masters of the Bison pitching staff, to develop a more effectively thrown Uncle Charley. With a new and sharp breaking hook, Cavarretta offered that Lewandowski had a very good chance of making the final cut. They wanted him to get closer to what Bowman was able to provide, a pitch that "looks like a slow curve but it breaks like a whip," player-coach Lowrey passed along to the News' Kritzer.

Bowman was slowly rounding into form. Drews was in excellent shape. Of him, Cavarretta had to say, "You have to discount his 9-won, 13-lost record with Oakland last season in the Pacific Coast League. He was pitching for a poor ball club. But look at the rest of his record. He pitched 197 innings and struck out 109 while walking 62 men. He won't beat himself by walks." Cavarretta likened Drews' arm to that of Early Wynn and Bob Feller, adding that Drews would continue to be a good pitcher until his legs failed him, and there was little chance that that would be coming soon. Drews liked to run and was usually at the head of the pack when it came to finishing wind sprints about the ballfield.

Mario Picone's pitching responsibilities were temporarily suspended. The hurler continued to complain of a sore arm and had been told to refrain from any throwing at all for the next three days. Hopefully, the newly arriving Fred Hahn would be found with an intact left wing.

As for the outfield, Joe Brovia notified the Bisons that he was down with the flu in his Santa Clara, California, home. He hoped to be leaving for Florida on March 30. His lateness meant that he probably would not be able to appear in a lineup until the middle of the week to come. In Brovia's absence, Ray Coleman, a five-year major leaguer with several good seasons with the St. Louis Browns and Chicago White Sox, showed up to ask for a tryout. Coleman had been the star center fielder on the Bisons' 1949 squad, hitting .295, slugging 23 home runs and driving home 113. His performance that year had catapulted him back to the majors for three more seasons. He had struggled with Havana in 1954, hitting only .192 in 17 games, and in 1955 with Class D Mayfield in the Kitty League, he had appeared in only 30 contests. He was trying to make a comeback at age 34. Stiglmeier was unable to help him, citing the current veteran status of the team the Bisons were already fielding.

Tommy Hughitt stopped in again to watch practice. Cheektowaga Councilman Joe Neibert and his wife also arrived to visit with Stiglmeier for a day or two. They were on their way home from vacation at Delray Beach.

March 29, Thursday

It was another rigorous workout day under a hot sun. John Blatnik, Bill Serena, Clyde Vollmer and George Bullard were given an extra 30 minutes at the plate to make up for missed batting practice, as they were the last of the position players to make it into camp. Blatnik and Serena impressed Cavarretta with their stick work, and the skipper himself looked sharper at the dish. Several drives cleared the fences, and one of Easter's plunked a police car that was stationed behind right field. The officer relocated his vehicle. Blatnik was stuck in the head by a pitch from Harry Nicholas but his helmet liner protected him from injury. At the end of batting practice, the quartet of Easter, Ortiz, DeMars and Serena went through a series of infield drills that left them nearly ready to collapse.

Cavarretta then rewarded his men with a day off on Friday before Saturday's first exhibition outing. The manager offered his words of appreciation to the men for the spirited work they had put forth for 12 consecutive days. They had earned the breather, he commented. This would also give them time for observance of Good Friday services. Drews took the opportunity to drive home to his family, some 200 miles south.

For the media's benefit, Cavarretta opened up about sign stealing. Cy Kritzer of the News recorded the following: "Our club has one great asset. One of the best sign stealers and tipoff readers in baseball. In ten days we have found that two or three of our pitchers are easy to read. Especially for a sharpie like Peanuts Lowrey." Lowrey had been able to call every pitch thrown by lefties Bob Schultz and Bill Froats in the six inning intra-squad contest that took place on Monday. Schultz was gripping his fastball on the cross-seams and changing his grip for a curve, a habit that likely cost him four or five games the previous year, Cavarretta surmised. Froats was bringing the ball over his head for his fastball but stopping in front of his face for the curve. With sluggers like Easter, Blatnik,

Ortiz, Serena and Vollmer, having knowledge of the pitch coming in could help immeasurably. On the other hand, some batters might not want to know what the pitch was likely to be. Cavarretta said he had never wanted to know. It could be dangerous for the hitter if the tipoff was inaccurate.

Perhaps a better way to determine what was coming, Cavarretta suggested, was to watch the middle infielders and see which way they moved just before the pitch was thrown. A step or two to the right for a righthanded batter could mean a curveball was coming and was likely to be pulled. A step or two to the left might signal a fastball that the hitter couldn't get around on so quickly. But veteran middle infielders would often feint in the opposite direction just to confuse the hitter as to what might be coming. Baseball is a game of deception as much as anything else.

March 30, Friday

The day off for the players meant a black bass fishing expedition for Bob Schultz and John Blatnik. Others took off for golf or swimming. Cavarretta, Lowrey and Stiglmeier stayed on at camp to work.

Stiglmeier, keeping the telephone close at hand in anticipation of possible deals, said he had agreed to take a look at the Kansas City Athletics' pitcher Cloyd Boyer, who was coming with a $7500 price tag—and a sore arm, cautioned Kansas City's general manager Parke Carroll. Stiglmeier made no promise other than to look. Elsewhere, he was still after Carl Sawatski, trying to get the White Sox to come down to an offer he had put forth, and also talking with Lee McPhail of the Yankees, Gene Martin of the Phillies and John McHale of the Tigers. McHale was trying to come up with replacements for the three men included in the franchise sale who had decided to retire: Mel Hoderlein, Pierce McWhorter and Bill Killinger.

All of the men in camp, with the exception of Harry Nicholas, Bill Serena and Roger Bowman, who were staying with their families, were living in the Oaks Hotel and talking baseball in the lobby after the workouts. This was leading to good team chemistry, Stiglmeier noted, adding, "I haven't heard a gripe. Every man seems happy and proud to be wearing the Buffalo uniform, and we're going to try to keep it that way." The key to a winning ball club, he went on, was maintaining a "happy" club, and in this respect an independent team such as the Bisons had an advantage over farm system prospects. "Our players have a feeling of some security," he stated. "They are veterans for the most part and are not worried that one bad day and they will be on their way to a lower classification," he told Kritzer. They were not just numbers who could be lost in a large farm system operation of upwards of 250 players, a fate that could cost some of them confidence in their abilities. Local residents were also chipping in to help the players feel personally welcomed, loaning fishing boats and equipment and even golf clubs to the men.

Cavarretta was approached for his thoughts about the team and volunteered his plans for base coach duty, given that "coach" Peanuts Lowrey would frequently be leaving his coaching box to take the field or pinch-hit as "player" Peanuts Lowrey. Or he, Cavarretta, might be on the field. In such instances, the manager would need other men to assume the first- or third-base coaching responsibilities. He was going to try out veteran pitchers Karl Drews, Milt Jordan and Johnny Weiss in the upcoming exhibition games. Catcher Pat Tomkinson and outfielder Clyde Vollmer would also get a look. Cavarretta said he was considering sending in the righthanded-hitting Vollmer for the lefthanded-swinging Joe Brovia when the team was at home, given Offermann Stadium's cozy left-field dimensions.

The manager planned to carry a squad of nine pitchers, four outfielders, six infielders and two catchers after the league cut-down day in mid-May. He would be one of the infielders and could also take a stint in the outfield, if required. He had increased flexibility with Lowrey's ability to play outfield or at second or third. For the first road trip, he added, he would take 25 men. Their play would dictate his final cuts in May.

March 31, Saturday

The day off must have given the men the rest they needed. They took a 5-4 win from Double A Augusta at the Tigers' Lakeland farm club site, but just barely. Cavarretta fielded a lineup of Bullard in center, DeMars at short, Serena at third, Easter at first, Blatnik in right, Ortiz at second, Vollmer in left, Tomkinson catching and righthanded pitcher Vic Stryska on the mound. Easter proved the offensive star for the Bisons, collecting three hits, one of them a triple, scoring two runs and driving home one more. Bill Serena tripled, doubled, scored once and drove home a baserunner in his five official trips to the plate.

Buffalo scored one run in the fourth inning, two in the sixth and two more in the seventh to take a 5-0 lead into the ninth. Stryska pitched three strong innings to start the game for the Herd, followed by Ed March who blanked the Augusta men for three innings more. Dan Lewandowski got past the Tiger farm club in the seventh and eighth frames, despite giving up four safeties, but the bottom of the ninth was another story. Four more hits sent the Buffalo boy to the showers before Cavarretta turned to John Weiss to choke off the rally. The line on Lewandowski read 2⅔ innings pitched, eight hits and four earned runs.

The Bisons nearly missed the contest. A fleet of private cars provided by Bartow residents for the trip to Lakeland failed to show up. The players had to use their own personal vehicles. Augusta was piloted by former Bison manager Frank Skaff, fired after 48 games for leading the 1950 Buffalo squad into the cellar. The team had won the 1949 pennant under the previous year's manager Paul Richards, but in Skaff's defense he had been lacking the pitching and hitting that Richards had been able to call on.

Outfielder Joe Brovia finally arrived on this day from his California home but had to be left in Bartow to see the dentist, complaining of an infected tooth after taking early morning batting practice. If Joe Brovia hits like this with a toothache, his teammates wondered, what is it going to be like when he's healthy?! Among his drives were two that cleared the distant right center field wall. Complaining that he was several pounds underweight from his bout with the flu and the infected tooth, Brovia figured he would be ready to go in four to five days. The tooth was pulled. Froats, Donovan and Picone were also left back at Bartow to rest.

APRIL

Sunday, April 1, Easter Day

Hopes awakened by the advent of spring were on notice even among the Bisons' veterans. No fool he, slick-fielding Billy DeMars was certain he could get another shot at the bigs after a solid year as a full-timer in Buffalo. He had changed his stance, he advised, following a dip in average and power from his 1949 Buffalo numbers. His production that year—.278, with 18 doubles and six home runs—had won him a berth with the 1950 St. Louis Browns, but the best he could manage in the American League was .247, with no power at all. Demoted to San Antonio in the Texas

League, DeMars saw his 1951 average plummet to .232 before he sought out the help of batting instructor Al Vincent. Vincent had gotten him to choke up the bat, hold it even with his shoulders and stop pretending he was a slugger. Reducing the arc of his swing by 15 inches and holding back for a better look at the pitch had seen him bounce back to hit .282, .261, .299 and .283 over the past four seasons. Given the chance with the Bisons, he believed, he was sure he had a return to major league ball in front of him. He pointed to Eddie Joost for comparison, noting that Joost had returned to take over as starting shortstop for the Philadelphia Athletics after a strong season with Rochester while he was in his early 30s.

The same dream was there for other men such as Serena, Easter, Drews and Rodin, all of them anticipating a call to a major league club at the close of the 1956 season. Younger men, Buffalonians all, suiting up in the Detroit fold, had dreams of making it for the first time. Pitchers Nick Koleff (Lackawanna High School) and Jimmy Lumadue (Riverside) were on the Durham roster. Tonawanda native Al Henningham, late of Erie County Technical, was hurling with the PONY League Jamestown, New York, entry. Cy Williams' son Bobby, the former Timon shortstop and pitcher, was currently working out with the Valdosta, Georgia, club but hoping for advancement to Class B Terre Haute, Indiana. That was where pitcher Al Dwyer from Geneva was going.

The only Bison not in camp, pitcher Duane Pillette, was listed on the Bison roster but was still working out with the Cleveland Indians. Trade rumors had him headed to the Philadelphia Phillies, where general manager Ray Hamey had put in a call to Stiglmeier to discuss a deal. Cleveland manager Al Lopez had said that Pillette's arm was sound but that he simply did not have room for him in camp. He had other younger pitchers available. Should Pillette stick with the Phillies, Buffalo would likely get two pitchers—one on option and one outright. One of the men Stiglmeier had in mind was Jim Owens from Bradford, Pennsylvania. Only 22 years old, the impressive righthander had already won 82 games in five seasons of organized ball, the last two spent with Triple A Syracuse. The club could have used his arm in the Easter Day exhibition contest against the Richmond Virginians, the New York Yankees' International League farm team.

Led by new manager Ed Lopat, a 12-year Yankee junk ball artist (166 wins), the Vees clobbered Cavarretta's charges by a score of 12-2. The Bisons took the lead in the bottom of the first on scores by Bullard and DeMars, but Karl Drews was touched for four runs in the third and Roger Bowman gave up eight—six earned—in his 2 1/3. Harry Nicholas finished up, pitching 3 2/3 innings of two-hit ball. Cavarretta offered that it would take a while yet for his pitchers to get in shape and be able to sustain hard throwing.

Bullard and Serena notched two singles apiece. The Bisons' infield combination of DeMars, Ortiz and Easter pulled off two twin killings, but the club also hit into two double plays. The Herd was gifted with seven walks but left 10 men on base.

Attendance for the game was about 150, the Bartow locals being joined by several more Buffalo visitors to the camp. Paul Zalewski and his son Pete, a Canisius High School pitcher, were there. Also putting in appearances were Bison shareholders S.S. Doby, a Hamburg pharmacist, and his wife, and former Buffalo Bills head football coach Red Dawson, whose 1948 team had won the AAFC Eastern Division title in a playoff game against the Baltimore Colts. The run had ended there; the Bills succumbed to the Cleveland Browns in the league championship. Tommy Hughitt was once again in attendance and feted Stiglmeier, Cavarretta, Lowrey and shareholders in attendance at his Eagle Lake vacation home after the game.

April 2, Monday

Discussions with the Yankees were bearing fruit. New York offered to option 25-year-old pitcher Constantine Nicholas (Gus) Keriazakos. The player, who they had just picked up in a trade with the Kansas City A's, had made a brief appearance with Washington in 1954 and had also dropped one game in five appearances with Kansas City in 1955. Most of 1955, however, was spent with Savannah (Sally League) and Columbus (American Association). His record in the minors was 14-7 with a 2.61 ERA. Stiglmeier was interested in the deal, provided the Yankees could help cover part of the salary. Given this day's outing against Miami, Buffalo needed to be interested in any potential new hurler who might be on the market.

Keriazakos had been signed to a reported $67,500 bonus by the Chicago White Sox following an outstanding career at Montclair (New Jersey) High School, where he also happened to set the state high jump record. He had started his first major league game in 1950 at the age of 19 but had lasted only two innings, requiring further seasoning.

For the second day in a row, the opposition collected 14 hits off Bison pitching. At the Marlins' camp at Plant City, Florida, Cavarretta started his usual lineup of Bullard, DeMars, Serena, Easter, Blatnik, Ortiz, Vollmer and Tomkinson. Despite managing only four safeties, the Bisons put together a four-run second inning via a hit, two walks, a hit batsman and two Miami errors.

Milt Jordan started on the mound and breezed through the first two innings until loading the bases with two out in the third frame. A bases-loaded triple and two following safeties sent Jordan to the showers on the short end of a 5-4 score. Bob Schultz came on in relief to give up a hit that scored the sixth run charged to Jordan. Schultz allowed the Marlins two more tallies in his three-plus innings pitched. John Weiss held Miami scoreless over two frames. The Bisons got one back in the ninth. Miami 8, Buffalo 5.

The Bisons also got their first look at Ed Bouchee, rookie Miami first baseman, who hit safely three times. Former Bison slugger Billy Kelly, now scouting for the Chicago Cubs, called Bouchee the best-looking prospect in the minors. Buffalo left six men on base and hit into three double plays, making it six twin killings in three contests. Asked about it after the game, Cavarretta agreed that this would be a challenge, with only Bullard in center field having any speed. On the other hand, he noted, the team was built for power and Offermann Stadium was a perfect setting for his long-ball swingers. He predicted 150 home runs and big-inning outbursts that he believed would offset the double-play balls.

President Taylor made it into Plant City for the final three innings. He hoped for a better look at the team in their game on Tuesday at Lakeland, when the Bisons would be taking on the Tigers' Charleston club of the American Association.

April 3, Tuesday

Now it was the Bisons' turn to amass 14 hits. Every man in the starting lineup, except for Serena and starting pitcher Bill Froats, connected for a safety. Joe Brovia, starting in right field and hitting third, lined out three singles. DeMars and Tomkinson each had two. Peanuts Lowrey made his first appearance of the season, playing in place of Blatnik in left field and singling in his only official time at bat. He also scored twice, the only Bison to do so. Despite the club's slowness of foot, Lowrey and Ortiz pulled off a double steal.

Three Bison hurlers, Froats, Donovan and Picone, shut out the Charleston Senators on four hits.

Cavarretta was pleased with what he saw but added that Froats had still more work to do. He was throwing a slider for the first time, the nickel curve taught to him by Detroit fireballer Virgil (Fire) Trucks. Froats gave up no hits and fanned three, but he allowed four walks. Donovan pitched the middle three innings and gave up two hits. A fine relay play from Brovia to DeMars to Tomkinson blocking the plate nabbed a runner at home to save the shutout. Mario Picone threw the last three frames and he, too, surrendered but two safeties. Buffalo 6, Charleston 0.

The Herd hit into another double play but also turned three in this contest, one of them a nifty 3-6-3 relay from Easter to DeMars to Easter. Brovia's bat had made him Cavarretta's likely starting right fielder, with Blatnik and Vollmer contending for the left-field position and Bullard ranging between them in center.

For more on the pitching front, Stiglmeier advised that he was in discussions with righthander Joe Coleman, a 10-year major league veteran just released by Detroit. The 32-year-old had won 13 games and lost 17 for Baltimore in 1954 and split last season with Baltimore and the Tigers, going 2-2. Former Bison manager Jack Tighe, now a Detroit coach, had recommended Coleman highly.

It was also reported that Detroit had asked for waivers on Buffalonian Babe Birrer, who had then requested to be optioned to Buffalo. The former Kensington High Schooler had made his impressive major league debut with the Tigers just last year. Winning four and losing three, the Babe had put on a Ruthian show on June 19, 1955, against the Baltimore Orioles. Relieving Frank Lary in the sixth inning with no one out, Detroit up by 5-4, Birrer set down the side. He then clubbed two three-run homers in his only two at-bats and held Baltimore scoreless for the final three frames. Detroit won the contest, 12-4. Lary got credit for the victory. Birrer got a well-deserved nickname.

April 4, Wednesday

Three Bison pitchers combined for a second straight shutout, this time over the visiting Denver Bears, the New York Yankees' affiliate in the American Association. Vic Stryska, though hit sharply, faced only nine men over the first three innings, the beneficiary of a DeMars-to-Easter double play after a walk. Stryska struck out two. Karl Drews hurled innings four through seven, giving up the only three hits the Bears would muster for the afternoon. He also fanned three. Ed March was untouched in the eighth and ninth.

The offense got it going in the bottom of the third on a bases-loaded walk to Easter that plated Lowrey, starting in center field in place of Bullard. Three more runs came home in the fourth, thanks to a Blatnik double, a walk to Ortiz and singles by Tomkinson, Lowrey and DeMars. Brovia's triple in the seventh scored DeMars. Hank Nasternak made his first plate appearance of the spring and walked for Stryska in the third inning. He was erased when he ran into an infield bouncer stroked by Lowrey. The Herd turned two more double plays and was victimized for one. Buffalo 5, Denver 0.

It was a cash payout day for the Buffalo players, with two stockholders on hand to award prizes for various feats: William L. Collins, retired Niagara Mohawk vice president, and Paul E. Fitzpatrick, president of American Lubricants of Buffalo as well as a top Florida tomato grower and cattle breeder. DeMars was the big winner, collecting $39.33 for his hitting and fielding. Blatnik took home $35.33. Joe Brovia and Peanuts Lowrey got $15.33 apiece. Luke Easter won $12; Bill Serena, $10; and Pat Tomkinson, $4. Stryska, Drews and March split the $10 prize for most effective pitching. Big Luke was offered $100 for a home run with the bases loaded in the third, but all he could manage was the walk that drove home the game's first run.

Club president Taylor was also a money winner this day. He and his son, a resident of Denver, had had a bet since Christmas Day on the game's outcome. He cheerfully reported that he had just sent his son a wire—collect.

Cavarretta got bad news about his pitching staff. Babe Birrer had been claimed off waivers by Baltimore. The skipper had been planning on Birrer as a starter. On the other hand, veteran righthander Jim Walsh had joined the team that afternoon after holding out from the Pacific Coast League San Francisco Seals. The Seals had finally given him his outright release. A reliever with Pittsburgh in 1950 and 1951, Walsh had pitched effectively in the Pacific Coast League and had put together an 8-10 record with last year's sixth-place finishers.

There followed bad news about the receiver corps. It looked unlikely that Carl Sawatski would be in a Buffalo uniform in 1956. It was reported that he would be heading north with the White Sox and that manager Marty Marion was thinking of carrying three catchers.

April 5, Thursday

Buffalo entertained the Miami Marlins in Bartow, and the rival International Leaguers scored against Cavarretta's mound crew for the first time in three games, managing two runs. Meanwhile, the Bison offense was making life difficult for the visitors. Buffalo racked up seven runs of their own and again notched double digits in hits, this time with 11.

Bullard, back from a brief illness, was once again the starting center fielder and leadoff man. DeMars followed him at shortstop in the number 2 hole. Lefty swingers Brovia, in right, and Easter, at first, batted third and fourth. John Blatnik hit next and played left field, with third baseman Bill Serena following him. Ortiz at second and Rodin, making his first catching start, rounded out the lineup, followed by starting pitcher Harry Nicholas.

The Bisons staked Nicholas to a three-run lead in the first on a walk to Bullard, a single by De-Mars, Easter's double and a second two-baser from Serena. The Marlins scored a single run in the second. The Bisons notched two more in the fourth, with DeMars scoring on a wild pitch.

Roger Bowman took the mound in the fourth and gave up only one hit in his three innings, but he yielded five walks. Miami bunched the free passes and a single in the fifth to score their second and final run of the game. A bases-loaded walk to Easter drove in the Bisons' sixth tally in the sixth inning, and Clyde Vollmer, substituting for Blatnik, hit a long single to score Easter. John Weiss pitched the last two frames for Buffalo, striking out three, walking two and keeping the Marlins hitless. Buffalo 7, Miami 2.

Buffalo turned two double plays, with Ortiz the pivot man on each. Bill Serena hit into a double play for the second game in a row. Struggling at the plate, Serena had now struck out six times in his last 10 at-bats. Lowrey went in for Brovia late in the game, as did Cavarretta for Easter. Two Buffalo products, catcher Don McAndrews and Hank Nasternak, also saw playing time. McAndrews handled Weiss's knuckler with ease but did not get a chance to hit. Nasternak pinch-hit for Bowman in the sixth and grounded out.

The hot spring bats thus far belonged to Billy DeMars and Joe Brovia. DeMars was hitting .366 with 11 hits in 30 trips to the plate; Brovia, the late starter, had gone seven for 12, a torrid .583 batting mark. The News' Kritzer overheard one of the Herd veterans commenting, "If we keep Joe happy and pepped up, he will tear the league apart."

International League president Frank J. Shaughnessy visited the camp this day on his circuit of International League training sites, conferring with general manager Stiglmeier and president Taylor. Stiglmeier made known the Bisons' need for one more pitcher, another outfielder and, especially, a catcher. Shaughnessy replied that even the Yankees were looking for another receiver for the Denver Bears, and that he could not recall when catchers were in such short supply. The Bisons, he said, were extremely lucky to have picked up Pat Tomkinson when they did. On the brighter side, Shaughnessy praised Brovia's cuts at the plate, noting that he was a sure contender for the league batting title if he continued in this vein. He also had good words for Serena's rifle-like arm at third and Easter's unanticipated maneuverability at the first-base sack. Down at least 20 pounds from his Ottawa playing weight of last season, he estimated.

Shaughnessy's greatest accolades were for DeMars' shortstop acrobatics. He'd never seen him looking so sharp. Should the Bisons get pitching help, Shaughnessy added, they were definitely first-division contenders.

April 6, Friday

The Herd made it four wins in a row, sending visiting Charleston down to defeat for the second time in two meetings. As against Miami, the Bisons again connected for 11 safeties. Four hits never left the infield, but the team also counted three doubles, a triple and the spring's first home run, a two-out, two-run shot by Easter in the sixth after a Bullard leadoff bunt single. Speed and power, a dangerous combination. Gifted with seven walks, a hit batsman and four errors, Buffalo tallied 10 runs and surrendered but three.

Bob Schultz pitched the scoreless first three innings for Buffalo. The Bisons notched single runs in each of those frames. Red Donovan hurled the middle innings and was touched for four hits. Along with a free pass, the Charlestons scored single runs off him in the fourth and fifth. The Bisons got those back with a pair in the fourth and then Easter's long blast over the right-field wall in the sixth. Bill Froats worked the final three frames and allowed the third Charleston run in the seventh. He fanned four to offset three base hits and a walk. Buffalo sent home their last three runs in the bottom of the seventh to end the scoring.

Bullard led the hit parade with three singles, while Easter and Serena each collected a pair of extra-base hits. Bullard, DeMars, Easter and Tomkinson each scored twice. Easter now could count 11 RBIs for seven games.

Nor did the Bisons shine only on offense. The infield turned four double plays with Ortiz brilliant at second, handling eight chances and demonstrating why he had twice been selected as the International League's All-Star Second Baseman. Third baseman Serena, no slouch himself, contributed seven assists. Cavarretta again spelled Easter in the late innings, and in this game the versatile Lowrey went in to give Ortiz a breather. Tomkinson caught the whole game. Buffalo 10, Charleston 3.

Cavarretta would need at least another week to evaluate his pitching, he said. He could only tell so much while his hurlers were being limited to these short three-inning stints. On the other hand, he had fine words of praise for both Bullard and DeMars. Regarding the young center fielder, Cavarretta volunteered that "he has the equipment" and he could "go a long way" if he, Cavarretta, and player-coach Lowrey could just keep him believing in himself. As for DeMars, the skipper reported that the Bisons had just turned down a trade proposal for him, calling the shortstop "a key man on our club." Again, Kritzer was there to provide the reporting for the folks back home.

April 7, Saturday

Shutout pitching and timely hitting propelled the Bisons to their fifth straight win, this time on the road at Haines City, Florida. The victims were their International League rivals, the Richmond Virginians, and it was payback time for the 12-2 thumping the Herd had endured at the beginning of the week at the hands of this same nine. For the second day in a row the Herd erupted for 10 runs, knocking out nine hits and receiving 11 free passes. Taking advantage of two Richmond errors, seven of the Bisons' runs were unearned.

Cavarretta started himself in the cleanup spot at first base in place of Easter. Luke had remained back at Bartow, nursing a painful instep from a foul ball he had struck in the previous game's outing. The skipper collected two hits, one of them a two-run triple in the third inning to drive in the first runs of the game off Richmond starter Jim Coates. The Vees' second hurler was Ed Cereghino, a New York Yankee $75,000 bonus baby back in 1951, who committed a throwing error in the fifth that gave Buffalo two unearned runs without the benefit of a hit. He was then scorched for five more unearned Buffalo tallies in the seventh. Pat Tomkinson provided the big blow, a bases-clearing double to right. The Bisons picked up their 10th run in the ninth off John Gebhard.

On the hill for Buffalo, Karl Drews became the first Bison hurler to go more than three innings. The big righthander threw six, giving up no runs, allowing four hits, striking out three and walking none. Drews made a strong case to become the Bisons' opening-day pitcher. Southpaw Fred Hahn worked the last three frames, allowing only one safety and setting three men down on strikes. Buffalo 10, Richmond 0.

Lou Ortiz matched Cavarretta's pair of hits, good for two RBIs. Buffalo hit into two more double plays but also counted two of their own, DeMars to Ortiz to Cavarretta and then Lowrey (replacing DeMars at short) to Ortiz to Cavarretta. Buffalo boy Don McAndrews came on for Tomkinson at catcher and struck out in his only two times at the plate.

Another aspiring Buffalonian had even worse luck. General manager Stiglmeier announced the release of free agent Hank Nasternak, the man being evaluated for utility infield backup. A sore arm from an automobile accident in the fall of 1955 and failure to produce at the plate had led to the decision. Announcing to the press that he was "finished with pro ball," Nasternak offered no complaints. "Phil Cavarretta gave me a good chance," he told the Courier-Express's Bill Coughlin.

April 8, Sunday

At home in Bartow for the fifth straight day, the Herd made it six in a row, this time at the expense of Buffalo's own Tommy Van Remmen, who started on the mound for the Augusta Tigers. Van Remmen, Timon High graduate and PONY League Rookie of the Year in 1954 with Jamestown, suffered from wildness in the six innings he worked. He allowed only five hits, but he walked eight and was victimized for all of Buffalo's runs in the 6-3 verdict.

George Bullard led off the bottom of the first with a walk, moved to third on a double by DeMars and was sent home by Cavarretta's sacrifice fly. Easter was again absent from the lineup due to the sore foot. Brovia's single cashed DeMars. In the fourth, Van Remmen walked the first three batters. Ortiz brought home Brovia and Blatnik on a hard single to left and Serena scored all the way from first on an error by the outfielder.

Righthander Harry Nicholas hurled the first five innings for Buffalo and kept the Tigers scoreless despite three hits and three walks. Center fielder Bullard contributed two superb catches in the second and Serena added a leaping catch of a line drive in the fifth. Lefty Roger Bowman came on for Nicholas in the sixth and was immediately assaulted for three straight doubles and a single, putting Augusta back into the game at 5-3. A fine throw by catcher McAndrews to Ortiz at second cut down a stealing Augusta baserunner to end the Tiger uprising.

Augusta manager Frank Skaff kicked up such a tirade over the call that umpire Stan Muñoz finally tossed him from the game, but Skaff would not leave, even upon threat of forfeiting the game to the Bisons. Umpires Mitchell and Muñoz finally determined that it wasn't worth their while to argue any longer in a meaningless exhibition game. Skaff continued to coach from his third-base box for the rest of the game. Bowman shut down the Tigers thereafter, no doubt benefitting from any future close calls the arbiters were required to make.

Brovia batted cleanup and was the only Bison to collect two hits, scoring once and driving home a run. McAndrews replaced Tomkinson and again went hitless in his one plate appearance.

Cavarretta gave a vote of confidence to Van Remmen following the game, despite the youngster's wildness. "That boy is going right to the majors," he predicted. He was tipping off his curveball, Cavarretta pointed out, and the manager and Brovia had taken advantage of it. Once he had that straightened out he would progress rapidly, the Buffalo skipper added.

President Taylor expressed his pleasure with the team's performance. Not certain upon his arrival in camp if the team could be a contender, Taylor had seen six wins in a row, a Buffalo run-scoring advantage of 44 to eight, shutout strings of 21 and 16 consecutive innings by his pitchers, and only one Buffalo error in 36 frames. "They have the will to win," he told the News' Kritzer. "It shines all over them." He was particularly impressed with George Bullard, both for his fly-catching abilities and his speed on the base paths. "He looks like a $50,000 player," he commented, a fleet center fielder who could run down long drives and keep his team in the game with his defense.

Taylor also offered the following assessment of the team's fortunes: "This club has the power to carry average pitching. I'll make one prediction: Buffalo, barring bad injuries, will score more runs than any International League club...And I believe, too, that the Bisons will make fewer mistakes." With that said, the president, following a morning meeting with Buffalo businessman and Bison shareholder Leonard Simon, was content to fly back to Buffalo to attend to his other business ventures.

Stiglmeier was more than contented. He had just finalized the purchase of 34-year-old Pete Castiglione from the Toronto Maple Leafs. An eight-year major league ballplayer with several solid seasons with the Pittsburgh Pirates, Castiglione brought the infield utility skills that the ball club had been seeking. Able to play shortstop, third base and second, and even take a turn in the outfield in a pinch, Castiglione had batted .293 in 64 games for Jack Kent Cooke's second-place Toronto ball club in 1955. Peanuts Lowrey knew Castiglione well. They had been teammates on the 1953 and 1954 St. Louis Cardinals. Castiglione would add more than his glove work, Lowrey commented. He had led the National League in pinch-hitting in 1950 with a .318 average (7 for 22) and had a lifetime pinch-hit mark of .299 (16 for 54). Castiglione was expected to arrive from the Toronto camp at Ft. Pierce on April 9.

Stiglmeier had been forced to make the purchase, he reported, because major league clubs had reneged on their promises to option another infielder to the Bisons. The purchase price was undisclosed but rumored to be in the neighborhood of $3000. "Now, if we can buy a seasoned catcher we will have a strong bench," he offered. Stiglmeier said he still had hopes for a deal for Carl Sawatski.

April 9, Monday

The Herd's six-game winning streak came to a halt, but they were not charged with a loss. Buffalo and the Detroit farm team Durham Bulls played to a 14-inning 7-7 tie at Bartow. The game was called by mutual agreement after more than three hours of play. Cavarretta sent 19 men into the fray, including himself and Lowrey, and Brovia smote a mighty three-run home run that must have carried 450 feet over the center-field fence, but the talk of the players afterwards was the pitching display put on by Lackawanna High School product Nick Koleff.

The 20-year-old, residing at 176 Harding Street in South Buffalo, had been signed to a Detroit contract by Buffalo's Cy Williams after a starring career at Lackawanna and a brief MUNY League experience with the Kicks squad. Koleff had won 15 games in each of his first two professional seasons and was being groomed by his manager, Johnny Pesky, to pitch the Durham opener in the Class B Carolina League the next week. What he showed this day on the mound was that he might already be too good for that level of competition.

Durham jumped to a five-run lead in the top of the first. Lefthander Bob Schultz started for Buffalo and put the leadoff batter on with an errant throw to first base. A walk to the number two batter, a successful double steal, another walk and four Durham singles chased home the five tallies before Schultz could get the third out. Over the next four frames he allowed only one hit, no walks and no runs.

Buffalo answered in the bottom of the first, scoring two runs of their own on two free passes and two Durham boots. The first Bison hit did not come until the third, when Brovia sent his thunderous shot to center to knot the ballgame at 5-5. The Bisons went ahead by two in the fifth when Koleff came on to pitch. He was clipped for singles by DeMars, Brovia (his third RBI) and Easter. Had it ended there, Brovia would have been the star of the day, but Koleff then took both the ball and the game in hand.

After allowing the go-ahead runs, Koleff shut the door on the Bison batsmen and nailed it tight. For the next nine innings, from the sixth through the fourteenth, he pitched no-hit ball. He set nine batters down on strikes and seemed even faster in the fourteenth than he had in the fifth. The best Buffalo could manage in that span was four walks.

Kritzer quoted Cavarretta after the game: "I think we saw a new pitching star born today." Koleff credited his success to the development of a curveball, thanks to the guidance of Willis Hudlin, the former Cleveland Indian ace and now the Tigertown pitching coach. "I couldn't throw a good curve until Hudlin showed me how to get the right spin on the ball. And he gave me a new grip." According to his teammate Bob Taylor, a resident of Blasdell, New York, Koleff had been the best pitcher in the Tiger camp over the past two weeks. "I'm glad we didn't have to face that boy under lights," was Easter's contribution.

It was a sloppy game afield. Durham booted two and the Bison defense committed six miscues. Ortiz was charged with three, two of those coming in the top of the ninth to help Durham score the two unearned tallies that tied the game and sent it into five extra scoreless innings.

Buffalo hits were limited to five. Brovia had his second game in a row with two safe knocks. Buffalo pitchers walked five men; Durham hurlers gave up eight free passes. Eleven Bisons went down on strikes. Thirteen Durham batters fanned. Buffalo hit into three double plays and turned one. Don McAndrews started at the catcher's spot and went 0 for five. He walked against Koleff in the fourteenth and was run for by Lewandowski.

Brovia's continued bat display was noted by several major league clubs considering their pinch-hitting needs. Cash offers, however, were not what general manager Stiglmeier was looking for. Player help was what was needed. Speaking of which, both Castiglione and Keriazakos had yet to show up, although more Buffalo fans had put in an appearance. Sloan police chief John Piekarski and his three daughters had arrived to spend the week on vacation.

April 10, Tuesday

The first rains of spring training gave the Bisons and their Terre Haute opponents the day off. Settled in at the Oaks Hotel, the players were grateful for a respite from the grind. Cavarretta was not quite so sanguine. His veteran players had rounded into much better condition than he had hoped for, he said, but he didn't want a lengthy period of rainout idleness that could set them back considerably.

The delay was helpful for at least three of the team. Eric Rodin's aching right shoulder was not responding to Jimmy Mack's heat treatments and his otherwise effective job behind the plate had been offset by his inability to throw. Milt Jordan's ailing elbow was also getting a chance to rest. The more direct overhand delivery that Mack had suggested was creating a different kind of strain on the arm and adding to his woes. Fortunately for Mario Picone, the unanticipated day off also gave him the additional rest needed to make him feel that his arm was finally ready to go.

Good news arriving with the rain was the presence of Pete Castiglione and Gus Keriazakos in camp. Castiglione would provide the critical infield backup the club so badly needed. Keriazakos would add a fresh righthanded arm to the mound crew. The "Golden Greek," as some had called him after his signing bonus from the White Sox, had not thus far lived up to his heralded expecta-tions. Only now, after five professional seasons, was the talented young New Jerseyite beginning to demonstrate his gifts. He was coming off his best year in organized baseball in 1955, a record of 11 wins and 2 losses with the Sally League Savannah A's (with an ERA of 1.67) and a promotion to Triple A Columbus, where he had won three and lost five. His presence brought the number of pitchers in camp to 15. The Bisons would add one more when the Duane Pillette scenario was resolved. Cavarretta's plan was to carry nine hurlers for the season.

The rain provided a good opportunity to corner Stiglmeier and ask for his outlook on the team. Being back in baseball after a 12-year hiatus had reenergized the 67-year-old general manager, who was only too happy to share his observations. He offered his evaluation of the league for the gathered newspapermen.

Brooklyn-backed Montreal, 1955's first-place finishers, again had to be rated as the favorites. Speed, power and defense were still there, even though they might not be as strong on the hill. The Red Wings had not been showing much in spring training, but they could count on seasoned pitching to help their cause. The new Miami club, the previous year's Syracuse squad, which had finished fifth, had been rejuvenated by the new ownership and blessed with a strong-looking crop of rookies from the Philadelphia Phillies' organization. They would be the youngest team in the league.

Richmond had a new tie-up with the Yankees and old pro Ed Lopat at the helm and could count on the strength of the Yankee farm system to make them competitive. The Columbus Jets would again have a working relationship with the Kansas City A's and could be the most improved team in the league. Manager Nick Cullop had strong pitching he could call on. Bob Kusava looked particularly impressive, and behind him were Ray Herbert, Jim Miller, Walt Craddock, Leroy Wheat and Bob Spicer. The big bats were outfielders Russ Sullivan and Bill Stewart, and the club had strengthened itself considerably with the addition of ex-New York Giant Ray Noble behind the plate.

The Havana Sugar Kings were a mystery. After finishing in third place the previous year, the club had been training in Mexico away from the eyes of their competitors. Manager Reggie Otero would likely once again call upon speed to put with some excellent pitching as was the case in 1955, but they did not look to have much power. They continued their linkage with the parent Cincinnati Reds.

All these teams would certainly be strengthened after the May 15 cutdown date of the major league ball clubs, but that meant that meant that the two independent teams, Toronto and Buffalo, had to get away quickly on the season to remain in the first division. Stiglmeier credited the Maple Leafs with the best set roster in the International League, likening the Canadians to the Bisons except for better pitching. Buffalo had a chance, he felt, if the team could play .500 ball on the opening road trip to Miami, Havana, Richmond and Columbus. For the road trip and the spacious ballparks they would visit, the club needed to emphasize defense to go with pitching. Once home in Offermann Stadium, the power could be unleashed to keep the team competitive.

Buffalo would be a first-division club—of this Stiglmeier was sure—if the organization could land a reliable catcher to share the duties with Pat Tomkinson. The spirit on the team was outstanding, he said. The men were going out of their way to help the club save investor dollars, chasing down batting practice balls for reuse and driving their own cars to away exhibition games, after the plan for Bartow to provide transportation had fallen afoul of insurance concerns. Stiglmeier relayed to the News' Cy Kritzer that Joe Brovia, whose home run wallop had rendered one ball unusable, had noted, "This is the happiest ball club I've ever been on. Everybody tries to help everybody else. And everybody is giving his best."

Stiglmeier's wife had arrived in town and would stay on to accompany him to the team's April 18 opening game in Miami. More fan arrivals were Harold Conley, a South Buffalo real estate developer, and Carl Latham of Niagara Falls. Both men and their wives had looked in on the club's progress en route to a vacation in Ft. Lauderdale.

April 11, Wednesday

The sun returned and so did the Bisons' winning ways, but not before overcoming wind gusts, dust storms and shaky second-line pitching that again sent them into extra innings to pull out the victory. The game was played at the Tigers' Lakeland facility and once more against Frank Skaff's Augusta Senators, whom the Herd had defeated 6-3 on the previous Sunday. However, on this day the Bisons struggled to capture a win by the narrow margin of 9-8.

Vic Stryska started for the visiting Bisons and proved that the recommendation by Buffalo's own Ray Dabek, now a catcher for the Texas League Dallas Eagles, had been worth the look-see. Dabek had caught Stryska in winter ball in the Caribbean and thought that the solid righthander had something to offer. A 24-game winner in his first professional season, Stryska had progressed admirably until he had reached Double A. Only 2-2 with Class B Galveston in 11 games the previous season, Stryska, now a free agent, held the Senators to two hits and no runs in five innings of work, striking out two and walking only one. What's more, it was his third outing of training camp, with yet a run to be scored against him.

Stryska "knows how to pitch, and has all the equipment to be a real fireman," said Cavarretta, speaking to the News of the role he had in mind for the hurler. He pointed out that the pitcher was keeping the ball low in the strike zone, throwing a sinker that was tough for lefthanders and a curve that had righthanders lunging, plus a slider he was able to get across for strikes. Keeping the ball low, Cavarretta continued, meant double killings and avoided the home run ball, "the chief requisite for a reliever."

Solo home runs by Easter, his second of the training session, and Ortiz, his first, staked the Bisons to a two-run lead. Red Donovan took over to pitch the sixth and seventh, but was no mystery to the Augusta hitters. They racked up seven tallies. Donovan walked three and gave up four hits, but it was Joe Brovia's misplay of a fly in right that cost the pitcher three unearned runs. Each team committed two errors, which figured in the scoring as Buffalo bounced back to tie the game with a five-run eighth. Pete Castiglione, playing his first game as a Bison and coming on in the sixth for Serena at third, singled home a run. Ortiz slashed his second hit of the day and singled in two more. Roger Bowman kept Augusta off the scoreboard in the eighth and ninth.

Ortiz slammed a two-run home run in the eleventh to send the Bisons ahead. Buffalo boy Dan Lewandowski had surrendered an Augusta hit and a walk in the tenth but kept the runners from scoring. In the eleventh he was greeted with a triple and a double to make the score 9-8 before bearing down to retire the next two men. His walk to the next hitter put the winning run on base and resulted in Cavarretta's call for John Weiss to get the final out. George Bullard tracked down a drive to deep center.

Cavarretta used 18 men in the game, with Castiglione by far the best of the substitutes. Pete had two hits, two runs and an RBI in three at-bats. Ortiz's three blows were good for five RBIs. Easter nearly had two home runs. His second hit was a double off the center-field wall. Augusta outfielder Fleming, who had earlier been offered to the Bisons by Detroit but had been turned down by Stiglmeier, had four hits in six trips.

April 12, Thursday

Buffalo traveled to Plant City, where Miami stopped the Herd's winning streak at eight. Mario Picone, making his first appearance since April 3, took the 4-2 loss. Picone gave up a double to International League rookie Ed Bouchee to start the bottom of the second and retired the next batter, but then surrendered a run-scoring single. Two walks loaded the bases and two runs came home on a Texas Leaguer that dropped in front of Brovia in right. Picone permitted four walks in his three innings pitched, his timing likely off due to a lack of work stemming from the sore arm.

The Bisons got their two runs in the third and seventh, Ortiz scoring the first and doubling home the second. Gus Keriazakos followed Picone to the mound and registered an impressive first outing for his new team with three innings pitched, no runs, one hit, three strikeouts and one walk. An eighth-inning triple and a sacrifice fly against Milt Jordan brought home the Marlins' final tally. Miami 4, Buffalo 2.

Easter cracked two sharp singles and a deep fly to center that was pulled in right in front of the fence. Castiglione pinch-hit a single to make him three for four in a Buffalo uniform. The Bisons turned one double play and were the victims of two.

Cavarretta's concerns about his pitching corps received some instant relief with the news that 10-year major league veteran Joe Coleman had been added to the roster. The big righthander—6 feet, 2 inches, and 200 pounds—had been given his release the previous week by Detroit. In 1948 with the Philadelphia Athletics, Coleman had posted 14 victories and earned a save in the 1948 All-Star game, won by the American League. He followed that season with 13 more victories for Philadelphia in 1949. In his last role as a starter, Coleman had won 13 and lost 17 for the 1954 Baltimore Orioles, earning enough votes to place him 19th in that year's MVP calculation. One of those wins had been a one-hitter against the Yankees. Last year, with Baltimore and Detroit, he had appeared in 23 games, winning two and losing two as a reliever.

The Bisons cut two pitchers after the ballgame. Unconditional releases were given to Dan Lewandowski and Ed March.

Mr. and Mrs. Howard Gunnison, vacationing at St. Petersburg, added to the list of Buffalo residents dropping in on spring training sessions.

April 13, Friday

The Bisons dropped their second straight road game in Lakeland by losing to Durham by a score of 4-2, but the major concern on this day was the state of catcher Pat Tomkinson's throwing hand. Tomkinson caught a foul tip off his right hand in the second inning and had to leave the game. Business manager Harry Bisgeier, now in camp, drove him for an immediate checkup at the Tigertown headquarters. Detroit's trainer in charge of the farm system, Bill Harper, ruled out the need for medical attention. He advised Tomkinson to rest the hand for a couple of days as well as staying out of the batting cage. Buffalo rookie Don McAndrews took over behind the plate.

Karl Drews started and threw five complete innings, giving up a two-run home run in the second. He held Durham to five hits, striking out three and walking none in his last warmup before Wednesday's league opener in Miami.

Buffalo got a run back in the fifth on Brovia's single to score McAndrews, but Durham retaliated and ran the score to 4-1 with a pair off Fred Hahn in the sixth. Buffalo ended the scoring in the top of the seventh on singles by Bullard, DeMars and Clyde Vollmer. Nick Koleff set down the Bisons with no hits in the eighth and the ninth. Buffalo left 10 men on base.

Buffalo's catching situation was critical. Tomkinson was their only experienced receiver who was healthy. Eric Rodin was still suffering with a sore arm and Don McAndrews, 0 for two this day, was now 0 for 12 for the spring. Stiglmeier was continuing his desperate search for another seasoned catcher.

Cavarretta stated that Drews would start for him in the season opener unless Miami overloaded the lineup with lefthanders. Froats was counted on as the manager's second starter and Keriazakos might be third in the starting rotation. Cavarretta was impressed with his outing against Miami. Tomkinson credited Keriazakos with the best curve he'd seen this spring, whether he was receiving or hitting.

Joe Brovia got some extra morning attention in the outfield before the club left for the game at Lakeland. As a 17-year-old, Brovia had worked out as a pitcher with the San Francisco Seals until manager Lefty O'Doul had gotten a look at him in the batting cage. He was sent to El Paso as an 18-year-old and wound up hitting .383 as an outfielder. Following his military service and marriage, a more mature Brovia made it to the Triple A Pacific Coast League in 1946 and had stayed there ever since as a steady .300-plus power hitter. He was especially dangerous with the short right-field fence in Portland as a member of the Beavers from 1949 to 1952. The altered stance he adopted during that period had allowed him to average 20 home runs annually and close to 100 RBIs regardless of the size of the ballpark in which he later found himself. He was keen to prove that Cincinnati should have given him more of a chance in 1955 to be an everyday player and not limit him to a pinch-hitting role. "I'd like to have my greatest year for Buffalo," he told the News' Kritzer, just to prove wrong those who had given up on him.

However, having his greatest year for Buffalo would depend greatly on his fielding. No one had yet confused Brovia with Bullard in the outer gardens, nor even with Blatnik or Vollmer. To support Joe's drive for success, Cavarretta and Lowrey had him out in right field for a pregame session in Bartow, Cavarretta driving liners and flies into the outfield with Lowrey posted several yards off to give him pointers.

The work appeared to have paid off in the afternoon in Lakeland, when Brovia started charging the ball as it was hit to him and not waiting for it to come to him. "Joe will come through for us," Lowrey commented. He likened Brovia's situation to that faced by Philadelphia Phillies outfielder Del Ennis. Ennis had learned to become confident and relaxed as an outfielder, and Lowrey believed that Brovia could make a similar adjustment. As with his hitting, it was simply a matter of being relaxed, he said.

"Honestly," said Brovia, "no one ever tried much to teach me how to field. Maybe it's not too late to learn. I'd like to work at it." With a manager like Cavarretta, it was certain that Brovia was going to get his chance to make this effort.

April 14, Saturday

Buffalo got back on the winning beam in the team's contest against the Class B Terre Haute Huts, scoring an unearned run in the last of the tenth inning to pull out a 4-3 victory.

Harry Nicholas started for Buffalo and made a strong statement to become Cavarretta's fourth starter. He held the Huts to two singles and no runs in six strong innings. He fanned five and issued no walks. Brovia's booming two-run double gave the Herd the lead in the fifth. Jim Walsh took over in the seventh for Nicholas and immediately gave up three hits, three runs and the lead. He then settled down and pitched scoreless ball in the eighth and ninth.

Easter tied the game in the ninth with a sacrifice fly following three bases-loading walks. The winning run in the tenth was another gift. Pete Castiglione, sitting on third base with his third hit of the day, scored on a two-out misthrow to first following a dropped third strike. The veteran Castiglione bluffed a run to the plate, distracting the young Terre Haute catcher, who then threw wildly to first, hitting Bob Schultz, the batter, in the leg. Schultz picked up the save and a bruised thigh. Walsh was credited with the win.

Buffalo played errorless ball again, turned one double play and hit into two. The Bison bats pounded out 11 hits, but timeliness was a concern. Eleven men were stranded on base.

Lowrey started in center field in place of Bullard and scored the tying run in the ninth. Bullard had reported in the morning with eye irritation from Wednesday's blowing dust and traveled to Lakeland with Harry Bisgeier for a consultation. Small cysts on each eyelid were removed, and the center fielder returned to Bartow, suited up and eventually pinch-hit for Walsh. Cavarretta caught up with his center fielder after the game and reiterated the need for the youngster to relax. He was back to thinking he was a home run hitter, the manager told him, and he was swinging for the fences again. What the Bisons needed from Bullard, he was told, was to get on base. The men behind him would drive him home.

Don McAndrews was behind the plate in place of Tomkinson and went hitless in three at-bats. Tomkinson, although injured only the day before and advised to rest, replaced McAndrews in the late innings as Cavarretta tried to squeeze out the winning run in regulation time with a substitute batsman. Having to use Tomkinson in the game only demonstrated the dire state of the Bison catching situation.

It was now apparent that catcher-outfielder Eric Rodin's sore arm was not going to respond. The Bisons returned his contract to the New York Giants and began a fevered search elsewhere for a capable receiver. Cavarretta, Bisgeier and Stiglmeier again worked the telephones, reaching out to their contacts. The Phillies, Stiglmeier reported, were close to making a decision on Duane Pillette. If he stayed with that club, Philadelphia would offer the Herd the services of a yet-to-be designated pitcher as well as catcher Lou Heyman. Heyman was a 35-year-old career minor leaguer who had hit only .206 and .194 in part-time duty with Syracuse in 1954 and 1955.

Cincinnati was offering catcher Matt Batts, a nine-year major league part-timer with a .269 batting average. He had seen action in 26 games with the Reds in 1955, hitting .254. With American Association Indianapolis, he had hit .231 in 51 contests. The sticking point was the asking price: $10,000 for the purchase, plus an annual salary of $9000. This was much too rich for the cash-strapped, community-owned Bisons.

Another long shot was help from Toronto, if the Chicago White Sox came through on a promise made to Rudy Schaefer, the Maple Leafs' general manager. Schaefer had let Stiglmeier know that he might be receiving Earl Battey from the Sox. If that indeed turned out to be true, Toronto would loan catcher Sam Hairston to the Bisons. Hairston, now 36, had had a cup of coffee with the White Sox in 1951 and was a durable catcher who had hit a respectable .268 with Triple A Charleston in 1954 and an outstanding .350 with Class A Colorado Springs in 1955. Although Stiglmeier was still holding out hope for the services of Carl Sawatski, the general manager would jump at the chance to have Hairston if it was possible. Cy Kritzer quoted him as saying, "We have to have a catcher now. Can we wait? Not after what happened Friday [to Pat Tomkinson]."

April 15, Sunday

Buffalo and Miami gave the spectators a preview of what they might expect in the season opener on Wednesday in Miami. Hitting was scarce—four for the Bisons, five for the Marlins—but walks were plentiful and missed opportunities rampant. Each side surrendered nine walks; each committed an error. Buffalo left eight men on base; Miami left 10.

Bill Froats started for the Herd and kept Miami off the board in his three innings of work. He gave up only one hit and struck out five, but he also walked four men. Miami made the most of two hits and a walk allowed by Joe Coleman to make the score 1-0 in the fifth. Following his manager's orders, Bullard got on base in the sixth and scored the tying run on an Easter single. Miami took the lead in the ninth off Roger Bowman. An Ortiz boot, an intentional walk and a bases-loaded walk with two out produced one run. A base hit by former National League All-Star Sid Gordon produced two more.

In the Bison half of the ninth, Miami reliever Henry Mason speared leadoff hitter John Blatnik's line drive straight back at him only at the last instant. Shaken, Mason then walked the next three batters before he was taken out. Pinch-hitter Bill Serena drove in one man on a fielder's choice and George Bullard stroked a two-run single to make it 4-3, but the rally ended there. Miami 4, Buffalo 3.

Don McAndrews caught the game for the Bisons and continued his woes at the plate. He was 0 for three. The Marlins also stole four bases off the young catcher. Lou Heyman, the subject of purchase talks by the Bisons and the Phillies, caught the game for Miami. He was 0 for two.

The pitcher-catcher deal with the Phillies was still being worked on at the end of the day. Stiglmeier and Cavarretta were desperate for a catcher, but Pillette, the Buffalo hurler candidating with the Phillies, had been rained out of his scheduled appearance against Boston. Philadelphia still wanted one more look at him before they would conclude the transaction.

Immediately following the game, the Miami club left for their home base in a fleet of automobiles. Cavarretta headed out to spend a day with his family, who were vacationing in Pompano Beach. Karl Drews, likely the opening-day starting pitcher, drove to his home in Hollywood, Florida, from where he would commute during the Miami series. The remaining 27 men on the roster were scheduled go with general manager Stiglmeier on the next morning, traveling first by bus to Lake Wales and then by train to their Miami destination, the Leamington Hotel. The club would have a final workout in Miami stadium on Tuesday afternoon in preparation for the Wednesday night April 18 opening game of the season.

The Bisons finished their spring training record with 9 wins, 5 losses and a tie. Miami finished with 11 won, 8 lost, but ominously took three out of the four games against the Herd.

April 16, Monday

The purchase of catcher Lou Heyman from the Miami Marlins, talked about for some while, was provisionally agreed to on this day. The matter was still pending the Phillies' decision on Duane Pillette. Don McAndrews, hitless in the spring but showing form defensively despite the previous day's four stolen bases, was sent out to Syracuse, now an Eastern League ball club, leaving the Herd with two veteran catchers. Pat Tomkinson was the likely the starter with Heyman serving in a backup role. Although a fine receiver with a good arm, Heyman's work in the batter's box left something to be desired.

A big man at 6 feet, 3 inches, and 230 pounds, the 35-year-old Heyman had three times slugged 30 or more home runs at the lower rungs of baseball classification, but at Triple A Syracuse in 1954 and 1955, he had fared poorly. In addition to his dismal batting averages, he had homered only seven times in 1954 and had improved to only nine roundtrippers the following season.

The catcher who general manager Stiglmeier and manager Cavarretta had really wanted, Carl Sawatski, had been sent to Toronto by the Chicago White Sox for the sum of $10,000, a figure less than the Bisons had offered, Stiglmeier pointed out. Regardless, Stiglmeier vowed that he would continue his search for another quality receiver from a major league club.

Cavarretta surprised the newspapermen by announcing that lefty Bill Froats would be his opening day hurler. Veteran Karl Drews, with plenty of major league experience, had been hinted at, but the spring training contests with the Marlins had forced Cavarretta to recognize the Miami club's lineup of strong lefthanded batters. Froats' lefthanded slants were more likely to neutralize Miami's Ed Bouchee, Larry Novak and Dave Mann, as his work on the day before had shown.

Johnny Blatnik was likely to start in left. He collected two sharp singles in the Grapefruit League finale against the Marlins. Cavarretta would start Pete Castiglione at third base on the strength of his .400 hitting in spring training.

April 17, Tuesday

A new day brought a new lineup change for the opener. Cavarretta had decided to go with Bill Serena at third after all, to face the likely Miami starter, Thorton Kipper. Serena had stood in well against the 25-year-old righthander in the spring training ballgames. And Heyman's catching role with the club was finalized. The Phillies, keeping Pillette, would be sending the Herd another pitcher as promised.

Stiglmeier had asked for righty Jim Owens, a proven 17-9 and 15-11 with Syracuse in the past two campaigns, and only 22 years old—or perhaps the highly regarded 21-year-old southpaw Seth Moorhead, 8-13 in his rookie International League season with the same club. Both young men were destined for successful major league futures. Stiglmeier wanted Buffalo to be their final stop before reaching the bigs. The Phillies replied that their decision would be forthcoming at the May 15 cutdown date.

With Bill Veeck at the helm, the opener was being trumpeted in Miami as the city's first Triple A League appearance. Officials spoke in terms of a crowd of perhaps as many as 15,000 fans, and perhaps several hundred of those would be vacationing Buffalo rooters. Stiglmeier was fielding a plethora of ticket requests. Roxie Gian, a Bison board member and the owner of four ponies that would be racing at Gulfstream Park, would be there, as would another Gulfstream aficionado, Frank Lillich. Dan Carnevale, manager of the 1955 Buffalo team, sent his well wishes to the Bisons' new operation.

THE 1956 BUFFALO BISONS
MANAGEMENT

All images courtesy of 1956 Buffalo Bisons Scorebook

Harry Bisgeier,
business manager

John C. Stiglmeier,
general manager

Reginald B. Taylor,
president

THE 1956 BUFFALO BISONS

STAFF

Image of Jimmy Mack courtesy of 1956 Buffalo Bisons Scorebook; images of Max Felerski and John Boersma courtesy of SUNY Buffalo State Courier-Express Collection

Max Felerski,
stadium superintendent

Jimmy Mack,
trainer

John Boersma,
groundskeeper

CHAPTER 6: THE 1956 SEASON

CY KRITZER OFFERED the fans his analysis of the International League in a column that appeared in the April 17 edition of the Buffalo Evening News.

Montreal's Royals, winners of five pennants in the past 11 seasons, appeared loaded again. Skipper Greg Mulleavy could rely not only on the big bat of 1955's Triple Crown winner, Rocky Nelson (.364 average, 37 home runs, 130 RBIs), but would also call on a potent outfield of George Shuba in left, Jim Williams (.329) in center and Bob Wilson (.317) in right. With Nelson at first, Chico Fernandez at short and Clyde Parrish covering third, Montreal had three returnees from what International League president Frank Shaughnessy the previous year had called "baseball's best defensive infield." Charley Neal's replacement at second would be either the slick-fielding George (Sparky) Anderson, making the leap from Mobile, or Harry Schwegman, .306 at San Antonio. The Royals could count on Dick Teed as a dependable receiver, but pitching-short Brooklyn might create a similar pitching shortage north of the border.

Bruno Betzel's Toronto Maple Leafs had finished in second place in 1955, but this year the Toronto manager believed he had the horses to take over the top spot, especially with the addition of long-ball–hitting catcher Carl Sawatski. International League All-Star Hector Rodriguez returned at shortstop, slugging Mike Goliat would be at second and the pride of Pisgah, Iowa, Loren Babe, would cover third. Lou Limmer (28 home runs) was scheduled to share first base with Ed Stevens. In the outfield, Betzel could call upon the multitalented Sam Jethroe in center field (24 stolen bases), flanked by hard-hitting Bill Wilson (down from Kansas City) in left and Lew Morton in right. Betzel would feel happier with yet another outfielder and hoped his mound crew could make up for the loss of 19-game winner Jack Crimian, now with the American League Kansas City club.

The Havana Sugar Kings, 1955's third-place finishers, had not made major changes to their roster. Reggie Otero would continue to rely on the speed, defense and pitching that allowed his squad to outscore their opponents by 688 runs to 611, resulting in an 83-70 record. New additions of the youthful Ultus Alvarez in the outfield and Forest (Woody) Smith at third could add some much-needed punch at the plate. Otero could surely count on reliable pitching from 37-year-old Pat Scantlebury and expect that he would be ably supported by 26-year-old Rudy Minarcin (5-9 with Cincinnati's Reds in 1955; a 16-game winner with Buffalo in 1951). Given the warmth of the climate, Havana pitching might overpower other teams' hitting in the early weeks of the season.

The Rochester Red Wings under Dixie Walker planned to count on 20-year-old rookie center fielder Mel Nelson and veteran, proven hitters on either side of him: Allie Clark (.308, 23 home runs) in left and Tom Burgess (.285, 10 home runs) in right. Dick Rand and Ebba St. Claire would return behind the plate. Buffalo's own Stan Jok would anchor the infield at third base. Eddie Kasko, obtained from Richmond, would play shortstop. The biggest question marks were on the right side of the infield, with rookies Ron Plaza at second and Neal Herweck at first. The team's greatest strength was in the veteran pitchers it could send to the mound: Cot Deal (7-4), John Mackinson (9-7) and Duke Markell (13-13).

The fifth-place Syracuse Chiefs of 1955 had become the Miami Marlins of 1956, and manager Don Osbourne liked the new look his squad had taken on. His strength would be in his young pitching corps, headed by 21-year-old Turk Farrell, 12-12 with the previous year's Chiefs. Major league veteran catcher Gus Niarhos was now on hand to guide this youthful mound crew. Outfielders

Larry Novak and Mel Clark were likely to be sandwiched around newcomer Dave Mann in center, a leadoff speedster from Wayne University in Detroit who had been clocked at 6.2 seconds in the 60-yard dash and 9.8 in the 100. Twenty-three-year-old lefthanded-swinging first baseman Ed Bouchee, a .313 hitter with 22 home runs for Eastern League Schenectady in 1955, had the spring training camps talking Rookie of the Year about his skills. Veteran major leaguer Sid Gordon, now 38, would be Osbourne's player-coach at third base and offer both wisdom and power to the team after compiling a 13-year-career major league total of 202 homers. He hit .243 in 1955 for the New York Giants. Mickey Micelotta and rookie Wilbur Johnson would battle it out for short, while Bob Tomkins returned at second.

The Columbus Jets under Nick Cullop had made the most extensive changes in the league, picking up former major league catcher Ray Noble (three years with the Giants) from the previous year's Havana squad, and virtually overhauling the entire infield. Third baseman Johnny Lipon came over from Havana with Noble, and first baseman Clint McCord, a fine defender, was obtained from Richmond. Up the middle, Pacific Coast Leaguer Ray Rose (Oakland) had arrived to play shortstop, and Frank Verdi would shift from third to second to cover the considerable hole left by the departed Spook Jacobs. A healthy Bill Stewart (.299 and 12 home runs in a season shortened by injury) and another outstanding year from Russ Sullivan (.319 and 29 long balls) would make the outfield the power source for the club. "Another big bat in the outfield," Cullop stated, "and we're on our way." Mound additions of veterans Bob Spicer and Bob Kusava and newcomers Glenn Cox and Ray Herbert might help to solve last year's pitching deficit.

Tail enders in 1955, the Richmond Virginians were bound to improve with the presence of new manager Eddie Lopat, the former Yankee pitching great. Lopat would guide the team from both the dugout and the mound. Al Cicotte (26) and International League veteran Niles Jordan would also be slated for regular mound duty. Lopat was still looking for another starter and some strong hitting, hopefully to be supplied by center fielder Al Van Alstyne and the $40,000 Yankee bonus baby, first baseman Frank Leja.

As for Buffalo, power, principally in the person of first baseman Luke Easter, would make the Bisons a factor in the league. Direction from manager Phil Cavarretta meant that the veteran team would be unlikely to make many mistakes. Another catcher and a starting pitcher would enable the Bisons to make a significant impact on the league.

Veteran sportswriter Bill Coughlin of the Courier-Express, a man who had covered the Bisons for 35 seasons, echoed Kritzer's assessment in his own column on the same day. Coughlin felt the Bisons had a legitimate chance at a first-division finish. This was his best prediction for the club since the Tigers had assumed ownership of the team and fielded the 1952 squad.

A veteran lineup contrasted sharply with the previous year's "Detroit youth movement" and should result in greater success. Of the starting nine, only center fielder George Bullard (26) and catcher Pat Tomkinson (29) would be south of the 30-year mark, and only Bullard would provide any speed. Still, the new Bison power lineup of Easter, Ortiz and Serena in the infield, and outfielders Blatnik, Vollmer and Brovia should ably offset that limitation. Especially when considering the short outfield fences in Offermann Stadium.

Defensively, Bullard would need to range far into left and right center field to assist his slower outfield teammates. Ortiz at second and DeMars at short should turn out to be the equal of or surpass any keystone combination in the league, with Pete Castiglione an effective backup at any of three positions and able to hit as well. Still looking at the middle, a stronger-hitting catcher to alternate with Pat Tomkinson remained an ongoing need. Serena, at third, had a cannon for an arm.

The veteran mound crew, barring a "wholesale collapse" from past performance, should prove more than capable. Coughlin listed Karl Drews, Bill Froats, Harry Nicholas, Mario Picone, Gus Keriazakos and Joe Coleman as highly regarded starters, with Vic Stryska waiting in the wings. If Cavarretta planned to carry a squad of nine hurlers, Roger Bowman, Jim Walsh, Larry Donovan, John Weiss, Fred Hahn and Milt Jordan would contend for the remaining two positions. And there was still the "pitcher-to-be-named" to come down from the Phillies.

Cavarretta's managerial experience at the major league level and Lowrey's acquired wisdom from a 13-year major league career assured effective team guidance. These men would even be able to step into the lineup as the occasion demanded. Even more impressive to Coughlin's eyes was the confidence of the players in the straightforward, unflagging efforts of general manager John C. Stiglmeier. Stiggy was committed to respond both to the men's varying needs and, more importantly, put a winning team on the diamond. Having been let down by the White Sox in the Sawatski matter, Stiglmeier was still looking for that elusive solid second receiver.

BUFFALO BISONS INTERNATIONAL LEAGUE SCHEDULE: 1956

April

S	M	T	W	T	F	S
			18 @ Miami	19 @ Miami	20 @ Miami	21 @ Havana
22 @ Havana @ Havana	23 @ Havana	24 @ Richmond	25 @ Richmond	26 @ Richmond	27 @ Richmond	28 @ Columbus
29 @ Columbus	30 @ Columbus					

May

S	M	T	W	T	F	S
		1 BYE	2 Miami	3 BYE	4 Miami	5 Havana
6 Havana Havana	7 Havana	8 Columbus	9 Columbus	10 Columbus	11 Richmond	12 Richmond
13 Richmond Richmond	14 Montreal	15 Montreal	16 Montreal	17 Montreal	18 @ Toronto	19 @ Toronto
20 @ Toronto @ Toronto	21 @ Montreal @ Montreal	22 @ Montreal	23 @ Montreal	24 BYE	25 Rochester	26 Rochester
27 Rochester Rochester	28 Toronto	29 Toronto	30 Toronto Toronto	31 @ Rochester		

June

S	M	T	W	T	F	S
					1 @ Rochester	2 @ Rochester
3 @ Rochester	4 BYE	5 @ Havana	6 @ Havana	7 @ Havana	8 @ Miami	9 @ Miami
10 @ Miami @ Miami	11 BYE	12 Havana	13 Havana	14 Havana	15 Miami	16 Miami
17 Miami Miami	18 @ Columbus	19 @ Columbus	20 @ Columbus	21 @ Columbus	22 @ Richmond	23 @ Richmond
24 @ Richmond	25 Columbus	26 Columbus	27 Columbus	28 Columbus	29 Richmond	30 Richmond

July

S	M	T	W	T	F	S
1 Richmond Richmond	2 BYE	3 Montreal	4 Montreal Montreal	5 Montreal	6 @ Rochester	7 @ Rochester
8 @ Rochester	9 Toronto	10 Toronto	11 Toronto	12 Toronto	13 @ Montreal	14 @ Montreal
15 @ Montreal @ Montreal	16 @ Toronto	17 @ Toronto	18 @ Toronto	19 @ Toronto	20 Rochester	21 Rochester
22 Rochester	23 All-Star Game	24 @ Richmond	25 @ Richmond	26 @ Richmond	27 @ Columbus	28 @ Columbus
29 @ Columbus @ Columbus	30 Miami	31 Miami				

August

S	M	T	W	T	F	S
			1 Miami	2 Miami	3 Havana	4 Havana
5 Havana Havana	6 Rochester	7 Rochester	8 Rochester	9 Rochester	10 Toronto	11 Toronto
12 Toronto	13 @ Havana	14 @ Havana	15 @ Havana	16 @ Havana	17 @ Miami	18 @ Miami
19 @ Miami @ Miami	20 BYE	21 Richmond	22 Richmond	23 Richmond	24 Columbus	25 Columbus
26 Columbus Columbus	27 @ Rochester	28 @ Rochester	29 @ Rochester	30 @ Rochester	31 Montreal	

September

S	M	T	W	T	F	S
						1 Montreal
2 Montreal	3 @ Toronto @ Toronto	4 @ Toronto	5 BYE	6 BYE	7 @ Montreal	8 @ Montreal
9 @ Montreal						

INTERNATIONAL LEAGUE BALLPARKS, 1956

Illustration of Offermann Stadium courtesy of Bruce Barber; illustrations of other ballparks originally published in Buffalo Bison 1959 Sketch Book for Press – Radio – Television.

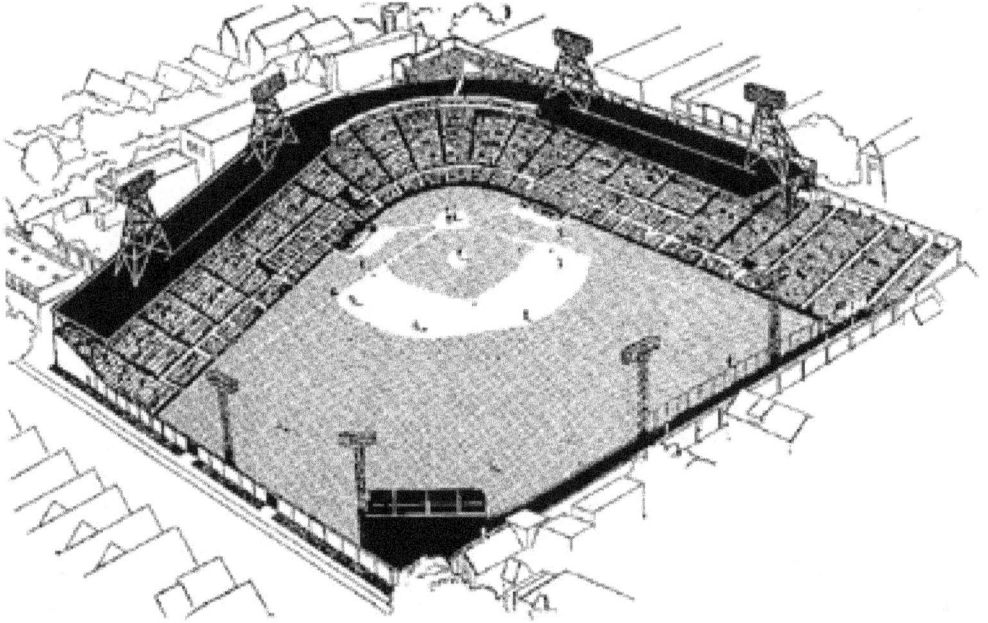

Offermann Stadium, Buffalo, New York

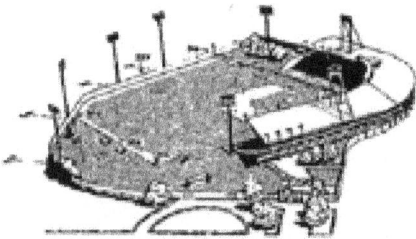

Jets Stadium, Columbus, Ohio

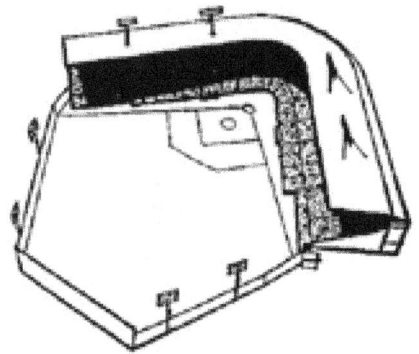

Maple Leaf Stadium, Toronto, Ontario, Canada

INTERNATIONAL LEAGUE BALLPARKS, 1956

All illustrations originally published in Buffalo Bison 1959 Sketch Book for Press – Radio – Television.

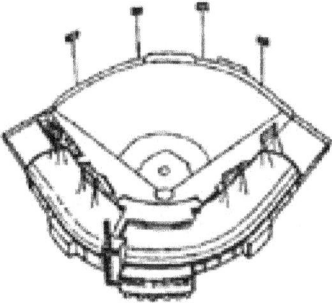

Miami Stadium, Miami, Florida

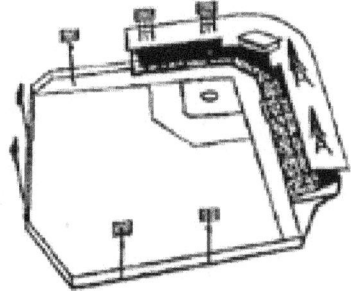

Parker Field, Richmond, Virginia

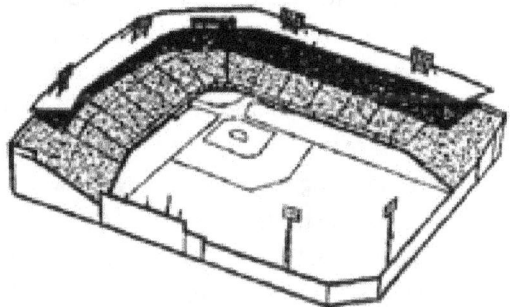

Delorimier Stadium, Montréal, Québec, Canada

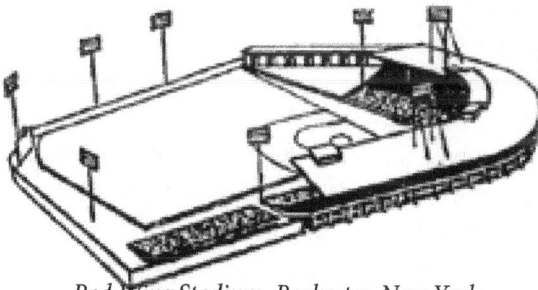

Red Wing Stadium, Rochester, New York

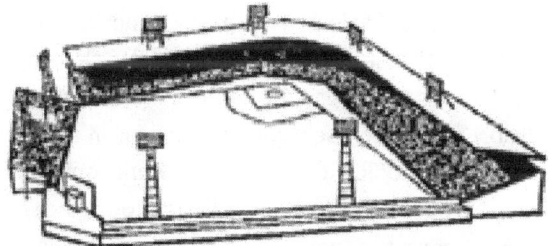

La Gran Stadium, Havana, Cuba

Game 1—Wednesday, April 18, Miami, Florida: Miami 10, Buffalo 3
> *The newly relocated and newly named Miami Marlins took the*
> *season opener from the new community-owned Buffalo Bisons.*

```
Game 1 – April 18, 1956
Buffalo          002 100 000 – 3  7  0
Miami            005 010 04x – 10 11  0
WP – Greenwood (1-0)    LP – Froats (0-1)
```

The best the Herd could manage was to salvage a tie from the third-inning, benches-clearing fisticuffs.

Buffalo opened the scoring in the top of the third, Pat Tomkinson leading off with a double against Thornton Kipper. Froats walked but was forced out at second by Bullard, Tomkinson moving to third. A walk to DeMars loaded the bases and Tomkinson scored on a fielder's choice from Brovia. With two down, Easter clubbed a double to the centerfield wall, 400 feet away. Bullard scored but Brovia held at third. Blatnik went down with two men on to end the inning.

Five walks and four hits in 2⅔ innings undid Froats. One of those blows was a run-scoring drive to right center by Sid Gordon that Bullard got a glove on but could not capture. Ed Bouchee also sent a liner to center that Bullard appeared to misplay, resulting in a triple that finished Froats. Cavarretta called on righthander Harry Nicholas to relieve, but Miami manager Don Osbourne countered by sending in the lefty-swinging Larry Novak to hit for the righthanded Ed Mierkowicz. Novak made Osbourne look like a genius, taking Nicholas deep to right field and off the light standard for a home run, boosting the score to Miami 5, Buffalo 2. Cavarretta protested to no avail that the ball had bounced back into the park and should not have been ruled a homer. Vic Stryska replaced Nicholas and got the final two outs.

Buffalo made it 5-3 with a run in the fourth. Ortiz singled with one out and was sent home by another single by pinch-hitter Clyde Vollmer. Bob Greenwood took over the mound for Osbourne and ended the scoring. He was good for five innings of two-hit ball until the Bisons threatened again in the ninth.

Lefthander Fred Hahn took on the pitching chores for Cavarretta in the bottom of the fourth. He, too, was on the hill for five frames but gave up a single Miami tally in the fifth and then was battered for four more in the eighth. Hahn was touched for six hits and six walks.

Buffalo's attempted rally in the ninth fell sadly short. With one out, Tomkinson collected his second hit of the day and Castiglione walked in a pinch-hitting role for Hahn. Osbourne once again turned to his bullpen and called on Ed Zinker to face Bullard. The Bison center fielder, who had been robbed of at least a double by a fine outfield play by Mel Clark in the seventh, sent a scorching line drive that shortstop Bobby Micelotta gloved with a circus catch, throwing to second to double up Tomkinson and end the contest. Froats took the loss; Greenwood got the win.

BISON TALES: Because it was opening day in a new city, and because Bill Veeck was in charge of the Miami front office, there were fireworks out beyond center field to inaugurate the Marlins season—in addition to the fireworks that took place on the field. Music was played and speeches were made before the game, and tightrope walker Josephine Berosini traversed a 150-foot wire strung between two outfield light stanchions, 80 feet above the ground. Finally, making a helicopter land-ing on the pitcher's mound in the second inning, Satchel Paige sent up a dust storm that delayed the game for several minutes. He then strolled out to a large easy chair that had been provided for him in the Miami bullpen.

Veeck even brought in baseball clown Max Patkin to entertain the crowd with his antics as the Marlins' first-base coach for the first three innings. His gyrations may have distracted Froats.

The baseball-type boxing match in the sixth inning came after Hahn had given up a leadoff infield single to Miami's Dave Mann. The lefty then picked Mann off base. The ensuing rundown saw even Blatnik coming in from left field to participate before Hahn could make the tag. Mann's complaints to the umpire brought words from Blatnik to quit his bellyaching, whereupon Mann responded with language that Blatnik said he was not going to take, and the two men set to swinging.

Whether actual blows were landed is a matter of speculation. Both men were ejected, likely to face $25 fines from the league office. Peanuts Lowrey took over Blatnik's duties in left.

Bobby Micelotta played a big part in the Miami win. Osbourne had decided to go with Micelotta instead of rookie Wilbur Johnson at short. Micelotta collected three hits and drove home three runs in addition to his timely fielding contributions.

Potential help for the Bison pitching staff appeared when former major leaguer Max Lanier showed up for a tryout. Lanier, out of baseball for two years and just released by the Marlins prior to today's game, had been making a comeback attempt. Stiglmeier and Cavarretta promised the veteran they would give him a chance to show his stuff. Lanier boasted a record of 108-82 in 14 major league seasons, most of them with the St. Louis Cardinals.

The Courier's Bill Coughlin noted the presence of many dignitaries and Buffalo and Western New York residents who put in appearances at the game. International League president Frank J. (Shag) Shaughnessy was there, as was U.S. senator George Smathers, Miami mayor Randy Christmas and a Democratic contingent from Chicago led by Col. Jack Arvey. Of course, John C. Stiglmeier and Bison business manager Harry Bisgeier were there, as were their wives. The Courier-Express also sent columnists Joe Glaser and Frank Lillich to observe. Former Courier reporter and now sports editor of the Ft. Lauderdale News, Joe Kolb, was on hand, too.

Spectators from the Buffalo area included: Dr. John Gabbey, Joe Radice, Mrs. Joseph A. Schutz, Rose Stiglmeier, Clara Munzel, Betty Sawtelle, Dr. Dexter F. Levy and son, Sam Abelson, Mr. and Mrs. John Piekarski and their three children, Eddie Meys, Roxie Gian, Mr. and Mrs. Vincent Brun, Gloria Smith, Andy Olson, Terry Gregory, Jimmy Quinn, James Sexton Jr., Harold O'Connor, Bill Wright, Mr. and Mrs. Frank Porzella and son, Dr. Frank Kean, Marge Lasker, Roy Siegel, Mr. and Mrs. Barney Lepper, Joe Schinstock, Jerry Sullivan, Marge Sullivan, Henry Duch, George Schillinger, Florence Nesslin, Herbert Whiting, Mr. and Mrs. William Davis, Mr. and Mrs. Martin Lee, John Ganson, Charley Hall, Albert Gerspach, Gerry Gallagher, Joe Springer, Mr. and Mrs. Ed Labelle, Bernie Flynn and George Parker.

They hoped for a better result from the next day's contest. Cavarretta was likely to go with Drews on the morrow.

FULL 1956 SEASON BOX SCORES MAY BE DOWNLOADED AT: https://tinyurl.com/2p992ahr

Game 2—Thursday, April 19, Miami, Florida: Buffalo 6, Miami 1

Shining defense and aggressive baserunning gave Karl Drews the first Bison victory of the year.

```
Game 2 – April 19, 1956
Buffalo          000 004 011 – 6  7  1
Miami            100 000 000 – 1  5  2
WP – Drews (1-0 )         LP – Anderson (0-1)
```

Drews walked five and allowed five hits in the first three innings, but defensive gems by George Bullard and Pat Tomkinson in the first inning and a bang-bang double play by Billy DeMars and Lou Ortiz in the second kept the Marlins to only one run after two.

With one out in the first, Ben Tompkins walked and came in to score on singles by Larry Novak and Sid Gordon. A walk to Ed Bouchee loaded the bases. Mel Clark's high fly ball deep to center was hauled in by Bullard, who then unleashed a strike to Tomkinson at home. The Bison catcher came out in front of the plate, took Bullard's throw on the short hop and blocked the charging Novak from scoring, applying the tag for an inning-ending double play. Novak's spikes cut Tomkinson's shoe in the process, but the catcher had saved his team a crucial run. "One of the greatest block plays I've ever seen," Cavarretta offered in the postgame wrapup. The wizardry of DeMars to Ortiz to Luke Easter closed the door on a Marlin threat in the second.

From the fourth inning on, Drews was untouchable, with corner-finding curves and crossfire fastballs keeping the Miami batters off balance. The Bisons finally broke through for him in the sixth.

DeMars' bunt single led off and a walk to Brovia followed. Easter's single cashed DeMars and put Brovia on third. Cavarretta sent Lowrey in to run for Brovia. Miami manager Osborne turned to Don Cardwell to quench the rally, but this time the bullpen failed him. Cardwell could not find the plate, giving up a wild pitch that scored Lowrey and sent Easter to third. Nicholas ran for Easter. Cardwell then walked Blatnik and Serena to load the bases.

A sharp ground ball from Lou Ortiz seemed destined for a double play, but Serena's hard slide into second dumped Miami's Tompkins and allowed Nicholas to score from third and Blatnik, a slow runner, to make it all the way home from second. That finished Cardwell's night and the scoring for the Herd in the sixth. The Bisons added two more unearned runs in the eighth and ninth, Ortiz sending Serena home with a sacrifice fly and Cavarretta, now at first base for Easter, bringing home DeMars on a solid single.

BISON TALES: Drews had hurled the first complete game of the season. Gus Keriazakos was on tap to pitch tomorrow night. The Herd would leave after the game for a flight to Havana.

Buffalo was still waiting for a Phillie hurler to join the team in exchange for the big club keeping Duane Pillette. Max Lanier worked out for the team but Cavarretta was still pondering a decision.

Game 3—Friday, April 20, Miami, Florida: Buffalo 8, Miami 6

Late power off the bench brought the Bisons a come-from-behind extra-inning win.

Game 3 – April 20, 1956

Buffalo	000 000 140 3 – 8	14	2
Miami	200 000 120 1 – 6	11	1
WP – Stryzka (1-0)	LP – Zinker (0-1)		

Miami starter Gene Snyder was forced from the game by a blister. In seven impressive innings, the hard-firing lefty had yielded only one run and had set nine Bisons down on strikes.

Miami got two first-inning runs off Gus Keriazakos and it could have been more, save for a dazzling backhand stop by Lou Ortiz behind second. The Bisons got their lone run off Snyder in the seventh, when Pat Tomkinson scored on George Bullard's sacrifice fly. Miami added another run in the bottom of that frame.

Buffalo bats got going in the eighth against Snyder's replacement, Bob Cain. First up, Luke Easter walked. John Blatnik doubled him to third. Harry Nicholas went in to run for Easter and Peanuts Lowrey for Blatnik. Enter new Miami hurler, Ed Zinker. Bill Serena's fielder's choice scored Nicholas. Ortiz walked. Lew Heyman (catching for Tomkinson after the latter had been tossed in the seventh for arguing balls and strikes with plate umpire Harry Schwarts) struck out. But Phil Cavarretta put himself in as a pinch-hitter for Keriazakos and crushed the first Bison home run of the season over the right-field wall. Buffalo 5, Miami 3.

Bob Schultz took the hill for the Herd in the bottom of the eighth. He fanned two but also walked two, and Cavarretta called for Bill Froats. Froats walked the only man he saw and was re-placed by Joe Coleman. Ben Tompkins greeted Coleman with his second double of the day to knot the game at five apiece. Coleman finally got Ed Mierkowicz to retire the side.

With Vic Stryska replacing Coleman on the mound, Buffalo won the game in the tenth. Lew Heyman's homer put the Bisons one up. Billy DeMars bunted for his fourth hit, Stryska singled, and Clyde Vollmer, pinch-hitting, doubled both men home for the 8-5 Bison lead. Three scratch hits produced a sixth Miami run in the bottom of the tenth, but Fred Hahn came in to get the final out.
BISON TALES: Cavarretta's blow was the first league pinch-hit home run of the campaign.

Ed Bouchee picked up a four-stitch gash in his left knee trying to break up a double play in the first. DeMars got the force out at second.

Game 4—Saturday, April 21, Havana, Cuba: Havana 8, Buffalo 3

Three Sugar King home runs sent the Bisons down to
defeat in the opener of the four-game series.

Game 4 – April 21, 1956

Buffalo	100 001 100 – 3	6	1
Havana	202 020 20x – 8	9	4

WP – Marrero (1-0)   LP – Jordan (0-1)

Buffalo had gotten on the board first, George Bullard legging out a first-inning infield hit and going to second on an errant throw by third baseman Woody Smith. One out later, Brovia sent him home with a single. Havana went ahead in the bottom of the first, 2-1.

Angel Scull, leading off for the Sugar Kings, was plunked by a Milt Jordan fastball to put a runner on first. He didn't stay there long. Number-two hitter Juan Delis sent him scampering home with a double. Nino Escalera singled and Havana was up, 2-1. The Cubans added two-run home runs from Smith in the third and Ultus Alvarez in the fifth to make the score 6-1 in Havana's favor.

Bill Serena got one back for the Herd by smacking his first homer of the year to lead off the sixth inning. Havana starter Connie Marrero—five years as a Washington Senator pitcher with a record of 39-40, and seven wins and three losses last year with Havana—set down the next three men in order. Jordan called it a day after completing the sixth frame, giving way to pinch-hitter Pete Castiglione in the seventh.

Buffalo tried again in the seventh. DeMars got a life on Smith's second throwing error of the night and wound up on second. As he had in the first, Joe Brovia sent home the runner on second with a clean single to right. Jim Walsh started the seventh in relief of Jordan but was cudgeled for yet another two-run blast. Smith walked and Ultus Alvarez cracked his second homer of the night with a man on. That finished the evening's scoring.

Joe Hatten, 39-year-old veteran of seven major league seasons with Brooklyn and the Chicago Cubs (record: 65-49), kept the Bisons hitless and scoreless in the eighth and ninth. The Buffalo record for the year evened at two and two. Havana pleased their fans with a won-3, lost-1 start to their season.

BISON TALES: The Bisons' two hurlers had no strikeouts on the night and walked four. Two of those walks scored.

Cavarretta's two pinch-hitters, Castiglione in the seventh and Blatnik in the ninth, both flied out. The manager said he would call on Froats to start the first game of the scheduled Sunday doubleheader. He was uncertain who he would pitch in game two.

Following Cavarretta's Friday night pinch homer, Pat Tomkinson made it two Buffalo firsts in two days. He picked up a $25 fine for the previous day's outburst in Miami. It was the first one levied this season by league president Frank J. Shaughnessy.

Games 5 and 6—Sunday, April 22, Havana, Cuba: Buffalo 5, Havana 4; Buffalo 3, Havana 1

Old pros in the field and young arms on the mound led the Herd to a
doubleheader triumph over the speedy Sugar Kings.

Game 5 – April 22, 1956 (first game of doubleheader)

Buffalo	000 000 110 3 – 5	6	0
Havana	000 100 010 2 – 4	9	2
WP – Drews (2-0)	LP – Amor (1-1)		

Game 6 – April 22, 1956 (second game of doubleheader)

Buffalo	101 100 0 – 3	6	0
Havana	001 000 0 – 1	5	2
WP – Nicholas (1-0)	LP – Bracho (0-1)		

The two victories matched the total wins Buffalo had managed in all of 1955 in Gran Stadium. With four wins and two losses, the Herd was now in second place in the International League standings, a game behind Toronto's Maple Leafs.

In game one, Larry Donovan, 23 years old, held the Cubans to seven hits and a single run in seven innings of steady work, giving up only one base on balls and fanning two. Down by a run after Havana had scored in the fourth, the Bisons knotted it in the seventh on George Bullard's single and a double by Joe Brovia. Peanuts Lowrey entered the game to run for Brovia. In the eighth, with two down and Pete Castiglione on first, pinch-running for Bill Serena who had walked, manager Cavarretta called on himself again to pinch-hit and drew a walk to move Castiglione to second. Bullard's second single of the game scored Pete and gave the Bisons the lead. Mario Picone came in to preserve the win.

The Cubans were not yet ready to concede. Juan Delis walked to lead off the bottom of the eighth. Picone struggled against Nino Escalera before he got him out. Cavarretta called in Karl Drews to retire Woody Smith. Drews didn't have the same fortune against Ultus Alvarez, who pounded him for a double, moving Delis to third. Amado Ibañez's ground out brought Delis home and tied the score once again. Drews closed out the inning without further damage.

Drews blanked Havana in the ninth and Cuban starter Vicente Amor followed suit against the Bisons, having to this point given Buffalo only three base hits. The Herd collected that many again in the next frame, breaking through for three tallies. Pat Tomkinson led it off with a double to right. With one out, Bullard walked and Billy DeMars punched a single to left to score Tomkinson. Lowrey, now playing for Brovia, lined a double that sent Bullard and DeMars across the plate and gave Buffalo a three-run lead, just enough to win.

Drews gave up a hit and two walks, and suddenly the bases were loaded with Angel Scull, Juan Delis and Nino Escalera aboard. A ground out by Woody Smith scored a run. Cavarretta went back to the bullpen and turned to Vic Stryska. Stryska got the inning's second out, threw a wild pitch and walked two more men, forcing in a run. Joe Coleman, the inning's third Buffalo pitcher, finally stuck out Asdrubal Baró on a full count with the bases loaded. Drews was credited with win number two on the season. Coleman saved it for him.

In the second game, potent hitting from the first two Bisons in the lineup gave the Herd the victory in a contest in which they never trailed. Billy DeMars slugged his first home run of the season in the first inning to give starter Harry Nicholas the lead. A second run came in the third inning when George Bullard tripled and DeMars chased him home with his second hit of the game. Nicholas surrendered an Asdrubal Baró home run in the bottom of the third to make the score 2-1, but the Herd got that one back in their next turn at the plate. Shortstop Pablo Bernard, who would make three errors on the day, gave a life to Bill Serena, leading off the inning, by muffing his grounder. Lou Heyman's base knock moved Serena to third. Bullard singled him home with a rocket to center field for his second hit of the afternoon. That took care of the scoring for both clubs.

Nicholas threw a seven-inning complete game for his first victory of the campaign. He spaced five hits, fanned seven and walked only three in an impressive outing. For their part, the Bisons collected only six hits, with Bullard and DeMars at the head of the order garnering two apiece and driving in all three runs. Pete Castiglione went in to run for DeMars in the third and stayed in the game at shortstop. John Blatnik spelled Joe Brovia in right midway through the game and Cavarretta performed a like role for Luke Easter at first base. Peanuts Lowrey started the game in place of Clyde Vollmer in left.

BISON TALES: With the sweep of the doubleheader, the Bisons now found themselves the sole possessors of second place in the league with a 4-2 record, one game behind the 4-0 Maple Leafs and a game ahead of a four-way tie for third place: Rochester, Havana, Montreal and Columbus had all started the season 3-3. Miami was 2-4 and Richmond stood at 1-5. Perhaps a first-division Bison finish was not such an unlikely outcome.

Pat Tomkinson had hit safely in each of the first five games of the season, going six for 16 for a .375 average. Manager Cavarretta rested him for Lou Heyman for this second game. Heyman came through with a base hit in two official at-bats.

Heat and humidity were significant factors when playing in Cuba, particularly for the pitchers and catchers, and for big men like Easter and Brovia. Hence, Cavarretta's decision for the lineup changes and substitutions in game two.

Keeping the ball low, Nicholas finally found a way to silence Ultus Alvarez's bat. Alvarez had slugged Bison pitching for four hits in eight plate appearances in the first two games of the series, including two home runs, a double, three runs scored and five driven home.

John Weiss was scheduled to be Cavarretta's candidate to take the hill for the final game of the series. He would likely face off against Charlie Rabe, a youngster whose promise was being touted by the Cincinnati Red Legs, the major league affiliate of the Havana club.

Game 7—Monday, April 23, Havana, Cuba: Havana 1, Buffalo 0

His own ninth-inning miscue with the bases loaded pinned the loss on Buffalo starter John Weiss.

```
Game 7 – April 23, 1956
Buffalo          000 000 000 – 0   3   1
Havana           000 000 001 – 1   6   1
WP – Rabe (1-1)          LP – Weiss (0-1)
```

Weiss had been working on a knuckleball in spring training and unveiled it against the Cubans. He was hoping the same pitch that had sent Ben Flowers (12-9 with the 1955 Bisons) back to the majors would be the key to a similar promotion for him.

The Sugar Kings were hard pressed to make solid contact off Weiss' offerings and had managed only four hits, plus four walks, through eight frames. No one, it seemed, including Weiss, was quite sure where the knuckler would wind up. At the same time, the Bison bats were anemic against the Cubans' 24-year-old Charlie Rabe, a sparkling 21-7 with the previous year's Single A Sally League Columbus club. Rabe was looking to jump two classifications and was showing thus far that he could do it. A nifty curveball had set eight Bisons down on strikes.

Only in the eighth did the Herd threaten. Center fielder Angel Scull pulled in a 400-foot blast off the bat of George Bullard leading off the frame. Billy DeMars then worked Rabe for a walk. Peanuts Lowrey flashed the hit-and-run sign from the batter's box and DeMars was off with the pitch, but Nino Escalera, the Cuban first baseman, snagged Lowrey's line drive toward the hole for the easy unassisted double play.

John Blatnik, sent in to hit for Joe Brovia in the ninth, stayed in the game in right field. Juan Delis, a thorn in Buffalo's side throughout the series, led off the Havana half of the ninth inning with a slicing drive down the right-field line that Blatnik got a glove on but could not hold. Delis wound up at third base, credited with a triple.

Cavarretta ordered Ultus Alvarez and Asdrubal Baró walked intentionally to load the bases and then pulled the infield in. Pinch-hitter Don Nicholas, batting for Dutch Dotterer, hit a ball directly to DeMars, who threw home for the inning's first out. Rabe batted for himself.

The pitch from Weiss was in on the fists, where he wanted it, but Rabe managed to squib the ball back to the mound where Weiss gloved it and then dropped it. Alvarez came in to score the winning run. The official scorer generously awarded Rabe a hit on what should have been an in-ning-ending double-play ball.

BISON TALES: It was a tough game to lose. In the locker room, Blatnik commented that Delis' blow would likely have hooked foul if he had not gotten a glove on it.

The Sugar Kings' manager Reggie Otero made two winning calls. The first was to bench the er-ratic Pablo Bernard and move Juan Delis to shortstop. The second was to allow his lefthanded-bat-ting pitcher to dig in against the righthanded-throwing Weiss in the ninth.

The Bisons got to bed at 2:30 in the morning following the contest, catching only three hours of sleep before the scheduled flight to Richmond, Virginia.

Cavarretta had reason for some satisfaction as his club flew into Richmond. He had pegged his team as a legitimate first-division contender and after seven games they were in a three-way tie for second place, one and a half games behind the undefeated Toronto Maple Leafs. George Bullard,

Cavarretta's designated center fielder "if he could hit .275," had fashioned a .269 average thus far. Bullard with five runs scored, and DeMars with six, were leading the club in that category. DeMars was hitting a cool .360 to top all regulars.

It was the skipper himself who was showing the way at the plate: two hits in five at-bats for a .400 average, a home run, a pinch walk and four RBIs, tying cleanup hitter Luke Easter for the lead in RBI count. The catching staff, a question mark in spring training, was leading most of the other ballplayers in hitting. Pat Tomkinson could claim a .315 average and Lew Heyman was at .500 (two for four with a homer). Old pro Peanuts Lowrey was hitting .285.

The rest of the men were struggling, and the famed power had not yet shown itself. The club had managed only four home runs to date, less than adequate to offset hitting into nine double plays. The Bisons had turned eight. The club as a whole was hitting an anemic .211, while the opponents had managed a .252 mark against Bison hurlers. More problematic to Cavarretta had been the bases on balls. Buffalo pitching had surrendered a total of 42 free passes, an average of six per game. This had to change if the Herd expected to win consistently.

Karl Drews, Harry Nicholas and John Weiss had turned in three starting gems, even though Weiss had dropped the 1-0 decision in yesterday's second game. The bullpen still had not yet established itself. Cavarretta was still looking for consistency.

Fifteen pitchers were at this point listed on the roster, and five or six of them would eventually be released. Cavarretta wanted to see what each man could do in at least a couple more outings before deciding whom to keep and whom to let go. There was also the matter of the pitcher yet to come from the Phillies, and that arm would factor into the manager's decisionmaking.

International League Standings
April 24, 1956

	W	L	Pct	GB	
Toronto	4	0	1.000	—	
Buffalo	4	3	.571	1½	
Havana	4	3	.571	1½	
Rochester	4	3	.571	1½	
Columbus	2	2	.500	2	
Montreal	3	4	.429	2½	
Miami	2	5	.286	3½	
Richmond	2	5	.286	3½	

Game 8—Tuesday, April 24, Richmond, Virginia: Buffalo 2, Richmond 0

*Lefthander Roger Bowman made his claim for a permanent spot on the roster
by throwing a three-hit shutout on a bitterly cold evening.*

Game 8 – April 24, 1956

Buffalo	200 000 000 – 2	7	0
Richmond	000 000 000 – 0	3	1

WP – Bowman (1-0)   LP – Coates (0-1)

The combination of a humming fastball and a sharp breaking curve set five Vees down on strikes. The only flaw was the continuation of far too many walks—Bowman gave up seven, including three in one inning. However, the lefty induced a comebacker to the mound that turned into a 1-6-3 double play to end the threat.

Jim Coates started for Richmond and gave up the game's only runs in the first inning. George Bullard walked to lead off and moved to second on Billy DeMars' single. A walk to Luke Easter loaded the bases. Bill Serena, fighting a 0-for-10 drought, stepped in against Coates with two men down and delivered a two-run single. That was it for the scoring.

Coates surrendered five more hits in the next six innings, gave up one more base on balls and struck out three, but he kept the Bisons in check after that ruinous first frame. Breaking out of his slump, Serena went two for four. Lou Ortiz, hitless in four games, picked up a single.

Buffalo suffered a close call on a run-down play in the seventh. Buddy Carter and Vic Morasco had singled, putting runners on first and second. A missed call sent Morasco running to second base while Carter remained anchored there. Bison catcher Lew Heyman alertly threw to shortstop DeMars to trap Carter. Carter got back safely to second, but Morasco was retired on DeMars' throw to Easter. On the play, Morasco collided with the big Buffalo first baseman and knocked him out of the game with a bruised leg. Cavarretta took over first base for the remainder of the contest.

Bison Tales: Easter was fortunate the collision wasn't worse. Morasco had taken pains to avoid spiking him, he said. Hopefully, time in the Richmond whirlpool bath would make him ready to play again in a day or two.

The Bisons were angry about having to play on such a frigid night, especially after navigating a tricky obstacle course just to get to the stadium in time for the start. With only three and a half hours of sleep after the previous night's Havana game, Buffalo had caught a 6:30 a.m. airport bus to make their flight out of Cuba. In Miami, after clearing customs, they then caught taxis for their next flight to Washington, D.C. Yet a third flight brought them to Richmond, and then a bus to their hotel at 5:15 p.m. A bath, a sandwich and still another bus ride brought them to the ballpark.

Perhaps Richmond had thought the Bisons would be too tired to put up much of a fight. Cavarretta had asked them to do their best. As veterans, they had responded.

DeMars was nursing a sore left leg that was taped before the game. Heyman was in to sub for Tomkinson, who was battling a sore throwing arm. Tomkinson did receive some excellent news in the eighth inning—his wife had just given birth to a 7-pound, 14-ounce baby girl.

Game 9—Wednesday, April 25, Richmond, Virginia: Buffalo 3, Richmond 0

Bill Froats' shutout moved Buffalo into sole possession of second place,
a half-game behind Toronto.

Game 9 – April 25, 1956

Buffalo	000 030 000 – 3	7	0
Richmond	000 000 000 – 0	5	1
WP – Froats (1-1)	LP – Nardella (0-2)		

As in Monday's contest, the Bisons scored all their runs in one inning, bunching a walk and three hits to score three times in the fifth.

Virginian pitcher Wimpy Nardella had held the Bisons to only one hit over four innings, but he gave up a walk to Bill Serena to start the fifth frame. Cavarretta lined a single off the glove of Richmond first baseman Tom Hamilton. Lou Ortiz singled up the middle to send Serena across the plate with the first run of the game. Froats dumped a one-out single into short right to drive in Cavarretta. George Bullard's foul sacrifice fly to deep right plated Ortiz.

For the second night in a row, Richmond had big trouble against a lefty. Froats fanned 10 men, including striking out the side in the seventh. He gave up five hits, but none after the fourth inning. Three stellar defensive plays saved the shutout.

In the second, Peanuts Lowrey, playing left field, ranged far to his right to haul in a long drive from Hamilton near the line. The next batter, Moe Thacker, solved Froats for a double. Thacker then tried to score on a sharp single to left by Dee Phillips, but Lowrey's barehanded pickup and throw to home to the 230-pound Lou Heyman stopped the 210-pound Richmond runner cold, a foot in front of the plate. In the third, a bang-bang 6-4-3 double play ended the last Richmond threat with two men on.

BISON TALES: Buffalo substitute players proved Cavarretta's point that "a team is only as strong as its bench." Lowrey had started the last two games in left in place of John Blatnik. Heyman again took on the catching chores for Pat Tomkinson, the latter having added a heavy cold to his sore throwing arm. Pete Castiglione subbed for the ailing Billy DeMars and Cavarretta manned first base so that Luke Easter could continue to recuperate from Monday's collision.

Despite too many walks, pitching was a bright spot for the club. The staff had five complete games in nine starts and two consecutive shutouts. Bison hurlers had allowed only one run in their last 31 innings. Cavarretta planned to carry a nine-man pitching staff. Froats, Roger Bowman, Karl Drews, Gus Keriazakos, Larry Donovan, Harry Nicholas and John Weiss had all proven themselves in the starter role. Joe Coleman, Bob Schultz, Jim Walsh, Vic Stryska, Fred Hahn, Mario Picone (sore arm) and Milt Jordan (sore arm) were vying for the two other spots.

Cavarretta went two for four in the game, but the manager's 39-year-old back meant he couldn't play for very long without rest. Easter was probably out of the lineup until Sunday but could likely pinch-hit if needed. DeMars was still out for tomorrow and Larry Donovan had a sore shin after a batting practice line drive.

Buffalo schools would be closed at 1:45 p.m. on Home Opening Day, May 2, to allow the children to attend the ballgame.

Game 10—Thursday, April 26, Richmond, Virginia: Richmond 1, Buffalo 0

There was a third straight shutout tonight, but this time it was the Bisons who wore the collar.

Game 10 – April 26, 1956

Buffalo	000 000 000 – 0	4	1
Richmond	100 000 00x – 1	8	1

WP – Cicotte (2-0)   LP – Drews (2-1)

Karl Drews allowed the Virginians only six hits over seven frames, but it was the one first-inning fastball to third baseman Buddy Carter that cost him the ballgame. Carter put it over the left-field fence for the game's only run.

Drews, the old pro and former Yankee, had the bad luck to come up against the Yankees' starting righthander of the future, Al Cicotte. Plagued by past wildness, the 26-year-old had found some magic under the tutelage of former Yankee mainstay, Eddie Lopat. "I was wild and every manager I played for talked to me about getting control," Cicotte said after the game, but not Lopat. "You're one of my starting pitchers," Lopat had said, advising him to "keep on firing and aim for the middle [of the plate]."

A blazing fastball combined with "the best slider most of us have ever seen" held the Herd to four singles. Cicotte gave up four bases on balls, but he also struck out six and kept the ball down. The Vees turned three double plays.

The Buffalo power hitters continued to struggle. Joe Brovia hit into a double play in the fourth with two men on and no outs. Cavarretta said later that Brovia was pressing and might need a day off. Luke Easter pinch-hit for Lou Ortiz with the bases loaded in the seventh and two out and was one of Cicotte's six strikeout victims. Easter was so incensed at the call that he was thrown out of the game by plate umpire Joe Linsalata.

The Bisons kept trying. Clyde Vollmer, hitting for Drews in the eighth, got a single, but nothing came of it. Milt Jordan got himself into a jam in relief of Drews in the eighth and was literally knocked out of the box. After giving up a base hit and a walk, Joe Tesauro lined an infield single off Jordan's knee, rendering him unable to continue. Fred Hahn registered the last two outs and held the Vees scoreless.

John Blatnik, batting for Brovia, scratched a one-out base hit in the top of the ninth to put the tying run aboard, but Bill Serena received the same third-strike call that had undone Easter. That left it up to Cavarretta. The manager slammed a 3-2 pitch off the right-field wall, just foul, before tapping out, pitcher to first, to end the game.

BISON TALES: Buffalo bats ended the cool night on a cold note. With the club hitting only .214, Cavarretta, 0 for three, dropped his team-leading average to .363. He commented that no pitcher should be able to shut out this lineup.

The Bisons dropped into a third-place tie with Montreal, each a half-game behind both Toronto and Rochester, who were tied at the top.

Game 11—Friday, April 27, Richmond, Virginia: Buffalo 10, Richmond 2

Ten hits, including 3 home runs, answered Cavarretta's question
about where the team's power had gone.

Game 11 – April 27, 1956
Buffalo	010 105 300 – 10 10 3	
Richmond	001 001 000 – 2 9 3	
WP – Keriazakos (1-0)	**LP – Starr (0-1)**	

Gus Keriazakos scattered nine hits to pick up the complete-game win, his first of the season. Lou Heyman, subbing behind the plate for the injured Pat Tomkinson, was the offensive star of the game, while George Bullard ranged far to turn in three fine catches in center field.

Keriazakos and Richmond starter Dick Starr were locked in a tight game until the Bisons erupted for five runs in the sixth inning. Buffalo had drawn first blood on Heyman's solo home run in the second. Richmond tied it in the third. The Bisons broke back on top when Bill Serena scored on Keriazakos' ground out in the top of the fourth. In the sixth, Luke Easter led off with a single, followed by Bill Serena's second homer of the season to right center. Clyde Vollmer singled after Serena's blow, Lou Ortiz walked and Heyman struck again, doubling home both baserunners. Another single by Bullard and an error loaded the bases. Heyman came home on Peanuts Lowrey's sacrifice fly.

Joe Tesauro doubled home the second Vee run in the bottom of the sixth to make the score 7-2, but Heyman was not yet finished. Serena and Ortiz singled in the seventh and the Bison catcher clubbed a three-run homer over the left-field wall.

BISON TALES: Before the game, Richmond manager Ed Lopat echoed Cavarretta's previous night's comments. The Bisons, he said, "should be a big-inning team" with nearly every man in the lineup liable to light up the scoreboard.

Heyman ended the night with three hits, two of them home runs, three runs scored and six RBIs. It was easily the best night of his International League career. A slugger in the lower minors, reserve catcher Heyman now led the club with three roundtrippers and seven RBIs. Heyman enthused about being with the Bisons and added he hoped he could continue to contribute to the team's success.

Cavarretta, his back still aching, subbed for Easter in the eighth to give the limping first baseman a rest. On Cavarretta's orders, Joe Brovia was given the night off while Clyde Vollmer played right field and picked up a hit and scored a run.

Another hurler was the target of a line drive for the second straight game. Richmond reliever Bill Voiselle had to leave after completing the eighth inning, after having been struck in the knee by a line shot hit by Pete Castiglione. At least Voiselle recovered and got the out. The ball off Jordan's knee the previous night went for a hit.

The injury report: in addition to Cavarretta and Easter, Billy DeMars was out with a leg ailment, Pat Tomkinson had a sore throwing arm and Jordan was limping from last night's affair.

The cold weather may have been a factor in the game's six errors, three for each team. The Bisons were now a half-game out of first place.

Saturday, April 28, Columbus, Ohio: Rainout

Heavy rains accompanied by thunder and lightning postponed the evening's contest. It was a welcome opportunity for Cavarretta's men to get some needed rest. The extra day off would benefit the ailing: Tomkinson, Easter, Cavarretta, DeMars and Jordan. Brovia was suffering from general exhaustion. The only complaint raised was by the Jets' general manager, Harold Cooper, watching a weekend night's ticket sales get washed away by the storm.

Only manager Cavarretta, trainer Jimmy Mack and 18 players had been able to make it in time for the scheduled first pitch, suffering through a bumpy airplane ride from Washington, D.C. and just beating the storm into Columbus. Business manager Harry Bisgeier, his wife and eight hurlers were arriving on a later carrier, whenever it was able to make it in.

Uncertain travel connections were continuing to afflict the ball club. Another early-morning bus departure from Richmond to D.C. preceded the airline confusion. This evening's rest would be thoroughly enjoyed, as a Sunday doubleheader was on tap for the next day.

Games 12 and 13—Sunday, April 29, Columbus, Ohio: Columbus 1, Buffalo 0; Columbus 2, Buffalo 0
Buffalo had 10 hits on Friday in a 10-2 win. In this outing,
the club could manage only two hits in each game and was shut out twice.

Game 12 – April 29, 1956 (first game of doubleheader)
| Buffalo | 000 000 000 – 0 2 0 |
| Columbus | 000 001 00x – 1 3 0 |

WP – Herbert (2-0)   LP – Donovan (0-1)

Game 13 – April 29, 1956 (second game of doubleheader)
| Buffalo | 000 000 0 – 0 2 2 |
| Columbus | 000 101 x – 2 6 0 |

WP – Kume (1-1)   LP – Nicholas (1-1)

The pitching was going great guns, but where had the offense gone again? The double loss dropped the Herd into fourth place, two games behind league-leading Rochester. They had now been shut out four times in 13 games.

In game one, Larry Donovan turned in a second straight strong performance, yielding but three hits and two walks while fanning three. As with his first outing the previous Sunday, his effort was good enough to win, except that when Donovan took the mound the Buffalo bats were suddenly going silent.

Jet starter Ray Herbert was even more effective than Donovan. Herbert allowed only a pair of singles, walked but two and set down seven on strikes. Two Jet double plays foiled any potential Buffalo threats.

The game's only run came in the bottom of the sixth. Russ Rose led off with a single. Herbert sacrificed down the first-base line and Easter fielded the ball in what he thought was foul territory, but umpire Frank Guzzetta ruled it a fair ball. Easter had to race Herbert to the bag for the putout and thereby lost the chance to catch Rose at second on a throw to Billy DeMars. Frank Verdi, next up, singled to left center and Rose came home to score.

The Bisons turned a double play to snuff out an earlier Columbus threat, but the call on Herbert's sacrifice bunt took away that possibility in the sixth.

In the seven-inning second game, Mike Kume held the Bisons without a hit for five innings. Pat Tomkinson, catching for the first time in six games, broke up the no-hitter with a clean single to center leading off the top of the sixth. Peanuts Lowrey came on to pinch-hit for starter Harry Nicholas and failed in two sacrifice attempts to move the runner into scoring position. Finally, Lowrey hit into a double play. George Bullard followed with the single that might have plated Tomkinson, had the sacrifice worked, but Billy DeMars was retired on a soft fly to center and that was it for the Bisons for the day.

Catcher Billy Shantz, brother of Kansas City Athletics' pitcher Bobby, batted in both of the Columbus runs. Bill Stewart reached Nicholas for a single in the fourth inning and came home on Shantz's two-out double. Al Pilarcik singled in the sixth, went to third on a single by Butch McCord and scored on Shantz's ground out.

It was a silent Bison locker room in the aftermath, Cavarretta's the only voice to be heard, and a frustrated voice it was. He had no criticism for any of the men, however. He had inserted himself as a pinch-hitter for Donovan in the ninth and had experienced the same difficulty they had in picking up the ball from the haze behind center field.

BISON TALES: No one was hitting this night. The weather stayed gray and on-and-off rainy and windy throughout the evening. Columbus got only three hits in the first game, only six in the second.

Lou Heyman almost put another one out of the park in game one, foiled by a leaping stab of the ball by Columbus left fielder Bill Stewart. A pair of drives off the bats of Johnny Blatnik and Bill Serena in game two came just short of the fences after the breeze out to left field died suddenly in the fifth inning.

The team slump puzzled Karl Drews, now in his 17th professional season. On every ball club he had been on usually someone was hitting, but for this Bison roster no one was.

Following the single game scheduled for tomorrow, the Bisons were headed to Buffalo for the home opener on May 2. Stadium preparations were under way with a thorough cleaning of the facility and a grooming of the outfield grass and infield. Buffalo had been blessed with a series of excellent groundskeepers, so the ballpark's rich green grass and deep red infield dirt would, as always, be a delight for the fans to see and a joy to play on for the fielders. Buffalo was known for having the best infield composition in the league, and outfielders swore by the resiliency of its turf.

The colors of the emerald grass and the reddish infield dirt were offset by the crisp white of base lines, batter's box, bases and the pitching rubber. Add to this the deep green of the general admission seats, the red of the boxes, the colorful advertising signs on the left- and right-field walls, the green hitter's background in center and the imposing black scoreboard in right center field and the park was an artist's palette of wonder.

Game 14—Monday, April 30, Columbus, Ohio: Columbus 4, Buffalo 2

Columbus swept the series, taking the third and final game on
a frigid night that kept attendance down to 623.

Game 14 – April 30, 1956
Buffalo   010 001 000 – 2 9 1
Columbus   001 300 00x – 4 9 0
WP – Wooldridge (2-2)   LP – Weiss (0-2)

The Bisons matched the Jets with nine safeties apiece, but the difference was in the timing. Columbus bunched five of their blows in the fourth inning, scoring three runs and chasing starter John Weiss from the game.

The Bison scoreless string of 19 innings came to an end in the second when Bill Serena, Lou Ortiz and Pat Tomkinson all singled off Floyd Wooldridge to give the Herd a short lived 1-0 lead. Billy De-Mars' first error of the season put Russ Rose on base to lead off the bottom of the third. Two outs later, Johnny Lipon singled to knot the score at 1-1.

Three Jet scores put the game away in the fourth inning. Bill Stewart opened the frame with a single and moved to third on Al Pilarcik's double. Butch McCord, third batter of the inning, sent a slow roller toward second on which Ortiz had no play but to try to get Stewart at the plate. The gamble failed. McCord was credited with an infield hit, Stewart scoring. Weiss settled down to retire the next two batters, but the two-out bugaboo struck when both Woolridge and Frank Verdi hit safely, driving home Pilarcik and McCord. Fred Hahn came out of the bullpen to retire Lipon and stop the bleeding.

Wooldridge gave up a second Buffalo run in the sixth. Clyde Vollmer, who had replaced Peanuts Lowrey in left when the starter injured his leg diving for a catch, singled and moved to second on a wild pitch. Easter's ground out put him on third. Another ground out, this one from Brovia, brought him home.

Glenn Cox replaced Wooldridge in the seventh after Pat Tomkinson and pinch-hitter Pete Castiglione both singled. Cox was masterful with runners on first and third and none out. He got Bullard, DeMars and Vollmer on 12 pitches—a strikeout, a popup and a harmless fly to center.

The Bisons couldn't solve Cox. He walked two in the eighth, but a timely strikeout got him out of trouble. Bullard and DeMars singled in the ninth, but two additional strikeouts and Easter's weak tap back to the mound ended the ballgame.

Hahn held the Jets scoreless for two-plus innings. Vic Stryska did the same in the seventh and eighth.

BISON TALES: Tomkinson had gone three for six with an RBI in his two games since coming back from the sore arm. Easter was now hitless in his last 11 official at-bats and Brovia 0 for 14. Eight Buffalo men struck out, and 11 men were left on base in this game.

The Bisons left for Buffalo immediately after the game with an estimated arrival at Central Station at 11:10 a.m. A simple overnight train ride would be a welcome respite from the hectic plane and bus connections they had been subjected to since leaving Cuba.

HOME OF DREAMS
Tuesday, May 1: Scheduled Day Off
Offermann Stadium, Buffalo

Construction of Offermann Stadium had begun during the 1923 baseball season, and the Bisons continued to play there on the previously existing ball grounds while the new ballpark was being built around them. The stadium opened for business as a new facility on April 30, 1924.

The Bisons had been playing at this site at the corner of Michigan Avenue and East Ferry Street (Woodlawn Avenue provided the barrier where the right-field fence was located) since 1889, when the wooden ballpark was called Olympic Park (Olympic Park II for the historians). The stadium name, but not the structure itself, was changed in 1907. It became known as the Buffalo Baseball Park. In 1924, it was rechristened Bison Stadium. It was given the name Offermann Stadium in 1935 following the death of the then club president, Frank J. Offermann.

The International Association Bisons played at this site in 1889. In 1890, the Players League baseball squad usurped the grounds for the one season that league was in existence. Cornelius McGillicuddy (Mr. Connie Mack), later owner and long-time manager of the American League Philadelphia Athletics (and to be enshrined in the Baseball Hall of Fame), was the catcher and one of the investors in the Players club and lived on Gelston Street near the Niagara River, within easy walking distance of the ballpark for a fit young man (a little under two miles).

The minor league Bisons, then members of the Eastern League, returned to Olympic Stadium (II) in 1891. The Bisons had been playing here ever since, as members of the Eastern League, then the Western League, finally returning to the International League in 1912.

Babe Ruth had played here in 1914 as an International League rookie pitcher with the Baltimore Orioles. He defeated the Bisons in the 1914 home opener (5-3) and was to return later that year as a pitcher with the International League's Providence Grays. He had returned on a number of occasions as a barnstormer and for exhibition games against the Bisons, on those occasions as a member of the New York Yankees. He had had favorable words about the new concrete and steel stadium that was being erected on his visit in 1923.

The ballpark seated perhaps 15,000 fans at a pinch, though more could be squeezed in behind temporary ropes strung across the outfield. Balls finding their way in to the patrons gathered there were considered ground-rule doubles. A single deck of general seating (slatted wood with foldup seats) underneath the roof ran from the right-field corner around home and past the visitor dugout along the left-field line. Box seats hugged the field from the home dugout (right-field line) to the visitor dugout (left-field line). Concrete stepped bleachers seating about 2,000 ran from the metal fence barrier—where the wooden general admission seats stopped—to the left-field corner. Bullpens were sandwiched in between the foul lines and the seats in both right-field (home team) and left-field (visitor) corners.

Still other fans could watch a ballgame without paying the Bisons for a ticket. Two-story houses across Woodlawn Avenue provided second-floor porch seating for residents and their friends. There were also houses immediately behind the left-field wall. These establishments did not offer second-story porches but rather built bootleg bleachers on top of their garages to provide viewing platforms. At one time or another, the ball club erected a small scoreboard and then some signage above the wall in left field to interfere with vision from the bootleg seats.

The grounds were a hitter's delight and a pitcher's nightmare from the start, no matter what the year or the name of the ballpark or its configuration. For the new construction of Offermann Stadium, the distance down the left-field line was only 321 feet, with the power alley in left at 325. It was 346 feet to left center and only 385 to straightaway center field. Just to the right of center, where the scoreboard met the centerfield fence, the distance measured 400 feet. It was 380 feet at the juncture of the scoreboard with the right-field wall. In right field, right center was measured at 366 feet. It was 297 feet down the right-field line to the wall.

Nor did fences prove a challenge. During the deadball days, the original wooden fences stood 12 feet high all around. They were replaced in 1923-1924 with 12-foot high concrete barriers. As the ball got livelier, the fences proved even less of an obstacle to the home run.

Frustrated with the non-paying fans on the rooftop bleachers behind the left-field fence, president Offermann had a wooden fence of 10 feet in height added to top of the left-field wall for the ballgame of June 27, 1934. This new "elevated fence" was constructed while the Bisons were on a road trip out of town. Not only did the raised fence prevent the club from losing money to the bootleg viewers, but it produced more income by adding another deck for advertising signage. The existing 12-foot concrete walls in left and right were already in use for this purpose.

A huge, black, manually operated scoreboard dominated center field. It took a couple of years after the stadium was opened for the scoreboard to be installed, and at first there was a gap between the ends of the scoreboard and the fences. A ball that rolled behind the scoreboard was still in play and usually meant a home run. Those gaps were quickly filled with additional fencing.

Traditionally, the scoreboard, including the advertising signage placed above it, had been spoken of as 60 feet in height, though a more precise measurement might have called it closer to 50 feet. Nevertheless, tradition being strong within baseball, 60 feet it remained for the opening ballgame. The scoreboard was so massive that it allowed for not only the lineups of the Bisons and that day's opponents, and the inning-by-inning score of the game, but up-to-date scores of all of the other International League clubs as well.

The right-field fence had always stayed at the original height of 12 feet. Not so the wall in left.

In 1947, while the Bisons were on a road trip, a 10-foot wire screen fence was added atop the left-field barrier, making the height of the wall an imposing 32 feet. Bison manager Paul Rapier Richards had become incensed by the "phoney" home runs being hit in Offermann by visiting teams against his Bisons. The home club was at a disadvantage, not having sufficient righthanded power to utilize against the visitors.

The first game back from the road trip took place on June 16, 1947. On the first pitch of the game from Buffalo's Ted Gray, Newark right fielder Ford Garrison clubbed a home run to left field over the newly installed screen. The Bisons eventually won the game in the bottom of the ninth inning when Buffalo center fielder Clint Conatser hit a one-out, two-run home run—over the newly installed screen.

The first International League night baseball game took place on this diamond on July 3, 1930. The Bisons fell to Montreal, 5-4.

The first International League All-Star game was played in Offermann. The South team prevailed over the North squad by a 6-1 score on July 7, 1942.

In-season exhibition games against the New York Yankees and Detroit Tigers and other major league clubs had taken place here. In October 1921, in a baseball cause célèbre, Babe Ruth was denied use of the ballpark for having directly challenged the authority of the commissioner of baseball, Kennisaw Mountain Landis.

Traveling Negro League teams and their ballplayers, including Luke Easter and Satchel Paige, had brought their magic to the ballpark in years gone by. Luke and Satchel would return for the 1956 season. The New York Black Yankees had called Offermann home for a number of games, as had the Indianapolis Clowns in 1953, with their slender rookie shortstop Henry Aaron.

The ballpark had seen multiple uses beyond baseball: political rallies, religious events and boxing matches. Buffalo boxing great Jimmy Slattery won the final match of his career here on June 19, 1934, defeating Eddie Kaminski.

The Buffalo High School football championship (Harvard Cup) was initiated at the ballpark in 1904, Masten Park High School defeating Central High School by a score of 28-5. With the 1926 construction of All High Stadium behind Bennett High School, the amateurs departed but not the pros. Semipro football squads and the professional Buffalo All-Americans, the Buffalo Bills and the Buffalo Rangers suited up here until Civic Stadium was constructed in 1937.

Fans cheer on the Bisons at the home opener
Photo courtesy of SUNY Buffalo State Courier-Express
Collection

Game 15—Wednesday, May 2, Buffalo: Buffalo 7, Miami 0

If it hadn't been opening day with 11,008 paying customers on hand,
it would have been a rainout.

Game 15 – May 2, 1956
Miami   000 000 000 – 0 7 2
Buffalo   102 100 30x – 7 12 0
WP – Drews (3-1)   LP – Anderson (1-2)

The rain could not dampen the home crowd's enthusiasm to see the Bisons at work nor the players' determination to break out of a three-game tailspin. The win put them back in the first division.

Raindrops started at 12:05, and a downpour arrived at 1:00. The start of the game was delayed by 40 minutes and there were several rain delays during the contest. Groundskeeper Max Felerski and his nine assistants were on the field as much as the players and the umpires, repairing infield divots and the footing at home plate. They could do little about the lakes in the outfield. The umpires let the game play out, only calling for the lights to be turned on in the fourth inning.

George Bullard got the Bisons going in the first inning. Nicked by a John Anderson pitch to lead off, he promptly stole second base despite the treacherous footing. Joe Brovia broke his hitting drought with a one-out single to put the Herd up 1-0. Two more runs came in the third. Bullard singled and Brovia went the other way, sending a drive over the left-field screen for his first home run of the year. He and Easter had both said they would start to hit when they reached Offermann Stadium. Lou Ortiz's single and a two-out single by Bullard made it 4-0 in the fourth.

Drews allowed seven hits and four walks but fanned nine. The Marlins threatened twice. They loaded the bases in the sixth on a walk to Dave Mann and consecutive singles by Ben Tompkins and Ed Bouchee with no one out. The muddy footing likely kept Mann from scoring. Miami cleanup hitter Sid Gordon then hit a skidder to the right of the mound that Drews barehanded and flipped to Tomkinson at the plate for the force out on Mann. Drews bore down, striking out the league's leading hitter, Bob Bowman, and doing the same thing to Bob Micelotta. Miami filled the sacks again in the seventh, but Billy DeMars fielded a one-out grounder from Tompkins, fed Ortiz at second for the force there, and the quick relay to Easter at first kept the inning scoreless.

The Herd picked up its last three runs in the seventh, when Big Luke blasted his first of the season with DeMars on base ahead of him. Easter's shot soared over the 380-foot mark near the scoreboard in right center. Bill Serena added the game's final run on a bases-loaded, two-out single by Drews.

BISON TALES: After the game, Drews said he had pulled a muscle in his side on the Gordon play in the sixth. He would take time off to rest.

Easter was swinging a heavier bat in this game. He had stopped in Cleveland on the way north to pick up his family and had also brought with him some of his own lumber from home.

Easter was certainly a popular man. Two fans, devotees of the Bisons, Luke Easter, and concession manager Frank Christie's 9000 cases of beer, jumped the low barrier to the field and raced to congratulate the big first baseman. The overzealous and overly lubricated fans were escorted from the premises. After the game, young fans swarmed about Easter, shouting, "we want Luke." The other Bisons had to surround him to get him safely into the dugout and down to the dressing room.

Easter also heard that he was to be fined $50 for his "indecent comments" to umpire Frank Linsalata during the Richmond series. General manager John Stiglmeier had a few "comments" himself about league president Frank (Shag) Shaughnessy in response.

Though pleased with the opening-day results, Cavarretta noted that the team needed to hit better than they had to date, and that injuries were to be avoided at all costs. With no major league agreement, it would be difficult to replace injured men. The manager praised his pitching staff and the output from his catching corps. He had been aware, he said, of Tomkinson's ability to handle pitchers, but he was pleasantly surprised at the slugging from both Pat and Lou Heyman.

Attendance would have been greater had it not been for the rain that shortened the pregame ceremonies. Club president Reginald B. Taylor, Myrt Power (the $64,000 winning baseball expert) and Mrs. Stanley Berny, a club director, headed the procession that gathered at home plate following the flag raising in center field by the Marine Corps color guard. With Stan Barron as master of ceremonies, Taylor, Mrs. Power and manager Cavarretta made abbreviated remarks. Mayor Steven Pankow, seated next to the Bison dugout, made the first-pitch opening peg to Cavarretta.

Allie Heerdt, 74, of 231 Fox Street, a star on the old Buffalo Germans basketball team, came to his 62nd opener despite having a cold. When it was over, Heerdt vowed he would never again attend a baseball game in such weather. Neither he nor Frank Rausch, 72, of 155 Merrymount Drive could recall such a rainy opening game. Rausch had come for his 58th opening contest. He and his wife left in the fifth as more rain arrived. Harry E. Gentile, 67, drove in from Ransomville, a 35-mile trip, for his 40th home opener. George Obernauer, secretary of the Buffalo Bowling Association, was on hand, too, not having missed an opener since World War I.

The weather made it impossible for George H. Fuerschbach, 90, to keep alive his string of 68 consecutive home openers, but Charley Swanz was there at the press gate for the 29th straight year. And a man who had been a devoted opener presence for 25 years, but who had never once seen any of the action, was on hand yet again. The No. 4 Oxford Avenue resident, 87-year-old Harry Phillips, was still selling bags of peanuts at the corner of East Ferry Street and Michigan.

B.B. Kasmier of 230 Weiss Street, Chester Baker of 147 Mills Street, Dick Tafelski at 230 Springville Avenue in Eggertsville and Joseph Logan of 241 Fancher Avenue, Kenmore, all voiced their support for community ownership.

Youthful fans did, too. Pat Tomkinson's 16-year-old brother Wayne was out working behind the scoreboard. Wayne was a first-string catcher at McKinley High and playing in the Cornell Cup High School series. Larry Hudson, 14, of 141 Dellwood Road and Albert Schriber, 12, of 285 North Ivyhurst Road, both of Eggertsville, were the first two in line at the bleacher entrance. They were students at Amherst Central Junior High. They arrived at 11:00 a.m. with sandwiches, popcorn, potato chips and candy bars in hand.

Children from the German Roman Catholic Orphan Home and the Protestant Home for Unprotected Children were treated to the game, courtesy of the Greater Buffalo Ad Club. George H. Hochreiter headed up the committee that also provided the youth with popcorn, peanuts and other favorites from Frank Christie's stock of refreshments. On hand for the opener were 100,000 hot dogs and rolls, 9000 cases of beer, 80 gallons of coffee, 350 cases of soft drinks, 5000 bags of peanuts and 2000 boxes of popcorn.

Thursday, May 3, Buffalo: Scheduled Day Off

The International League schedule had programmed the Bisons and Marlins for a two-game series, with an idle day in the middle. It gave Cy Kritzer from the Evening News a chance to talk to Joe Overfield, Buffalo's baseball historian without equal, to ask if there had ever been a wetter opener. Not for a game that was actually played, Overfield replied.

Back in 1924, when Offermann Stadium was officially opened, the Bisons had had to wait seven days to play their season home opener. The scheduled April 30, 1924, opener was called in the second inning due to rain. Wet grounds prevented the teams from taking the field on May 1. May 2 brought snow and cold. May 3, 4 and 5 were all rained out as well. The club finally took the diamond on May 6, playing a doubleheader and defeating New Jersey in both games. The coldest opener, Joe added, was in 1926, when snow forced a halt to play after five innings.

The day off also gave a chance to learn more about two larger-than-life newcomers to the International League: Luke Easter (Buffalo) and Satchel Paige (Miami). At 6 feet, 4 inches, and 230 pounds, Luke had been known for mammoth home runs in ballparks from coast to coast. Easter revealed to the Courier-Express's Frank Lillich that he had played in Offermann when toiling in the Negro Leagues. Asked about the 60-foot-high centerfield scoreboard 400 feet away, Easter said he had cleared that barrier once, if not twice, in those underreported days. He was looking forward to playing half his games here at the Buffalo ballpark where, now that he had his own bats with him from home, he could reach any fence. Luke was calling Cleveland home now and was part owner of a sausage factory there.

Of his longtime friend and former Cleveland Indians teammate Satchel Paige, Luke said that the pitcher's longevity was attributable to staying relaxed, liking a good laugh, keeping his legs in shape by hunting in the off season and keeping fit on the dance floor. Women found Paige quite attractive; he had no lack of partners when the dance music started. Relaxing with the guitar or a ukulele might have also helped. As to his age, well, who could be sure about that? (Easter had to be careful here; his own self-reported 34 years might be a few short of the mark.)

Bill Veeck, the man who brought both Easter and Paige to the Indians and who, in 1947, had signed the American League's first African-American player, Larry Doby, estimated that Paige could be as young as 56. Not too young to have already tossed a shutout against Montreal in the current season. Easter explained Paige's routine for keeping his arm in shape. He warmed up with the outfielders, going out to left field and throwing to the plate five or six times, then moving to center to repeat the process and finally ending up in right. But Paige's throws were on a line to the catcher without a hop. What might ruin someone else's arm kept Paige's loose, Easter advised. "Paige has got you," Luke went on, "if you watch his motion and take your eye off the ball." His fastball was still alive. His only weakness, Luke commented, was fielding bunts.

Veeck had more to say about Paige. As quoted to Cy Krtizer, "He is an amazing fellow. He knows a lot about any subject you bring up. Take flying for instance. Satch knows all the air routes and how to operate most planes. He owns a new plane and flies it everywhere himself." Reportedly, Paige was being paid $15,000 in 1956, the highest salary in the league.

Joe Brovia was the big winner in the opener's cash and prizes department. He took home $40 (a 10-spot for his home run, $5 for each of his three RBIs, another $5 for the first single, $5 more for a run scored and the final $5 for a putout). The home run also brought him a $50 savings bond, a $10 hat and a case of beer. George Bullard collected $25 in cash as well as a case of oil and a traveling case. Drews claimed $45 in cash, $5 for each of his first three strikeouts, $15 for winning the game and another $15 for being the game's outstanding performer. Easter's home run was worth $10, plus an additional $20 from the members of the Junior Chamber of Commerce. DeMars, Ortiz and Easter split $45 three ways for their seventh-inning double play.

Friday, May 4, Buffalo: Rainout

Overnight rain and continued early showers made the field unplayable. It was a day of lost revenue. Finances would be a concern all season long, and makeup doubleheaders wouldn't offset attendance lost from two separate games.

President Reginald B. Taylor, with an eye on the bottom line, met with Cavarretta to discuss a cutdown of the roster. The Bisons were suiting up 26 men, five over the league maximum, and the Phillies were still to send another hurler as part of the Duane Pillette deal. Cavarretta hoped to be able to view each starter three times before deciding which pitchers to cut, but rainouts had been interfering with those plans.

The Bisons take the field at the home opener
Photo courtesy of SUNY Buffalo State Courier-Express Collection

Game 16—Saturday, May 5, Buffalo: Havana 9, Buffalo 2

Havana capitalized on early opportunities, whereas timely hitting escaped the Bisons.

Game 16 – May 5, 1956

Havana	143 000 001 – 9	12	0
Buffalo	000 200 000 – 2	9	3
WP – Lane (2-1)	LP – Froats (1-2)		

Bill Froats' wildness hurt him from the outset. He walked leadoff man Don Nicholas and number two hitter Angel Scull and gave a single to Nino Escalera for a run. A strikeout and a double play helped him escape further damage.

Buffalo couldn't score in the bottom of the first despite three hits. George Bullard singled leading off against Havana starter Jerry Lane, but Billy DeMars, next up, grounded into a double play. Singles by Joe Brovia and Luke Easter were wasted when Bill Serena flew out.

Havana attacked Froats again in the second. Pablo Bernard and Dutch Dotterer singled with one out, and Froats loaded the bases by walking Lane. Nicholas doubled for two runs to finish Froats. Reliever John Weiss was touched for a two-run single by Scull that made it 5-0.

It got worse in the third. Juan Delis doubled, and Weiss walked Forest (Woody) Smith and Dotterer. Lane singled home Delis. Nicholas singled for two more. It was 8-0 by the time Weiss could retire the side. He was able to hold the Kings scoreless in the fourth.

The Bisons got their runs in the last of the fourth on back-to-back homers. Bill Serena hit his third of the season over the left-field fence. Clyde Vollmer hit his first of the year to almost the same spot. Lane then shut the Herd down for the remainder of the game. Joe Brovia walked in the fifth, but Luke Easter's liner was turned into an unassisted double play by Nino Escalera at first. Tomkinson got a two-out infield hit in the ninth.

Joe Coleman took over for Weiss and pitched shutout ball for three frames. Jim Walsh entered after Coleman went out for a pinch-hitter and yielded an unearned run in the ninth. Cavarretta stepped in to pinch-hit for Walsh in the ninth but took a called third strike.

BISON TALES: In attendance tonight were 3370 chilly fans. Jerry Lane spent part of his youth in Buffalo and attended Seneca Vocational High School.

Sunday, May 6, Buffalo: Rainout of Doubleheader

Rain wiped out play for Sunday. Meanwhile, X-rays showed that Bill Serena had suffered a se-verely sprained thumb in Saturday's loss and would need Pete Castiglione to fill in for him at third for the time being. Cavarretta might also be out of action after having an infected tooth pulled. Peanuts Lowrey would step in for the manager.

Game 17—Monday, May 7, Buffalo: Buffalo 6, Havana 2

The win featured two home runs by Luke Easter,
a near brawl after a pitch went behind Easter's head and sharp Buffalo fielding.

Game 17 – May 7, 1956

Havana	101 000 000 – 2	6	2
Buffalo	010 103 01x – 6	5	0

WP -Keriazakos (2-0)   LP – Minarcin (1-2)

Gus Keriazakos threw a complete game in front of fewer than 2000 fans on a 30-plus degree evening, but it didn't look like Gus was on his game when he started. Don Nicholas, leading off for the Sugar Kings, took Keriazakos' first offering over the screen in left to give the Sugar Kings a 1-0 lead. Gus was lucky it wasn't more. Clyde Vollmer made a leaping stab of Woody Smith's line drive to the wall in left and turned it into a double play, Vollmer to Lou Ortiz to Luke Easter, to get Nino Escalera at first.

Rudy Minarcin, a 16-game winner for the Herd in 1951, started for Havana. Easter tied the con-test in the second inning, scorching a Minarcin pitch over the 380 mark in right center.

Nicholas' double in the third scored Pablo Bernard and put the Marlins ahead once more. Mi-narcin and Easter faced off again in the fourth, and again Big Luke came out on top. His drive into the right-field light tower tied it at 2-2.

DeMars kept it that way with a diving stab of Angel Scull's liner with two on in the top of the fifth. The Buffalo shortstop then led off the bottom of the frame with a single. After Joe Brovia fanned, it was Easter and Minarcin confronting one another for the third time. The hurler's first pitch sent the Buffalo first baseman sprawling. The second went behind his head.

Easter started for the mound, bat in hand, but plate umpire Lou Linsalata and Cavarretta head-ed him off. Minarcin had stepped forward but then went back to the hill. Havana manager Reggie Otero ordered an intentional walk for Easter and then, frustration showing, Minarcin plunked Clyde Vollmer to load the bases. Lou Ortiz unloaded them with a double on the left-field line that also fin-ished Minarcin. Umpire Linsalata walked the Miami pitcher over to and down through the Buffalo dugout to get to the showers.

A sixth Buffalo tally came in the eighth with Ortiz on second after a throwing error by Bernard. Pete Castiglione's base knock sent him home.

Bison Tales: The game started with Ken Roberts umpiring behind the plate, but he took a serious fall into the Bison dugout in the fourth after racing over to make the call on Tomkinson's foul ball. Dr. Leonard Berman, the Bisons' physician, gave him sedatives to cope with the pain and had him transferred to hospital via ambulance. Linsalata took over behind the plate.

Game 18—Tuesday, May 8, Buffalo: Columbus 5, Buffalo 2

Another cold night saw only 1625 fans turn out to watch the
Bisons go down to a 5-2 defeat. Buffalo also lost another third baseman.

Game 18 – May 8, 1956
Columbus   030 000 101 – 5 14 1
Buffalo   000 101 000 – 2 7 2
WP – Kuzava (3-1)   LP – Bowman (1-1)

Al Pilarcik led off the second inning for the Jets with a single. Ray Noble also singled on a drive to left that Blatnik gloved but then dropped as he crashed to the turf. When Pilarcik tried for third, Blatnik's throw to Pete Castiglione at the base should have caught him, but the ball took a bad hop and struck Castiglione in the face, knocking him out. Pilarcik was safe, Noble took second on the throw and a limping Peanuts Lowrey had to go in to replace Castiglione. Pilarcik scored on a ground out to the right side. A single by Russ Rose plated Noble. Rose scored on Bullard's throwing error on a Frank Verdi hit.

Buffalo loaded the bases in the fourth with none out but could only manage one run. Ortiz doubled to lead off, followed by a walk to Easter and an error on Blatnik's infield grounder, but Jet starter Bob Kuzava caught Brovia on a called third strike and Lowrey could only bounce into a force play at second to score Ortiz. Tomkinson rolled out to end the inning.

The Herd also loaded the bases in the sixth, but once more could notch only a single tally. Easter singled, went to second on Blatnik's hit and came home on Lowrey's double. A walk to Tomkinson with one out loaded the bases. Lou Heyman went in to pinch-hit for Bowman. Kusava registered a strike on his first pitch but exploded when his second offering was called a ball. So strong was his protest that he was thumbed from the game for the first time in his 15-year career. Jet manager Nick Cullop called in the righthanded Floyd Wooldridge to take over and Cavarretta, playing the percentages, replaced Heyman himself. Swinging lefthanded, Cavarretta, completed the at-bat by fanning on the next two pitches. Bullard's drive was captured in right, and the Herd stranded three runners.

Wooldridge held the Bisons to one hit and one walk in relief. Columbus got insurance runs in the seventh and ninth off Bison reliever Fred Hahn, who walked two and allowed four hits.

Bison Tales: Pitcher Jim Walsh received his unconditional release this day. Cavarretta was desperate to find someone to take over third base if Castiglione could not come back from this evening's injury. X-rays showed a slight fracture of his nose. The Bisons were also in need of righthanded outfield help. Blatnik had taken a tumble in today's game and Vollmer was still hurting from being hit by a pitch the night before. Lowrey's leg also really needed to be rested.

About 75 members of the Amherst Kiwanis Club and the Amherst Central High School Band, under the baton of John Krestic, led the cheers from behind the Bison dugout. Bison fans were being urged to throw foul balls back onto the field, saving $2 for each replacement.

Wednesday, May 9, Buffalo: Rainout

Bad weather led to the third rainout of the home stand, hurting not only the bottom line but the pitching staff as well. The idleness prevented the men from staying sharp and kept Cavarretta from getting an adequate look at his hurlers prior to cutting the number down to nine. The front office was worried about reducing the payroll. If there was any good news from the delay, it was that Bill Serena, Pete Castiglione and Peanuts Lowrey got another day off to get healthier. One of them was needed to cover third base. Castiglione's right eye was swollen nearly shut. Clyde Vollmer could also rest his arm.

Game 19—Thursday, May 10, Buffalo: Columbus 7, Buffalo 2

Only 1240 overcoated fans watched as Karl Drews struggled against both the Columbus Jets and home plate umpire Joe Kane.

Game 19 – May 10, 1956

Columbus	101 030 002 – 7	11	0
Buffalo	000 100 001 – 2	11	3
WP – Herbert (3-1)	LP – Drews (3-2)		

Drews and Kane couldn't agree on a strike zone, and Peanuts Lowrey complained that a called third strike in the fifth had nearly knocked him down. When Easter opened up about it from the on-deck circle, Cavarretta had to hustle in from the third-base coaching box to keep his slugger in the ballgame.

Kane and the Bison dugout had a running dialogue all night, and not a pleasant one. In the ninth inning, Kane came over to the Bison bench and threatened to clear it. Base umpires Bob Smith and Frank Guzzetta intervened to calm the situation and walked Kane back to the plate.

Drews may have lost his sharpness due to inactivity, not having pitched in a week. He was also likely angry at himself for giving up two-out run-scoring singles to Russ Sullivan and Bill Stewart in the first and third innings. Buffalo got one back in the fourth on a Joe Brovia double and Lou Ortiz single, but Columbus added three in the fifth, aided by two errant pickoff attempts by Drews. Joe Coleman shut down the Jets in relief until they scored two unearned runs in the ninth, helped by an errant throw by a limping Peanuts Lowrey fielding a bunt at his third-base position.

Buffalo's second run came in the bottom of the ninth on a Billy DeMars sacrifice fly with the bases jammed. Lowrey's single loaded them again, but Easter bounced out to end the contest.

BISON TALES: The defeat was Buffalo's fifth straight against Columbus and kept the Herd in fifth place in the league, one game under .500.

Cavarretta did not blame umpire Kane for his team's defeat, saying the Bisons weren't hitting. No regular was over .300 and 11 men were left on base in the game. The team obviously needed extra batting practice. But he did lodge a formal complaint with International League president Frank Shaughnessy. Kane, he said, had cursed at both catcher Lou Heyman and pitcher Joe Coleman, who had relieved in the fifth.

Pat Tomkinson's bat had stopped producing hits on the home stand and had started producing boos. Perhaps he was pressing before the home crowd. Cavarretta started Heyman behind the plate. Pat got a pinch-hit single in the ninth.

Friday, May 11, Buffalo: Game suspended due to rain

The rain in Spain stays mainly on the plain, but in Buffalo it was also turning out to be a consistent visitor to Offermann Stadium this season. The Bisons made it into the second inning against the visiting Richmond Virginians before the heavens opened up and blew a squall into town. The teams resumed play after a 58-minute delay, only to encounter a new and heavier downpour that turned the infield into mud while the Vees were at the plate. The 0-0 game was to be continued in late June and would be part of a doubleheader when Richmond next visited. The 2140 fans on hand had rainchecks to use whenever they chose.

Manager Eddie Lopat's Richmond squad was struggling coming out of the gate, with a record of only 8-15. However, the New York Yankees had strengthened their former hurler's club with the additions of pitchers Jim Coates and Al Cicotte, plus shortstop Jerry Lumpe and outfielder Lou Skizas. Coates was 14-8 with Binghamton and Birmingham the year before. Cicotte had a 4-4 record with Birmingham and Denver. Lumpe hit .301 with Birmingham after returning from two years of military service. Skizas put up a monster 1955 at Denver, hitting .348 with 21 home runs and 99 runs driven home in only 112 games. He added a much-needed big bat to the lineup.

General manager John C. Stiglmeier also announced Buffalo roster moves. Pitcher Milt Jordan was released. Outfielder Joe Caffie was purchased from the Cleveland Indians system. Caffie, a former Cleveland Buckeye in the Negro Leagues, joined Luke Easter as the second African American on the team. At 25 years old, Caffie was a 5-foot, 10-inch, 180-pound speedster who would add youthful legs to the outfield and take some of the strain for coverage off Bullard. Caffie was a lefthanded swinger but a righthanded thrower. He had batted only .261 the previous season, splitting his time between Triple A Indianapolis and Syracuse, but stole 28 bases. He and Bullard would add a go-go dimension to the Buffalo attack.

Cavarretta still wanted to get an honest look at what his pitching corps could do. The rain had hampered this effort. Gus Keriazakos would toe the slab on Saturday, if the elements allowed. The manager then planned to send lefty Bob Schultz to the mound in Sunday's doubleheader. Larry Donovan had been tapped to pitch the opening game with Schultz to follow. Cavarretta had also moved Bill Froats to the bullpen, telling him to stick with his fastball and curve and stay away from the slider that was getting him into trouble.

Lopat had had to revise his pitching assignments due to Buffalo weather conditions. He would be on the mound on Saturday and throw Jim Post and Wimpy Nardella against the Herd on Sunday. Lopat was 1-1 for the year. At 38, he was still sorting out his strategy for his dual role as pitcher-manager for his club. Initially, he had intended to pitch the seven-inning second games of doubleheaders, but he had found that no matter which game he started—the first or the second—he was too tired to perform well in his managerial role in the final contest. Thus, his intention was to hurl the nine-inning game on Saturday. He had heard the stories about Offermann being a death-trap for lefthanders but had confidence that he could prevail against such odds. After 166 wins in 12 big-league seasons, plus a won-4, lost-1 record in World Series play, Lopat had reason to have confidence.

Off the field, general manager Stiglmeier confirmed that he had been offered a $15,000 post with the New York State Liquor Authority, and it was an offer both especially hard to accept and especially hard to refuse. Stiglmeier admitted that his two great loves were politics and baseball. To take the state job would mean sacrificing his general manager duties with the Bisons. After considering the offer, Stiglmeier reportedly met with manager Cavarretta and coach Lowrey, and then with the team in the dressing room, honestly laying out the situation. If he were to take the job, Stiglmeier was said to have commented, it would only be with the provision that he could spend his weekends in his (already unpaid) general manager role with the team. He reaffirmed his commitment to keeping Buffalo in the International League and exhorted the players to give their best to the club and to the city.

Joe Caffie slides home
Photo courtesy of SUNY Buffalo State Courier-Express Collection

Game 20—Saturday, May 12, Buffalo: Virginia 4, Buffalo 1

Two old reliables showed up in the Buffalo ballpark—
Steady Eddie Lopat and the rain. Neither helped the Herd.

Game 20 – May 12, 1956

Richmond	400 000 – 4	7	0
Buffalo	100 000 – 1	4	2

WP – Lopat (2-1)   LP – Keriazakos (2-1)

Lopat showed 2300 fans that he still had plenty of the junk-ball skills that helped him to 166 big-league victories over 12 seasons, plus a record of 4 wins and 1 loss in five World Series. Tonight, he only had to throw six innings before rain called a halt to the proceedings and the contest went into the books as a completed game.

All the scoring took place in the first inning while the rain was light. Gus Keriazakos, starting for the Bisons, got the leadoff hitter, but Dee Phillips got a life on Billy DeMars' errant throw that pulled Easter off the bag. Joe Tesauro had hit well against the Bisons in Richmond and now beat out a double-play grounder to keep the inning alive. Tom Hamilton reached Keriazakos for a single, putting men on first and third. Next up, Jerry Carter stung Keriazakos for a double, scoring Tesauro and moving Hamilton to third. Both men came home on a double by Jerry Lumpe, starting his first game for the Vees at shortstop. Cavarretta stuck with Keriazakos for one more batter, and right fielder Dick Getter proved that a wrong decision. Getter collected the third double of the inning to put Richmond ahead 4-0. Cavarretta brought in Froats, who retired the side. Keriazakos had lasted only two-thirds of an inning and had given up four unearned runs.

The Bisons got one back in the bottom of the first. George Bullard parked a Lopat pitch over the left-field wall for his first home run of the season, but after that hoorah there was nothing more to come. The scoring was over for the evening.

Lopat scattered three more hits in six innings, walking one. Froats gave up three hits in 5⅓ frames, walking three. The game was stopped due to the increased downpour after the Virginians had batted in the top of the seventh. The umpires called it a completed game after a 35-minute wait. The field was unplayable. The official line score reverted to the end of the sixth.

BISON TALES: Morning batting practice had had to be put off because of the weather. It was not certain the extra swings would have made much of a difference against Lopat.

Lumpe was impressive, collecting a double, a single and a triple in three at-bats. Early closure of the game cost him the opportunity to go for the cycle. He also started two double plays.

Buffalo stayed in fifth place in the league, one game behind Columbus and 2½ games ahead of Richmond, Miami and Havana, tied for sixth.

In major league news: Brooklyn's Carl Erskine this day threw the second no-hitter of his career, stopping the New York Giants at Ebbets Field, 3-0. Carl Furillo saved the day with a backhand stab of a drive to the right center field scoreboard off the bat of Ray Katt. In the eighth, Jackie Robinson dove to his left and speared a rocket hit by Willie Mays. A ninth-inning blow to right by Whitey Lockman hooked foul at the last minute. Robinson, Duke Snider and Roy Camapanella drove in the Dodger runs.

Game 21—Sunday, May 13, Buffalo: Virginia 7, Buffalo 4

Richmond took the opener of the scheduled doubleheader.
Rain started in the sixth inning of game one and washed out game two.

Game 21 – May 13, 1956
Richmond   300 200 200 – 7 9 0
Buffalo   001 210 000 – 4 7 2
WP – Nardella (1-3)   LP – Schultz (0-1)

Lefty Bob Schultz made his first start as Cavarretta continued to look at his pitching staff. Vee leadoff man Len Johnston drew a walk. With two out, cleanup hitter Al Van Alstyne parked a two-run shot over the left-field wall. Jerry Carter, next up, homered to add a third score.

In the second inning, Jerry Lumpe singled for his fourth hit in four plate appearances. When Moe Thacker added another single, Schultz's day was over. Fred Hahn came in to put out the fire.

Buffalo got a run in the third when Hahn singled and scored on Lou Ortiz's sacrifice fly, but Lumpe and Richmond were not yet done. Lumpe got yet another hit in the fourth inning, followed by Thacker's two-run blast to left. The Herd answered in their half. Serena singled to lead off and Easter, next up, drove a mammoth shot over the right center field wall, a distance of easily 440 feet. Lou Ortiz made it a one-run game when he smacked his first homer of the year in the fifth.

Joe Coleman, now pitching for Buffalo, finally retired Lumpe. It took an off-balance, barehanded flip of the ball by Ortiz on a slow roller in the sixth. Richmond got two unearned runs in the seventh inning, helped by an errant throw by DeMars. The Bisons' half of that frame was unbelievable.

Ortiz, Brovia and Serena walked with two out to bring Easter to the plate, and that brought lefthander Niles Jordan in to relieve. Easter crashed to the ground on an inside pitch on a two-and-two count, claiming the ball had struck him on the wrist. The ball, however, rolled into fair territory where Jordan fielded it and ran to first base, calling for the force out. Plate umpire Bob Smith ruled the out and the Virginians ran off the field.

Now, Cavarretta, Peanuts Lowrey and Ortiz raced to the plate to protest that Easter had been hit by the ball and was entitled to first base, with a run scoring. At home plate, Easter lay face down on the ground with trainer Jimmy Mack attending to him while Lowrey looked on. Ortiz argued with umpire Smith, Cavarretta raised Cain with umpire Guzzetta, and Richmond manager Ed Lopat complained to umpire Kane. Jordan insisted that he had retired Easter. Umpire Smith insisted that Easter was faking.

The arbiters finally decided that the pitch had hit Easter's bat and was a foul ball, satisfying no one. Discussion ended when the men in blue tossed Cavarretta and Ortiz out of the game, sent the Virginians back onto the field and ordered Easter back to the plate. Easter fanned on the next pitch. Castiglione went in to play second base. A last-ditch, bases-loaded, two-out Buffalo effort failed in the eighth on Castiglione's fly out.

Game 22—Monday, May 14, Buffalo: Montreal 8, Buffalo 4

The red-hot Montreal Royals, fresh off a nine-game home winning streak, made it 10 in a row. Buffalo fell to a fifth straight defeat.

```
Game 22 – May 14, 1956
Montreal       003 002 300 – 8  12  1
Buffalo        100 100 002 – 4   6  4
WP – Kipp (3-2)        LP – Bowman (1-2)
```

George Bullard doubled off Montreal lefthander Fred Kipp to lead off the Bison half of the first inning. He scored on a misplay by the Royals right fielder Bob Wilson. This was the first Buffalo first-inning lead in a week's time.

Bob Bowman started for the Herd and held Montreal off for two innings. They got to him in the third. George (Sparky) Anderson looped a pop-fly double into left to open the frame. The Bison infield moved in, expecting a sacrifice, but Kipp instead swung away for a single. Leadoff man Jimmy Williams drew a free pass, filling the sacks with no one out. A sacrifice fly from Chico Fernandez tied the score. With two out, two men on and first base open, Cavarretta had Royals slugger Rocky Nelson intentionally walked. The strategy would have worked, save that Easter misplayed a grounder hit by Oscar Sardinas and the Royals scored two unearned runs.

Buffalo got one back in the fourth inning. John Blatnik doubled to lead off and Joe Brovia walked. Both men moved up on Clyde Vollmer's ground out. A ground out by Lou Heyman plated Blatnik. The Bisons left the tying run on third as Bowman went down on strikes.

Montreal surged back to add a pair of runs in the sixth, helped by three singles, a passed ball from Heyman and Bullard's error in center. They put the game away with three more tallies in the seventh. Wilson's single and Brovia's drop of Nelson's fly ball put two on. Sardinas emptied the bases with a drive over the right-field fence. Half of the runs off Bowman were unearned.

John Weiss took the mound for Buffalo and held Montreal hitless and scoreless in the eighth and the ninth. Lou Heyman cracked a two-run home run to left with Blatnik on base in the bottom of the ninth. It was Heyman's fourth of the year, tying him with Easter for the club lead.

BISON TALES: The 24-year-old Kipp threw a mixture of curves, knucklers, sinkers and sliders. Cavarretta batted Easter fifth and Brovia seventh against the lefty. The impressive outing might find Kipp shortly being called up to the Dodgers, now that Billy Loes had been sent to Baltimore.

Buffalo gave Bob Schultz his outright release and returned Mario Picone to Toronto. Picone's arm had not improved and Toronto would refund the purchase price. Buffalo needed to cut three more to get down to the 21-man roster limit, including a pitcher and an outfielder.

General manager Stiglmeier contacted league headquarters to discuss the quality of the officiating. The previous night's ejections would cost Cavarretta and Ortiz $25 each. To date, six Bisons had been fined by the umpiring crews. Veteran players let their objections be known when the umpiring was not up to par.

Montreal manager Greg Mulleavy referred to Sparky Anderson as "another Eddie Stanky." Not great skills, "he just beats you."

Tuesday, May 15, Buffalo: Rainout

Buffalo was rained out for the sixth time in the opening home stand. The Bisons were looking at eight future doubleheaders to make up the postponements. This was going to prove a significant hardship for the many veterans on the club. In a long season, the hot days of summer would sap the strength of even the fittest men.

At the till, the Herd had estimated losses from ticket sales and refreshments at nearly $35,000. General manager Stiglmeier had called upon everyone to "tighten the purse strings." He had been encouraged by the fan turnout thus far, despite the weather, and was hoping this loyalty would continue when the better weather arrived.

Cavarretta was dismayed at the failure of both Brovia and Easter to hit with men on and planned to bench both of them for the Wednesday contest. Newly acquired Joe Caffie would go in right field in place of Brovia. Cavarretta would replace Easter at first base, if his back would allow it.

The team's batting had fallen off. The warmer weather in Miami and Havana made it easier for the veterans to loosen up, but the cold encountered in Richmond and at home in Buffalo had made that much more difficult. It had been affecting their swings. Cavarretta had planned to be a player-manager this season, but it now remained to be seen if that was possible. He intended to give himself a couple more games to see what he could do. If he couldn't produce, he would place himself on the inactive roster to make room for another man who could.

The roster paring continued. Vic Stryska was released this day, reducing the pitching staff to nine men. One of the outfielders was still to be cut, but that would still leave the club with yet another man to go to reach the 21-player limit by midnight Thursday, May 17. Cavarretta had to decide if that last man would be himself.

Johnny Blatnik had been the exception to the hitting of late. His three-for-four performance on Monday night raised his average to a sky-high .393. The next closest hitter was Tomkinson at .289. Cavarretta, 0 for his last five at-bats, was down to .285.

Luke Easter and Lou Heyman were leading the club with four home runs apiece. Serena had hit three. Heyman had 10 RBIs. Of the pitchers, only Drews (3) and Keriazakos (2) had more than one win.

International League Standings
May 15, 1956

	W	L	Pct	GB
Rochester	18	9	.667	—
Montreal	19	10	.655	—
Toronto	15	9	.625	1½
Columbus	12	11	.522	4
Buffalo	9	13	.409	6½
Havana	10	16	.385	7½
Richmond	10	17	.370	8
Miami	9	17	.346	8½

Wednesday, May 16, Buffalo: Rainout

Buffalo's chilly, rainy, miserable weather was due to a stationary low-pressure trough which had affected all of New York State and Pennsylvania and southward into Maryland. Weatherman Barney Wiggin had predicted a "slow recovery," with cloudy skies, scattered showers and daytime highs in the middle 50s.

The weather had been bad for both baseball and farming. Genesee County farmers had been advised to forego planting peas and turn to other crops. Frosts had nipped blossoms and delayed pollination on fruit farms. No one was happy with the weather except umbrella makers.

Games 23 and 24—Thursday, May 17, Buffalo: Buffalo 3, Montreal 0; Montreal 1, Buffalo 0
Karl Drews blanked the Royals in game one.
Gus Keriazakos was a hard-luck loser in the second contest.

Game 23 – May 17, 1956 (first game of doubleheader)
Montreal   000 000 0 – 0 3 1
Buffalo   100 110 x – 3 9 2
WP – Drews (4-2)   LP – Harris (2-2)

Game 24 – May 17, 1956 (second game of doubleheader)
Montreal   100 000 000 – 1 5 1
Buffalo   000 000 000 – 0 5 0
WP – White (3-1)   LP – Keriazakos (2-2)

The early-morning temperature at the airport was 32 degrees, breaking a record that had stood for 65 years. May 17, 1891, had registered a balmy 34. A cold wind made it hard to hit and hard to pitch and kept the crowd down, too.

Drews' shutout in game one ended the Herd's five-game losing streak. In this seven-inning first game, Drews held the Royals to three singles, fanned six and did not walk a batter. The Bisons pounded out nine hits, two apiece for Lou Ortiz, Bill Serena and Luke Easter in the middle of the order. Cavarretta did not make good on his threat to bench Luke, and the big man showed his gratitude. Batting in the fifth hole, Easter's first-inning single cashed Ortiz with the game's initial run. In the fourth, Easter drove a Bill Harris offering high over the right-field wall for his fifth home run of the year. George Bullard doubled in the next inning and Ortiz sent him across the plate with a sharp single up the middle, the last run of the game.

Drews faced only one real threat from the Royals. It came in the fourth inning when speedy leadoff hitter Jimmy Williams got a life on Serena's error at third. Drews retired Chico Fernandez, but Bob Wilson reached the pitcher for a single to center and Williams motored to third. The dangerous Rocky Nelson, Montreal cleanup hitter and 1955's triple crown winner (.364, 37, 130), stepped to the plate. Drews was equal to the task. Nelson hit a hot grounder to second that Ortiz gloved, flipped to DeMars for the force on Wilson, and DeMars' relay to Easter made it out number three of the inning. It was the second Bison double play of the game.

Joe Caffie did start in right field in place of Joe Brovia. He batted second, putting the two Buffalo speedsters at the top of the order. Caffie rapped a single in three at-bats.

Baserunning lapses and failed opportunities made Gus Keriazakos a 1-0 loser in game two. It was another hard-luck outing for Gus. Back on May 12, his last start, a Bison error opened the door to four unearned Richmond runs in the first inning. Keriazakos dropped that rain-shortened, six-inning game by a 4-1 decision.

In today's contest, he allowed only one earned run in the first inning. It turned out to be the only run of the game. Two base hits sandwiched around a walk led to the score.

Jimmy Williams reached on a single to start the game. Chico Fernandez and Bob Wilson were easy outs, but Keriazakos pitched too carefully to Rocky Nelson and walked him, moving Williams into scoring position at second. Oscar Sardinas followed with a double and Williams scored. The Bisons played catchup baseball for the remainder of the game but could not prevail against the Royals' Frank White.

White spun a five-hitter against the Herd, walking six. The Bisons had chances and could not capitalize. George Bullard doubled to open the game and was left stranded at second. Johnny Blatnik made a mental error in the fourth after lining a drive off the left center field wall. He pulled up coming into second with a sure double, then tried to take an extra base when he saw center fielder Williams miss the carom off the fence. Williams, however, recovered quickly and threw Blatnik out at third.

In the seventh, Blatnik drew a walk to lead off. DeMars singled him to second. With no one out, Pat Tomkinson bunted to move the runners up. White, off the mound, threw wildly to third to catch Blatnik, but the throw sailed into short left field. Blatnik scrambled to his feet, raced for the plate and was cut down by an accurate peg from left fielder Oscar Sardinas.

With two men still on, Peanuts Lowrey was sent in to pinch-hit for Keriazakos and drew a walk to load the bases. Bullard, up next, looped a ball to center field that DeMars was sure would fall, but the speedy Williams came in to make the catch. DeMars, halfway down the line, had to hustle back to third to tag up, losing his opportunity to come home on what could have been a game-tying sacrifice fly.

Lou Ortiz's single in the eighth, his third hit of the day, raised some hopes, but Bill Serena bounced into a double play to end that chance. Lastly, Joe Brovia pinch-hit for Tomkinson with two out in the ninth, looking for the long ball that would tie the game. Joe swung and missed at a third strike.

BISON TALES: There were to be no Annie Oakleys at Offermann Stadium this season except for the working press. The board of directors decided back in the spring that no free passes were to be given out. President Reginald Taylor, general manager Stiglmeier and business manager Harry Bisgier all paid for their seats —and for those of their guests, as did the directors. The club needed the income to meet expenses. Taylor had six box seats and paid $600 for this privilege.

Clyde Vollmer, hitting only .162, was given his outright release earlier in the day.

Each team only collected five safeties in the second game. The cold affected control, with each side giving up six walks.

The Bisons ended their first home stand with a won-3, lost-7 mark. Two of those victories were shutouts by Drews. Easter bashed five home runs, a double and hit .324. This day's blanking was the fifth time the Herd had taken the collar this year. The team headed off to Toronto.

General manager Stiglmeier reported that the club's reserves to purchase new players had been wiped out by the poor gates resulting from the weather. The team was not broke, but they needed strong attendance on the next home stand to boost the coffers and meet the payroll.

Game 25—Friday, May 18, Toronto, Canada: Buffalo 5, Toronto 4

A four-run rally in the ninth with two outs, plus 10 innings of shutout relief, gave the Herd the victory. All the Bison runs were unearned.

Game 25 – May 18, 1956

Buffalo	000 000 004 000 1 – 5	9	0
Toronto	020 200 000 000 0 – 4	5	3
WP – Hahn (1-0)	LP – Romberger (1-0)		

Bill Froats started for the Herd and lasted three innings. He gave up four hits and three free passes and was charged with all four Leaf runs. The first Toronto hit was a two-run home run by center fielder Bill Wilson in the bottom of the second, following a base on balls to Ed Stevens. The roof fell in on the Bison pitcher in the third and Cavarretta called in Joe Coleman with one more run across, two on base and no one out.

Coleman walked two more, including pitcher Ed Blake, with the bases loaded to score the fourth run. From that point on the Bison pitching staff was virtually unhittable. In his four innings, Coleman allowed no hits. He did walk two more, but he also fanned six. Fred Hahn took over in the eighth and pitched six innings of one-hit ball, walking two.

Buffalo, meanwhile, could manage only one hit off Toronto starter Ed Blake through eight innings. In the ninth, the Herd rallied to tie the game at four apiece. There was a costly error by shortstop Hector Rodriguez and an odd choice of play by second baseman Mike Goliat. George Bullard got the Bisons rolling with a single. Joe Caffie's ground ball to Goliat was dropped by Rodriguez at second on the force attempt, Bullard safe on the error and Caffie now on first on the fielder's choice. Blake coaxed fly outs from Ortiz and Serena, but Easter grounded a ball behind second that Goliat knocked down and then threw to first instead of going for the force on Caffie at second. The lumbering Easter beat the throw, being credited with a hit and loading the bases.

Blake walked John Blatnik, a former Leaf, to bring Bullard home with the first Buffalo run. Ex-Leaf Billy DeMars sent Blake to the showers with a single that scored Caffie. Cavarretta went to the bench for lefty-swinging Joe Brovia to hit for Pat Tomkinson against the righthanded Dutch Romberger, now on in relief. Brovia made Cavarretta look like a genius, doubling to the right center field gap to score Easter and Blatnik. The game was knotted at four apiece.

It was a story of goose eggs for the next three frames until Caffie bunted for a base hit to lead off the top of the 13th inning. He then promptly stole second base and hurried to third on catcher Earl Battey's wild throw. Romberger bore down to get Lou Ortiz on a short fly ball and Bill Serena on a foul out, Caffie holding. He next carefully walked Easter after falling behind in the count. Noting how deep Toronto third baseman Loren Babe was playing, John Blatnik fooled everyone and bunted down the third-base line. Romberger and Babe could only watch and hope the ball rolled foul. It stayed inside the line, and Caffie scored the game winner.

Hahn set the Leafs down in order in the last of the thirteenth to pick up the comeback win.

Game 26—Saturday, May 19, Toronto, Canada: Toronto 5, Buffalo 4

Buffalo starter Harry Nicholas gave up only five hits in six innings,
but three of those were long balls that made the difference.

Game 26 – May 19, 1956

Buffalo	120 010 000 – 4	7	0
Toronto	201 002 00x – 5	6	1
WP – Hetki (2-1)	LP- Nicholas (1-2)		

It was a seesaw contest for the first six innings. Buffalo took the lead in the first, 1-0, when Joe Caffie hit his first home run of the year over the right-field wall off Leaf starter Johnny Hetki. Nicholas relinquished the lead in the bottom of the frame. Loren Babe, the Buffalo boy from Riverside, drew a walk. Former Bison outfielder Archie Wilson bashed his second home run of the year. The Leafs were up by one.

Archie had led the league in home runs (30) back in 1951, when he was the Herd's left fielder, earning the 27-year-old a call up to the Yankees at the end of that season and a starting spot in the Bombers' outfield in 1952. He lasted only three games with New York before being sent on to the Washington Senators and then the Boston Red Sox. Wilson hit .228 in 47 games in the bigs that season, but had swung the stick well again since his return to Triple A. In 1955, with Toronto, he batted .319 and drove in 119 runs.

Buffalo jumped in front with two more runs in inning number two. DeMars doubled to lead off and Lou Heyman was plunked in the hip by a pitch. Nicholas sacrificed, the runners moving up. With George Bullard at bat, Heyman was ruled safe on a pickoff attempt from Toronto catcher Carl Sawatski to second baseman Mike Goliat. Goliat went into such a rage he was tossed from the game, to be replaced by Walt Derucki. Hetki got Bullard on strikes but then gave an intentional pass to Caffie to load the bases. Lou Ortiz foiled the strategy, cracking a sharp single to right to bring home DeMars and Heyman.

Sam Jethroe, former Negro League standout and the 1950 National League Rookie of the Year with the Boston Braves at age 33, powered his third home run in the third inning, knotting the game at 3-3. Easter put the Bisons ahead once more in the fifth, driving a solo shot over the right-field wall, his sixth homer in 12 games.

Toronto scored the winning runs in the sixth. With two men out, Ed Stevens looped a single off Nicholas and Lew Morton lined his third homer of the season over the right-field fence. John Weiss relieved Nicholas for the seventh inning and Bill Froats hurled the eighth. The Leafs were held scoreless, but the damage had been done.

Buffalo wasted the chance to tie it in the ninth. George Bullard ran his hitting streak to seven games by leading off with a triple, but Hetki bore down and induced short fly balls from Caffie, Ortiz and finally Serena to end the ballgame.

BISON TALES: Eight Bisons went the strikeout route. Heyman was a victim three straight times after his hit-by-pitch in the second inning. Buffalo left eight men on base. By contrast, Toronto left one runner.

Despite the loss, the Herd hung onto fifth place in the International League. At 11 won, 15 lost, the Bisons were one half-game behind fourth-place Columbus and one half-game up on sixth-place Richmond.

Games 27 and 28—Sunday, May 20, Toronto, Canada: Buffalo 4, Toronto 0; Game 2 suspended due to curfew

Roger Bowman threw a strange shutout: two hits and nine walks.
Buffalo scored all their runs in the seventh inning.

Game 27 – May 20, 1956 (first game of doubleheader)

Buffalo	000 000 400 – 4	4 1
Toronto	000 000 000 – 0	2 1

WP – Bowman (2-2)   LP – D.Johnson (4-2)

In game one, it was a shutout contest between two wild hurlers. Through the seventh, Toronto's Don Johnson had allowed only a single to DeMars, who thereby ran his hitting streak to five games (.300), but the hurler had walked five.

Toronto pulled off two double plays to frustrate the Bisons' efforts. Buffalo recorded one. In addition, DeMars turned in three dazzling plays at short and Bowman escaped a bases-loaded fourth by fanning Earl Battey.

John Blatnik was due to lead off the Buffalo seventh, but Cavarretta turned to the lefthanded-swinging Joe Brovia as a pinch-hitter to face the Toronto righthander. Brovia came through with a ringing double, his second two-bagger in three pinch-hit appearances in this series. Harry Nicholas, running for Brovia, took third on a long fly out to right by DeMars. Johnson fell behind Peanuts Lowrey, pinch-hitting for Heyman, and then intentionally walked him to get to Bowman. Cavarretta let the pitcher hit for himself, and Bowman sent a fly ball deep enough to left that Nicholas could come in on the sacrifice fly. Johnson had two down with only one run in, but he was not yet out of the inning.

Bullard coaxed a walk, putting runners on first and second and bringing Joe Caffie to the plate. The Bison right fielder stung Johnson with his second home run in two days, a three-run blast that gave Bowman a sizable lead that he would hold onto. Dutch Romberger made his second relief appearance of the series to retire Ortiz and end the inning. He kept the Herd hitless and scoreless thereafter, but his efforts came too late.

Toronto's last gasp was snuffed out when Easter made a leaping stab of Ed Stevens' line drive with two men on in the eighth to preserve the shutout and the win.

Game 28 suspended: The Bisons led Toronto, 5-1, in the second game when the 6 p.m. curfew was called. The Herd grabbed a two-run lead in the first off Leaf starter Bill Fischer. George Bullard and Joe Caffie singled back to back to lead off. Bullard scored on Joe Brovia's ground out and Caffie came home on a Luke Easter single.

Toronto got a run back in the bottom of the fifth off Buffalo starter Larry Donovan when Ed Stevens, pinch-hitting for Fischer, doubled home Hector Rodriguez. Dutch Romberger came on in the sixth to pitch for Toronto but was pounded for three more runs. Lou Ortiz doubled and came in on Joe Brovia's single. Luke Easter hammered his seventh home run of the year to make it 5-1.

Toronto had the bases loaded and no one out in the last of the seventh and final inning of game two when curfew was called. The teams would resume the game in Buffalo on July 16.

Games 29 and 30—Monday, May 21, Montreal, Canada: Montreal 13, Buffalo 3; Montreal 1, Buffalo 0

The Bisons had left by train for Montreal immediately following the calling of the 6 p.m. curfew in the previous day's second game at Toronto. Today's doubleheader was billed as a showdown between the International League's two top home run hitters, Montreal first baseman Rocky Nelson with nine and Buffalo first-sacker Luke Easter with seven (counting the suspended game). Both men would shoot for the short right-field wall at Delormier Downs, but it was the other men on the field who would provide the fireworks. Pitching dominated in game two.

Game 29 – May 21, 1956 (first game of doubleheader)

Buffalo	000 300 000 –	3	8 1
Montreal	035 023 00X –	13	16 1

WP – Nishita (3-1)   LP Drews (4-3)

Game 30 – May 21, 1956 (second game of doubleheader)

Buffalo	000 000 0 –	0	4 0
Montreal	010 000 x –	1	5 0

WP – Harris (3-2)   LP – Keriazakos (2-3)

In game one, Buffalo's Karl Drews was not on his shutout form. The Royals pounded him for six hits and five runs in two innings. He left with no one out in the third and two men on. Joe Coleman fared no better. He was tagged for nine safeties in his five innings of work. The two runners Drews left on came around to score and Coleman was charged with six more tallies—two of those unearned—before being relieved by John Weiss in the eighth. Weiss kept Montreal off the scoreboard in his one frame of relief.

After a scoreless first, Drews gave up singles to Rocky Nelson and George Shuba to start the second. Clyde Parris hit a three-run shot into the right field screen above the home run marker. The first four men Drews faced in the third got on base: Bob Wilson doubled, Nelson walked, Shotgun Shuba stung a second double and Parris singled. Enter Joe Coleman and two more hits, the second of them a two-run double to Montreal hurler Bill Nishita. The Royals led 8-0.

Buffalo tried to make a game of it with three runs in the top of the fourth. Lou Ortiz doubled to start the inning and moved to third on a Joe Caffie single. An infield hit by Brovia held Ortiz at third but allowed Caffie to reach second to load the bases. Ortiz scored on a ground out by Easter, with the other men advancing. Caffie crossed the plate on a base hit by Castiglione, and Brovia followed immediately after him when the ball got away from Royal catcher John Roseboro for an error. Next man up, Serena, drew a walk to keep the rally alive, but an acrobatic leap at second by the Royals' Sparky Anderson snared Heyman's screaming liner toward right and Serena was doubled up easily. Anderson flipped the ball to shortstop Hector Fernandez to make the tag. Little did they know it at the time, but the Bisons' offense was done for the day.

Montreal's defense kept the Herd from doing any further damage to the Hawaiian-born Nishita. The Royals turned four double plays.

In game two, Keriazakos got out of the first inning with two men on base, but Montreal picked up the game's only run in the second after two were out. Sparky Anderson, four for four in game one, bunted for his fifth straight hit of the day. Opposing pitcher Bill Harris followed with a double that found the gap between George Bullard and Joe Brovia and rolled all the way to the right center field fence. Anderson, off at the crack of the bat, circled the bases to score, beating the relay from Bullard to Lou Ortiz to Pat Tomkinson.

There were no chances for either side after that. Game two was an errorless and low-hitting affair. Keriazakos surrendered only five safeties in total. Harris gave up only four. Each man allowed one walk. Montreal turned one double play, a figure matched by the Bisons.

BISON TALES: DeMars was ailing again after rupturing a blood vessel in his right arm in the suspended second game in Toronto. Castiglione had to take over for him in the third inning of that contest and started both of this day's games at short.

Joe Brovia was back in the starting lineup in right field on the strength of his two pinch-hit doubles in three at-bats in the Toronto series.

Now it was Bill Serena's bat that was dry. Cavarretta sent Peanuts Lowrey to third to start game two. Peanuts was 0 for three, but no one was hitting Bill Harris today.

Even though he wasn't in the lineup, Serena came away from the game with a bruised knee. Ortiz was so disgusted at a third strike call that he threw his bat, the projectile sailing into the Bison dugout and finding the unsuspecting Serena.

Dixie Howell, winding down his catching career after seven major league seasons with Cincinnati and Brooklyn, had been substituting for Montreal manager Greg Mulleavy and had guided the Royals into first place. Mulleavy was in Detroit to attend the funeral of his mother-in-law. Howell was hitting .429 as a pinch-hitter, and under his command the Royals had taken four out of five games against second-place Rochester and now this doubleheader win over the Bisons.

The twin-bill loss dropped the Herd into seventh place, only percentage points behind sixth-place Havana. Each club was 7 1/2 games behind the front-running Royals. Miami was now occupying the cellar, 1 1/2 games behind the Herd.

Game 31—Tuesday, May 22, Montreal, Canada: Montreal 8, Buffalo 4

Montreal took their third straight of the series and the fifth of their six games against the Bisons. A four-run seventh inning did it.

Game 31 – May 22, 1956

Buffalo	200 020 000 – 4	8	0
Montreal	300 001 40x – 8	13	0
WP – White (4-0)	LP – Froats (1-3)		

Royals starter Frank White picked up his second win against Buffalo, but he had to work for it. Peanuts Lowrey banged a two-out base hit in the first inning and Joe Brovia, back at cleanup, sent a tremendous drive over the centerfield wall to jump the Herd out to a two-run lead.

Bill Froats started on the hill for the Herd and gave the lead right back. Hector Rodriguez drew a one-out walk and Bob Wilson poked a single to put two men on, but Froats' curveball fooled Rocky Nelson, who went down swinging. The curve didn't fool Clyde Parrish. The Montreal third-sacker drove a Froats offering over the distant left-field wall, giving him two three-run homers in two days, plus the lead to the Royals.

Buffalo went back on top in the fourth. Froats and George Bullard drove out back-to-back base hits. Joe Caffie's fielder's choice eliminated Froats at third, but Peanuts Lowrey came through with the third single of the inning to drive in Bullard and knot the game at 3-3. Brovia's single sent Caffie home with the Bisons' fourth run.

The Royals tied it in a combative last of the sixth. Wilson singled again and then tried to score on Clyde Parris' double to left center. The relay from Bullard to Castiglione to Tomkinson stopped him at the plate, but Tomkinson came up swinging at the runner who had crashed into him trying to jar the ball loose. Wilson swung back and both benches emptied. No one got hurt but both Tomkinson and Wilson got thumbed. Parris came home on a single by Jim Williams.

Froats couldn't get a man out in the seventh. John Roseboro got it started with a single and was credited with a stolen base after being picked off at first. Luke Easter's throw to DeMars was high at second and Roseboro slid safely under the tag. Did this unhinge Froats? He hit Sparky Anderson with a pitch to put runners on first and second and no one out. White's sacrifice was so good that he wound up on first base with a bunt base hit and the sacks were loaded. Cavarretta called on John Weiss to relieve.

Interim Montreal manager Dixie Howell called on himself to pinch-hit for Oscar Sardinas. Howell ripped Weiss for a two-run single and a two-run lead. Hector Fernandez's ground out moved the runners up. Cavarretta went to Fred Hahn to face George Shuba, the latter having replaced the ejected Wilson. In the lefty-versus-lefty matchup, Shuba cracked yet another single and the lead was up to four. Hahn allowed one more base hit before retiring the side. Joe Coleman finished the game for Buffalo. Buffalo could muster nothing more against White.

BISON TALES: Parris had six hits in 11 at-bats in the series, four of them for extra bases. Anderson was seven for nine and had raised his league-leading average to .474.

Wednesday, May 23, Montreal, Canada: Weather Postponement

Management postponed the game due to cold. The temperature dropped to the low 30s, and so did the fan turnout. The game would be made up on the Bisons' next trip to Montreal.

On a positive note, league president Frank J. Shaughnessy stated that Pat Tomkinson would not be fined for the donnybrook that took place Tuesday night. He ruled that Bob Wilson was the aggressor and would be the only one fined ($25). It was the only battle in Montreal in which the Bisons came out on top.

Thursday, May 24, Buffalo: Scheduled Day Off

The Bisons had a second day off following the "cold out," thanks to the International League schedule. The won-two, lost-four road record had dropped the Herd into seventh place in the standings. The curfew-called game in Toronto still wasn't completed and couldn't yet be called a win, even though Buffalo was leading by a 5-1 margin in the last of the seventh. In baseball there was no telling what might happen.

Thirty games into the season, Cavarretta's major concern was who he could put into the fourth position in the lineup who would drive in some runs. Luke Easter had batted cleanup in 17 games but had produced only 7 RBIs hitting in that slot, batting but .257. Bill Serena was tried there for six games but did not drive in even one run in 21 official at-bats. He averaged only .242. Joe Brovia had occupied that position on five occasions but had hit only .200. In the most recent road game against Montreal, Joe did collect two hits in four trips to the plate, scored a run and drove home three. Cavarretta was hoping Brovia could continue this pace when the club began its home stand on Friday against the Rochester Red Wings.

It wasn't just the cleanup hitters. Few on the team were hitting. Not counting the suspended game, John Blatnik was leading the squad with a .306 mark, but the only other regular over .250 was Pat Tomkinson at .265. Challenged by the acquisition of Joe Caffie and losing his starting place in right field, Brovia managed a turnaround in his hitting performance and continued to hit the ball when he was reinstated as a regular. Joe went 5 for 13, a .384 average that brought his season average up to .233. He had five RBIs on the trip.

Pete Castiglione finally found his place at the plate, going 5 for 12 on these games away from home and hitting at a .412 clip. But the road pitching was disastrous for Serena and Ortiz. Bill went 1 for 17 and was now down to .192. Ortiz collected but 2 hits in 21 plate appearances, dropping his average to .229. Bullard was leading the team with 14 runs scored. Easter, Brovia and Ortiz each had 12 RBIs.

Defensively, the club had suffered from DeMars' absence due to a ruptured blood vessel in his throwing arm. With DeMars out, and with Serena on the bench and Lowrey filling in for him at third, the left side of the Bison infield was a decided weak spot.

The pitching was the club's strong suit, much to the surprise of many. Drews, the four-game winner, had an ERA of 2.45. Gus Keriazakos was a hard-luck loser at 2-3 with an ERA of 1.87. Lefthander Bob Bowman was 2-2 and had held the opposition to 1.74 runs per game. Starter Joe Coleman's ERA was 1.66 with no decisions. Larry (Red) Donovan had a record of 0 wins, 1 loss and the team's best ERA at 1.13. Harry Nicholas (1-2, 3.99) and reliever Fred Hahn (1-0, 4.05) had shown bright spots. John Weiss (0-2 as a starter) had made himself a strength out of the bullpen. He had held opponents scoreless in five relief outings until Montreal managed a run off him in the game on Tuesday, May 22. Only lefty Bill Froats at 1-3 and an ERA of 6.27 had not yet gotten untracked.

Game 32—Friday, May 25, Buffalo: Rochester 8, Buffalo 7

Buffalo lost a seesaw affair marked by errors, wildness and a Stan Jok 10th-inning home run to fall into the cellar behind Havana.

Game 32 – May 25, 1956
Rochester	020 300 002 1 – 8	10	0
Buffalo	050 000 011 0 – 7	7	2
WP – Markell (4-2)	LP – Hahn (1-1)		

Rochester scored two in the second inning when Tom Burgess got aboard on a Pete Castiglione error and Jay Van Noy hit an opposite-field home run off Bison starter Harry Nicholas.

Luke Easter started the Buffalo second by drawing a walk. Lou Ortiz, next up, drilled a homer over the left-field screen and suddenly the score was tied. With one out, Pat Tomkinson and Nicholas both singled and George Bullard sent a scorching line drive to the base of the scoreboard for a triple, driving home both baserunners. Obviously rattled, Rochester's John Mackinson walked Joe Caffie, who immediately set out for second base. The throw from Rochester catcher Dick Rand was too late to catch Caffie, and on the play Bullard executed the second half of the double-steal by racing home. Buffalo led 5-2.

The Red Wings knotted the score in the fifth. Allie Clark drew a walk and came home on Jay Van Noy's double. Mel Nelson's high fly ball down the left-field line just cleared the wire fence near the 321-foot marker for a two-run homer to make it a tie ballgame. Cavarretta called Fred Hahn in to relieve.

Hahn shut down the Rochester attack and Mackinson did the same to the Herd until Bill Serena slugged his fourth home run in the eighth. Buffalo was back in front by one.

Stan Jok, from Riverside in Buffalo, sent in to play third base for Van Noy when Hahn came into the game, singled off Hahn to lead off the Rochester ninth. Pinch-hitter Fred Huesman sent a sure double-play grounder to Castiglione that the shortstop flubbed. With two on and no outs, Nelson blooped a single into short right to score Jok and tie the game once more. Then Hahn couldn't find the plate and walked Mackinson, loading the bases. Cavarretta left Hahn in to get the next two batters, but a walk to Joe Cunningham gave Rochester the lead.

Pat Tomkinson tied it back up, leading off the ninth with his first homer of the year. Duke Markell relieved and got the next three Bisons.

Stan Jok hit the third Rochester home run of the game off Hahn in the tenth for the game winner. John Weiss relieved Hahn to get the third out. Markell set the Herd down one, two, three.

BISON TALES: Billy DeMars' throwing arm swelled up on him during infield practice so that he couldn't play. A pulled muscle was suspected. Earlier in the day, John Blatnik put in a request for voluntary retirement. He planned to take a position at the Workman's Compensation Bureau in his home state of Ohio. On the double steal pulled off by Bullard and Caffie, the theft was Bullard's 10th of the year. The team had 14 total.

Fans had now begun to throw balls hit into the stands back onto the field to help the bottom line. Fans who did not do so were getting booed.

Game 33—Saturday, May 26, Buffalo: Rochester 13, Buffalo 7

Sixteen Rochester hits sent the Bisons down to a
fifth straight defeat and kept the Herd in last place.

Game 33 – May 26, 1956

Rochester	313 000 600 – 13	16	1
Buffalo	012 000 400 – 7	9	2

WP – Deal (5-2)   LP – Bowman (2-3)

Offermann stadium's reputation for being hard on lefthanders was borne out this night. Lefty Roger Bowman, starting for the Bisons, lasted only an inning and a third. Reliever Bill Froats, another southpaw, was battered for nine runs. Buffalo got seven runs off Cot Deal, the Rochester righty who started and won the game. It was a dangerous park for righthanders, too.

The contest was played in the rain—what else was new? Bowman gave up a walk and four singles in the first inning, leading to three Red Wings tallies. An unassisted double play pulled off by Easter kept it from being worse. Rochester's Cot Deal, an excellent hitting pitcher, pulled a home run over the right-field wall to start the second frame. After a John Huesman single and a one-out walk to Joe Cunningham, Cavarretta pulled the plug on Bowman. Bill Froats came in to retire the next three men.

Buffalo got one back in the home half of the second on a Bill Serena walk, Luke Easter's sharp single to right field and Pat Tomkinson's sacrifice fly. The Red Wings added three more in the third. Stan Jok hit his second solo homer in two nights. Mel Nelson and Deal both singled. A double by Ed Kasko chased the two runners home.

Down 7-1, Buffalo would not quit. George Bullard opened with a double in the bottom of the third and Joe Caffie drew a walk. Serena and Easter picked up RBI singles to make it 7-3.

Goose eggs reigned for the next three innings. The offense opened up again in the seventh when 10 runs crossed the plate, six of them by Rochester. Froats, being given a chance by Cavarretta to work his way through his wildness, allowed two walks, four singles, a double and a home run by Gene Green. The Red Wings batted around, Dick Rand making both the first and the last outs, popping to Ortiz each time.

Three of Buffalo's four runs in the seventh were scored on Peanuts Lowrey's first home run of the year, driving home Bullard and Caffie ahead of him. A two-out single by Pete Castiglione brought Serena home from second. Duke Markell came in for Deal and got Tomkinson to end the inning.

John Weiss pitched the final two frames for Buffalo, allowing one hit but no runs. Rochester reliever Duke Markell was again unhittable.

BISON TALES: The Bisons were now a half-game behind seventh-place Havana and needed player help in a big way. Cavarretta had placed himself on the inactive list but might have to return to the active roster when the weather got warmer. General manager Stiglmeier was looking to friends in the major leagues for assistance.

International League president Shaughnessy made yet another ruling on the Tomkinson-Wilson fight. Wilson would not be fined after all. No one was to blame. It's baseball.

Games 34 and 35—Sunday, May 27, Buffalo: Buffalo 5, Rochester 4; Buffalo 7, Rochester 5
Karl Drews snapped the losing streak with a 12-inning complete-game effort in game one.
Lou Ortiz's grand slam won the second.

    Game 34 – May 27, 1956 (first game of doubleheader)
    Rochester   100 200 100 000 – 4 13 3
    Buffalo   022 000 000 001 – 5 10 0
    WP – Drews (5-3)   LP – Faszholz (2-5)

    Game 35 – May 27, 1956 (second game of doubleheader)
    Rochester   203 000 0 – 5 11 1
    Buffalo   101 100 4 – 7 8 0
    WP – Bowman (3-3)   LP – Mayer (0-1)

In the first game, Drews gutted out the win, giving up 13 hits and four walks, but coming through in the pinch with the aid of the Bison defense. As in the two preceding games, Rochester struck first.

Ron Plaza got a one-out Texas Leaguer in inning one and scored on Allie Clark's hit up the middle. The Bisons responded in the home half of the second frame. Luke Easter led off with his eighth home run of the year over the left-field wall to knot the score at 1-1. Lou Ortiz, next up, connected for a single, and all men were safe when Serena's grounder was misplayed by Rochester hurler Gary Blaylock. The error resulted in a run when Drews' sacrifice fly to center plated Ortiz.

The Herd added two more in the third. Easter coaxed a one-out walk and Bill Serena slammed a Blaylock fastball for an opposite-field home run over the right-field barrier. It was Bill's fifth of the season. Drews had a 4-1 lead.

Rochester clawed back to 4-3 with a pair of runs in the fourth. Back-to-back doubles by Clark and Tom Burgess brought one home. Burgess scored when Jay Van Noy dumped a pop single to right just out of the reach of a charging Joe Brovia. Rochester tied it up in the top of the seventh. Mel Nelson singled, moved to second on Stan Jok's pinch-hit ground out to the right side, and took third on Ed Kasko's infield single up the middle that Ortiz knocked down but couldn't make a play on. Plaza's grounder became a fielder's choice and a run batted in when Ortiz and Pete Castiglione couldn't turn the double play. Nelson scored.

Defense kept Drews in the game until the Bisons could manufacture the winning run in the twelfth. Castiglione started two 6-4-3 double plays. Peanuts Lowrey ran down a liner from Mel Nelson in left field and made a perfect throw to Easter to double up Van Noy at first. Serena made two diving grabs to his right to snuff out two sure doubles. Drews came up big in the eighth, fanning Jok with men on first and third.

Joe Caffie scored the winner on a two-out infield error charged to Joe Cunningham. Caffie waited out the only walk issued by Rochester reliever Jack Faszholz, then moved to second on Lowrey's crisp line-drive single to left. Faszholz looked like he was out of trouble after Serena hit a major league popup in front of the mound. Van Noy tore in from third to make the play and Cunningham did the same from first. Catcher Gene Green called for Cunningham to take it. Faszholz called for Van Noy. In the mix-up, the two men collided and the ball popped out of Cunningham's glove. Caffie, running all the way, crossed the plate with the winning run.

With Rochester first-ball hitting in the 11th and 12th innings, Drews had to use only nine pitches to get the last six outs.

In the seven-inning second game, Gus Keriazakos just didn't have it. Again, the Red Wings scored in the first frame, taking a 2-0 lead. Allie Clark doubled home Ron Plaza after two were out. Tom Burgess singled in Clark.

George Bullard doubled leading off the bottom half of the first, and Luke Easter singled him home to bring the Bisons within one. The Red Wings, however, added three more runs in the top of the third and sent Keriazakos to the showers. Joe Cunningham walked, Tom Burgess singled and catcher Dick Rand cracked a two-out, three-run homer over the left center field wall. John Weiss took over the mound for the Bisons.

Bullard doubled once again in the bottom of the third. This time, Caffie singled him home. Buffalo got an unearned third run in the fourth frame. Serena was hit by a pitch to lead off, moved to third on a throwing error by Van Noy and came home on Bullard's fielder's choice.

Weiss and Joe Coleman pitched effectively in relief, keeping the Bisons in the game for the dramatic confrontation at the finish. Meanwhile, Duke Markell had replaced Rochester starter Gary Geiger on the mound in the sixth inning, but he was not as dominant today. Buffalo managed a hit off him in the sixth. In the seventh, with one gone, Joe Caffie beat out an infield bouncer and Peanuts Lowrey walked. In came the lefthanded Ed Mayer to face Luke Easter.

Easter moved close to the plate on Mayer's warmup pitches to watch his delivery. Rochester manager Dixie Walker called out from the bench to "knock down the big so-and-so" and the hurler did just that, hitting Easter in the right shoulder with one of the throws. Bat in hand, Easter headed toward the Rochester bench, but he was restrained by plate umpire Walter Ryan and other Bisons. Luke resumed his on-deck position close to the plate and Mayer sent another warmup pitch whizzing close to the big first baseman's head. Both benches emptied after this incident but only words were thrown, no punches.

When Easter finally stepped in to bat, Mayer fell behind in the count and Walker ordered an intentional pass to load the bases. Righthander John Mackinson was called on to face Lou Ortiz. Ortiz had homered off Mackinson in game one of the series and now he did it again. The third pitch went high over the screen in left. The walkoff blast was Ortiz's third home run of the season and the Bisons' first grand slam.

BISON TALES: The visitors' dressing room was reached through the Bison dugout. After the game, Easter was waiting there for Walker with a bat in his hand but had no intention of using it. He merely wanted to send a message about being thrown at when he was not at the plate and ready for such tactics. Ortiz, a Red Wing from 1950 to 1954, said that throwing at the on-deck batter was common in the St. Louis Cardinal organization.

Havana lost two to Columbus today, and the double win pulled the Bisons out of the cellar.

Game 36—Monday, May 28, Buffalo: Buffalo 4, Toronto 3

Still riled from the Rochester series, the Herd made it three victories in a row
with a ninth-inning win against the Maple Leafs.

```
Game 36 – May 28, 1956
Toronto          002 000 100 – 3  10  1
Buffalo          010 200 001 – 4  11  1
WP – Donovan (1-1)      LP – Miller (0-1)
```

For a change, Buffalo scored first. Lou Ortiz singled in the second inning against Toronto starter Don Johnson, moved to second on Pete Castiglione's one-baser and came home on Pat Tomkinson's sharp single to right center.

Toronto captured the lead in the third. Larry Donovan, pitching for Buffalo, gave up a single to Loren Babe. One out later, Ed Stevens, hitting but .183 and with one home run, hit the second pitch he saw over the 367-foot sign in right center.

Buffalo reclaimed the lead in the fourth. Ortiz started it this time with a double. Bill Serena got a walk. Castiglione got his second hit of the night to score Ortiz and move Serena to third. And now the Bisons pulled off their second double steal in three days: Serena, age 31, and Castiglione, 35, showing the youngsters that their elders could do it, too. Serena's marker put Buffalo back on top.

Serena slid around the tag attempt by Toronto catcher Carl Sawatski, beating the throw home from Mike Goliat. Johnson protested the call by throwing his glove high in the air, earning an immediate trip to the showers. Leafs manager Bruno Betzel joined him in short order after offering his views on the call. John Hetki was pressed into mound service and retired Pat Tomkinson to end the inning.

Hetki held Buffalo to one hit in the two-plus innings he worked. Meanwhile, the Leafs got the tying run in the seventh. Sam Jethroe drew a walk and came around on a Serena overthrow at first.

Castiglione led off the ninth with his third hit of the night. Tomkinson singled, and the Bisons had runners on first and second with no one out. Bill Miller, now on the mound for Toronto, was replaced by Dutch Romberger. Cavarretta sent Billy DeMars up to pinch-hit for Donovan. Everyone knew the sacrifice was coming, but DeMars' bunt was so well placed that no one could make a play. It was a hit, loading the bases. George Bullard went down swinging at a third strike for the first out, but Joe Caffie swung at Romberger's first pitch and lined a sharp single into right field. Castiglione crossed home plate with the game winner.

BISON TALES: Lou Kahn managed Toronto after Betzel was banished in the fourth. Stevens had three hits and could have had a fourth, but for Bullard's leaping catch against the center-field wall in the fifth. Bullard's throw on the play doubled up the baserunner from first and saved at least one run and possibly two.

Buffalo was now only percentage points behind Richmond for sixth place in the circuit.

THE MINORS VERSUS THE MAJORS: I
Tuesday, May 29, Buffalo

Despite the recent if modest win streak by the team, the front office was encountering stiff resistance when it came to obtaining new players to shore up the club's weaknesses. An infielder to cover shortstop for the injured DeMars was critical; both Castiglione's range and his arm were only good as a stopgap measure. Blatnik's unanticipated departure created a need for another outfielder. Lowrey's 38-year-old legs could only go for so long. Brovia's bat was what had made him a regular, but thus far his bat production was not able to compensate for his glove deficiencies. A catcher with power was a desperately sought acquisition.

But the major league clubs had not been honoring their commitments to the Bisons, according to general manager John Stiglmeier. Only three organizations had aided the team. The Yankees made Gus Keriazakos available. The Red Sox sold Bill Serena to the Herd. And, most recently, the Indians had sent Joe Caffie. "The major leagues said last winter that community, home ownership was the salvation of minor league baseball, but they are not backing up their words," Stiglmeier was quoted in the May 29 edition of the Buffalo Evening News.

Stiglmeier was still keenly upset that Charles Comisky of the White Sox sent the slugging lefthanded catcher Carl Sawatski to the Maple Leafs. Stiglmeier thought he had a commitment that Sawatski would come to Buffalo if he did not stay with the major league squad. Millionaire Toronto owner Jack Kent Cooke likely had either more influence, or more money, or both to outbid the Bison offer. Nor did Pittsburgh give the Bisons a chance to sign the recently released catcher Toby Atwell. Upon learning of the impending release, Harry Bisgeier went to the Steel City to sign Atwell, only to discover that the Pirates had already sold the catcher to St. Louis in order to help the latter's American Association Omaha ball club.

Brooklyn, too, was faulted for their failure to allow a waiver claim for outfielder Bob Borkowski of the Montreal team. Despite International League president Frank Shaughnessy's protest, Borkowski was sent to the Pacific Coast League. Stiglmeier responded: "The major leagues are guilty of employing devious methods to help one another in their minor league operations." Given these irregular maneuvers of the major league operations, Stiglmeier put in a complaint to baseball commissioner Ford C. Frick.

Stiglmeier was a veteran baseball man who had been the general manager of the Bisons back in the 1940s. In that capacity, he had helped arrange the meeting of Frick and Shaughnessy with President Franklin D. Roosevelt that had resulted in the president's "green light" decision allowing baseball to continue play during World War II. Stiglmeier had met with Senator James M. Mead at that time to organize the meeting of the principals.

"Baseball has changed a great deal in 12 years," Stiglmeier lamented, harkening back to 1944 when he had last occupied a Bison front-office position. "Then, you could rely on a man's word and a promise was something that was made to be kept."

"If we don't get assurances of help," he added, going on to say that the team was willing to buy players, not seeking charity, "I am going ahead and ask for a congressional investigation. I know two members of Congress who will carry it out and I have an able lawyer who will fight the case. It may cost me personally a lot of money, but I'll spend it out of my own pocket to get justice for the stockholders of our ball club. We should have the right and the privilege to buy players.

"I have a file of correspondence ready to present to commissioner Frick. I hope that he can do something so that we have an equal chance against the monopoly of the majors in negotiating for players."

Stiglmeier was in a fighting mood. Baseball had better beware.

Billy DeMars and Lou Ortiz turn two
Photo courtesy of SUNY Buffalo State Courier-Express Collection

Game 37—Tuesday, May 29, Buffalo: Buffalo 7, Toronto 6

The Bisons bagged their fourth in a row. This time it was Bill Serena's
turn for the final-inning heroics in a come-from-behind win.

```
Game 37 – May 29, 1956
Toronto          020 112 000 – 6  11  0
Buffalo          300 002 002 – 7  11  1
WP – Coleman (1-0)      LP – Jacobs (2-2)
```

Buffalo started out with the lead for the second game in a row and gave starter Fred Hahn a three-run cushion in the first inning, thanks to two home runs. George Bullard chopped a single to deep short off Toronto starter Ed Blake to get aboard. Blake retired Joe Caffie and Peanuts Lowrey, but not Luke Easter. Luke's massive home run to left center field hit the roof of a house behind the double-tiered, 22-foot-high fence. Lou Ortiz batted after Easter in the order and he also followed Easter with the long ball. Lou's roundtripper cleared the left-field wall past the 345 marker. Buffalo led 3-0.

Hahn had won the start after several strong outings in long relief, but today he could not finish his assignment. He was gone before the end of two innings. Maple Leaf first baseman Ed Stevens, on a hitting tear against the Bisons, rocked Hahn for a circuit shot leading off the Toronto second. Hahn got the next two batters, but then Walt Derucki also took him deep for Toronto's second home run of the frame. When the Buffalo pitcher walked the next man, Carl Sawatski, Cavarretta went to the bullpen. In came John Weiss to retire the side.

Weiss hurled a scoreless third, but then gave up four runs and the lead in the next three frames. Stevens poled his second home run of the night during this outburst, and a throwing error by Bullard contributed to an unearned tally. It could have been worse. A fine throw by Peanuts Lowrey in left cut down Stevens trying to score on a Loren Babe base hit. Toronto was up 6-3.

Buffalo bounced back with two runs in the home half of the sixth. Pete Castiglione singled, followed by Pat Tomkinson's double to right center, Castiglione holding at third. Joe Brovia's pinch-hit ground ball to the right side scored Castiglione. Tomkinson came home from third on Joe Caffie's two-out line drive single.

Bill Froats threw the seventh and eighth and Joe Coleman the ninth to keep the score at 6-5 for Toronto. Tony Jacobs, the fourth Maple Leaf pitcher, blanked the Bisons in the seventh and eighth and retired Caffie and Lowrey to start the ninth, but Easter lined a base hit to center to keep the Herd alive. Now pitching carefully to Ortiz, Jacobs wound up walking him. Bill Serena got the game winner when he whistled a high drive off the second tier of the centerfield fence. Running at the crack of the bat, Easter and Ortiz both made it home to give Buffalo the victory.

BISON TALES: Ortiz's first-inning smash was his fourth base hit in four official at-bats: the game-winning grand slam on Sunday, two for two yesterday with a double, and today's home run, his fourth of the year. Easter's was his ninth. Lowrey's sparkling defense in left was a major factor in two of the four recent wins.

Games 38 and 39—Wednesday, May 30, Buffalo: Toronto 2, Buffalo 0; Buffalo 9, Toronto 1

Bill Fischer's shutout hurling snapped the Buffalo winning streak at
four in game one. Keriazakos finally got some run support to win the second.

Game 38 – May 30, 1956 (first game of doubleheader)

Toronto	010 000 100 – 2	5	0
Buffalo	000 000 000 – 0	6	0

WP – Fischer (2-0)   LP – Bowman (3-4)

Game 39 May 30, 1956 (second game of doubleheader)

Toronto	100 000 0 – 1	6	0
Buffalo	010 044 x – 9	12	0

WP – Keriazakos (3-3)   LP – Lovenguth (5-3)

In the first game, Roger Bowman, starting for the Herd, retired the side in order in the first. The Bisons could make no dent in Fischer in their half. Former Bison Archie Wilson, batting cleanup, led off the Toronto second and drove a Bowman fastball high over the wall in left center to stake the Torontonians to a one-run lead.

Ortiz tried to set up the tying run for the Bisons in the bottom of the second but was thrown out trying to stretch a double into a triple. His blow to center field rolled all the way to the 400-foot sign at base of the scoreboard, but the relay throw from Sam Jethroe to Mike Goliat to Walt Derucki at third base put him out. It turned out to be the Herd's best chance for a run. Fischer scattered five more hits and stranded seven Bisons on the basepaths. It was the first shutout of the year by a Toronto pitcher.

The Maple Leafs got to Bowman for their second run in the seventh inning after two men were down. Second baseman Mike Goliat led off the frame with a single but was erased on a slick double play from Bill Serena to Lou Ortiz to Luke Easter. First baseman Ed Stevens continued his hot hitting in this series and lashed a single. A walk to right fielder Bill Wilson moved him into scoring position. Derucki's only base hit of the game brought him home.

Bowman conceded only five hits—one less than Fischer. He and Fischer each allowed two walks. Buffalo turned in two double plays to snuff out Leaf chances. Bowman's outing was his third complete game of the season.

Archie Wilson liked swinging the bat in Offermann, despite yesterday's 0 for five. As the Buffalo left fielder in 1951, he had hit 28 out of the park and had been named the International League's MVP. That performance won him a trial with the Yankees at the end of 1951 and a 47-game stint in the majors the following year. He was a consistent .300 hitter with power in Triple A.

In the seven-inning second game, Gus Keriazakos threw a six-hitter and the Buffalo bats opened up. Lynn Lovenguth, former Bison, was on the hill for Toronto. A four-run outburst in the bottom of the fifth ended his day.

Archie Wilson drilled his second solo home run of the day and the Leafs took another first-inning one-run lead. The Bisons made it 1-1 in the second. It was a Lou Ortiz double that created the opportunity, and this time Ortiz stopped at second. Bill Serena's single made it a tie game. It stayed that way until the bottom of the fifth.

Lovenguth had been a .500 pitcher for Buffalo back in 1951 and 1952 and had pitched successfully thereafter with the Syracuse Chiefs, but he was never able to win again at Offermann since leaving the Bisons. He had lost nine straight in Buffalo coming into this evening's game.

Joe Caffie opened the fifth inning with a single. Peanuts Lowrey's sacrifice moved him into scoring position. Lovenguth pitched around Easter, walking him. The strategy looked good when Ortiz popped up for out number two, but then three straight hits followed. Serena cracked a sharp single to bring Caffie home with the tiebreaker and send Easter to third. Pete Castiglione's ground ball found eyes through the infield and scored Easter, Serena taking second. Lou Heyman, catching this second game, doubled high off the left center field wall, with Serena and Castiglione running with two outs. Both men crossed the plate to make it 5-1. That was it for Lovenguth. Leaf manager Bruno Betzel called in Tony Jacobs to retire Keriazakos.

The Bisons hammered Dutch Romberger for four more runs in the sixth. George Bullard and Caffie led off with singles. A third straight single by Lowrey plated Bullard, Caffie racing to third. Easter's towering sacrifice fly ball to center scored Caffie. Ortiz ended the surge by whacking his fourth home run of the home stand, his fifth of the year. Lowrey scored ahead of him. Romberger finally got Serena and Castiglione to close out the inning.

Keriazakos pitched a scoreless seventh to pick up his third win of the campaign.

BISON TALES: After the game, Lovenguth was overheard to remark, "Ugh! If I never see this park again, I'll be happy."

Manager Phil Cavarretta had reactivated himself as a player with the retirement of John Blatnik and no one else to replace him. Five different Buffalo pitchers won a game during the home stand. Ortiz slugged the ball at a .344 clip with four home runs, nine runs scored and nine driven home. Easter and Serena chipped in with a pair of homers apiece. Tomkinson was a .318 hitter. Castiglione, at .290, started six double plays.

International League president Frank Shaughnessy was in town to meet with general manager John C. Stiglmeier, promising his full support to the Bison executive's request to meet with baseball commissioner Ford C. Frick. He offered to go with Stiglmeier to the meeting, and to a call for congressional action if it came to that. The Bisons were asking the majors for a bona fide chance at signing available talent, such as with the Joe Caffie purchase from the Indians.

A holiday crowd of 7693 turned out to make the cash registers and the front office happy.

In International League news: As of May 30, Montreal's scrappy Sparky Anderson was leading all hitters with a .434 mark. Toronto's Rocky Nelson had nine home runs. Luke Easter was right behind him with eight, but Luke's ninth was still waiting to be officially counted from the suspended game. George Bullard was leading the league in stolen bases with 12.

Elsewhere, Tommy Van Remmen, the former Timon pitching standout, had been transferred from the Sally League Augusta, Georgia, squad to closer to home. He would now be hurling for the Eastern League Syracuse ball club.

Game 40—Thursday, May 31, Rochester, New York: Rochester 5, Buffalo 4

Four first-inning runs and two late walks spelled defeat for
Harry Nicholas and the Bisons in a well-fought 11-inning affair.

> **Game 40 – May 31, 1956**
> Buffalo   000 202 000 00 – 4 6 0
> Rochester   400 000 000 01 – 5 6 1
> WP – Blaylock (3-1)   LP – Nicholas (1-3)

Buffalo went down easily in the top of the first inning against Rochester starter Don Blaylock. Not so the Red Wings. Second baseman Ron Plaza led off for Rochester and drew the first of seven walks Nicholas would concede. Nicholas also gave a free pass to Eddie Kasko, batting second. Lou Ortiz knocked down Joe Cunningham's sharp grounder up the middle but had no play, an infield hit loading the bases with none out. Allie Clark, cleanup hitter, unloaded them with one swing, sending a grand slam home run over the left-field wall. Rochester had a 4-0 lead and nobody out.

Cavarretta stuck with Nicholas, and the Buffalo righthander recovered to retire Rochester in the first and hold the Red Wings scoreless for the next nine innings. Over that span, he allowed only three more base hits, walked four and set nine men down on strikes. Buffalo got two runs back in the fourth inning and tied it in the sixth.

Nine Bisons in a row had gone down against Blaylock until George Bullard bunted for a base hit to open the visitor half of the fourth. Joe Caffie's single to left moved Bullard to second. Peanuts Lowrey flew out for out number one, but Easter, batting cleanup, singled to right to drive home Bullard and send Caffie on to third. Ortiz's hot grounder to short was turned into a fielder's choice that eliminated Easter, Caffie scoring on the play as Ortiz beat the relay throw to first.

Buffalo tied it two innings later. Peanuts Lowrey drew a walk and Easter crashed his ninth home run of the year to deep right center field. (Ten, counting the suspended game, a total that moved him ahead of Rocky Nelson in the International League home run race.)

Blaylock reasserted his mound command and matched Nicholas with scoreboard zeros into the eleventh. He allowed only two more hits, both to Pete Castiglione, one of them a double that the Bisons could not convert into a score.

Tom Burgess, Red Wing right fielder, hitless for the night, coaxed the sixth walk out of Nicholas to open the bottom of the eleventh. Jay Van Noy followed him with a perfect sacrifice bunt to move Burgess into scoring position. Cavarretta, looking for the double play, ordered catcher Dick Rand walked to put runners on first and second. Nicholas got center fielder Mel Nelson on a popup to Bill Serena to make it two men down, but then manager Dixie Walker sent the switch-hitting Cot Deal up to bat for Blaylock. Deal stepped in lefthanded against Nicholas and sent a dribbler to right field just out of reach of Easter's glove. Burgess crossed the plate with the winning run.

Bison Tales: Ellis (Cot) Deal again showed his dominance against Buffalo. Winning his last six decisions as a pitcher and carrying a lifetime 11-3 record against the Herd, today it was his potent bat that did the damage.

Castiglione's two base hits gave him a six-game hit streak, 10 for 22 and a .454 average.

Friday, June 1, Rochester, New York: Weather Postponement

Today's game called off due to frigid weather.

Game 41—Saturday, June 2, Rochester, New York: Rochester 3, Buffalo 0

Buffalo not only lost a ballgame but, more critically,
a catcher. Pat Tomkinson suffered a deep spike wound on a tag-out play at home.

```
Game 41 – June 2, 1956
Buffalo          000 000 000 – 0   4   0
Rochester        000 002 10 x – 3  10   0
WP- Faszholz (3-5)        LP – Drews (5-4)
```

Continued frosty weather kept fan turnout under 1000 and Buffalo bats as cold as ice against Rochester starter Jack Faszholz. Only three Bisons reached as far as second base.

By contrast, Karl Drews was battered for 10 hits in seven innings. The Red Wings notched two runs in the bottom of the sixth. Ron Plaza opened with a base knock. Ed Kasko forced him at second and Joe Cunningham fanned, but then Drews hit Allie Clark with a pitch and Tom Burgess singled to score Kasko. Still with two out, Jay Van Noy's double off the right-field wall brought in Clark. Burgess tried to make it all the way home from first, but the relay from Caffie to Ortiz to Tomkinson blocking the plate caught him to end the inning. Ominously, Burgess' spikes ripped open Tomkinson's left foot on the tag play and carved such a deep wound that the Bison catcher had to be helped from the field to be stitched up. Lou Heyman went behind the plate.

Rochester's final run came on Faszholz's two-out double in the seventh inning, an infield hit by Plaza and a single by Kasko.

BISON TALES: The injury to Tomkinson showed how dire was the Buffalo roster situation. Billy De-Mars had missed the past 11 games with a muscle tear in his throwing arm, and now this.

In addition to not getting Carl Sawatski, the Bisons had not been given a chance to go after another White Sox catcher. Sam Hairston had hit .268 at Triple A in 1954. Chicago had given him a long look in spring training but then had returned him to Double A without telling Buffalo.

Baseball commissioner Ford C. Frick and John Stiglmeier had a meeting planned for June 7 in New York City, the Bison general manager wanting major league clubs to fulfill their commitments to the Bisons. International League president Frank Shaughnessy, as well as George Trautman, executive in charge of all minor leagues, would be there in support.

International League Standings
June 1, 1956

	W	L	Pct	GB
Montreal	28	14	.667	—
Rochester	27	18	.600	2½
Toronto	20*	18	.526	6
Columbus	20	21	.487	7½
Miami	20	24	.454	9
Richmond	20	25	.444	9½
Buffalo	17*	22	.416	9½
Havana	17	27	.386	12

*Not including suspended game of 5/20.

Games 42 and 43—Sunday, June 3, Rochester, New York: Rochester 7, Buffalo 6; Buffalo 8, Rochester 3

Buffalo's come-from-behind effort failed in the first-game loss,
but four Bison home runs earned the club a second-game victory.

Game 42 – June 3, 1956 (first game of doubleheader)
Buffalo   000 001 320 – 6 10 1
Rochester   002 050 00x – 7 13 0
WP – Russell (2-1)   LP – Keriazakos (3-4)

Game 43 – June 3, 1956 (second game of doubleheader)
Buffalo   102 130 1 – 8 10 0
Rochester   000 012 0 – 3   6 0
WP – Hahn (2-1)   LP – Deal (6-3)

The Red Wings jumped out to a 7-0 lead in running their winning streak to five in a row in game number one of the doubleheader. Gus Keriazakos, on the mound for the Herd, pitched two scoreless innings before giving up a pair of runs in the third. Another shutout inning followed, and then the roof fell in when Keriazakos couldn't retire a batter in the fifth.

All told, Gus gave up eight hits and three walks before John Weiss, Cavarretta's bullpen standby, was called upon. But Weiss was no mystery to the Rochester batsmen either. John was only able to retire two men. Cavarretta had to turn to Bill Froats to get the third and final out of the frame, but by then the home team had pushed five runs across the plate.

Lefthanded Rochester starter Kelton Russell held the Bisons in check until the sixth inning, when the Buffalo offense finally pushed one run across and broke a scoreless string of 19 innings. The Bisons got three more against the lefthander in the seventh. Two more Buffalo runners crossed the plate in the eighth before Rochester manager Dixie Walker went to his bullpen ace, Duke Markell.

Markell was back on his game in this afternoon contest, stopping the Buffalo onslaught and allowing only one Bison base hit over the last two frames. Cavarretta, reactivated to the roster on May 30 following John Blatnik's voluntary retirement, made his first appearance in the lineup since May 13. He pinch-hit unsuccessfully for Joe Coleman against Markell.

In game two, Fred Hahn pitched a complete game (seven innings), a six-hitter in his second straight starting role, bringing the Bisons back into the win column. Joe Brovia and Lou Ortiz each hit two home runs to provide the fireworks.

Cavarretta had sat Brovia in the first game against starter Russell's lefthanded offerings, although he had made an appearance as a pinch-hitter for Froats (unsuccessful). But Brovia was back in the lineup and batting third as the team faced off against the righthanded Cot Deal in game two. The lefthanded right fielder made the manager look good in his first at-bat, smashing a Deal fastball over the right-field fence to give the Bisons a rare first-inning lead.

While Fred Hahn was keeping Rochester scoreless, Buffalo picked up two more runs in the third. Brovia hit his second in a row, this time with Joe Caffie on base ahead of him. The Herd went up 4-0 the next inning. Lou Ortiz added to the long-ball attack by driving a solo blast off his former teammate over the left-field wall. Ortiz did it again the next inning, making it a three-run fifth by homering for the second time. Brovia and Easter scored ahead of him. With the score 7-0 in Buffalo's favor, Deal's hand had been played for the night and was found wanting.

Rochester got a run off Hahn in the bottom of the fifth on back-to-back doubles by Ed Phillips and Dick Rand. They added two more in the sixth when Gary Geiger, Deal's pitching replacement and a lefthander, drew a walk and moved to second on single by Ed Kasko. Stan Jok's long single with two outs—he slipped rounding first and had to hold at that base—plated Geiger and Kasko. Buffalo added an insurance run in the seventh on Caffie and Easter singles.

BISON TALES: The loss in the first game was the Herd's third in a row, but a bright spot was Billy DeMars' return to the lineup. Billy's three RBIs were his best one-game showing in that category in the season.

Brovia's long balls in game two, his third and fourth home runs of the year, gave the Bisons a much-needed lift. Joe's average had slumped to .218 and he had been riding the bench prior to this outburst. For defensive purposes, Cavarretta sent Peanuts Lowrey in to play left field in the seventh and shifted Joe Caffie to right to take Brovia's position.

Lou Ortiz picked up his fifth and sixth home runs of the year in a ballpark where he had starred from 1950 through 1954.

Fred Hahn's outing reflected the command noted in his previous long relief stints that had won him a spot In the starting rotation.

The Bisons had another day off on Monday to allow them to fly down to Havana to start a series there on Tuesday. The extra day would help the catching situation. Heyman caught both games after Tomkinson's injury on Saturday and could use the rest. Tomkinson hoped to be ready to play in a few days.

In the meanwhile, third baseman Bill Serena had spoken to Cavarretta and had offered to do some catching to spell Heyman. Bill had gone behind the plate for a number of games in the low minors when his managers were looking at the best position to get his potent bat into the lineup. He caught batting practice today and convinced Cavarretta he could handle it as a fill-in. The manager would then send Castiglione to third base if Serena took up the receiver position. DeMars was back at shortstop and started two double plays in game two.

The alternative was to recall Don McAndrews from Eastern League Syracuse. This would mean placing Tomkinson on the 10-day disabled list, something Cavarretta was loath to do. In addition, McAndrews was hitting poorly in Single A ball and was unlikely to hit the kind of pitching he would see two levels higher.

Buffalo was 10½ games behind first-place Montreal, but only 10 percentage points in arrears of sixth-place Richmond. A Bison win in Havana on Tuesday, coupled with a Virginian loss, would move the Herd into sixth place, one game ahead of the Vees, and pad their lead over Havana to 4½ games.

Monday, June 4, Travel Day Off: Rochester to Havana

For reasons unknown to anyone, Fred Hahn was bumped from the Bisons' flight from Rochester to New York City en route for the three-game Havana series. Hahn had to take a later plane, and by the time he arrived in New York the club had already left for Cuba. He finally caught up with the team on the island.

Game 44—Tuesday, June 5, Havana, Cuba: Havana 10, Buffalo 6

Joe Brovia's second pair of home runs in two consecutive games
was not enough to bring the Herd back from an early 10-2 hole.

Game 44 – June 5, 1956

Buffalo	002 000 202 –	6	13	1
Havana	205 300 00x –	10	12	0
WP – Sanchez (3-3)	LP – Weiss (0-2)			

Red Donovan had a short night: a hit batter and three singles, including Nino Escalera's two-run blow, in one-third of an inning. John Weiss came in to stop the assault. Joe Caffie's single and Joe Brovia's two-run shot to right off Havana's Jerry Lane tied it at 2-2 in the third.

The Sugar Kings got to Weiss in the bottom of the frame. Two men were in and two on when Cavarretta called in Joe Coleman to face Woody Smith. The Havana third baseman blasted a three-run homer to put the Cubans up by five. They added three more in the fourth off Coleman as Escalera hit a two-run roundtripper of his own.

Brovia's second homer of the night, again with Caffie in front of him, carried over the centerfield wall, some 450 feet away. Earlier in the game, Easter had just missed a home run to that same spot. He wound up with a double, but the Bisons could not bring him in.

Buffalo's last chance was to load the bases with two out in the ninth. Pete Castiglione's single scored George Bullard and Caffie, but Bill Serena's pinch-hit effort was stopped by Vicente Amor, Havana's fourth pitcher of the night.

BISON TALES: Cavarretta wondered about the humidity in Havana taking the edge off his hurlers' deliveries and affecting their stamina. Havana manager Nap Reyes was using his staff in "relays," short stints on the mound as a means of beating the heat.

Brovia wanted back in the starting lineup and had turned around his hitting in the past two games to get there. Tomkinson continued on the bench due to the spike wound and was not likely to play in Havana. His stiches would be removed when the club reached Richmond on Friday, June 8, with an assessment of his status at that time.

Buffalo (18-25, .419) was in seventh place in the standings, only 10 percentage points behind sixth-place Richmond (21-29, .429). A Buffalo win coupled with a Richmond loss would move the Herd into sixth position.

In International League news: Toronto hurler Don Johnson threw a seven-inning no-hitter against the Columbus Jets in Columbus, winning 2-0.

Game 45—Wednesday, June 6, Havana, Cuba: Havana 13, Buffalo 0

It was Buffalo's worst defeat of the year, with Havana amassing 18 hits off four
Bison pitchers and scoring eight times in the eighth.

Game 45 – June 6, 1956

Buffalo	000 000 000 – 0	4 0
Havana	100 301 08x – 13	18 0

WP – Scantlebury (3-1)   LP – Bowman (3-5)

The Bisons only managed four hits: two from Luke Easter and one each from Lou Ortiz and Bill Serena, back in the lineup this evening at third base. Otherwise, Cuban pitcher Pat Scantlebury was in complete control. In contrast, Buffalo's Roger Bowman was in trouble early and often.

Bowman was lucky to hold the Sugar Kings to one run in the first after giving up three base hits. He stranded more runners in the second and third but was finally reached for three more scores in the fourth. Two men were on base with singles when Scantlebury sliced a ball off the diving Ortiz's glove that went for a triple down the right-field line. The inning's fourth hit, this one from Hal Bevan, brought Scantlebury home.

Joe Coleman was the Herd's only bright spot. Bowman had gotten an out in the sixth frame but then gave up three straight base knocks to Don Nicholas, Pablo Bernard and Bevan to produce the fifth run against him. Coleman stopped the Cubans cold for an inning and two-thirds. After he went out for a pinch-hitter, the Sugar King bats opened up once more.

Bill Froats and Larry Donovan were battered in the eight-run eighth. Froats had pitched well in recent relief outings, but not tonight. He faced six men, allowing four hits and one walk and hitting Juan Delis with a pitch. Donovan took over and fared only slightly better. He got the side out, but not before he saw three runners charged to him (a baserunner from a fielder's choice, a walk and a hit) cross the plate. Froats was charged with five runs in zero innings pitched as he had been unable to retire a man. It was the worst inning the Bisons had suffered all year.

BISON TALES: Serena played third and hit the ball crisply, hopefully a sign that he was coming out of his slump. Pete Castiglione was once more at shortstop because Billy DeMars' arm was ailing yet again. According to Cavarretta, the team needed another catcher, another shortstop and an effective relief pitcher in order to make it out of the second division. A stomach ailment kept Caffie out of this night's starting lineup.

Cavarretta planned to throw Karl Drews against Havana in a bid to win the final game of the series, calling Drews the club's "stopper." Rumor had it that several major league scouts would be on hand to watch Drews' effort. The Detroit Tigers, the Chicago White Sox and the Baltimore Orioles were all hurting for pitching and might look to purchase the big righthander.

Drews was an eight-year major league veteran who had last pitched for the Philadelphia Phillies and the Cincinnati Redlegs in 1954. In that year, he put together a 5-4 record as a starter and reliever. Cavarretta said he would not part with Drews without getting at least four players in return who could help the Buffalo squad.

Game 46—Thursday, June 7, Havana, Cuba: Buffalo 5, Havana 4

*Karl Drews came through in his "stopper" role, going seven innings,
with John Weiss coming on to preserve the win.*

Game 46 – June 7, 1956

Buffalo	200 021 000 – 5	4	1
Havana	011 010 100 – 4	9	0

WP – Drews (6-3)   LP – Rabe (3-7)

For the second night in a row, Buffalo managed only four hits, but the blows were timely. The first one was Lou Ortiz's eighth home run of the year in the first inning, scoring Joe Brovia ahead of him. Brovia had picked up the first of the five walks Havana starter Charlie Rabe would concede in his less than five innings.

Havana got back in the ballgame when Nino Escalera hit a solo home run in the second inning and Juan Delis doubled home a runner in the third to tie it. Buffalo regained the lead with another pair of markers in the fifth, thanks to continued wildness from Cuban pitching.

Rabe got the first two batters, Lou Heyman and Drews, but then walked George Bullard. Peanuts Lowrey got the inning's only hit, a single that moved Bullard to third. Rabe fell behind Brovia and wound up walking him to load the bases. Yet another base on balls to Ortiz sent Bullard home to break the tie. Havana manager Nap Reyes turned to Rudy Minarcin to relieve Rabe, but Minarcin encountered similar troubles. Bill Serena stepped in against the reliever and he, too, benefitted from a walk. It was the fourth free pass of the inning and it scored Lowrey. The third out came when Luke Easter went down on strikes.

The Sugar Kings got one back in their half of the fifth as Nino Escalera sent a run-scoring single into center to make the score 4-3. But the Bisons added to their lead in their next at-bat. It was another story of walks with two outs. Billy DeMars and Lou Heyman both fanned, but Minarcin put Drews on base with a free pass. Bullard walked to follow him. Lowrey also walked to load the bases. Joe Hatten was called to the mound. But he then walked Brovia and Drews came home. It was to be Buffalo's final run of the night and, as it turned out, the game winner. Ortiz bounced into a fielder's choice to end the inning.

Hatten held Buffalo in check for the rest of the game. He gave up a base hit and walked only one more man. The Sugar Kings got a run back in the home half of the seventh on a Juan Delis run-scoring ground out. Drews finished the inning, but Cavarretta felt his hurler was suffering from the heat and brought in John Weiss to pitch the eighth and ninth frames. Weiss was up to the task, keeping the Sugar Kings off the scoreboard and allowing only one base hit.

BISON TALES: The victory moved the Herd into sole possession of sixth place, 11 percentage points ahead of Richmond. Buffalo's record was now 19 wins and 26 defeats, a winning percentage of .422. Richmond, with 21 wins and 30 losses, had a winning percentage of .411. The Bisons would next face off against fifth-place Miami for a four-game series. The Marlins were three games up on Buffalo with 23 victories and 24 defeats. A Buffalo sweep would take over fifth place from the Marlins.

THE MINORS VERSUS THE MAJORS: II
Thursday, June 7, Buffalo

While the ball club was on the road squaring off against its International League rivals, the front office was also out of town. General manager John Stiglmeier and business manager Harry Bisgeier had traveled to New York City to meet with the commissioner of baseball, Ford C. Frick. The ball team was striving for victories on the field. Management was seeking a win that would make available more able bodies for the lineup.

In a Special to the Courier-Express (printed on June 8, 1956), general manager John C. Stiglmeier was quoted: "We left the meeting with [baseball commissioner Ford Frick with] high hopes that Mr. Frick's personal prestige can produce the reinforcements our club needs." Stiglmeier and Bisgeier had met with Frick for almost three hours on June 7. A spokesman for the commissioner categorized the meeting as "very pleasant" and focused solely on the needs of minor league baseball.

The commissioner's office issued the following statement:

"Representatives of the Buffalo International League baseball club today [June 7] conferred with commissioner Ford Frick and explained the plight of their community-owned baseball club to obtain player help from the major league clubs.

"John Stiglmeier and Harry Bisgeier of the Buffalo club appeared accompanied by George Trautman, president of the National Association, and Frank Shaughnessy, president of the International League.

"The commissioner expressed sympathy with the Buffalo officials and at the end of the session that lasted for almost three hours the commissioner assured Messrs. Stiglmeier and Bisgeier that he would make every effort to help them solve their problems."

The spokesman noted that the commissioner was without power to direct major league owners to send players to the minor leagues. However, he had pledged to undertake to speak with the major league clubs and encourage them to allocate some of their player personnel to struggling minor league operations.

Stiglmeier realized that the commissioner's powers were limited as had been stated, but he believed that he had also demonstrated to Frick that several major league organizations had reneged on their promises and that the full extent of the contract by which Detroit had sold the team to the community had not been fully met. Frick asked for a copy of the contract.

The wheels were turning, but very slowly. Baseball did not easily embrace changes that could infringe upon the owners' nearly absolute control of a very tightly run operation.

Game 47—Friday, June 8, Miami, Florida: Miami 8, Buffalo 0

Young Don Cardwell crushed Buffalo's hopes for advancement
in the league standings with a three-hit, nine-strikeout performance.

Game 47 – June 8, 1956
Buffalo   000 000 000 – 0 3 0
Miami   000 030 05x – 8 9 2
WP – Cardwell (6-0)   LP – Nicholas (1-4)

Harry Nicholas pitched well through six innings but received no offensive support. Meanwhile, the 20-year-old Cardwell escaped a bases-loaded first inning and only got tougher. George Bullard and Joe Caffie drew walks to start the contest, but Cardwell settled down to retire Luke Easter and Joe Brovia. He pitched around the hot-hitting Lou Ortiz to yield his third free pass of the frame and load the bases. Bill Serena went down on strikes to end the inning. Cardwell did not walk another batter the rest of the game.

Bullard and Caffie got on base again to start the visitor half of the third inning, but Easter became a strikeout victim, Brovia sent a harmless fly to the outfield for out number two, and Ortiz grounded out. Two more men left on base.

The Marlins broke through against Nicholas in the fifth. Bob Micelotta reached him for a single and was followed by another one-baser by Jim Command. Cardwell came up with the big blow of the inning, a triple to right that eluded Brovia and rolled to the wall. A sacrifice fly by Cal Abrams scored Cardwell.

Manager Cavarretta pinch-hit unsuccessfully for Nicholas in the seventh, bringing Bill Froats to the mound. The Miami bats got to Froats in the eighth. Ben Tompkins singled. Froats walked Ed Bouchee. Bob Bowman popped out, but a Moose Johnson double scored Tompkins, and when Froats loaded the bases on a free pass to Glen Gorbous, Joe Coleman was called in to pitch. Joe was greeted by Micelotta with a two-run double to make the score 6-0. Cardwell's second extra-base hit of the night, this time a double, plated Gorbous and Micelotta. The Bisons went down quietly in the ninth.

BISON TALES: After Buffalo's ninth shutout of the year, Cavarretta was bemoaning the lack of a consistent cleanup hitter. The Herd had left 10 men on base in the series finale in Havana, and now nine more in this contest.

Lou Ortiz's six-game hitting streak was ended tonight although he continued to hit the ball sharply. He had gone 9 for 21, a .428 average with three home runs and seven RBIs.

Buffalo again encountered difficulties flying out of Cuba. The first flight had to turn back after 20 minutes when the pilot discovered he could not retract the wheels. Clearance to land was received after circling the airport four or five times. Looking down, the players could see ambulances gathered for a possible emergency.

A second plane's departure was delayed when it was noted that one of the engines was on fire. It took three hours before yet a third plane could take off, but for some reason Pat Tomkinson, Joe Caffie and Gus Keriazakos couldn't fly with the rest of the team. They had to take a later flight.

Game 48—Saturday, June 9, Miami, Florida: Miami 10, Buffalo 3

Buffalo left an even dozen on the basepaths as, again, timely hitting went missing.
Miami made 12 hits count for 10 runs.

Game 48 – June 9, 1956
Buffalo   000 020 001 – 3 7 0
Miami   030 041 11x – 10 12 1
WP – Greenwood (1-0)   LP Keriazakos (3-5)

Gus Keriazakos started for Buffalo and was the victim of his own wildness. He loaded the bases in the bottom of the second on three walks, bringing up Miami catcher Gus Niarhos. In a struggle of Gus versus Gus, Greek versus Greek, Niarhos won, clearing the sacks with a double. Miami took a 3-0 lead.

The Bisons made it momentarily close by scoring twice in the top half of the fifth. Held to two singles over four innings by lefty Seth Morehead, George Bullard slammed a leadoff double into left center field and scored moments later on a Peanuts Lowrey line single. When Joe Brovia also drove a double to the right center field wall to score Lowrey, Morehead's day was finished and Buffalo had the tying run on second.

Reliever Bob Greenwood took over and got Lou Ortiz on strikes, and then Bill Serena on a ground out to short. He walked Luke Easter to set up a force play, walked Pete Castiglione unintentionally and finally ended the inning by inducing a popup from Lou Heyman. The Herd left the bases loaded.

The first three men Keriazakos faced in the fifth solved him for base hits. Cavarretta called in John Weiss, but the Marlins continued with two more safeties, making it five in a row. Miami rang up four scores before Weiss could retire the side. The Marlins added single runs off Weiss over the next two innings. Bill Froats got the call for the eighth and was tagged for a solo home run shot by Bob Bowman.

Buffalo scored one run off Greenwood in the ninth. Bullard's double and Lowrey's short single put runners on first and third with one out. Bullard scored on an Ed Bouchee error at first on Brovia's grounder. Greenwood then got Lou Ortiz on a fly out, walked Bill Serena and got Easter to ground out to first to end the ballgame.

BISON TALES: Greenwood had set down 11 men in a row until Bullard's double in the ninth.

Buffalo signed new outfielder Ed Mierkowicz from the Columbus Jets. Mierkowicz had started the year with Miami, was traded to Columbus and now had been purchased by the Herd.

Ed was first signed to a baseball contract by Buffalo general manager John C. Stiglmeier back in 1944 at the recommendation of Detroit super scout Wish Egan. Mierkowicz hit .303 with 21 home runs for the Herd in 1945. In 1946, he hit .324 and 10 homers. He was a member of the 1945 World Series Championship Tigers and also saw brief duty with that club again in 1947 and 1948. He appeared in one game with the St. Louis Cardinals in 1950. Measuring 6 feet, 4 inches, tall and 205 pounds, Ed was a .300 Triple A hitter in 1953 and 1954 but had registered only a .256 mark in 1955.

Games 49 and 50—Sunday, June 10, Miami, Florida: Buffalo 5, Miami 3; Miami 3, Buffalo 2

Buffalo won the first game of the doubleheader behind
Larry (Red) Donovan, with relief help from "money pitcher" Karl Drews.

Game 49 – June 10, 1956 (first game of doubleheader)

| Buffalo | 000 000 500 – 5 8 0 |
| Miami | 000 000 030 – 3 6 2 |

WP – Donovan (2-1)   LP – Qualters (3-3)

Game 50 – June 10, 1956 (second game of doubleheader)

| Buffalo | 010 100 0 – 2 3 0 |
| Miami | 100 010 1 – 3 5 0 |

WP – Paige (4-2)   LP – Hahn (2-2)

In the first game, all the runs came in the seventh and eighth innings. Until that point, Donovan and his mound opponent, Tom Qualters, had been in command of the batters. A two-hour rain delay between the fifth and sixth innings may have been a factor in the outcome, leaving the footing uncertain.

Buffalo went on top first, scoring all of their runs in the visitor half of the seventh. Lou Heyman, struggling of late, blooped a hit into left field to start the inning and was replaced on the basepaths by Peanuts Lowrey. Donovan sacrificed the runner to second. Miami starter Qualters then had trouble finding the plate. George Bullard drew a walk. Joe Caffie was an easy fly out, but then Qualters walked Luke Easter to load the bases. Joe Brovia's hot shot up the middle was knocked down by shortstop Bob Micelotta, who threw wildly to second base as he was falling. The play was ruled a base hit and an error, with Lowrey scoring on the single and Bullard racing home on the errant throw. Easter wound up on third and Brovia on second as the Marlins threw to the plate in a vain attempt to catch Bullard.

Lou Ortiz, zero for five yesterday hitting in the cleanup position, but batting fifth tonight, came through with a single to left center that cashed Easter and moved Brovia to third. Miami looked to be out of it, but a Pete Castiglione grounder to Ben Tompkins was mishandled by the Miami second baseman and Brovia scored and Ortiz was safe at second. Lowrey, who had scored the inning's first run, came up for his first at-bat of the day. Miami manager Don Osborn made a pitching change, calling for Thornton Kipper.

Lowrey clipped a single over short to send Ortiz home and give Donovan a five-run lead. The Bisons needed all of those runs. Miami staged their own big inning in the bottom of the eighth.

Cal Abrams collected a one-out base hit that fell in front of Lowrey, now playing left. Tompkins followed with a double that put runners on second and third. Ed Bouchee, the next batter, turned on a Donovan delivery and sent it over the right-field fence. Cavarretta went to the mound and called to the bullpen.

Karl Drews, the "stopper," pitched scoreless ball for the remainder of the game. He walked two but did not allow a hit. It was Buffalo's first win in this four-game series.

A second game win for the Herd wasn't to be. In a low-hitting contest, a disputed double by Gus Niarhos and a hit batsman by Fred Hahn gave Miami the winning margin. Cavarretta was upset with the umpiring, but also with too many strikeouts by his team and not enough hitting with men on base.

Miami had taken the lead in the bottom of the first on a walk to Abrams, an infield out by Ben Tompkins and Bouchee's run-scoring single, but Buffalo came right back to tie it in the second on a fit of continued Marlin wildness. Gene Snyder was on the mound for Miami and gave up a single to Bill Serena. After getting Luke Easter on a fly ball, he then issued three straight walks to Pete Castiglione, Pat Tomkinson and Hahn. Serena's run knotted the game at 1-1, but no one could come up with the bases-loaded hit to break the game open. Angelo LiPetri came in for Snyder and closed the door on any further scoring.

Easter put the Bisons up by a run in the top of the fourth, sending a LiPetri pitch over the left center field scoreboard, 400 feet away. The lead lasted until the Marlins had their at-bats in the bottom of the fifth. Cal Abrams waited out a base on balls. Tompkins singled him to third. Bouchee's single brought him home with the tying run.

Satchel Paige relieved for the Marlins in the sixth inning. It was the first chance the Bisons had to see him this season. The ageless mound wizard retired the Herd in order for two innings, keeping them hitless and fanning four. Then he helped win the game with his bat.

Gus Niarhos was credited with a double down the left-field line that was ruled fair by plate umpire Frank Guzzetta. Cavarretta protested to no avail that the ball had hooked foul. Marlins manager Don Osborn let Paige hit for himself, and the lanky senior hurler blooped a base hit into left that had Niarhos holding at second. A ground out by Abrams moved the runners up one base and Cavarretta called for an intentional walk to Tompkins to set up a force at the plate. The plans went awry when Hahn nicked Bouchee on the forearm with his three-and-one pitch and Niarhos trotted home to score the game winner.

BISON TALES: Cavarretta was steamed about the outcome in the dressing room afterwards. Niarhos' ball was clearly foul, he said. He was also unhappy about the Bisons' paltry three hits, although one of them was Easter's 10th home run.

A chartered plane would bring the team home at 1:00 a.m., happy to be done with a road trip that saw them win three and lose eight. With the doubleheader split, Buffalo held onto its sixth-place position. Havana divided its two games against Rochester, as did Richmond against the Maple Leafs. The Bisons were one game ahead of Richmond and 2 1/2 in front of Havana.

Toronto, in first position, was 12 1/2 games distant. Fifth-place Miami had a 4½-game lead on the Bisons. The Columbus Jets were a game ahead of Miami and occupied fourth place in the first division, where the Bisons wanted to be.

Buffalo had a .408 winning percentage, based on 20 games won and 29 lost. The Herd also had a 5-1 lead over Toronto in the suspended 28th game of the season. That game looked like a win, but Toronto had the bases loaded with no one out in the bottom of the seventh and final frame.

Monday, June 11, Travel Day Off: Miami to Buffalo

Air travel was giving the Bisons as much trouble off the diamond as their opponents were on the field. On Sunday evening the club had to endure a last-minute rush to the Miami airport to catch their 1:00 a.m. Monday morning flight. The team had spent nine and a half hours at the Miami stadium to get in the rain-delayed doubleheader and barely had time to grab a bite to eat before busing to the airport. This flight to Washington, D.C., was uneventful, but motor trouble caused an hour's delay before the second plane could depart for Buffalo. Most of the men were unable to catch any shuteye.

Ed Mierkowicz would be joining the club on this day, and Cavarretta had plans to install him in left field and perhaps in the cleanup spot in the batting order. The move would allow Peanuts Lowrey to come in to play third base and give Bill Serena some time off until his thumb healed from the sprain sustained in the 16th game of the season. Pete Castiglione would shift to shortstop for Billy DeMars, allowing DeMars time to heal up from his ongoing arm problems. Cavarretta also would look at Mierkowicz's skills around the first-base bag. If he could do the job there, he might replace Easter when the Bisons were facing a lefthanded thrower.

It had been a disastrous road trip for the Herd, winning three games and dropping eight. Opponents outscored the Bisons by 30 runs, 69 to 39. The team endured three shutouts and lost three out of four one-run contests. From the mound, Drews won one game and saved another. Hahn and Donovan picked up the other victories.

Brovia led the club with four home runs on the trip but they came in two consecutive games, only one of which the team won. He scored seven times, drove home nine men and batted .275. Easter hit .324 and added two homers. Ortiz drove in 10 men and slugged three out of the park. Other than Easter and Brovia, only Lowrey (.269) hit over .250 in the 11 away games.

Injuries had been hurting the club on offense and defense. The pitching that was the club's strength in the early going had declined sharply, perhaps in part as a result of the defensive woes and Cavarretta's inability to find a cleanup hitter who could cash in the baserunners. Timely hitting would have allowed Cavarretta to go longer with his effective starters if the Buffalo batsmen had produced earlier in the games. The team had been in or near double-digit figures in men left stranded in many of their contests.

The production expected from Bill Serena's bat had been absent following his thumb injury. It was hampering him both in the field and at the bat. He hit only .100 on the road trip just ended. Behind the plate, Pat Tomkinson had now missed more than a dozen games due to various injuries. His hot start at the plate had cooled off considerably. Injuries had affected his timing as he was favoring the foot that had been sliced open in Rochester. Lou Heyman was pressed into everyday service on the road trip, and the heat and humidity in Cuba and Florida took their toll on the big man. He was only able to muster a .149 average in those 11 outings.

The key to the infield defense, Billy DeMars, had missed 18 games due to injury and had only been able to pinch-hit on three occasions. Pete Castiglione had filled in admirably, but DeMars' arm and range at shortstop were sorely missed. Everyday play was tiring Castiglione, and he could use a rest. George Bullard and Joe Caffie were usually reliable ball hawks, but Joe Brovia's defensive limitations were not being offset by his bat output. Cavarretta was substituting for him in the field in the late innings and had been platooning him against righthanders.

In International League news: Easter's chief rival for the league home run crown, Montreal's

Rocky Nelson, had been called up by Brooklyn. In 49 games Rocky was hitting .394 with 12 home runs and 37 RBIs. And, thanks in part to Nelson's perpetual assault on International League pitchers, Montreal was in first place. How the callup would affect the Royals' status at the top of the chart remained to be seen.

Club Statistics: 50 Games (including Game 28)

Pitchers	W	L	ERA	Notes
Drews	6	4	3.30	Club leader with 4 complete games, 1 save
Bowman	3	5	3.21	Little run support in his outings
Keriazakos	3	5	4.04	Could be 5-3 with support in earlier games
Donovan	2	1	2.30	Leading 5-1 in suspended Game 28
Hahn	2	2	4.24	Effective reliever moved to a starter role
Coleman	1	0	2.45	Most effective reliever on the team
Froats	1	3	8.16	Inconsistent control as starter or reliever
Nicholas	1	4	4.65	Ineffective starter in last 5 outings
Weiss	0	2	5.00	Ineffective reliever in last 5 outings

Hitters	G	AB	R	H	HR	BI	Avg
Easter	49	170	23	45	11	25	.264
Castiglione	36	104	5	27	0	7	.259
Tomkinson	30	81	6	21	1	4	.259
Ortiz	49	170	26	43	8	31	.252
Caffie	27	99	18	25	2	7	.252
Bullard	50	196	28	49	1	8	.250
Cavarretta	14	17	3	4	1	4	.235
Brovia	42	116	11	27	6	24	.232
DeMars	34	106	11	24	0	5	.226
Lowrey	40	98	12	22	1	13	.224
Serena	44	144	18	27	5	17	.187
Heyman	31	78	7	13	4	13	.166

Stolen bases: Bullard 14; Caffie 4.

Games 51 and 52—Tuesday, June 12, Buffalo: Buffalo 4, Havana 3; Havana 3, Buffalo 0

New Bison Ed Mierkowicz's bat and legs helped the Herd to a
come-from-behind triumph in the seven-inning opening game.

Game 51 – June 12, 1956 (first game of doubleheader)

Havana	000 201 0 – 3	7	0
Buffalo	001 000 3 – 4	7	1

WP – Bowman (4-5)   LP – Amor (2-2)

Game 52 – June 12, 1956 (second game of doubleheader)

Havana	000 200 010 – 3	6	0
Buffalo	000 000 000 – 0	7	0

WP – Gross (1-2)   LP – Drews (6-5)

In game one, Buffalo gave Roger Bowman a one-run lead in the third inning. Peanuts Lowrey singled off lefthander Charley Rabe to start the frame, moved to second on an infield out and came home on a two-out base hit off the bat of Pete Castiglione. The Sugar Kings bounced back to take the lead in their at-bat in the fourth.

Center fielder Nino Escalera roped a single off Bowman for one of his three safe blows in the game. Woody Smith, next man up, sent a line shot over the left center field wall to put the Cubans up by one. Pitcher Rabe helped his own cause in the sixth when he solved Bowman for a single. A base knock by Don Nicholas sent Rabe to third, and he scored from there when the Bisons turned a Castiglione to Ortiz to Easter double play. The threat of a big inning was erased, and the stage was set for the seventh-inning Mierkowicz heroics.

Rabe, tiring, gave up a leadoff single to Pete Castiglione to start the seventh. Lou Heyman doubled off the left-field wall just inside the line to send Castiglione to third. Harry Nicholas went in to run for Heyman and Cavarretta sent Mierkowicz up to pinch-hit, his first appearance in the Buffalo lineup. Havana manager Nap Reyes countered by bringing in righthander Vicente Amor to face Mierkowicz.

The outfielder's best days had been with Buffalo in 1944 and 1945 as a 20- and 21-year-old, but two subsequent beanings had short-circuited what had promised to be a solid career. The beaning as a Rochester outfielder in July 1951 resulted in a fractured skull that cost him the rest of that season.

Amor got two quick strikes, but his next pitch was too close to the plate and Mierkowicz smashed a high fly ball to left that struck the screen and just missed being a game-winning home run. Castiglione scored, but Nicholas was held up at third by Cavarretta, the manager not wanting to risk the tying run being thrown out at the plate. Mierkowicz, at second, represented the winning run.

Amor walked George Bullard to load the bases, looking for the force at the plate and a double play if possible. Instead, his control abandoned him, and he wound up walking Peanuts Lowrey to drive home Nicholas with the tying score. The sacks were full of Bisons and veteran Joe Hatten was called on to pitch to Joe Brovia. With a ground-ball pitcher on the hill, Havana pulled the infield in, looking for the home to first double play. Instead, Brovia sent a drive to right center field for the game-winning sacrifice fly. Mierkowicz tagged and easily beat the throw to home.

It was a thrilling win to reward the 4353 fans who had come out to watch the hometown heroes.

In game two, staff stalwart Karl Drews pitched well enough to win, but there were no similar last-inning heroics to pull out the victory. Buffalo's hopes ended with a broken bat.

Havana had whacked Bison pitching for 39 hits in the previous three-game series in Cuba, but in today's first game Bowman had yielded only seven. In the nightcap, Karl Drews limited the Sugar Kings to but four in his seven frames on the hill. Unfortunately for Drews, one of those was a two-run home run off the bat of Ultus Alvarez in the fourth inning.

Sugar King starter Don Gross was almost as stingy as Drews. The Bisons managed six hits off him in the seven-plus innings he worked but couldn't push over even one run. Moreover, the lefthander was possessed of a wicked fastball in this evening game that saw him fanning a total of 11 Buffalo hitters.

Pat Tomkinson had batted unsuccessfully for Drews in the seventh inning and Cavarretta sent John Weiss to the mound to keep the Cubans close. Instead, Havana manufactured a third run in the eighth on a pair of singles and two stolen bases. Don Nicholas sent a bouncer back through the box and into center field to put himself on base. He then stole second, and then he stole third against the Bison battery. Hal Bevan's one-baser to right made the score Havana 3, Buffalo 0.

Gross gave up a one-out single to Peanuts Lowrey in the eighth, followed by a two-out double to Lou Ortiz. That was enough for Havana manager Nap Reyes. He called on the righthanded Rudy Minarcin to relieve, and at first it looked like Buffalo was going to make it two comebacks in a row.

Minarcin walked Bill Serena, the first man to face him, bringing up Luke Easter with the bases full. The Bison first baseman delivered a long drive deep to right center that everyone thought was surely a home run, but the ball suddenly died and fell into center fielder Nicholas's glove near the scoreboard for the inning's third out. Heading back to the bench to pick up his glove for the ninth inning, a disgusted Easter tossed aside the bat that now sported a new, long crack down the barrel.

Pete Castiglione managed a single off Minarcin to open the last of the ninth, but he was left stranded. The Bisons had been shut out for the 11th time this season. They had left another 10 men on the basepaths.

Bison Tales: Pat Tomkinson's foot split open again in practice and he was ordered to give it a rest for at least three games. Even so, Cavarretta had to send him up to hit for Drews in the seventh to put a righthanded batter in against Gross' lefthanded delivery. Tomkinson's bouncer to second was an easy putout.

The club got word following the ballgame that Brooklyn was making a loan of infielder Jimmy Clark to help with the shortstop problem while DeMars was out of the lineup.

THE MINORS VERSUS THE MAJORS: III
Tuesday, June 12, Buffalo

On June 12, the Bisons announced that they had acquired Jimmy Clark from the Brooklyn farm system to help with the shortstop situation. Clark, a singles-hitting 28-year-old, had made the Double A Texas League All-Star team in 1955 with Oklahoma City when he hit at a .289 clip.

General manager Stiglmeier reported that he had heard from two major league general managers who previously had not been returning his calls. He had also heard from at least half a dozen more who had expressed new awareness of Buffalo's situation and a new willingness to help—not the case prior to the meeting with baseball commissioner Frick.

In addition to Stiglmier's and Bisgeier's efforts on behalf of the Bisons, word was received that Vincent M. McNamara, president of the PONY League, was going to ask George C. Trautman, president of the National Association of Baseball Clubs, and baseball commissioner Frick for the creation of a $100,000 emergency relief fund to assist minor league teams struggling to stay afloat. The same terrible spring weather that had cancelled ballgames for the Bisons had also affected McNamara's teams. They had lost irrecoverable revenue from games that had been sunk by the weather.

"The fund would be used at the discretion of the National Association president to assist leagues making application for assistance with the unanimous approval of league directors involved," McNamara had commented to the Buffalo Evening News. A representative of the National Association president would investigate applications and file a report within 72 hours.

McNamara was calling for his proposal to be put to a vote by the National Association members, noting that two of his PONY League members—Hamilton, Ontario, and Bradford, Pennsylvania—had had to cease play and withdraw from the league after only a dozen games had been played. He added that the six surviving league members were also in desperate straits.

National Association president Trautman responded that he was aware that a number of leagues were facing dire consequences, but he was not optimistic that any substantive plan to assist could be formulated for the 1956 season.

The wheels of organized baseball appeared to be organized to move very slowly.

Game 53—Wednesday, June 13, Buffalo: Havana 4, Buffalo 0

The Bisons were shut out for the second consecutive ballgame.
Righthander Jerry Lane's darting slider held them to four hits.

Game 53 – June 13, 1956

Havana	000 011 200 – 4	10	0
Buffalo	000 000 000 – 0	5	2
WP – Lane (5-1)	LP – Nicholas (1-5)		

Cavarretta had stacked his lineup with three lefty hitters in a row—Joe Caffie, Joe Brovia and Luke Easter. The trio accounted for one walk.

Harry Nicholas, the Bison pitcher, matched Lane zero for zero until the fifth inning, when right fielder Don Nicholas, all 5 feet, 7 inches, and 150 pounds of him, took advantage of the short Offermann fences and popped a home run down the line in right, 297 feet away. Havana had a one-run lead. Woody Smith made it 2-0 with a more robust shot in the sixth, this one to left. The Cubans finally chased Nicholas in the seventh.

Pablo Bernard singled with one down, and manager Nap Reyes called upon his third-place hitter Hal Bevan to sacrifice to set up an insurance run with two men out. The move paid off. Nino Escalera singled sharply to left center and sent Bernard across the plate. Next up, Woody Smith drove the ball into the right center field gap almost to the wall, Escalera scoring and Smith holding at second with a double. That blow finished Nicholas and brought Larry Donovan to the hill. Ultus Alvarez popped up for the third out.

No more runs were scored. Ed Mierkowicz struck out pinch-hitting for Donovan in the bottom of the frame, and Joe Coleman threw the last two innings of two-hit ball. The best offense the Bisons could manage was Castiglione's ninth-inning double. He got as far as third.

BISON TALES: Havana was using a shift against Easter that they had started in the final game of the series in Cuba the past week. Shortstop Owen Friend was stationed just to the left of the second-base bag to cut off Easter's ground balls up the middle. Luke's power was really to left center. He was now hitless in his last 12 at-bats against the Sugar Kings.

Jim Clark played shortstop in this game, allowing DeMars to go on the disabled list to give his arm time to heal properly. Clark was hitless in four trips to the plate and made an error. Cavarretta praised his skills in pregame practice, likening him to Eddie Miller when Miller was a perennial National League All-Star in the 1940s for the Boston Braves and Cincinnati Reds.

Wedding bells rang out for the Bisons today. St. Joseph's New Cathedral rectory was the site of the morning wedding of 22-year-old Larry (Red) Donovan and his 20-year-old bride, Carolyn McAlary. Bride and groom both called Ionia, Michigan, their hometown. The bride's parents, Mr. and Mrs. Lee McAlary, were attendants. The bride's father was vice president of the Ionia County National Bank. The Rt. Rev. Msgr. Francis P. Garvey officiated.

Game 54—Thursday, June 14, Buffalo: Havana 9, Buffalo 6

Buffalo broke a scoreless streak of 18 innings with a four-run first-inning outburst, only to lose on a late-inning three-run homer.

```
Game 54 – June 14, 1956
Havana          023 100 030 – 9  11  1
Buffalo         401 000 100 – 6  12  1
WP – Sanchez (2-3)        LP – Froats (1-4)
```

Gus Keriazakos was the beneficiary of the Buffalo attack. Pat Scantlebury had shut out the Herd on June 6, but George Bullard made sure that wouldn't happen tonight. Bullard drove the sixth pitch of the evening over the left-field screen for his second home run of the season. Peanuts Lowrey, batting second, reached Scantlebury for a single, as did Ed Mierkowicz, starting tonight in right field in place of Joe Brovia. Lou Ortiz kept the hit parade going. His single scored Lowrey. Luke Easter made it five in a row, adding a single to right center, good for two RBIs. The Bisons had a four-run lead and nobody out.

Scantlebury finally asserted himself and retired the side. Havana got two back in the second frame. Owen Friend parked a Keriazakos pitch over the screen in left with Woody Smith on base in front of him.

The Sugar Kings took the lead in the third. Gus walked Pablo Bernard and Juan Delis with one out. Nino Escalera grounded to Easter, who got the out at second, but Ortiz's double-play relay wasn't in time. Woody Smith took advantage and lined a ball off the wall in left to tie the ballgame. Cavarretta went to the bullpen for Joe Coleman. Ultus Alvarez, the first man he faced, ripped a single to score Smith and put Havana one up.

Easter tied it up for Buffalo in the home half of the third. His home run, number 12 of the season, flew out of the park over the right-field fence between the light standards. The tie was short lived. In the top of the fifth, Don Nicholas and Pablo Bernard hit back-to-back doubles to make it 6-5, Havana. Cavarretta again went to his bullpen, this time for Bill Froats.

Froats got Delis to end the fourth and was in full command of the Sugar Kings until the eighth inning. He fanned six men, including four in a row. Buffalo tied the ballgame and chased Scantlebury in the seventh after Lowrey singled and, two outs later, scored on Easter's one-baser. Raul Sanchez took the hill and got the third out.

Froats' curveball deserted him in the eighth. Dutch Dotterer rapped a leadoff single. Sanchez got one, too. Nicholas popped up for an out, but Bernard sent the third ball of the night over the left-field screen and the Cubans had a three-run lead. Buffalo could do nothing against Sanchez. The Sugar King hurler retired seven men in a row in the seventh, eighth and ninth frames.

BISON TALES: Tomkinson, despite the spike wound, had to catch the ninth inning after Joe Caffie had pinch-hit for Lou Heyman. A new catcher, Norm Sherry, on loan to the Herd from the Dodgers, was still traveling from Ft. Worth.

Games 55 and 56—Friday, June 15, Buffalo: Miami 10, Buffalo 2; and Miami 11, Buffalo 3

This twi-night doubleheader loss to Miami dropped the Herd
back into last place in the standings, a half-game behind Havana.

Game 55 – June 15, 1956 (first game of doubleheader)

Miami	190 000 0 –	10	14	1
Buffalo	101 000 0 –	2	2	0

WP – Spring (5-4)   LP – Donovan (2-2)

Game 56 – June 15, 1956 (second game of doubleheader)

Miami	004 030 040 –	11	9	3
Buffalo	000 000 003 -	3	7	2

WP – Qualters (4-3)   LP – Hahn (2-3)

The outcome of the first game was decided in the second inning. Newlywed Larry Donovan had allowed a Miami run in the first inning on a double to Ben Tompkins and an RBI single by Ed Bouchee. A fine running catch by George Bullard on a ball hit into right center by Bob Bowman was turned into an easy double play on the throw to Luke Easter. Bouchee had thought the ball was going to drop and was headed to third. Buffalo tied it in the bottom half of the inning against Miami's Jack Spring. Ed Mierkowicz drew a walk, moved to third on a Lou Ortiz single and scored when right fielder Bob Bowman muffed Easter's easy fly ball.

Donovan couldn't get anyone out in the second. Nine men scored. Sid Gordon walked to lead off and Larry Novak and Bob Micelotta followed with singles to load the bases. Cavarretta turned to the bullpen. Roger Bowman took over the mound, but the first two men to face him, Jim Command and pitcher Spring, also hit singles to produce two runs and keep the bases full. The first out was registered when Cal Abrams went down on strikes, but then Tompkins walked to drive in a run and Bouchee singled for two more and Cavarretta again had to resort to his relief crew. This time it was John Weiss, who entered to give up a single to Bob Bowman that scored Tompkins. Gordon, who had led off the inning with a walk, smacked a three-run home run to center field. Weiss retired the next two men and the worst inning Herd pitching had endured all year mercifully ended.

Buffalo got a run back in the third. Jim Clark drew a walk and Weiss singled. Clark scored as Bullard hit into a rally-killing double play.

Three home runs and nine RBIs from the Marlins' right fielder Bob Bowman highlighted game two. Buffalo fell to defeat after wasting a first-inning opportunity to break the game open against $40,000 bonus baby Tom Qualters. George Bullard drew a leadoff walk, and then Qualters added to his troubles by walking Ed Mierkowicz and Luke Easter to load the bases with one out. The next batter, Lou Ortiz, hit a sharp ground ball right at third baseman Sid Gordon. Gordon stepped on the bag to force Mierkowicz and threw on to Bouchee for the inning-ending double play.

Fred Hahn was the victim of his own wildness and Bob Bowman's potent home run bat in the third. Cal Abrams, Bouchee and Gordon had all drawn walks to load the bases. Bowman unloaded them with a drive over the left center field wall, his second grand slam of the year and 12th homer of the season, tying him with Easter for top honors in the league.

Three more Miami runs came in the fifth, the last two on Bowman's second homer of the night.

This one was slugged to right. Gus Keriazakos, making his first relief appearance of the season, stopped the visitors effectively for two-plus innings. Joe Coleman hurled the eighth and ninth and was hurt by his own errors and yet another long ball from Bowman. This homer, with two mates aboard, went out in left. Miami scored four times in the eighth, three of the runs unearned.

Qualters walked seven men and gave up seven hits, but the Bisons couldn't break through against him until he tired in the ninth. Peanuts Lowrey smacked a pinch-hit single to lead off. Bullard doubled for his second hit of the night and Caffie collected his first, driving home both baserunners. Mierkowicz drew his sixth walk of the evening to put men on first and second.

Easter's ground ball was turned into a force play at second, but Mierkowicz's slide upended Ben Tompkins, whose throw to first went wild. Caffie raced home on the error. By this time, Qualters was complaining of a knotted muscle in his forearm. Angelo LiPetri came in to relieve and retired Ortiz and Pete Castiglione to give the Marlins the doubleheader sweep.

BISON TALES: Buffalo left 12 men on base in game two. The three, four and five hitters managed one hit in game one, none in game two. Mierkowicz walked three times in each game.

Joe Brovia was released to make roster room for the new catcher, Norm Sherry. Recently acquired Ed Mierkowicz gave the Bisons an adequate corps of outfielders and his glove would be an improvement over Brovia's. The critical needs still were for another catcher and a middle infielder. Tomkinson had to catch the second game instead of resting his injured foot. Heyman was exhausted from his workload.

Terrible weather had held season attendance down to 60,500, some 40,000 short of where the club had hoped to be at this time of the year.

Bob Bowman's 14 home runs had put him two ahead of Easter. Game two saw five errors.

Buffalo had now dropped five in a row for the third time this season and fallen into the cellar, one game behind the Sugar Kings. After taking three out of four from the Herd, the Sugar Kings split their doubleheader with Rochester and climbed into seventh position. Fourth-place Miami was now seven and a half games up on the Bisons.

International League Standings
June 15, 1956

	W	L	Pct.	G.B.
Montreal	38	20	.655	—
Rochester	36	23	.610	2½
Miami	31	29	.517	8
Columbus	30	28	.516	8
Toronto	28*	28	.500	9
Richmond	25	35	.416	14
Havana	24	36	.400	15
Buffalo	21*	34	.381	15½

*Not including suspended game of 5/20.

Game 57—Saturday, June 16, Buffalo: Miami 9, Buffalo 8

Buffalo's "stopper" was halted himself this evening by the
Miami run machine. The Bison losing streak reached six.

Game 57 – June 16, 1956

Miami	211 104 000 – 9	13	3
Buffalo	000 000 314 – 8	6	3

WP – Cardwell (7-1)   LP – Drews (6-6)

Again, Miami built up a huge early lead. Karl Drews was touched for eight hits and five runs in four innings. Among the blows were home runs by Ben Tompkins, Jim Command and, once again, Bob Bowman, his fourth in two days. Drews departed with no one out in the fifth.

Bill Froats got out of the fifth but was himself victimized for a big sixth inning. The Marlins scored four times thanks to errors by Jim Clark, Pat Tomkinson and Luke Easter, plus a walk and the three hits Froats gave up. Miami led 9-0.

Don Cardwell had shut the Bisons out back on June 8 in Miami and continued in that vein for six innings in this game, walking four but giving up only one base knock. Pat Tomkinson got walk number five to lead off the Buffalo seventh and the Bisons got a break when Tompkins fumbled a sure double-play grounder hit by Jim Clark.

Up to bat for Froats in a pinch-hit role, Bill Serena caught a Cardwell fastball and drilled it over the fence in dead center field for a three-run homer. It was Bill's sixth of the season and his first since May 27. Larry Donovan replaced Froats on the mound.

Luke Easter led off the eighth frame against Cardwell with a solo home run to almost the same spot as Serena's blast. Luke's number 13 put the Bisons down by five. A ninth-inning rally sent Cardwell to the showers. Clark reached base leading off on third baseman Sid Gordon's second error of the evening. Peanuts Lowrey pinch-hit for Donovan and walked on four straight balls. Thornton Kipper came in for Cardwell. He got George Bullard on strikes, but Joe Caffie poked a short single into center to load the bases. Ed Mierkowicz's double into the left-field screen scored a pair of Bisons. Enter Angelo LiPetri to pitch for Miami. Easter cracked a double of his own, to almost the same spot on the screen, making the score 9-8. With the tying run on second, the winning run at the plate and only one man out, Harry Nicholas came in to run for Easter as Lou Ortiz stepped into the batter's box. The Buffalo second baseman's drive to deep left center looked sure for extra bases, but left fielder Larry Novak made a last-second running stab of the ball for the out. Novak then spun and threw to second, catching Nicholas too far from the bag for the game-ending double play.

BISON TALES: As with the previous night's game, this contest featured plenty of home runs (five) and errors (six), plus the fatal baserunning mistake not shown in the box score.

In International League news: Toronto Maple Leaf hurler Lynn Lovenguth no-hit the visiting Richmond Virginians, 8-0.

Games 58 and 59—Sunday, June 17, Buffalo: Miami 5, Buffalo 3; Buffalo 3, Miami 2.

Miami took game one, but Roger Bowman finally hurled
Buffalo to a victory in game two to break the seven-game winless streak.

Game 58 – June 17, 1956 (first game of doubleheader)
Miami   301 000 001 – 5 9 0
Buffalo   000 000 003 – 3 8 1
WP – Farrell (2-0)   LP – Nicholas (1-6)

Game 59 – June 17, 1956 (second game of doubleheader)
Miami   011 000 0 – 2 6 0
Buffalo   012 000 x – 3 4 1
WP – Bowman (5-5)   LP – Morehead (1-6)

Falling behind early makes it difficult to win. Harry Nicholas had an unpleasant start to this contest.

Cal Abrams led off the first game with a 400-foot drive that struck the scoreboard just to the right of center and wound up at second. The smash must have unnerved Nicholas because he immediately walked Ben Tompkins and then gave up a home run ball to Ed Bouchee that sailed over the right-field fence for a quick Miami 3-0 lead. Three singles by Abrams, Tompkins and Bouchee in the third made it 4-0 and brought Fred Hahn in to pitch the fourth and try to make it close.

It was Hahn's best outing in some while, throwing five strong innings of three-hit, no-run baseball, and not allowing a baserunner beyond second. Norm Sherry made his first appearance in a Bison uniform in the eighth frame, pinch-hitting for Hahn and drawing a walk, but the Bisons were unable to score. Putting the leadoff batter on base in four of the first five innings had gotten the Herd nowhere. Miami turned four double plays to frustrate any potential rally.

The ninth inning saw Miami collect a fifth marker off Joe Coleman. Cal Abrams walked, stole second and scored his third run of the game on a two-out Moose Johnson single. John Weiss relieved Coleman to get the third out.

Down 5-0, Buffalo made a comeback in the ninth, but it was again too little, too late. Turk Farrell, on the hill for the Marlins, had given the Bisons only five hits through eight frames. Then Joe Caffie lined a single to right to start the final inning and Ed Mierkowicz coaxed a walk. The runners moved up on Luke Easter's ground out to first base. A second ground out to the right side from Lou Ortiz brought in Caffie with Buffalo's first run. Bill Serena, back in the starting lineup, slammed a ferocious drive to right center that rebounded off the concrete wall and skipped past center fielder Abrams. By the time Mel Clark in left field could track the ball down, Mierkowicz had scored easily and Serena had legged out a triple. Pete Castiglione kept the inning alive with a walk.

Satchel Paige became the new Marlin hurler, and Pat Tomkinson stepped in against him as the tying run. Tomkinson bounced a single into right field just beyond Tompkins' reach and made the score 5-3. The tying runs were now on first and second. Cavarretta went to the bench and sent Peanuts Lowrey up to hit for Weiss. Peanuts had been the hottest Buffalo hitter on the home stand (7 for 16, a .437 average, plus a walk), but as with last night the Bisons would come up short. Lowrey worked the count to 2-2, fouled off another offering, then lofted a fly ball to right that Bob Bowman circled under for the final out.

In the second game, it was Bill Serena's now-hot bat that made the difference, allowing Roger Bowman to even his record at 5-5.

George Bullard was tossed from the game in the bottom of the first for protesting a called third strike. Joe Caffie, sitting out against the lefthanded Seth Morehead, had to come in to replace him. Miami went ahead, as usual, in the second inning. Gus Niarhos' drive to left found the wall halfway up and dropped safely for a double, driving home Ben Tompkins, who had reached base on a walk. The Herd came back with a run of their own in the bottom of the frame to tie it. Pete Castiglione also waited out a walk, moving into scoring position while Norm Sherry, catching his first game in a Buffalo uniform, and Roger Bowman made outs. Caffie's ringing double to right center brought home Castiglione, but Morehead then retired Peanuts Lowrey to strand the go-ahead run at second.

The Marlins regained the lead in the top of the third. Cal Abrams, with his own hot bat in this series, pulled his third home run of the year just over the fence down the right-field line. The Bisons were not to be outdone in the home half of the third. Ed Mierkowicz, now a starting outfielder, stung a double into the left-field corner as the first man up. Lou Ortiz became a strikeout victim, but not so Serena. Bill clubbed his second home run within a 24-hour period. The ball that cleared the left center field barrier made it Buffalo 3, Miami 2. The game ended on that score. Roger Bowman allowed only two baserunners to get as far as second base in the final four innings.

BISON TALES: Rain delayed the onset of play by an hour and kept the crowd down to 2021.

Former Bison outfielder, now optometrist, Dr. Joseph A. Schultz on Friday past diagnosed Bill Serena with astigmatism. The condition hadn't affected him in the field, but at bat he had difficulty picking up the ball as it left the pitcher's hand. With prescription eyeglasses, Bill had hit two home runs and a triple in the last three games. Jim Clark went in to spell Castiglione in the fifth.

The Bisons left via train after the doubleheader for a four-game series in Columbus and would then travel on to Richmond for four more. They would return home on Monday, June 25. Billy De-Mars did not make the trip, staying in Buffalo to continue treatment for his arm.

Only Roger Bowman had any real effectiveness in this home stand, winning both of the club's victories. Of the batsmen, only Peanuts Lowrey cracked the .300 level. Pete Castiglione was next closest at .290. Luke Easter tagged a brace of home runs and drove home seven but struggled with a .193 average. Bill Serena, in the last three games, had two home runs, drove in six runners and raised his season average to from .187 to .194.

Roger Bowman stopped Ed Bouchee's 17-game hitting streak in the second contest. In the first four games of this Buffalo series, Bouchee had hit .467 with six runs scored and 10 driven home. Bouchee collected two walks and went down swinging once in his three plate opportunities against Bowman.

Game 60—Monday, June 18, Columbus, Ohio: Buffalo 5, Columbus 3

The Bisons beat Columbus for the first time of this season,
thanks to stingy relief pitching and masterful managing.

Game 60 – June 18, 1956				
Buffalo	000 005 000 – 5	10	0	
Columbus	300 000 000 – 3	10	3	
WP – Weiss (1-3)		LP – Herbert (5-3)		

Bill Froats got his first start since May 22 but was battered for five straight hits and three runs without retiring a man. Cavarretta called in John Weiss with two men on and no one out. Weiss retired the side on a fielder's choice and a Bill Serena to Lou Ortiz to Luke Easter double play. Weiss closed the door and kept it shut for five innings, aided by two more twin killings.

Ed Mierkowicz's unassisted double play in the second inning was unique. Columbus hurler Ray Herbert had rapped a leadoff double. One out later, with Herbert still at second, Russ Rose hit a sinking liner into right center that Herbert thought was sure to drop. He took off for third. Mierkowicz snagged the ball just before it hit the ground and kept running toward the infield, stepping on second base to complete the play.

Herbert had fanned seven men and allowed only two Bison safeties through five innings when Cavarretta changed the complexion of the game. Peanuts Lowrey batted for George Bullard in the top of the sixth. Bullard had been upset with the calls he was getting at the plate and Cavarretta wanted a cooler head in there.

The Bison player-coach bounced a single off shortstop Rose's glove for a base hit. Joe Caffie singled him to second. Mierkowicz made it three singles in a row, Lowrey crossing the plate on a misplay by the left fielder. Easter's ground out moved the runners up one base, and Ortiz stung a two-run double down the left-field line to knot the score at 3-3. Hot-hitting Bill Serena got an intentional pass to set up a force play at any base. Pete Castiglione's fly out to center made it two down, but now Cavarretta made his second move by inserting Pat Tomkinson to hit for Norm Sherry. Tomkinson's grounder to the right side was booted and the bases were loaded. Cavarretta's third move of the inning was to send up Jim Clark to bat for Weiss.

Hitless until now as a Bison, Clark punched the first pitch he saw into right field for two RBIs and a Buffalo lead. After Lowrey singled for the second time in the inning to reload the bases, Herbert was done. Floyd Wooldridge came on to get Caffie and end the outburst. He and Bob Spicer kept the Herd scoreless for the last four innings. Joe Coleman did the same in relief of Weiss, sitting down 12 men in a row.

BISON TALES: Heavy rain had forced the Jets ground crew to cover the infield with tarp, burn gasoline on the field to clear up puddles and turn over dirt to make the grounds playable. The park had been sold out to a local drug company and the Jets could not afford to not play the game.

Gus Keriazakos, slated to pitch, was confined to his hotel room by a sudden stomach ailment. Froats was a last-minute replacement for him.

Game 61—Tuesday, June 19, Columbus, Ohio: Buffalo 4, Columbus 2

Sharp hitting and pitching gave the Herd its third win in a row on a wet night.
Larry Donovan came up big with both arm and bat.

Game 61 – June 19, 1956
Buffalo   020 000 020 – 4 13 2
Columbus   000 000 110 – 2   9 1
WP – Donovan (3-2)   LP – Ceccarelli (1-5)

Donovan got the nod on the hill and subdued Columbus on three hits for the first six innings before tiring in the eighth and ninth. Buffalo got two runs in the second and held onto the lead the entire game, with two more tallies in the eighth frame for the game winners. Art Ceccarelli lasted five innings for the Jets. Bob Spicer replaced him in the sixth.

Luke Easter rapped his first hit in 15 times at bat in Columbus with one down in the second. Pat Tomkinson singled behind him. Joe Caffie's ground out moved the runners up, and Donovan came through with a solid base knock that sent both runners home for a two-run lead.

Jim Clark's error put Johnny Lipon on base to start the Columbus seventh. He came around to score on singles by Butch McCord and Ray Noble, cutting the Buffalo lead to one. Dave Melton, pinch-hitting for Spicer, executed a sacrifice bunt that moved both runners into scoring position, but here again Cavarretta's managerial prowess asserted itself. Spook Jacobs was intentionally walked to load the bases. Donovan bore down to get foul-ball popups from both Russ Rose and Ben Downs that Tomkinson gathered in behind the plate for the last two outs. Columbus stranded three.

Buffalo scored the two winning runs in the eighth inning against new Jet pitcher Floyd Wooldridge. Caffie beat out a bunt up the first-base line to start it off. Donovan sacrificed him to second. After Clark's pop out, Peanuts Lowrey banged his third single of the night (six in two evenings) to drive Caffie home. Lowrey alertly took second base on the high throw home by the left fielder trying to catch the fleet Caffie. Ed Mierkowicz rapped yet another single, and Lowrey scored the fourth Buffalo marker.

Columbus scored a run in the bottom of the frame. Russ Sullivan singled and came home two outs later on another single by Butch McCord. Donovan ran out of gas in the ninth. Fred Hahn got the last two outs to save the win.

Bison Tales: Donovan had a cracking fastball early in the game as well as a deceptive pickoff motion. He caught Spook Jacobs off guard in the first after the Jet second baseman had singled. Jacobs was erased in a rundown. The Buffalo bats broke out for 13 hits. Three Jet double plays helped to keep the score down.

George Bullard and Bill Froats had argued ball and strike calls in the previous game and got themselves thumbed out from the dugout in the fifth inning for the same behavior. The Buffalo win, plus Richmond's split of a doubleheader, lifted the Bisons a half-game out of the cellar.

Gus Keriazakos returned to Buffalo for medical evaluation of his ongoing stomach pains.

Game 62—Wednesday, June 20, Columbus, Ohio: Buffalo 7, Columbus 3

The Bisons must have liked the rain in Columbus.
There was more precipitation as well as a fourth straight Buffalo victory.

```
Game 62 – June 20, 1956
Buffalo          300 211 000 – 7  10  1
Columbus         010 000 110 – 3  10  0
WP – Drews (7-6)        LP – Cox (3-6)
```

Lou Ortiz's three-run first-inning homer was the big blow to back up Karl Drews' gritty pitching. Columbus starter Glenn Cox retired Pete Castiglione and Joe Caffie to start the game, but then got too careful with the middle of the order. Ed Mierkowicz walked, as did Luke Easter, both men with two hits in the previous game. Lou Ortiz, with doubles in his last two contests, slammed his ninth home run of the year over the left-field fence and the Bisons were off.

The Jets got one back in the second on an Al Pilarcik single and a long double by Frank Verdi, but Drews bore down and stranded the baserunner. Columbus put a man aboard in each of the next four innings, but Drews prevailed each time and the Jets piled up runners left on base.

The Bisons stung Cox for two more in the fourth. Easter opened with a single. Ortiz walked. A ground out to the right side by Peanuts Lowrey moved the runners up a base. The Jet hurler pitched around Bill Serena, walking him to load the bases and set up the double play. Pat Tomkinson flew out to short left field, but Drews whisked a single into center field to score both Easter and Ortiz. The Herd added another in the next inning. A blooper by Mierkowicz fell for a base hit. He was then credited with a stolen base to second as Columbus catcher Ray Noble had difficulty handling a low Cox pitch. Lowrey singled and Mierkowicz came in.

Lowrey's blow meant the showers for Cox as lefty Jim Miller took over. Buffalo got to him for their final score in the sixth. Tomkinson rifled a single to center, moved up on a free pass to Drews and came home on Castiglione's base knock.

The Jets added a run in the seventh on a Butch McCord leadoff double and a pinch-hit single by Dave Melton, and scored their third and final run in the ninth on Al Pilarcik's solo homer.

BISON TALES: Keriazakos was slated for a hospital stay in Buffalo to determine the nature of his stomach issue. Lou Heyman had accompanied him on the journey home, but Heyman was headed for sale or trade, as the younger Norm Sherry would now split the backstop duties with Tomkinson. Heyman's bat had fallen off to a .156 average after his early-season home run heroics. He had managed only five hits in his last 39 at-bats.

The good news was that Billy DeMars was ready to return to the lineup. Shortstop Jim Clark would return to St. Paul in the American Association. Clark had managed only one hit as a Bison, but it was a big one—his two-run pinch single won the opening game of this road series.

George Bullard would stay on the bench for the remainder of the Columbus series. Cavarretta wanted to prevent the bad blood between his outfielder and the umpiring crew from poisoning the Bisons' chances.

Game 63—Thursday, June 21, Columbus, Ohio: Columbus 6, Buffalo 3

The loss snapped Buffalo's four-game win streak and tumbled
the Herd back down to the cellar, a half-game behind Richmond.

Game 63 – June 21, 1956
Buffalo   001 011 000 – 3 7 1
Columbus   032 100 00x – 6 9 1
WP – Kume (4-2)   LP – Hahn (2-4)

The Jets' Mike Kume hadn't won since May 22, but he'd vanquished the Bisons 2-0 here in Columbus back on April 29 and was up to his old tricks once again. The old bugaboo about falling behind early struck Buffalo's Fred Hahn in the second. The lefty threw four wide ones to center fielder Al Pilarcik, and the following batter, Frank Verdi, moved him to second with a single. Butch McCord made it two hits in a row and brought in Pilarcik, but the Jets weren't finished yet. Kume laid down a perfect sacrifice bunt to move both runners up one base, and Spook Jacobs sent them home with the inning's third single.

Buffalo scored a lone run in the third, taking advantage of a Kume free pass. Pat Tomkinson walked to lead off and moved to second on Hahn's ground ball putout. Pete Castiglione brought him home with his first hit of the day.

The Jets answered with two long balls in the bottom of the frame. Ray Noble cracked a home run off Hahn to left. One out later, Pilarcik hit the ball over the right-field wall. Exit lefty Fred Hahn for lefty reliever Bill Froats. Bill got out of the inning without further damage, but the Jets reached him for still another run in the fourth. Russ Rose's two-out double plated McCord.

Tomkinson scored again in the fifth. As in the third, the catcher walked to lead off and moved to second on a ground out by the pitcher. A second single by Castiglione sent him home. Buffalo's final run came the sixth inning. Kume tried to sneak a change up past Easter, but the Bison first baseman abruptly changed the ball's direction and sent it high over the left-field barrier.

The seventh looked promising despite outs to Tomkinson and Cavaratta, pinch-hitting for Froats. With two gone, a single by Castiglione, another one from Caffie and a walk to Ed Mierkowicz loaded the bases. Easter worked the count to two balls and one strike but could only manage a high fly ball to Pilarcik in medium center. It was the Bisons' last chance. Kume shut them out the rest of the way. Joe Coleman threw two shutout innings in relief.

BISON TALES: Pete Castiglione became the first 1956 Bison to collect four hits in a game. Easter's homer put him two behind the Miami Marlins' Bob Bowman's 16 for the league lead. Billy DeMars still could not suit up and so Jim Clark's departure was delayed. Cavarretta used Clark as a pinch-hitter for Coleman.

The four-game Richmond series was next, and Buffalo hoped to take at least three, if not a sweep, and thereby leap over the Vees to escape the cellar. The R & W Stores had bought out Offermann Stadium, except for the box seats and the first five rows of reserved seating, for the Monday night return home on June 25. The remaining seats would go on sale Monday.

Game 64—Friday, June 22, Richmond, Virginia: Richmond 7, Buffalo 2

The Bisons got a run in the first inning, but Herd pitching
could not hold the advantage. Buffalo left another 10 men on base.

Game 64 – June 22, 1956

Buffalo	100 001 000 – 2	7	0
Richmond	130 000 03x – 7	12	1
WP – Post (5-4)	LP – Bowman (5-6)		

Pete Castiglione opened for the Herd with a leadoff first-inning base on balls off Richmond lefty starter Jim Post. Ed Mierkowicz singled him to third. Post uncorked a wild pitch going after Lou Ortiz and Castiglione beat the throw back to the plate from catcher Neal Watlington.

Richmond evened it in the bottom of the first. Dee Phillips cracked a one-out double off the Bisons' Roger Bowman and the Vees' new outfielder Bill Renna brought him home with a sharp single. Bowman allowed another hit in the inning but held the scoring to only one run. He had less success in the second. Jerry Lumpe, who had worn out Bison pitching back in May on his arrival to the International League from the Yankees, singled in his first at-bat today. A walk to Watlington moved him to second. Post punched a single into center and Lumpe scored to give Richmond the lead. Len Johnson's ground out made it two down with the runners advancing. Bowman got ahead of Phillips, but the Richmond first baseman made it a two-for-two day and singled to right to score two more.

Bowman steadied to hold the Vees without a run from the third through the seventh, allowing only two more base hits. Buffalo lost a big chance in the fifth when Post fanned both Peanuts Lowrey and Luke Easter with the sacks full. Bill Serena's triple to lead off the sixth cut the deficit to two after he scored on Pat Tomkinson's sacrifice fly. The Herd failed to capitalize on another threat in the seventh. Post walked both Lowrey and Easter with one out, bringing on a pitching change. Manager Ed Lopat called on Sonny Dixon, and the righthander easily handled Tomkinson and Cavarretta, the latter a pinch-hitter for Bowman. Dixon had Buffalo's number and stifled the Herd in the eighth and ninth.

Richmond, in the meanwhile, took advantage of Joe Coleman and then Bill Froats, who had been called in to take over for Bowman. Coleman walked third baseman Dick Getter, the first man to face him in the eighth. When Renna singled Getter to third, Froats was called in. Lumpe got his second hit of the day to score Getter. Buddy Carter singled Renna home. Froats retired second baseman Bobby Kline, but Watlington singled to score Lumpe, and the Virginians had three more runs before Froats could finally get the side out.

BISON TALES: Richmond had benefited from the major league cutdown day in May and did so once again with the new addition of Bill Renna.

A New York Yankee trade with Kansas City had sent first baseman Ed Robinson and outfielder Lou Skizas to the A's and brought outfielder Renna and pitcher Ed Burtschy to the Yankees. Renna, hitting .271 with the major league Kansas City club, was sent down to the Vees and now had six hits in his first four games for the Richmond club, including two homers.

Game 65—Saturday, June 23, Richmond, Virginia: Richmond 5, Buffalo 4

*Richmond came from behind once again to run the Buffalo losing streak
to three and push the Herd another game farther into the cellar.*

Game 65 – June 23, 1956
Buffalo   101 110 000 – 4 7 0
Richmond   000 220 001 – 5 9 3
WP – Nardella (4-5)   LP – Weiss (1-4)

Al Cicotte had shut the Bisons out, 1-0, back on April 29, but in this outing the Herd clipped him for a run in their first time at bat. Joe Caffie slapped a one-out single and stole second base as the Richmond hurler was retiring Ed Mierkowicz. Cicotte pitched around Luke Easter and walked him, preferring to face Lou Ortiz and create a force at any base. Ortiz foiled those plans by ripping a single, and the Bisons had a run. Caffie made it 2-0 in the third when he worked Al Cicotte for another one of the five walks the hurler would surrender. Again, Joe stole second base, as he had in inning one. Easter's base knock sent him home to pad the lead.

George Bullard, back in center field, made it 3-0 for Buffalo with a run in the fourth. Bullard singled and advanced on a walk to Billy DeMars. It was the shortstop's first game appearance since June 8, an absence of 18 games. When first baseman Dee Phillips misplayed the double-play relay on Tomkinson's grounder, Bullard's alertness kept him running and his speed allowed him to scramble home.

Harry Nicholas started for Buffalo and kept Richmond in check until the bottom of the fourth frame. It was home run balls that did him in. The Vees cut the lead to 3-2 on the strength of a Bill Renna two-run blast with Jerry Lumpe aboard. Joe Caffie's leadoff solo home run, his third of the year, restored the Bisons' two-run margin in the fifth inning, but the Herd could add no more, even as they loaded the bases against Cicotte with one out. Manager Ed Lopat went to his bullpen for Wimpy Nardella. DeMars popped out and Pat Tomkinson flew out to center, and the Bisons had blown a big chance.

Dee Phillips knotted the ballgame in the fifth with his own two-run shot, Neal Watlington scoring ahead of him. Nicholas got the side out without more scoring, but Cavarretta sent Bill Serena up to pinch-hit for him in the sixth and John Weiss took over the hill for the Herd in the bottom of that frame.

Nardella didn't allow the Bisons a hit for the rest of the game. Weiss stopped Richmond until the ninth, when Tom Hamilton led off by cracking a single to right and Jim Post went in to run. Buddy Carter's sacrifice moved Post to second. Weiss pitched around Al Van Alstyne, walking him to set up the double-play possibility, but Watlington made it all for naught with his second hit of the night, the game-winning single that scored Post.

BISON TALES: Peanuts Lowrey, pressed into additional service in Columbus when Bullard and the umpiring crew couldn't see eye to eye on balls and strikes, rested his 38-year-old legs in this game. Bullard went one for two and turned his speed into a run in the fourth, taking advantage of a Richmond infield miscue. Buffalo left nine men on base tonight. Lack of speed was a factor in the loss as well as the lack of timely hitting.

Games 66 and 67—Sunday, June 24, Richmond, Virginia: Richmond 11, Buffalo 1; Buffalo 5, Richmond 1

Buffalo broke a four-game losing streak with a five-run,
seventh-inning come-from-behind victory in the second game.

Game 66 – June 24, 1956 (first game of doubleheader)
Buffalo   000 000 010 – 1 13 1
Richmond   070 102 01x – 11 15 0
WP – Jordan (3-4)   LP – Donovan (3-4)

Game 67 – June 24, 1956 (second game of doubleheader)
Buffalo   000 000 5 – 5 9 0
Richmond   000 010 0 – 1 7 1
WP – Drews (8-6)   LP – Dixon (3-3)

In the 11-1 first-game defeat, there was little to cheer about. Starter Larry Donovan lasted only into the second inning. He was replaced by Joe Coleman, who lasted only an inning and a fraction himself. Bill Froats came on in the fourth and pitched into the eighth, when John Weiss relieved him to get the final two outs.

The Virginians amassed a total of 15 hits against the first three Bison hurlers, 12 singles and three doubles, and were gifted with four walks. They erupted for seven runs in the home half of the second inning, six of those charged to starter Donovan. Only Weiss was perfect in his two-thirds of an inning of work.

For their part, the Bisons collected 13 hits—all singles—off two Richmond pitchers, but all this effort resulted in only one tally. Vee starter Niles Jordan was constantly in trouble but the Bisons continually let him get away with it. Only in the eighth did the Herd finally get a run. Peanuts Lowrey had gone in to play second base to spell Lou Ortiz due to the heat and managed a base hit in his only time at bat. One out later, with Lowrey now on second, manager Phil Cavarretta singled him home.

Cavarretta had gone in to play first base as the Richmond heat was also affecting Luke Easter. The manager's blow was his first hit since April 25, the ninth game of the season. He had placed himself on inactive status on May 18 and then reactivated his player role on May 31. Since that latter date, the manager had gone hitless in five pinch-hit appearances.

The difference for Bisons was seen in not only the timeliness of the hitting but also team speed. Richmond scored 11 of their 20 baserunners. The Bisons scored only one of their 14. On the veteran Buffalo squad, only the youngsters George Bullard and Joe Caffie had the ability to easily take the extra base and put the pressure on the defense that leads to errors of commission or omission. Speed also keeps you out of the double play. The Bisons hit into two this game, the Virginians one.

In game two, last-inning heroics won the scheduled seven-inning second game for "stopper" Karl Drews. The Buffalo ace, despite seven hits in six innings of work, allowed no bases on balls and held Richmond to a solitary run in the fifth inning. Dick Getter doubled and was sent home on a single by Len Johnston. That was all the Vees would manage off Drews or any Bison pitcher in this second contest.

Sidearming Richmond hurler Ed Burtschy was part of the Yankee-Kansas City deal that had brought hard-hitting Bill Renna to the Vee lineup, and he showed the further value of a major league affiliation by throwing six shutout innings at the Herd. The Bisons threatened in the third when they loaded the bases with no one out, but Burtschy got Ed Mierkowicz to ground into a third to home to first double play. He followed this up by fanning Luke Easter.

Down a run, the Bisons sent five men across the plate in the seventh to claim a victory. Again, it was manager Cavarretta showing the troops how it was done. Billy DeMars flew out to left field as the leadoff batter, but Norm Sherry got a life when third baseman Buddy Carter fielded his grounder and then threw into the dirt at first. Tom Hamilton could not come up with the scoop.

Cavarretta sent George Bullard in to run for Sherry to get speed on the bases for the tying run. While he was making that maneuver, Vee manager Ed Lopat went to his bullpen for a change of his own. Sonny Dixon was called in to take over for the tiring Burtschy.

Manager Cavarretta made his second move of the inning, inserting himself as a pinch-hitter for Drews. The manager came through with his second hit of the day when his sharp single to right sent Bullard on to third. Pete Castiglione added his second safety of the game, rapping the ball into center field as Bullard trotted home to tie the score. Joe Caffie was next up, and he hit a line-drive gapper into right center. Cavarretta scored easily. Castiglione motored home from first as center fielder Bill Renna had difficulty picking the ball up from the wall. Caffie kept running and was waved home from third, his speed creating an inside the park home run when the throw from second baseman Bobby Kline was up the line.

Suddenly, the Bisons had a three-run lead. Ed Mierkowicz made it one more. He blasted a Dixon offering over the left-field wall for his first home run this season as a Bison. Lopat turned to the pen again and signaled for Dick Starr. The Richmond reliever got the last two outs.

John Weiss was Cavarretta's choice to take on the Virginians in the bottom of the seventh, and he did so in order. The win allowed the Bisons to split the series and finish at .500 on the road, four won and four lost.

BISON TALES: Joe Caffie owned a five-game hit streak, going nine for 22 for a .409 average in that span. He hit two home runs in the Richmond series—his third and fourth of the year—scored four times and drove in four runs. Cavarretta had also turned Caffie loose on the basepaths trying to manufacture runs. Joe stole three in this series and now had 12 for the year.

The second-game defeat snapped Richmond's six-game winning streak. The Bisons remained in eighth place in the league, now two and a half games behind the Virginians.

The Herd would stay overnight in Richmond, leave in the morning and be home in Buffalo in the afternoon to open a five-game set against Columbus that evening. Then Richmond would come in on the weekend to visit the Herd.

Game 68—Monday, June 25, Buffalo: Buffalo 4, Columbus 1

A crowd of 8232, the largest since opening day, watched heroics
from Fred Hahn and Ed Mierkowicz make it two Bison wins in a row.

```
Game 68 – June 25, 1956
Columbus        000 100 000 – 1  7  1
Buffalo         000 100 30x – 4  11  0
WP – Hahn (3-4)         LP – Kume (4-5)
```

Hahn's effort wasn't pretty (seven walks in addition to six hits) but it got the job done. Mike Kume, who had bested the Bisons and Hahn only four days earlier in Columbus, took the loss.

Each team scored once in the fourth. Leading off the inning for Columbus, Al Pilarcik worked Hahn for one of those seven free passes. Singles by Ben Downs and Frank Verdi gave the Jets the short-lived lead. Buffalo came right back to tie it in the bottom of the frame. Peanuts Lowrey's high fly to left was lost by Downs in the haze, bouncing off his glove at the last minute to put the Bison coach–left fielder on second. Norm Sherry brought him home with a single to left.

Sherry, sacrificed to second by Hahn, tried to score on Pete Castiglione's base hit but was nailed at the plate by a fine throw from center fielder Pilarcik. In the sixth, Cavarretta tried the running game again, looking to manufacture a run on a double steal with two outs. Lou Ortiz was on third when Billy DeMars took off from first. The Jets must have had the sign. Catcher Ray Noble's throw to second was cut off in front of the bag by Curt Roberts and fired back to Noble to catch Ortiz at the plate.

The Herd finally went ahead in the seventh. Hahn topped a ball down the third-base line that wound up being a single. Castiglione forced him at second, but Joe Caffie pulled the ball down the right-field line for a double to put two runners in scoring position. Ed Mierkowicz followed with his own double to left to send both men home. The Jets intentionally walked Luke Easter to face Ortiz, but Ortiz also walked to load the bases. Lowrey's sacrifice fly to center was deep enough to score Mierkowicz with the Herd's final run.

Cavarretta went in to pinch-hit—unsuccessfully—for Castiglione in the eighth and stayed in to play first base for Easter. Bill Serena went to third.

BISON TALES: General manager John C. Stiglmeier expressed his gratitude for the sponsorship by the R & W Supermarkets that had turned out such a large crowd. Al Hausbeck chaired the effort.

The Philadelphia Phillies were sending pitcher Ron Mrozinki to the Bisons as part of the Duane Pillette deal. The 24-year-old lefty reliever had pitched parts of the last two seasons with the Phils, winning one and losing three. His current record was 3-2 for Pacific Coast League Sacramento. Baseball commissioner Ford C. Frick had said that he would look more closely at the terms of sale of the Buffalo club by Detroit, and the details of the player agreement that was supposed to exist between the two organizations.

Frank Cannon, already a member of the ball club's board of directors, was named to succeed the late Herbert J. Vogelsang as club treasurer.

The Bisons again encountered travel delays. They reached the Buffalo airport shortly after 5:00 p.m., having to forgo batting practice and shortening the pregame warmups for both teams.

Games 69 and 70—Tuesday, June 26, Buffalo: Columbus 8, Buffalo 7; Columbus 10, Buffalo 2

Columbus bats erupted for huge, game-changer innings in deciding each contest.
The Bisons left 17 men on base in the two games.

Game 69 – June 26, 1956 (first game of doubleheader)

Columbus	020 006 0 – 8	11	0
Buffalo	000 402 1 – 7	11	1

WP – Spicer (2-2)　　　　LP – Nicholas (1-7)

Game 70 – June 26, 1956 (second game of doubleheader)

Columbus	210 070 000 – 10	14	2
Buffalo	010 110 000 - 3	9	)

WP – Cox (3-4)　　　　LP – Bowman (5-7)

In the seven-inning opener, bases on balls knocked Bison starter Larry Donovan out of the game even while he still owned a 4-2 lead. Relief pitching couldn't hold the Jets in check.

Columbus broke on top with a pair in the second inning. Columbus starter Bob Kusava drew one of Donovan's six walks. A Russ Rose single to left moved him to second. Both men scored on a double to the right center field gap by Curt Roberts. Buffalo went on top in the fourth.

Ed Mierkowicz led off with his home run number two to left. Peanuts Lowrey drew a walk after Lou Ortiz had been retired and came all the way round to score on a long single by Luke Easter. The big Buffalo first baseman stumbled rounding first and had to retreat to the bag on what would have likely been a double. Billy DeMars flew out, but Norm Sherry worked a walk and pitcher Donovan gave himself the lead when his single plated Easter. Sherry came home on Pete Castiglione's double down the left-field line and Buffalo had a 4-2 lead. Bob Spicer took the mound for Columbus, walked Joe Caffie to fill the sacks and got Mierkowicz on a fly ball.

Donovan walked the first two batters in the fifth, which meant the end of his day. Harry Nicholas relieved and got out of that jam, but then two doubles, a single and a triple gave the lead back to Columbus in the sixth and brought Joe Coleman in to pitch with two down. Cavarretta had left fielder Ben Downs walked intentionally to get to catcher Ray Noble. The ex-Giant foiled that plan by sending a Coleman delivery high over the left-field screen for a three-run homer. By the time Coleman got the last out, the score stood Columbus 8, Buffalo 4.

Bill Miller had replaced Spicer on the mound for the Jets, but the Herd knocked him out with two runs of their own in the bottom of the sixth. Norm Sherry walked to lead off, and George Bullard pinch-hit a single for Coleman. A walk to Pete Castiglione loaded the bases. The big inning was cut short on Caffie's sharp grounder that was turned into a double play, Sherry scoring. A base hit from Mierkowicz brought Bullard home and brought a new pitcher to the mound. Jake Thies got Ortiz on a fly to left.

Bill Froats held the Jets scoreless in the top of the seventh, and Peanuts Lowrey started the home half of the inning with a triple. Bill Serena, in for Castiglione defensively and batting in Easter's spot, walked. The crowd's hopes were dashed when Billy DeMars hit into a double play. Lowrey scored but the Herd was still short one run. Norm Sherry grounded out to end the game.

In game two, Columbus broke open a tight 3-2 ballgame with a seven-run fifth inning. Roger

Bowman started for Buffalo and gave up five hits and two walks in two frames. The Jets took a 3-0 lead. The Herd got one back in the bottom of the second. Bill Serena walked, and Pat Tomkinson doubled to put runners on second and third with two out. Peanuts Lowrey pinch-hit for Bowman and singled into short left to score Serena. Tomkinson had to hold at third and was left stranded. Buffalo made it 3-2 with another tally in the fourth. Lou Ortiz lofted a fly ball to left that struck the wall and left him on second base with a double. He moved on to third on Serena's ground out and came across to score when George Bullard hit a deep sacrifice fly to center. That was as close as the Bisons were going to get.

Bill Froats, in relief of Coleman, had pitched two scoreless frames before the Jets got to him in the fifth. Right fielder Russ Sullivan took a Froats curveball that didn't break and sent it high over the right-field wall for an opposite-field home run. That made the score 4-2. Froats stayed in to face six more batters, retiring one of them, allowing two to score and leaving the bases loaded. Larry Donovan was pressed into service despite his four innings in game one. The first man he faced was Billy Shantz, the Columbus catcher who had been penciled in at first to hit against Bowman. Shantz took Donovan's first pitch over the left-field screen for a grand slam.

Donovan stayed in the game and kept the Jets off the scoreboard for the last four innings. The final Buffalo run came in the bottom of the fifth. Joe Caffie singled, moved to second on Luke Easter's ground out and came home on a one-baser by Lou Ortiz.

BISON TALES: The Bisons hit into four rally-killing double plays in the first game.

The Herd remained in last place, but thanks to a Richmond loss at Rochester they were now only two games out of seventh. Front-running Montreal was ahead of the Bisons by 15 games.

Local boosters from the Lincoln Park Village Club of the Town of Tonawanda honored Pat Tomkinson this evening. Pat now lived in that town. Tomkinson caught game two and picked up a double in four trips to the plate.

In an effort to drum up attendance, the season's first Ladies Night was slated to be held on Wednesday night, to be followed by Masonic Night on Thursday. Plans were also under way for a Polish Night that was scheduled for August 8. A meeting to organize that event was planned for Wednesday evening at 8:00 p.m. at Sharkey's Restaurant at East Ferry Street and Moselle.

Other groups were being encouraged to follow suit to help boost the turnout.

Game 71—Wednesday, June 27, Buffalo: Columbus 7, Buffalo 6

Buffalo lost a tough one in the ninth on an error by reliever
Roger Bowman. Hitting into three double plays stymied the Herd offense.

Game 71 – June 27, 1956

Columbus	000 240 001 – 7	10	1
Buffalo	201 000 300 – 6	10	1

WP – Spicer (3-2)   LP – Bowman (5-8)

Buffalo grabbed a 3-0 lead against Jets starter Ray Herbert. Following Pete Castiglione's fly out leading off, Joe Caffie dropped a bunt single to put a runner aboard. Herbert then lost the plate, walking Ed Mierkowicz, Luke Easter, Lou Ortiz (run batted in) and Bill Serena (run batted in) in succession. A double play held the runs to two. The Bisons' next tally came in the third frame when Mierkowicz walked and came all the way home on Serena's double into left center.

John Weiss, making only his second start of the year as Cavarretta was searching for a rest for his battered pitching corps, threw three strong innings before succumbing to the Columbus bats in the fourth and fifth frames. Gil Dailey picked on a Weiss fastball and sent it over the screen in left with Al Pilarcik aboard in the fourth. Four more Jets runs came home the next inning, the big blow being Al Pilarcik's three-run blast just to the right of the scoreboard. Roger Bowman took over with the Jets in the lead by three.

Buffalo pulled back into a tie with a three-run seventh. Pete Castiglione got it going with a single, and the Bisons caught a break when second baseman Curt Roberts bobbled Caffie's double-play ball to make all hands safe. Mierkowicz flew out, leaving men on first and second, but Easter's sizzler to short took an unexpected hop over Russ Rose's head and sent Castiglione home with the first run. Bullard came in to run for Easter. Ortiz was out number two, but Serena blasted his second double to the scoreboard in right center and both the speedsters, Caffie and Bullard, made it home to tie it up. Bob Spicer took the mound for Columbus and got Peanuts Lowrey on a fly ball for the last out.

The Jets got the winning run in the ninth, starting with a pinch-hit single by John Lipon. Pinch-runner Art Ceccarelli made it to second when a Bowman pickoff throw bounced into the dirt and away from Cavarretta, who had taken over first base from Easter. Russ Rose cracked a single to drive in Ceccarelli. Spicer set down Buffalo in the bottom of the ninth. It was his second victory against the Herd in two days.

BISON TALES: A Ladies Night crowd of 1462 watched the Bisons hit into three more double plays and leave nine men on base. Billy DeMars' arm was still ailing, again forcing Cavarretta to play Castiglione at short.

Al Pilarcik now had 14 home runs, tying him with Easter for second place in the league. Miami's Bob Bowman had 16. Only 5 feet 9 inches, the lefty-swinging Pilarcik had been on a tear, hitting .381 since June 12, slugging home 10 runs in his last 19 games. He now led the league with 59 RBIs. In these past four games in Buffalo, he was hitting .461 (six for 13), with four runs scored, four driven in and a homer.

Game 72—Thursday, June 28, Buffalo: Buffalo 7, Columbus 6

*The Bisons broke their three-game losing streak, but it took
an extra inning to do it. Joe Coleman got the victory in relief.*

Game 72 – June 28, 1956

Columbus	101 001 003 0 – 6	12	1
Buffalo	010 010 310 1 – 7	13	0

WP – Coleman (2-0)   LP – Cox (3-5)

The game was a seesaw contest. Russ Rose doubled off Karl Drews leading off the game and later scored to give the Jets the lead. Lou Ortiz tied it in the second inning, slamming a mighty shot off Columbus' Bob Miller over the center-field wall just to the left of the scoreboard. It was Lou's 10th of the year. Curt Roberts' score in the third put Columbus back up by a run, but Buffalo answered in the fifth on singles by Bill Serena and Joe Caffie and a sacrifice fly from Pete Castiglione.

Columbus took the lead once more in the sixth as Frank Verdi's line single plated Gil Dailey. Buffalo responded when Drews' single in the seventh scored Peanuts Lowrey and Serena and restored the lead to the Herd. Drews himself scored when Ed Mierkowicz cracked a double off the left-field wall. Serena's eighth home run in the eighth inning gave Drews a three-run cushion.

The Jets came back to tie the game in the ninth. Ray Noble drove a Drews pitch out of the park in left center to start the inning. Drews retired Verdi, but then Butch McCord doubled and Cavarretta called in Harry Nicholas. Nicholas threw eight pitches, seven of them balls, walking pinch-hitter Ben Downs and going to a 3-ball, 1-strike count on Russ Rose. Ray Coleman replaced Harry, completed the walk (charged to Nicholas) to load the bases and then walked Curt Roberts to score McCord. Coleman got Russ Sullivan swinging for out number two, but he then walked Al Pilarcik and the game was tied. Gil Dailey took a third strike for the final out.

New Columbus hurler Floyd Wooldridge held Buffalo in check in the ninth to send the game into extra innings. Noble fanned leading off the tenth for Columbus but the Jets rallied on hits by Verdi and McCord before Coleman coaxed an inning-ending double-play grounder from pinch-hitter John Lipon.

Glenn Cox came in to pitch for Columbus. Ortiz lined a single to left, moved to second on a walk to Peanuts Lowrey and scored the game winner on Norm Sherry's clean single to center. Coleman got the win. Cox, who had beaten the Bisons on Tuesday, took the loss.

Bison Tales: George Bullard, newly back in the starting lineup, suffered a broken thumb in batting practice and would be out of action for three to four weeks. Caffie would take over in center field. Caffie now had a 10-game hitting streak with 18 hits in 43 appearances for a .418 average. He had scored eight runs and driven home four in that span.

Ron Mrozinski, from the Phillies, had arrived to pitch in the upcoming doubleheader.

A turnout of 2052 was present for Masonic Night and Worthington Pump Co. Night.

Games 73 and 74—Friday, June 29, Buffalo: Buffalo 4, Richmond 3; Richmond 6, Buffalo 3

New hurler Ron Mrozinski pitched the Bisons to the win in game one,
but Buffalo hit into five double plays in losing game two.

Game 73 – June 29, 1956 (first game of doubleheader)
Richmond   001 020 0 – 3 6 1
Buffalo   001 021 x – 4 10 2
WP – Mrozinski (1-0)   LP – Starr (2-2)

Game 74 – June 29, 1956 (second game of doubleheader)
Richmond   002 001 201 – 6 12 0
Buffalo   000 010 200 – 3 6 4
WP – Cicotte (7-4)   LP – Hahn (3-5)

To add to the roster woes, the Bisons were already down one more man before the day's games began. On top of George Bullard's broken hand the day before, hot-hitting Pete Castiglione (.369 in his last 11 games) had to keep to his hotel room with a stomach ailment. Billy DeMars, still not completely healthy, had to start at shortstop, but his arm woes showed as he committed two errors. Adding yet another insult in the first inning, Lou Ortiz suffered a shin bruise on a hard slide into second by Richmond's Len Johnston as he broke up the double play. Ortiz eventually had to retire in the fourth frame, forcing Cavarretta to bring Peanuts Lowrey in from left field to cover second. Phil, who had been spelling an under-the-weather Luke Easter at first base in the later innings, had to himself go into the game to play left field. Despite the jury-rigged lineup, the Bisons were determined to win.

The seven-inning first game was scoreless for the first two innings. New lefthander Mrozinski allowed a Richmond run in the third. The speedy Len Johnston coaxed a walk, moved to third on Dee Phillips' single and scored as Cal Neeman hit into a 6-3 ground out. Buffalo got it back immediately. Joe Caffie nicked a single off Richmond's Jim Coates and then turned on the speed to steal second. Ed Mierkowicz slammed yet another pitch high off the left-field wall, his favorite target, and scored Caffie on the double.

Richmond went up by two in the top of the fifth as Jerry Lumpe doubled down the line in left and Bill Renna walked. Neeman counted his second and third RBIs of the contest with a double into right center. But again, the Bisons came back in the home half of the inning.

Mierkowicz picked up his third hit of the game and Cavarretta, now batting in Ortiz's slot, drew a walk. Richmond manager Ed Lopat called Dick Starr in from the bullpen. Peanuts Lowrey's ground ball to short looked like a perfect double-play ball, except that Lumpe muffed it and the bases were loaded. Bill Serena, with five hits in his last two games, continued his hot streak and cracked a Starr offering just inside the third-base bag for the game-tying double. Mierekowicz and Cavarretta crossed the plate.

The Herd won it in their next at-bat. Joe Caffie waited out a walk. Mierkowicz made it a four-for-four day by singling Caffie to third with the go-ahead run. Easter then did what the cleanup man is supposed to do, sending a hard shot down to first that bounded over first baseman Dee Phillips' head for the game-winning blow. Mrozinski set Richmond down in the seventh and final inning and picked up his first win as a Bison.

In the second game, the Herd's banged-up lineup hit into five double plays, while the Virginian batters were ganging up on starter Fred Hahn. Hahn was battered for 11 hits and four walks in his seven innings of work.

Richmond pitcher Al Cicotte started the damage with a solo home run to right off Hahn in the third frame. Len Johnson, back on base yet again, this time with a single, came all the way home from first on a Dee Phillips double before Hahn could retire the side. During this inning, Pat Tomkinson got into an argument over balls and strikes with plate umpire Bob Smith and got tossed from the game. Norm Sherry had to sub for Tomkinson. This move cost Cavarretta his last position player and a potential pinch-hitter. This would be important later on.

The score stayed at 2-0 for the visitors until the fifth. In the top of the inning, Joe Caffie stole a sure double from Phillips with a running grab at the scoreboard. In the bottom of the inning, Billy DeMars drew a walk and Caffie, continuing his torrid hitting, doubled to right. DeMars, running on the pitch, scored on the blow.

Richmond jumped the lead back up to two in the sixth when Al Van Alstyne clubbed a solo homer to left center. The Vee bombardment continued in the seventh as they added another pair. Hahn yielded a single to Phillips, a double to Bill Renna and Leon Carter's base knock, good for two RBIs. The Virginians went ahead 5-1.

Buffalo bounced back to score twice in the home half of the seventh, but a double play started by Lumpe kept the runs to two. Cicotte got himself in trouble when manager Cavarretta, now left fielder Cavarretta, roped a leadoff single. The Vee hurler then lost control and walked Bill Serena and Norm Sherry to load the bases with no one down. Cavarretta, without a pinch-hitter to call on, let Hahn hit for himself. The Bison hurler sent a grounder toward the hole at short that Lumpe backhanded, ran after Serena to slap a tag on him as he was running by and then fired on to first to catch Hahn for the double play.

Cavarretta scored on the action and Sherry alertly made it to third when Phillips, after making the putout at first, fell into the coach's box in an effort to avoid the onrushing Hahn. Now, with two out, a runner on third and DeMars at the plate, Cicotte unleashed a wild pitch to let Sherry score the Bisons' final run.

John Weiss pitched the last two innings for Buffalo and gave up an unearned run in the ninth. Caffie dropped Carter's fly ball to center, and Cal Neeman doubled the runner home with the Vees' sixth and final tally. Sonny Dixon took over for Cicotte in the eighth and allowed two hits but no runs to seal the Virginian victory.

BISON TALES: Ortiz and Castiglione would likely be able to play the next day, but the club desperately needed able-bodied reserves to call upon. At the plate, Mierkowicz had raised his team-leading average to .333 by going six for seven on the day. Caffie's recent hot streak had him only a few points short of the .300 circle. Vee outfielder Bill Renna had his own 13-game hit string going.

An incensed Buffalo fan jumped onto the field to take on umpire Smith after Tomkinson had been thumbed from the game. Buffalo's batboy Jack Godfrey helped security detain the man before he was escorted to the exit.

Game 75—Saturday, June 30, Buffalo: Richmond 7, Buffalo 3

*Luke Easter's two home runs were offset by a four-run fifth by the visitors,
while the Bisons hit into four more twin killings.*

Game 75 – June 30, 1956
Richmond   000 042 100 – 7 11 0
Buffalo   000 201 000 – 3 11 1
WP – Burtschy (1-0)   LP – Donovan (3-4)

Larry Donovan for Buffalo and Ed Burtschy for Richmond matched goose eggs on the scoreboard for three innings until Luke Easter gave the Bisons a two-run lead in the bottom of the fourth frame. Ed Mierkowicz singled, and Luke's 15th of the year left the park over the left center field wall. The lead disappeared on Richmond's next at-bat.

Richmond left fielder Len Johnston, a pest on the basepaths in this series, punched a single to put one man on. Donovan walked the next batter, Bobby Kline, but got Jerry Lumpe on a popup. He then made the mistake of hanging a curveball to Bill Renna, and the Richmond right fielder sent the pitch high over the left-field screen for a three-run home run. The next batter, lefthanded-swinging Tom Hamilton, made it two home runs in a row by taking Donovan over the right-field barrier near the light standard. The Herd was down by two at this point, and it got worse.

Donovan couldn't make it out of the sixth frame. Cal Neeman, the leadoff man, slammed yet another double in this series. Burtschy was retired, Neeman holding second, but Johnston walloped a fly to deep center over Caffie's head and wound up on third base with a triple. Cavarretta stuck with Donovan, but only for one more out. Kline's hot liner to short was nabbed by DeMars for out number two. Donovan's first pitch to Lumpe was into the dirt and away for a wild pitch, and in came Johnston with the Vees' sixth tally. Now Cavarretta went to the bullpen. Bill Froats took over with a 1-0 count and got Lumpe to bounce out, Ortiz to Easter.

Luke hit his second homer of the night in the bottom of the inning, this one to straightaway center field just to the left of the scoreboard. That ended the Bison offense for the evening. Richmond added a seventh run to their final tally in the top of the seventh. Froats retired the first two batters, but Leon Carter singled to put a man on first. Froats went to 3-2 on Al Van Alstyne. On the next pitch, Carter, running on the full count, legged it all the way home on Van Alstyne's drive to right center, sliding in ahead of Mierkowicz's throw to the plate. Taking no chances, Van Alstyne held at first. That ended the scoring for both teams.

BISON TALES: Back from injury but still nursing a sore leg, Lou Ortiz fielded seven chances at second base. He was hitless in three official appearances but drew a walk. Pete Castiglione was back as well, though his duties were limited to pinch-hitting for Froats in the ninth. He got a single but was left on base.

Easter now had 16 home runs. Renna's home run was his sixth in 14 games since he joined Richmond. He had gotten a hit in every one of those contests.

Games 76 and 77—Sunday, July 1, Buffalo: Buffalo 13, Richmond 9; Richmond 3, Buffalo 2

Buffalo won the first-game slugfest, amassing 16 hits.
Roger Bowman took a tough, rain-shortened loss in the second.

Game 76 – July 1, 1956 (first game of doubleheader)

Richmond	030 220 020 –	9	14 1
Buffalo	004 161 01x –	13	16 0

WP – Coleman (3-0)   LP – Coates (3-9)

Game 77 – July 1, 1956 (second game of doubleheader)

Richmond	100 20 –	3	6 0
Buffalo	010 01 –	2	7 0

WP – Lopat (6-4)   LP – Bowman (5-9)

In game one, Harry Nicholas made it through the first inning, but he couldn't get anyone out in the second. He gave up a walk to Tom Hamilton, a single to Leon Carter and a three-run blast to Al Van Alstyne. Cavarretta went to his relief corps following Neal Watlington's single to center. John Weiss came on to put out the fire.

Buffalo answered in the home half of the third against Richmond's Ed Cereghino. Weiss led off with a hit, Billy DeMars walked, and a single by Joe Caffie and a triple off the bat of Ed Mierkowicz produced three runs and a tie. Richmond thought they were out of the inning when Mierkowicz got trapped off third base and Luke Easter grounded out, but Lou Ortiz smacked a solo home run, his 11th of the year, and sent the Bisons ahead by one. The hit also sent Cereghino to the showers. Jim Coates was called on to retire Peanuts Lowrey and the side.

The teams swapped the lead back and forth. The Vees went on top again with a pair of runs off Weiss in the fourth. Enter Joe Coleman to stop it there. The Herd tied it up in the bottom of the inning as Coates also surrendered a marker. Two more Vee runs off Coleman in their next at-bat, in the top of the fifth, regained the lead for Richmond, to make it 7-5.

The Bisons put an end to the back and forth by hanging a 6-spot on the scoreboard in the home half of the fifth. Coates was knocked out of the box and so was Dick Starr, who lasted only a third of an inning. Luke Easter unloaded on Starr with his third home run in two days, a three-run blow to right that capped the outburst. It was Luke's number 17. Wimpy Nardella became the third Richmond pitcher of the inning and the fourth of the game for the Virginians.

Buffalo added another run in the sixth, but the Vees fought back once more and scored twice off Coleman in the eighth on Renna's two-run shot to left center. Cavarretta, desperate for the win, called Karl Drews in to the mound. Buffalo's "stopper" this day became Buffalo's "closer." The big righthander allowed a hit to Hamilton before getting Carter on a grounder to end the inning. Bill Serena tripled in the Bison half of the eighth, coming in to score to make it 13-9 for the home team. That was the way it ended.

Drews got Val Alstyne on a popup to start the Richmond ninth. Watlington singled for his third hit of the day but then was erased on a game-ending double play. Caffie speared a liner off the bat of pinch-hitter Dick Getter and fired the relay to Easter before the baserunner could make it back to the bag.

Rain halted the second game after five innings. Buffalo wound up on the short end of the 3-2 score. Roger Bowman started for Buffalo and was touched for a run in the first when Len Johnston led off the game with a double and Bill Renna, keeping a 16-game hit streak alive, doubled him home with two gone. Bowman helped get the tying run in the bottom of the second, singling cleanly to right off manager-pitcher Ed Lopat of the Vees. Joe Caffie tripled him in. The Herd left Caffie stranded when second baseman Bobby Kline made a diving stab of Ed Mierkowicz's sharp liner. It was a critical lost run.

Richmond took the lead again in the fourth when Renna singled and Cal Neeman drove a Bowman pitch the opposite way for a two-run homer to right. Rain started falling in the fifth. Lou Ortiz picked on a Lopat junk ball and sent it screaming out of the park just to the right of the screen in the home half of that frame. The home run was Lou's second of the day and his 12th of the season, but that was to be the last offense the Bisons would have an opportunity to muster.

Lopat set the side down as the rain picked up. A 15-minute downpour and driving winds sent both teams to huddle in their dugouts while fans raced for cover against the left-field grandstand wall. The umpires finally decided the field was no longer playable and the game would go into the books as a five-inning completed affair.

BISON TALES: Buffalo's June record was its worst month of the year, winning but 12 games and losing 23 for a .352 average. The club was 7-11 on the road, 5-12 at home. The Bisons were stuck in last place, now two and a half games behind the seventh-place Havana Sugar Kings.

It was an ongoing story of injuries and lack of reserve personnel to call on, as major league teams had been reluctant to fulfill earlier commitments to help the Bisons in the player department. Without the independent finances that Toronto or the new Miami franchise could draw upon to purchase new players when needed, Buffalo was at the mercy of the big-league organizations. And at the same time, those very big-league clubs were faced with demands from their own farm system ball teams for aid. To help the Buffalo squad compete at the expense of their own affiliated teams would bring the latter down upon their necks. Navigating the operation of an independent club, without independent wealth, was a more difficult task than had been imagined.

With 76 games now in the books—the suspended game back on May 20 against Toronto still needed to be completed—the Buffalo Bisons Baseball Club, Inc. was halfway through its inaugural season as a community-owned enterprise. Management, players and fans would have the standings read differently, but simply to have made it this far was a great achievement.

The Bisons collected their highest hit and run totals of the season in Game 1. The teams combined for 30 hits, 11 of them for extra bases. Eight pitchers allowed 22 runs and doled out 12 bases on balls.

The Bisons were off for a day until the Montreal Royals came to town on Tuesday.

In International League news: Havana split a pair with Montreal on this date and so the Herd could not pick up any ground in their efforts to leave the cellar.

Elsewhere, in Rochester, Red Wing outfielder Gene Green erupted for three home runs and six RBIs against the visiting Columbus Jets in the first game of their doubleheader.

International League Standings
July 1, 1956

	W	L	Pct.	G.B.
Montreal	46	29	.613	—
Rochester	46	33	.582	2
Miami	39	35	.513	7½
Toronto	38*	36	.516	8
Columbus	40	41	.493	9
Richmond	36	44	.450	12½
Havana	34	45	.430	14
Buffalo	30*	46	.394	16½

*Not including suspended game of 5/20.

Club Statistics: 75 Games (including Game 28)

Pitchers	W	L	ERA	Notes
Drews	8	6	3.55	Club leader with 5 complete games, 1 save
Bowman	5	9	4.46	Tied with Drews with 5 complete games
Coleman	3	0	3.80	All wins have come in relief
Donovan	3	4	4.24	Leading 5-1 in suspended Game 28
Keriazakos	3	5	4.25	Out of action since mid-June
Hahn	3	6	4.93	ERA jumped from 4.33 in last month
Weiss	1	4	4.69	Has shown effectiveness in relief
Froats	1	4	7.90	Continues to struggle as starter or reliever
Nicholas	1	7	6.31	Continues to struggle as starter or reliever

Hitters	G	AB	R	H	HR	BI	Avg
Mierkowicz	27	92	16	29	2	12	.315
Caffie	53	193	21	58	4	18	.300
Castiglione	60	190	20	55	0	13	.289
Easter	77	260	34	69	17	45	.265
Sherry	13	34	4	9	0	4	.264
Ortiz	75	264	35	69	12	45	.261
Lowrey	65	172	25	45	1	18	.261
Tomkinson	46	81	6	21	1	4	.259
Bullard	67	237	34	61	2	10	.257
Serena	68	201	28	45	8	31	.223
Cavarretta	18	23	5	5	1	4	.217
DeMars	44	141	13	30	0	8	.212

Monday, July 2, 1956, Buffalo: Day Off

A day off after Sunday's lengthy and rain-bedeviled doubleheader gave the field a chance to dry out and, more importantly, the Bisons a chance to heal up. Billy DeMars was not yet 100 percent, according to Cavarretta, and was off his hitting stroke. Pete Castiglione's stomach condition would benefit from a day of rest, as would Lou Ortiz's leg. To add to these woes, Luke Easter was limping badly after smacking a foul ball off his instep in the doubleheader.

Peanuts Lowrey had been steadily in the lineup following George Bullard's broken thumb and consequent loss to the outfield. Lowrey's legs needed a rest. The same could be said for manager Phil Cavarretta's back. With Lowrey rested, the coach could return to left field, provided Ortiz's leg was well enough to send him back to second. Or Castiglione might be called on to fill in at either position—provided he was ready. Cavarretta looked uncomfortable with his left-field patrol duty on Sunday. He also might have to fill in for Easter at first if the big man was unable to go against Montreal.

On a more positive note, Bill Serena was two for two in each of Sunday's games, a sign that he was finding the range at the plate and that his earlier hand problem had cleared up. In his last seven games, he had gone 11 for 22, a .500 average with five runs scored and eight driven home. Bill had been hitting for power, too. Among his 11 hits were three doubles, a triple and a home run. Equally important had been getting his glove back into the lineup and the best arm at third base in the league. Serena could not only hit doubles, but he could prevent them.

Joe Caffie's hitting streak now stood at 15. This torrid pace with the stick (24 for 61, .393) had raised his average to just a hair over .300. He joined Ed Mierkowicz (.315) as the only two Bisons in that esteemed batting circle. Easter's five RBIs in the first game on Sunday was the highest one-game total a Bison had manufactured since Lew Heyman's six back on April 27 against the same Virginians.

The Bisons desperately needed the bats to wake up to support a pitching staff that had under-gone an onslaught from opposing batters. In 35 games in the month of June, Bison hurlers had sur-rendered 206 runs, an average of 5.88 scores per contest. In contrast, the Buffalo offense had sent only 131 men across the plate, an average of 3.74 and more than two runs behind their opponents. The Herd also caught the goose egg five times in June. For the season, now half over, Buffalo had been shut out 12 times.

Karl Drews had been the only steady mound performer in the past month, winning three and losing the same. He also nailed down a fourth Bison victory in two innings of relief work, though he did not figure in the decision. John Weiss had been the club's most effective reliever until manager Cavarretta attempted to use him as a starter in this current home stand.

Losing starter Gus Keriazakos to an as yet undetermined stomach ailment was a blow to the pitching corps. When and if he would be able to return was uncertain. It was hoped that the arrival of Ron Mrozinski would help. Mrozinski won his first start. Every pitcher but Bill Froats had seen his ERA climb in the past month.

Injuries had hurt the defense by limiting the range of some who could play and keeping others with better defensive skills sidelined.

Games 78 and 79—Tuesday, July 3, Buffalo: Montreal 11, Buffalo 1; Montreal 10, Buffalo 0

Buffalo suffered its worst doubleheader defeat all year.

With 16 hits in each game, first-place Montreal outscored the Bisons 21 to 1.

Game 78 – July 3, 1956 (first game of doubleheader)

Montreal	051 041 0 – 11	16	1
Buffalo	000 100 0 - 1	7	0

WP – Harris (8-4)   LP – Drews (8-7)

Game 79 – July 3, 1956 (second game of doubleheader)

Montreal	015 002 200 – 10	16	2
Buffalo	000 000 000 – 0	5	1

WP – Kipp (12-3)   LP – Mrozinski (1-1)

The day off didn't help much. Pete Castiglione was back in the lineup in game one, well enough to take over shortstop for Billy DeMars. Luke Easter was not available due to the bruised foot, so Phil Cavarretta played first base. Lou Ortiz hit cleanup and was back in at second, allowing Peanuts Lowrey to return to left field. Surely the club had a chance with Karl Drews starting, but today Drews became just a pitching target to hit against—as he had been back on May 21 when the Royals battered him for seven runs in two innings up in Montreal.

The Royals broke open the first-game seven-inning affair with a five-run second inning against the big Buffalo righthander. George Shuba led off by pulling a pitch over the right-field wall. Clyde Parrish and John Roseboro followed with doubles in the gaps to score another. Dixie Howell's ground out moved Roseboro to third, and the Montreal runner slid safely under the tag when Castiglione tried to catch the runner at the plate on Sparky Anderson's ground ball hit to deep short. With Anderson now on first via the fielder's choice, Drews gave up a two-out, two-run four-bagger to Jimmy Williams, this one flying over the left-field barrier. Montreal had a five-run lead, but it didn't stop there.

The first three batters in the third found Drews for two singles and a walk to bring forth a pitching change. Cavarretta walked to the mound from his first-base position to take the ball from Drews and turn it over to reliever Bill Froats, who had come in from the right-field bullpen. Bob Wilson scored on Howell's sacrifice fly before Froats could end the inning.

Buffalo was having little success against Montreal lefty Bill Harris, but did count an unearned run in the fourth. Peanuts Lowrey and Bill Serena both singled and Lowrey scored from third when Williams dropped Cavarretta's fly ball to center. Harris nailed the door shut after that, and that run was all the offense Buffalo would generate in this initial contest.

Froats himself succumbed to the Montreal batsmen in the fifth frame. The first six men to face him got on base. After a Howell single that brought home Shuba and Parris, and a two-out single by pitcher Harris that scored Roseboro and Howell, Cavarretta again made the short trip over to the pitching rubber. John Weiss took over as the third Bison hurler of the day. He ended the fifth without another run scoring.

However, Weiss was touched for the eleventh Royals tally just an inning later on singles by Parris and Roseboro. Parris came home on a Howell ground out, Ortiz to Easter, giving the Montreal catcher a total of four RBIs for the first game.

In game two, Buffalo fared even less well against Fred Kipp. The second lefty they saw this day gave them only five safeties and not a single run.

Cavarretta juggled his lineup the best he could. Pete Castiglione was stationed in left field. Peanuts Lowrey moved to right. Billy DeMars went back in at short. And Cavarretta replaced himself at first base with the righthanded-hitting Ed Mierkowicz. Joe Caffie was the only lefthanded swinger still in the lineup, but all of Cavarretta's revisions made no difference to the game's final outcome. Ron Mrozinski, making his second start for the Herd, was bombed for 10 hits in two and two-thirds innings, showing none of the effectiveness he demonstrated against Richmond back on June 29.

Montreal took the lead with a second-inning run on Sparky Anderson's RBI double. The Royals then drove Mrozinski from the mound in the third. Before Harry Nicholas could be called in to register the third out, Montreal had added five more tallies. Nicholas was able to hold the visitors at bay in the fourth and the fifth frames, but then he, too, was hammered for two more runs in the sixth and yet another pair in the seventh.

Down by a score of 10-0, Pat Tomkinson popped out in a pinch-hitting role for Nicholas in the eighth and John Weiss came in to throw a hitless ninth. Kipp had the Bisons thoroughly handcuffed. **BISON TALES**: Joe Caffie hit safely in game one to extend his hitting streak to 16 games, easily the longest such accomplishment by a Bison this season. Joe hit .390 for this period. Kipp broke the string by keeping him hitless in four plate appearances in game two.

Mrozinski complained to Cavarretta of a sore shoulder. He would undergo testing. The last thing the Bisons needed was yet another injured player.

With the Royals managing 16 hits in each game, Jimmy Williams found the range for home runs in each outing. The Royals slugged a two-game total of seven doubles and four homers. Buffalo got a two-bagger from Bill Serena in the first game and another by Pete Castiglione in the second. Both Bison pinch-hitters were successful in game one. Tomkinson was not as fortunate in the evening set-to.

Lowrey, with singles in both the twilight and evening contests, now had a seven-game hit streak going. He had gone 8 for 25 and a .320 average. Mierkowicz's seven-game string was stopped in the nightcap. His was a torrid 12 for 26, pounding the ball at a .461 clip.

Montreal had now taken six out of seven games against the Bisons. A disappointed crowd of 3893 was on hand to watch the unfortunate spectacle. The teams would meet again on Wednesday for a Fourth of July doubleheader with hopefully a better fan turnout and a bigger bang on the field from the home team.

Games 80 and 81—Wednesday, July 4, Buffalo: Buffalo 5, Montreal 4; Buffalo 5, Montreal 2
Home run heroics and two complete games propelled
the Bisons to a holiday twin-killing sweep over the first-place Royals.

Game 80 – July 4, 1956 (first game of doubleheader)
Montreal	000 000 040 – 4	11	2
Buffalo	005 000 00x – 5	6	1

WP – Hahn (4-5)   **LP – Walz (6-5)**

Game 81 – July 4, 1956 (second game of doubleheader)
Montreal	000 000 2 – 2	4	1
Buffalo	011 000 3 – 5	6	0

WP – Donovan (4-4)   **LP – Nishita (3-4)**

Squaring off in the club's third doubleheader in four days, Fred Hahn hung on to win the nine-inning opener despite a costly Buffalo error that paved the way for four unearned Montreal runs. The Bison hits were again few on this day, but they were timely.

It was a 0-0 ballgame going into the bottom of the third of game one when Hahn worked a walk off righthander Bob Walz. Successive bunt singles by Pete Castiglione and Joe Caffie loaded the bases. Lou Ortiz lined a single to left hit so hard that only Hahn could score, and the bases remained filled. Luke Easter changed all that on a two-two count, driving a Walz fastball for a grand slam home run over the centerfield fence. It was Luke's 18th of the year. Today it was Buffalo's turn to grab the early multi-run lead.

Montreal found Hahn for 11 safeties and the lefty gave up three walks, but the Royals couldn't get the key hit to bring the runners home. Hahn kept the shutout going by stranding nine baserunners, including Dixie Howell, who had tripled with two outs in the fifth inning. A Castiglione to Ortiz to Easter double play helped.

The league leaders got back in the ballgame in the top of the eighth. Clyde Parris singled to lead off and Ron Diering followed with a base hit of his own, putting runners on first and second. Al Ronning, next up, sent a tailor-made double-play grounder to Bill Serena, but the Buffalo third baseman made a bad throw to second that pulled Ortiz off the bag and left everyone safe. Now the Royals had their own bases-loaded, none-out scenario. Hahn got Howell on a popup to short and struck out second baseman George Anderson with a nasty curve, making it two down, but he could not get past George Shuba. Pinch-hitting for pitcher Dave Cole, the third Royals hurler, Shuba parked his own four-run shot over the right-field wall to make it a one-run game. It was Shuba's third grand slam of the season.

Ed Mierkowicz punched a single off Frank White in the bottom of the inning, but the Bisons could not move him around for an insurance run. Hahn gave up one more hit in the ninth but hung on to take the win. It was his fourth complete game of the year and gave the bullpen a greatly needed rest.

In game two, Red Donovan spun a four-hitter to pick up the victory. Lou Ortiz hit the game-winning home run in the last inning.

Donovan had been shelled in three straight appearances since getting married back on June 13, but on this day he was dominant, giving up only two hits and striking out five through the first six frames. Montreal starter Glenn Mickens was tough as well. Again, the Bisons were held to but six safeties in the game.

Buffalo got a single run in the second when Bill Serena scored on Mickens' wild pitch. Joe Caffie's run made it 2-0 in the third while Luke Easter was hitting into a double play. It stayed that way until the scheduled seventh and final inning.

Donovan allowed his first walk of the night to put George Shuba on base. Clyde Parris sent a sharply hit ground ball between first base and second but right into the path of the advancing Shuba. Parris was credited with a hit, but the baserunner was called out for interference. It was a break for the Bisons. Harry Schwegman, the next man up, pounced on Donovan's two-strike offering and sent it over the right-field wall for the game-tying two-run homer.

Bill Nishita, the Montreal righthander who had come on in the sixth, had stopped the Bisons on one hit over three innings of relief in the opener. His luck wouldn't hold up in game two.

Pat Tomkinson got the rally going with a leadoff single to right center. Donovan sacrificed him to second. Pete Castiglione's grounder sent the Bison catcher on to third with two out. Caffie was then intentionally walked to get to the slower Ortiz and set up a force play at second. Ortiz went to a full count before slamming Nishita's last pitch of the game over the left-field screen for the game-ending three-run homer.

BISON TALES: Easter's 18th home run had put him back atop the International League home run race. Bob Bowman, with whom Luke had been tied, had been idled following a rib injury sustained in breaking up a double play. Easter said he might soon start wearing eyeglasses to correct a recently discovered weakness in his right eye. Serena's average had picked up nearly 40 points since donning his lenses. Ortiz's 13 homers made him second on the team to Easter.

News was received that George Bullard was lost to the club for at least three more weeks with his hand injury. It was also learned that Karl Drews had been suffering from an old tendon injury that had swollen his right elbow. It was likely he would miss his next turn on the mound.

Only 3086 fans turned out for the doubleheader, and attendance figures were worrying the front office. With half of the home dates played, and with makeup doubleheaders costing the team single-game attendance numbers, the club had drawn only 88,457 fans. The break-even goal for the season was 250,000. The team was currently looking at a deficit of 75,000 fans or more, and there was no telling how the weather might affect future dates.

In International League news: As of July 4, Havana's Hal Bevan had taken over the batting leadership of the league, hitting at a .348 clip. Montreal third baseman Clyde Parris was second at .341. Sparky Anderson, also of the Royals, shared the third position with Columbus' Al Pilarcik at .331. Richmond's Bill Renna had his 16-game hitting streak stopped on July 2. Since joining the Vees, he had gone 25 for 56, a .446 mark, with seven home runs, five doubles and a triple. Lynn Lovenguth of Toronto and Fred Kipp of Montreal were leading the circuit with 12 wins each.

Thursday, July 5, 1956, Buffalo: Rainout

The Bisons experienced their first rainout since May 16 and would head off to Rochester for a three-game set on Friday, Saturday and Sunday. The games that were postponed in Montreal on May 23 and Rochester on June 1 were just too cold to play on those nights.

The Herd would return to town for a four-game series against Toronto starting on Monday the 9th. Vince McNamara was chairing a committee that was working to turn out 7000 city, county, state and federal employees to help boost the Bisons' recent success on the field as well as answer the club's need for a shot in the arm for the pocketbook.

Speaking of arms, the two complete game victories in the doubleheader were a major help to the staff. Karl Drews was slated to be examined at Buffalo General Hospital for the old tendon injury that had resulted in a swollen right elbow and now his right hand. He would not take the hill until that issue was resolved, according to team physician Dr. Leonard I. Berman.

Newcomer Ron Mrozinski complained that his left arm had stiffened up after he was knocked out of the box on Tuesday. Trainer Jimmy Mack planned to work on the arm to see if this was a temporary matter that could easily be resolved, but Mrozinski's status was unclear.

Gus Keriazakos had returned to the club but with an unpleasant diagnosis and an uncertain future. His stomach complaint was diagnosed as ileitis, an infection of the small intestine similar to that recently suffered by President Dwight David Eisenhower. The President had undergone surgery on June 9 to correct his condition, from which he had satisfactorily recovered. It was uncertain whether Keriazakos would need surgery and, if so, how long this would keep him out of action. It was still unknown how long a recovery would take and when Keriazakos might again be available to pitch.

Casting about for pitching help, team management noted that Timon High School product Tommy Van Remman had put together a 3-1 record with the Terre Haute Tigers in the Three-I League (Illinois-Indiana-Iowa), but his club had just folded. Despite Terre Haute being in Class B, might the Tigers be willing to allow Van Remman to show what he could do in his hometown? He had been a 16-game winner at Jamestown (Class D) in 1954 and in 1955 had won 11 more in a season split between Class B and Class A. A move to Triple A (the Bisons) from B would be a very big jump, indeed.

And then there was the mystery of Bill Froats. Cavarretta was at a loss to explain the lefthander's inability to harness his skills when he took the mound. He managed very well when he was called in with the Herd behind, but give him a lead and his command vanished. The manager wonderd if it could be a lack of confidence, and he was racking his brain to come up with a solution that would enable Froats to achieve success. The team desperately needed the contribution he could be making.

John C. Stiglmeier reported that he was in talks with Miami about outfielder Mel Clark. Bullard's loss to injury had reduced the outfield corps to three men—Lowrey, now playing in left; Caffie, reassigned to center; and Mierkowicz, stationed in right. Cavarretta substituted in left field for two games, but his bad back made him unable to perform at the level the team needed. Pete Castiglione also patrolled left field for one game. Pete was not an outfielder, but his athletic skills enabled him to do a passable job.

Lowrey had said he intended to play regularly, but he might not have anticipated this much time in the field. His 38-year-old legs needed rest from time to time, especially when the club was playing a schedule of doubleheader after doubleheader.

The Bisons missed Bullard's speed on the basepaths in addition to his coverage in the outfield. Joe Caffie was the only man available to Cavarretta who could really run. Speed was a potent weapon that put pressure on the pitcher and the defense and led to runs.

Game 82—Friday, July 6, Rochester, New York: Buffalo 5, Rochester 3

Two former Red Wings helped run the Herd's winning streak to three.
It was Rochester's fifth straight loss.

Game 82 – July 6, 1956

Buffalo	230 000 000 – 5	13	0
Rochester	000 020 100 – 3	7	0
WP – Bowman (6-9)	LP – Faszholz (5-10)		

Buffalo got all its runs in the first two innings, with the first three men in the order doing all the scoring. Pete Castiglione led off against his former Rochester teammates by tripling to left center off starter Jack Faszholz. Joe Caffie, up next, slashed a hit off first baseman Joe Cunningham's glove to plate the first run. Lou Ortiz, who as a Red Wing had helped to win many a contest for Rochester with both his bat and his glove, drew a walk.

When Faszholz's first two offerings to Luke Easter were also called wide of the plate, that was all that Red Wing manager Dixie Walker was willing to see. Out went the call to the bullpen and in came a usual Buffalo nemesis, Cot Deal, while off to the showers went Faszholz. Deal retired cleanup hitter Easter and did the same to Ed Mierkowicz, batting fifth, but he didn't have the same fortune with Peanuts Lowrey. Lowrey's one-baser brought Caffie home and gave Buffalo pitcher Roger Bowman a two-run lead.

The Bisons made it 5-0 in the second after two were out. Deal had retired Norm Sherry and Bowman, leading off, but Castiglione singled for his second straight hit and Caffie then did the same. Ortiz stepped in with the two men aboard. The former Rochester All-Star second baseman took Deal's second offering high over the left-field wall at the 370-foot mark. It was Lou's 14th of the year and his second straight game with a game-winning three-run homer.

Bowman turned in a steady performance until he tired in the eighth and ninth. Red Wing third baseman Ed Phillips and catcher Dick Rand had reached him for back-to-back solo home runs in the fifth inning, but he had then regained control until the eighth. Deal's solo home run in that inning made the score 5-3.

Bowman gave up two leadoff hits when the Red Wings came to bat in the bottom of the ninth. Allie Clark doubled and Gene Green followed with a single, Clark holding at third. Cavarretta put out the call to the bullpen for Joe Coleman. Coleman got fifth-inning home run hitters Phillips and Rand out in succession: Phillips hit a popup to Ortiz and Rand sent a sharp bouncer to Bill Serena at third. Bill turned the latter into the game-ending 5-4-3 double play.

BISON TALES: Deal allowed only four Buffalo hits over the last seven innings, but all the damage had already been done. Easter decided not to wear his new eyeglasses and went 0 for four. Castiglione, Caffie, Ortiz and Lowrey all collected three hits in the game.

With his back to the plate, Castiglione made a running catch of a short fly ball into left field in the sixth that was the fielding gem of the night.

Game 83—Saturday, July 7, Rochester, New York: Buffalo 13, Rochester 5

John Weiss led the way for Buffalo with a complete game victory and
a two-run homer. Ed Mierkowicz drove in five baserunners.

Game 83 – July 7, 1956
```
Buffalo          304 023 010 – 13  13  0
Rochester        002 010 002 -  5  12  2
WP – Weiss (2-4)         LP – Markell (5-4)
```

To give his starters a rest, Rochester manager Dixie Walker sent reliever Duke Markell to the mound to make his first start of the year. As in the previous day's contest, Buffalo jumped on top in the first. Joe Caffie singled and held at third on Lou Ortiz's double. With two outs, Ed Mierkowicz slugged Markell for his third home run as a Bison. Buffalo was out in front, 3-0.

Markell pitched a scoreless second and went out for reliever Gary Blaylock, who started the third. Blaylock lasted for only one out. Caffie worked a walk, and this time he scored on Ortiz's second two-bagger. Luke Easter was given a free pass and both runners came home when Mierkowicz this time connected for a double. Peanuts Lowrey flied out to left, but Ed scored on a Bill Serena single that meant the showers for Blaylock. Manager Dixie Walker handed the ball over to Ed Donnelly. Shortly thereafter, Walker joined Blaylock in the dressing room. Norm Sherry hit an easy 4-6-3 double play grounder to end the inning, but Serena was ruled safe at second and Walker bounced back on the field to argue the call. He lost both the argument and his place on the bench. He got tossed from the game.

Rochester scored two in the bottom of the inning. Ed Kasko, Joe Cunningham and Tom Burgess all hit consecutive singles for one run. Allie Clark's single brought home Cunningham.

Weiss added two to the Bison total in the fifth, slamming his first home run just inside the left-field foul pole to score Norm Sherry, who had doubled. Donnelly was the victim. Tom Burgess got to Weiss for a Rochester solo home run in the last half of the frame. Buffalo scored yet again in the sixth. Easter doubled; Mierkowicz moved him to third with a single. Lowrey walked to load the bases. Serena got his second hit of the night to send Easter across the plate. Donnelly balked, allowing Mierkowicz to score. Lowrey came home with a third run on Kasko's throwing error.

The 13th Buffalo tally was tacked on in the eighth inning off the fourth Red Wing hurler, Kelton Russell. Ortiz singled for his third hit of the night, moved to third on Mierkowicz's third safety of the evening and scored on Lowrey's sacrifice fly. Weiss, with a 13-3 cushion, allowed two Rochester runs in the bottom of the ninth. Ron Rand doubled and Dick Plaza singled. Cunningham's two-out base knock brought both runners home. Weiss got Burgess for the last out.

BISON TALES: The Herd had won four in a row. Lou Ortiz had scored and driven home at least one run in each of the games and had had back-to-back three-hit outings.

Outfielder Mel Nelson pitched the ninth for the beleagured Red Wing pitching staff. He gave up no hits and struck out one.

Game 84—Sunday, July 8, Rochester, New York: Buffalo 8, Rochester 1

The Bisons swept the three-game series and took their fifth win in a
row as Harry Nicholas pitched his best game of the year.

    Game 84 – July 8, 1956
    Buffalo   001 203 002 – 8 12 1
    Rochester   000 000 010 – 1 2 1
    WP – Nicholas (2-7)   **LP – Mackinson (10-5)**

Rochester starter John Mackinson blanked the Bisons until the third inning. Pete Castiglione opened the scoring with a triple to left center, coming home on a double to right by Joe Caffie. Luke Easter's double, a walk to Ed Mierkowicz and a second free pass to Peanuts Lowrey loaded the bases in the fourth. Bill Serena's single to left sent Easter over the plate and brought Cot Deal in to take over the mound from Mackinson, still with the bases full. Norm Sherry's sacrifice fly scored Mierkowicz.

The Bisons solved Deal in the sixth. Caffie poled a home run to right, his fifth of the season. Ortiz dumped a single into left. Easter slammed a triple off the wall in center to score Ortiz, and the Buffalo first baseman made it home himself when Lowrey punched a single to right center between the outfielders.

Nicholas had been experimenting all season long with a slider that had been good only for producing home runs from the opposing batters. He had become the club's leader in home runs allowed. Today, dispensing with the slider and focusing on his curve and a tailing fastball, he had held Rochester hitless for seven innings. Ten Red Wings went down on strikes, somewhat offset by eight walks.

Shortstop Eddie Kasko led off the Rochester eighth with a topped ball down the third-base line that became the Red Wings' first hit. Bill Serena made a barehanded pickup, but his throw was just late. Two walks followed to load the bases and a ground out by Jay Van Noy manufactured a run without a ball having left the infield.

Buffalo picked up two unearned runs with two out in the ninth against the new Rochester reliever Mel Wright. Caffie singled for his third hit and Ortiz's ground ball was thrown away by Ron Plaza for a two-base error, putting runners on second and third. Easter lined a double to right and Caffie scored easily, with Ortiz just beating the throw to the plate. DeMars went in to cover second base in the ninth for a winded Ortiz.

BISON TALES: Mackinson had brought a 7-0 record into the series in Buffalo back on May 25 and had been battered by the Bison hitters in two of those contests. Although he was not charged with any decisions back then, his record since that time had been 3-5, including this game's loss.

It was Nicholas' first win since April 22, when he also allowed only one run. It was the Herd's fourth complete game in the last five.

Bison hitters collected a dozen safe blows off three Rochester hurlers. Easter's three hits were all for extra bases: two doubles and a triple. Since the 11-1 and 10-0 drubbings at the hands of the Montreal Royals on July 3, Buffalo had outscored the opposition 36 to 15 and put together the current five-game win streak.

Game 85—Monday, July 9, Buffalo: Toronto 9, Buffalo 5

The red-hot Toronto Maple Leafs, winners of 11 of their last 12 games,
snapped the Bisons' five-game win streak.

Game 85 – July 9, 1956
Toronto   500 102 010 – 9 11 0
Buffalo   003 000 011 – 5   9 2
WP – Hetki (5-3)   **LP – Hahn (4-6)**

The Leafs jumped in front with a five-run first-inning barrage off Buffalo starter Fred Hahn. Lead-off man Sam Jethroe doubled, followed by a walk to Hector Rodriguez. Another double by Mike Goliat brought Jethroe home and put men on second and third. Cavarretta brought the infield in to cut off the run at the plate, but the plans went haywire. Archie Wilson sent a grounder to Pete Castiglione at short, but Norm Sherry dropped the throw home and Rodriguez scored. Sherry picked up his second error on the play when his throw to first was wild. Bill Wilson, next up, drove the ball over the left-field fence for three more tallies.

A fine throw from Ed Mierkowicz to Sherry in the second inning cut down Jethroe at the plate, saving a run. Buffalo then got three runs in the third. Sherry started it with a single. With two out, Leaf starter John Hetki walked Joe Caffie and gave up a bloop single to left to Lou Ortiz to load the bases. Luke Easter cleared them with a triple to right center, a ball that bounced past outfielders Bill Wilson and Jethroe on the carom. Hetki stayed in the game and walked Mierkowicz, but center fielder Wilson turned in a diving, tumbling catch of a Peanuts Lowrey fly ball to end the Buffalo comeback.

Hahn gave way to Bill Froats in the fourth after Archie Wilson had doubled home Rodriguez with the sixth Toronto run. Two innings later, Froats walked Goliat and Archie Wilson tagged him for a home run. The next batter, Bill Wilson, was hit with a Froats fastball up and in. Earlier in the game, Hetki had hit both Castiglione (throwing arm) and Mierkowicz (left arm). The umpires called both managers out to put a stop to any more retaliation.

Gus Keriazakos took the mound for Buffalo in the eighth, his first appearance since June 15, when he had been sidelined by the stomach ailment that was finally diagnosed as ileitis. Gus allowed a run on singles to Hector Rodriguez and Bill Wilson and his own wild pitch.

Mierkowicz slugged a solo home run in the home half of the eighth. It was his number four of the season. Sherry hit a solo home run in the ninth, his first of the year.

Bison Tales: The Civil Service Employees Night attendance was a disappointing 3191. The good news for Buffalo was that Keriazakos was back to help the pitching staff.

Leaf defense cut off several Bison scoring opportunities. Goliat, in short right field, snared an Easter line drive in the first inning labeled "extra bases." Bill Wilson made a leaping catch off a drive by Caffie as well as his play on Lowrey in the third. Rodriguez stabbed an Easter liner in the eighth and turned it into an unassisted double play, just before Mierkowicz's home run blast.

Tuesday, July 10, Buffalo: Rainout

Rains made the grounds impossible to play. General manager John Stiglmeier and field manager Phil Cavarretta made the call at 4:30 p.m. The teams would take the field tomorrow and play a doubleheader to make up the postponed contest. This was the eighth home date on which a game had been cancelled or called early due to rain, including one doubleheader lost to the elements. This bad luck had likely cost the Bisons 20,000 in home attendance.

Buffalo remained stuck in last place, 13½ games behind front-running Montreal, but even at that they were now two games closer to the top than in June. The Bisons were a stubborn three games behind both Richmond and Havana, which were tied for sixth. The Herd had lost one more game (49) than those two (48) but had played four fewer games due to postponements.

Hall of Fame first baseman George Sisler was in town to watch this series. He was now scouting for the Pittsburgh Pirates, always short of pitching. Former Bison slugging first baseman, Billy Kelly, representing the Chicago Cubs, was here as well, as was Dale Jones who scouted for the Philadelphia Phillies. Toronto's Lynn Lovenguth might be on everyone's mind. The Leaf righthander's contract was owned outright by Jack Kent Cooke, so any transaction would be a straightforward deal not involving a trade with any other club. The bird dogs might be wanting to see if Lovenguth could pitch his way out of his Offermann Stadium jinx.

Luke Easter had been making a late push for fan selection to the International League All-Star squad for the upcoming game against the Milwaukee Braves, to be held in Toronto on July 23. Luke had bashed five hits in his last two games, all for extra bases—three doubles, plus a triple in one outing. Two of his outs the day before had come on sizzling liners right at the infielders. He had also driven home three men in each of those contests. On top of this, he was tied for the league home run leadership with Al Pilarcik of Columbus. Both men had 18 homers. Miami rookie Ed Bouchee had been the consensus first-base choice until Easter's recent offensive outburst.

Unfortunately for Luke, the onslaught had come too late. The conclusion of fan balloting for the All-Star team positions had just been just announced, with no Bisons among the starters.

Over 19,000 votes were cast in the eight league cities. The following starters were selected: righthanded pitcher, Lynn Lovenguth, Toronto; lefthanded pitcher, Fred Kipp, Montreal; catcher, Carl Sawatski, Toronto; first base, Ed Bouchee, Miami; second base, Sparky Anderson, Montreal; shortstop, Jerry Lumpe, Richmond; third base, Clyde Parris, Montreal; outfield, Bob Bowman, Miami; Al Pilarcik, Columbus; and Bob Wilson, Montreal. Other players would be added to the squad by Montreal manager Greg Mulleavy.

Luke Easter and Lou Ortiz both finished third in votes at their respective positions. How different the season might have gone for Buffalo had Stiglmeier been able to secure the All-Star Carl Sawatski from the Chicago White Sox.

In International League news: A late report had it that Al Pilarcik had been recalled by the Kansas City A's. He had been hitting .326, good for third in the league. He was first in RBIs with 75 and had in his last game just pulled himself into a tie with Luke Easter for the home run leadership with 18.

These roster maneuvers were part of the problem for minor league clubs affiliated with big-league programs. Columbus ownership was particularly unhappy. The Jets were a locally owned operation, but with a strong player tie to the major league A's. Buffalo did not face the problem of these abrupt player recalls, but the Bisons were handicapped by the lack of reinforcement players that were needed when the frontliners went down with injury. At times like that, the Herd was at the mercy of whatever big-league club would agree to help out.

Games 86 and 87—Wednesday, July 11, Buffalo: Buffalo 3, Toronto 1; Toronto 7, Buffalo 3

Larry Donovan pitched his way onto the International League All-Star roster in the first game.

Back to back to back home runs made the difference.

The Bisons couldn't catch up in the nightcap.

Game 86 – July 11, 1956 (first game of doubleheader)

Toronto	000 100 0 – 1 5 0	
Buffalo	000 300 x – 3 6 0	
WP – Donovan (5-4)	LP – Lovenguth (13-6)	

Game 87 – July 11, 1956 (second game of doubleheader)

Toronto	000 320 002 – 7 11 0	
Buffalo	000 110 001 – 3 10 1	
WP – Wojey (1-1)	LP – Bowman (6-10)	

All-Star team manager Greg Mulleavy had said that Red Donovan could earn a berth on the league's elite roster depending on how he did in this game against Toronto. Donovan made a strong argument for his selection.

In game one, the Buffalo righty and Toronto's righthanded ace, Lynn Lovenguth, matched shut-out pitching for the first three innings. The Maple Leafs broke through with a run in the top of the fourth. A Donovan fastball struck Leaf second baseman Mike Goliat on the elbow, the resultant pain forcing him out of the game. Walt Derucki came in to run and play second. Ed Stevens' single moved Derucki to third. Carl Sawatski—the catcher Buffalo couldn't get—sent a sacrifice fly deep to right that brought Derucki home.

Buffalo's big bats won it in the last half of the fourth. Lovenguth had allowed only a single to Luke Easter and a walk prior to this, but Lou Ortiz led off with a well-stroked home run over the left-field screen to tie the score at 1-1. It was Lou's 15th. Next up, Easter continued his hot streak and gave the Bisons the lead with one swing of his lumber. Luke's 19th of the year soared its way over the right-field wall. Ed Mierkowicz made it three consecutive home runs, driving his number five over the left center field barrier. Leaf manager Bruno Betzel stuck with Lovenguth for one more hitter, but when Peanuts Lowrey rocketed a single to left, it was four base hits in a row and time for the righty to come out.

Tony Jacobs came in to retire the Bisons in the home half of the fourth, and Dutch Romberger pitched the last two innings for Toronto. Easter picked up his third hit of the day off Romberger, but he was the only baserunner the Maple Leaf relievers would allow. Donovan continued his mastery of the Leaf batsmen. His fastball was sailing inside to righthanders and kept them loose at the plate. Archie Wilson was plunked by a Donovan pitch. Donovan walked only one man, the dangerous Sawatski.

In game two, the Herd again fell behind, but this time couldn't overcome the deficit. Each side was once more scoreless until the fourth frame, when a blown call at second base put the Bisons in a hole. Bill Wilson's two-out base hit off Roger Bowman put a man on first with Loren Babe on deck. Babe's grounder to Lou Ortiz at second was flipped to Billy DeMars for the force at second base and out number three, but umpire Paul Roy didn't see it that way. He ruled that Wilson had beaten the throw. Buffalo protested in vain and the Leafs took advantage of the situation.

Instead of the inning being over, Toronto had another life and with two men on. Ed Stevens, up next, cranked a Bowman curve over the right-field fence. The Maple Leafs were suddenly up by three.

Bill Serena got one back for Buffalo in the bottom of the inning with his solo shot to left center off Toronto's Don Johnson. It was Serena's ninth of the year. But the Leafs added two more in the top of the fifth. Hector Rodriguez beat out an infield grounder for a base hit and scampered home on Archie Wilson's double to the gap in left. Wilson scored on Babe's base hit.

Lou Ortiz got his second home run of the day in the Bison fifth to get another run back and make it 5-2. Johnson walked the next batter, Easter, but then had to leave the game with a wrenched back. It was a bad break for Johnson but may have turned out to benefit Toronto. Pete Wojey was called in at short notice and retired the side. He went on to hold the Bisons scoreless until Lou Ortiz banged his second home run of the game and third of the day in the bottom of the ninth. Lou's solo shot had now given him 17 for the year, only two behind Luke Easter. Wojey allowed three additional hits in the five innings he worked, striking out five and walking only one.

Toronto had preceded Ortiz's ninth-inning blast with two runs off Coleman. Rodriguez singled and Archie Wilson forced him at second—the correct call this time—but Bill Wilson made it a moot point by taking Coleman deep with a home run of his own. Bowman went out for a pinch-hitter in the eighth and Joe Coleman hurled the ninth. Buffalo wound up on the short end of a 7-3 final score.

BISON TALES: Word was received following the doubleheader that Donovan's pitching had indeed won him the spot on the International League All-Star team. Greg Mulleavy also selected Easter for the honor.

Luke's special eyeglasses were delivered before the doubleheader, but he decided against them at the last minute. He was three for three with two singles and a home run in game one, adding two singles and two walks in the second contest.

The second-game loss made Roger Bowman the team's first double-digit loser. There was no one on the squad with double-digit wins. Karl Drews was the closest with eight victories. Bill Froats learned that his mother, Marguerite M. Froats, had died at age 53. Bill was heading home for the funeral arrangements in New York and would be lost to the team for several days.

How the roster woes were mounting! Froats' absence left Cavarretta three men short on his pitching crew—Karl Drews with the sore tendon, Ron Mrozinski with the bad arm and now Froats on compassionate leave. The book was still out on whether Gus Keriazakos had the strength to pitch after his stomach ailment and layoff. Billy DeMars' arm was still not up to par, but he was forced into action anyway because Castiglione couldn't throw at all after being hit by Hetki's pitch on Monday.

The Bisons were the only team in the league against whom the Leafs had a losing record. The Herd had won six of 10 and led 5-1 in the yet to be finished suspended game of May 20.

Game 88—Thursday, July 12, Buffalo: Toronto 14, Buffalo 4

Toronto batters wore out the Bison pitching staff with 14 runs on 18 hits,
including three home runs by ex-Bison Archie Wilson.

Game 88 – July 12, 1956
Toronto	222 412 100 – 14	18	0
Buffalo	000 002 002 - 4	14	2

WP – Blake (9-5)   **LP – Weiss (2-5)**

No Buffalo hurler looked good except for Fred Hahn, who kept Toronto scoreless in the last two innings. Cavarretta had been hoping to save the lefty for the opener of the upcoming series in Montreal. The Maple Leafs scored at least one run in every inning until Hahn's appearance in the seventh with no one out and 14 runs across.

John Weiss started for Buffalo, and Archie Wilson opened the onslaught by homering over the left-field screen with a man aboard in the first. Weiss didn't get a man out in the second, giving up three more hits before giving way to Gus Keriazakos. Toronto scored twice more, both runs charged to Weiss. The Leafs added a pair in the third off Keriazakos when Wilson connected for his second two-run blow to almost the same spot in left. Keriazakos gave way to Joe Coleman in the fourth as the Leafs scored four more runs. Archie Wilson hit his third home run in three consecutive plate appearances. This one came with the bases empty.

Coleman didn't have the answer Cavarretta needed. Toronto battered him for five tallies in his brief stint. Hahn had to come in with no one out in the seventh to retire the side.

Ed Blake threw a complete game against the Herd even though he gave up 14 base hits in the process. Joe Caffie connected for the first Bison run in the bottom of the sixth, when he stroked his sixth home run just fair down the line in right over the 297-foot sign. Lou Ortiz cracked a followup single and wound up on third on another prodigious double by Luke Easter to the base of the scoreboard. Ed Mierkowicz's single plated Ortiz but the Bisons couldn't add more.

Buffalo got their final two in the ninth on Bill Serena's 10th roundtripper of the year, scoring Peanuts Lowrey ahead of him. Pete Castiglione, pinch-hitting, and Billy DeMars, with his first hit in 15 at-bats since reentering the lineup, each singled to raise some diehard hopes, but Blake stopped the rally there.

BISON TALES: Archie Wilson now had nine home runs for 1956, seven of them struck against Buffalo and six of them coming in Offermann Stadium. Wilson had 28 homers and was the league MVP as a Bison left fielder back in 1951.

Castiglione was limited to pinch-hitting or running until his arm healed. Billy DeMars was struggling at the plate since his return to short.

Manager Cavarretta was tossed out of the game in the fourth inning for complaining too much about plate umpire Harry Schwarts' call on Lou Ortiz's at-bat. Ortiz hit a pop fly near the stands that was touched by a fan, preventing catcher Carl Sawatski from making a play. Schwarts called Ortiz out for fan interference.

Games 89 and 90—Friday, July 13, Montreal, Canada: Montreal 8, Buffalo 4; Montreal 3, Buffalo 2

Friday the 13th lived up to its reputation for Buffalo: two defeats, three injuries and an uncertainty about meeting the payroll.

Game 89 – July 13, 1956 (first game of doubleheader)

Buffalo	100 003 0 – 4	6	1
Montreal	015 020 x – 8	10	1

WP – Cristante (5-4)   LP – Hahn (4-7)

Game 90 – July 13, 1956 (second game of doubleheader)

Buffalo	000 000 200 – 2	8	0
Montreal	000 030 00x – 3	7	1

WP – White (8-6)   LP – Nicholas (2-8)

Luke Easter drove in all four Buffalo runs in the seven-inning first game. His first-inning, two-out double off Montreal starter Leo Cristante scored Joe Caffie, who had walked. The run gave the Bisons the only lead they would have all day. Ron Mrozinski started for the Herd but had to leave after two as his sore arm acted up on him once again. The league's leading hitter, Clyde Parris, smacked his 10th home run to lead off the Montreal second and tie the game at 1-1. It was his first of four base hits in this game.

Fred Hahn, on to pitch for Buffalo in the third, showed none of the skill he had demonstrated against Toronto the night before. The Royals raked him for five runs on three hits and two walks. The last two tallies were unearned after Joe Caffie dropped Cristante's fly ball to center. Things got even worse in the fifth. Bill Serena tore open his right hand stabbing at a smash down the line by Cristante. Montreal scored twice more in that frame, while Bill was taken to the hospital to have his hand sewn up. He would be lost to the team for at least a week.

Pete Castiglione, sore arm and all, was pressed into duty to take over Peanuts Lowrey's spot in left field. Peanuts came in to play third. Billy DeMars, with a bad arm himself, would cheat in the hole to compensate for Lowrey's weak arm at third. With a limited pitching staff, Hahn would have to throw more innings and hope the Bisons could break through against Cristante.

They finally did so in the sixth. DeMars worked Cristante for a one-out walk. Lou Ortiz singled after Caffie was retired. Luke Easter, now wearing his new spectacles, clubbed his 20th home run of the year far over the short right-field Delorimier Stadium wall to make the score 8-4. Easter's smash ended Cristante's afternoon and brought Bob Walz to the hill. He fanned Ed Mierkowicz to end the inning.

The Bisons got no more runs, but they did suffer a third injury before the final out was recorded. With the Bisons at bat in the top of the seventh and Pat Tomkinson called in to pinch-hit, Peanuts Lowrey went out to the bullpen to catch warmup throws from Harry Nicholas, Buffalo's game two starter. One of the pitches struck the bullpen plate and bounced up, catching Lowrey behind the ear and knocking him cold. Montreal trainer Gene Harvey raced out to the Buffalo pen to revive Lowrey; Buffalo trainer Jimmy Mack was at the hospital seeing to Serena's injury.

After the last out was made, the Bisons sat down to plan their attack for the nine-inning affair.

Staying out of double plays was high on the list. Three twin killings had snuffed out a number of chances as Cristante gave up four bases on balls in the five-plus innings he pitched.

In the second game, bases on balls did in Harry Nicholas. Nicholas had gotten away with eight walks in his win over Rochester back on July 8, but the Royals took advantage of the opportunities given today and bunched two free passes and three hits in the home half of the fifth inning to win the ballgame.

Nicholas walked Al Ronning and Sparky Anderson to put two men aboard with one out. Royal pitcher Frank White stung Nicholas for a long single to left center that scored both runners, Anderson taking advantage of the weak Buffalo arms. White went to second on the throw to the plate. He scored the winning run himself as Dick Williams, the next hitter, also rapped Nicholas for another base knock to right.

Manager Phil Cavarretta's jury-rigged lineup found Castiglione (sore arm) playing third base and Cavarretta himself (bad back) in left field. Serena was at the hospital and Lowrey was on the bench trying to overcome the headache he was experiencing following his accident in the bullpen at the end of the first contest.

Cavarretta, who had wangled a pinch-hit walk in the first game, showed his men how it was to be done by banging two singles in game two. With his club down by three, the manager opened the Buffalo seventh with a base hit. He moved to second on Billy DeMars' single and scored when Pat Tomkinson made it three one-basers in a row. White seemed to settle down, retiring Lowrey (headache and all), who was pinch-hitting for Nicholas, and getting Castiglione on a short fly to left, but Joe Caffie came through with the fourth single of the inning to score DeMars and load the bases. That also finished White for the night.

Bob Walz made his second successful relief appearance on the day and fanned Lou Ortiz to leave the score at 3-2 in favor of the Royals. Joe Coleman pitched two innings of hitless ball for the Herd. Walz allowed only one base hit to the Bisons in their last two at-bats.

BISON TALES: With the double win, Montreal moved back into first place by a half-game over the rain-idled Maple Leafs.

Gus Keriazakos has been lost to the club for the season, unable to recover from his ileitis. On loan from the New York Yankees, his contract had been transferred back to Denver in the American Association. Gus was a steady hurler who lacked run support in several of his losses before the illness. His absence was yet another blow to the crippled Buffalo pitching staff.

Prior to Bill Serena's hand injury in game one, Cavarretta had contemplated using him on the mound and had even gotten permission from league president Frank Shaughnessy to reclassify him as a hurler. In his youth, Serena's strong arm had served him well as a pitcher until his bat determined that he had to play every day.

Lou Ortiz's potent 11-game hitting streak (.476, 4 home runs, 11 RBIs) was stopped in the second game. Luke Easter's monster seven-game streak was also halted (.583, 3 home runs, 12 RBIs).

CLUB FINANCES AT A CRITICAL LOW
July 13, Buffalo

General manager John C. Stiglmeier reported that the Bisons had only enough resources on hand to meet the payroll through August 15. Rainouts had cost the club at least $70,000 in revenue. The lack of a major league tie-up meant the team had no salary support for its players and had to rely solely on gate receipts.

The team would finish the season and the men would be paid fully as contracted. That was certain. The Bisons had had to take out a $25,000 performance bond as a condition of joining the International League as a newly owned entity. Thus, any financial shortfalls accruing during the full season would be made up by the insurance company, but this would then subject the club to a lien against the sale of the franchise.

No one wanted to sell the Bisons. However, the lack of a major league affiliation was proving more of a burden than had been anticipated. The major league clubs, understandably, had sought first to shore up their farm clubs or teams with whom they had working relationships. The days of "gentlemen's understandings" that Stiglmeier had referred to in the opening days of the season, if ever they had truly existed, were now long gone. In the current atmosphere, "gentlemen" only seemed to respond to threats of antitrust hearings and congressional action.

The club was desperately searching for a new income source for the 1956 season as well as for a working relationship for next year. As to the former, Stiglmeier was not certain where such monies might come from. As to the latter, the business aspects of the game were nowhere so evident as in the callups of Montreal first baseman Rocky Nelson by Brooklyn and the Columbus Jets' star center fielder, Al Pilarcik, by the Kansas City A's. Brooklyn had a deep well of talent and Montreal had not been significantly harmed by Nelson's absence. The Royals were currently in first place. Kansas City, on the other hand, was less fortunate than Brooklyn, and thus even less fortunate was Columbus. The Jets' general manager, Hal Cooper, was so incensed by the Pilarcik move that he had said the Kansas City–Columbus working arrangement would not be renewed for 1957. The Jets were struggling to break into the first division, where playoffs became a part of the postseason and produced extra revenue. The Jets currently stood five games behind the fourth-place Miami Marlins.

The Buffalo brass had to look at this Kansas City–Columbus fracture as potentially good news for the Herd, even with the Pilarcik fiasco. Kansas City would still need a Triple A tie-up in 1957, and it might well be Buffalo they would turn to. Each program would have to balance their specific needs against that of the other. As for other teams, Stiglmeier and president Reginald B. Taylor had also been in talks with the Phillies. Philadelphia had let it be known that they might have considered an arrangement with Buffalo had the sale of the club to the community gone through a few weeks earlier than it did.

Philadelphia had had a working relationship with the Syracuse Chiefs in 1955. When the Syracuse club was sold to Miami interests, according to the Phillies' farm director Gene Martin, Philadelphia was obligated to continue with that connection as part of the terms of sale. The Bisons were on good terms with Martin, and the Phillies would prefer to have their top farm club closer to the City of Brotherly Love.

Behind the scenes, the Miami ownership combo of Bill Veeck and Sid Salomon was strongly rumored to be seeking to buy the Detroit Tigers. Should they be successful, the Detroit club would undoubtedly switch its working relationship to the Marlins, leaving the Phillies to find a new Triple

A partner. Or, it could be that a group headed up by Toronto owner Jack Kent Cooke was the successful bidder in the Detroit sale. In this scenario, the Tigers and Toronto would have the relationship. This could open the door for a Buffalo–Chicago White Sox connection. This latter arrangement was perhaps the only likelihood under which the next Carl Sawatski would land in Buffalo, able to take aim at the short right-field Offermann wall.

It seems the "game" of baseball ain't nothin' but a "business" after all.

Offerman Stadium, Buffalo New York 1956

Game 91—Saturday, July 14, Montreal, Canada: Montreal 5, Buffalo 0

The Buffalo losing streak had now hit four games,
but worse than the shutout was Joe Caffie being knocked cold in the first inning.

Game 91 – July 14, 1956
Buffalo   000 000 000 – 0 8 0
Montreal   200 100 02x – 5 7 0
WP – Nishita (4-5)   LP – Froats (1-5)

The pitching matchup featured Bill Froats, back from his mother's funeral in New York City, against Bill Nishita. Nishita, with a 1-1 record against the Bisons, scattered eight singles against a Buffalo offense that could never find traction. Froats, for his part, stifled the Royals' hitters on four safeties over seven frames, but two of his three walks proved costly.

Froats walked the leadoff man, Jim Williams, in the bottom of the first. It looked like he might escape with no damage done as he retired the next two men, but Clyde Parris, five for seven the day before, sent a shot to straightaway center field that sent Joe Caffie off in hot pursuit. With his eye tracking the ball, Caffie ran full tilt into the center-field wall and crumpled to the ground, the ball bouncing off toward left center.

Williams circled the bases and so did Parris with an inside the park home run. Manager Cavarretta, again playing left field, chased after the ball but caught up with it too late. After the play was concluded, the Bisons and a number of the Royals took off for center field to see to Caffie. Though knocked out for several minutes, Joe eventually got to his feet and walked slowly off the field, turning down the offer of a stretcher that had been brought out to him.

Cavarretta had to juggle his lineup to complete the inning and the game. Peanuts Lowrey, the starter at third base, now went to center field. Pete Castiglione took over the hot corner, no matter the condition of his arm. The only position player left to call on was catcher Pat Tomkinson. Serena was in uniform but unable to play due to the injured hand.

The Royals got a third run in the fourth frame. Chuck Diering walked leading off but was erased on a fielder's choice, John Roseboro taking first. With two down, Nishita singled and then Williams doubled Roseboro home. John Weiss came in to hurl the eighth for Buffalo and was touched for singles by Wilson, Diering and Roseboro for two additional runs.

BISON TALES: Although Caffie was complaining of dizziness, his condition was not as serious as was feared. Medical evaluation had found him to be suffering from no more than the immediate shock to his system. The next day's lineup would have to wait to see how Caffie could manage. Serena's stitches were due to come out in four days, but he wouldn't grip a bat for a week.

In International League news: Brooklyn had recalled shortstop Chico Fernandez from the Royals but was sending last year's American Association All-Star shortstop, St. Paul's Jack Spears, to take his place, thus keeping Montreal competitive.

In major league news: Boston Red Sox lefthander Mel Parnell no-hit the Chicago White Sox, 4-0, in Fenway Park, a venue that hadn't witnessed such a feat in 30 years. Parnell gave credit to his middle infielders and to Jim Piersall for running down a long drive by Luis Aparicio.

Games 92 and 93—Sunday, July 15, Montreal, Canada: Montreal 5, Buffalo 1; Buffalo 2, Montreal 0

The Buffalo losing streak reached five in a row before
Larry Donovan threw a three-hit, 2-0 shutout to win game two.

Game 92 – July 15, 1956 (first game of doubleheader)
Buffalo   001 000 000 – 1 4 1
Montreal   010 001 12x – 5 10 1
WP – Kipp (14-4)   LP – Bowman (6-11)

Game 93 – July 15, 1956 (second game of doubleheader)
Buffalo   000 000 2 – 2 6 1
Montreal   000 000 0 – 0 3 1
WP – Donovan (6-4)   LP – Mickens (4-5)

In a first-game battle of southpaws, the Bisons were no match for International League All-Star selectee Fred Kipp in the nine-inning affair. The 13-game winner kept the Buffalo offense silent, allowing only four base hits and one base on balls. Roger Bowman was on the mound for Buffalo and toiled well until tiring in the late innings. The Bisons kept the score down by turning three double plays.

It was a close ballgame for six innings. Montreal catcher Dixie Howell opened the scoring in the bottom of the second by clouting a solo home run over the faraway left-field fence. Buffalo tied it one inning later. Pete Castiglione sliced a double to right with one out. Joe Caffie went down on strikes, but Lou Ortiz picked up Kipp's only walk of the day to keep the inning alive. Luke Easter then belted a single to right on which Castiglione scored, with Ortiz holding at second. Ed Mierkowicz bounced into a force play for out number three and an end to the Bison scoring in game one.

The Royals came back to take the lead in the sixth on the first of Bob Wilson's doubles and a single by Chuck Diering, and they were back at Bowman in the seventh, too. Sparky Anderson coaxed a walk and stole second base. Kipp helped himself with a clean single to center and Anderson scampered home with the run.

Montreal added a final pair of markers off Bowman in the eighth. New Royal shortstop Jack Spears, who had arrived in the city in the morning in time to suit up for game one, helped himself to four wide ones from Bowman and took first base. He moved on to third in front of Wilson's second double of the afternoon, this one to the left-field corner. Diering's second single brought both baserunners home, adding two more RBIs to his stats.

Lacking effectiveness from the bullpen, Cavarretta was going as long with his starters as he could, hoping they would hold the games close until the Bison bats woke up. There was not much hope for the latter against Kipp this day. Kipp's record was now 14-4. Bowman had fallen to 6-11, but his pitching deserved a better fate.

The seven-inning second game wasn't decided until the final frame. Larry Donovan showed why he belonged on the All-Star team. He fanned five, walked one and scattered three Montreal singles in tossing the shutout.

Glenn Mickens was the pitcher of record for the Royals and was helped out by three Montreal double plays that stymied the first couple of Buffalo thrusts to break into the scoring column. He had been stingy, allowing the Herd only three hits through six.

The Bisons doubled their hit total in the seventh inning and scored the two runs it would take to salvage the last game of this five-game set. The rally started with two outs. Norm Sherry roped a single to begin it and manager Cavarretta followed suit with his own base knock. Billy DeMars, next man up and not usually a long-ball threat, connected with a Mickens pitch that he slugged over the head of center fielder Chuck Diering and against the right center field scoreboard. Sherry scored easily. Cavarretta was running at the crack of the bat and was waved home at third, beating the relay standing up.

Donovan pitched a one-two-three bottom of the seventh. Buffalo had their first victory of the road trip.

BISON TALES: Joe Caffie played both games and was hitless in seven trips to the plate. Cavarretta sent catcher Norm Sherry out to play left field in game one against the lefthanded Fred Kipp. Cavarretta played left in game two to face the righthanded Glenn Mickens. Cavarretta got a double and a single and a walk in three at-bats.

Billy DeMars was spiked in the leg on a first-inning tag play at second. Fortunately, it was a superficial nick, but it still took trainer Jimmy Mack five minutes to tape it shut.

Donovan had been brilliant in his last three outings, throwing three complete seven-inning wins, allowing only 12 hits and three runs in 21 innings. He had struck out 14, walked three and could boast of a 1.28 ERA for that span.

The Bisons headed off for Toronto for a regularly scheduled game on Monday and the completion of the curfew-suspended contest of May 20. Buffalo commanded a lead of 5-1 in the curfew game, but the Maple Leafs had the bases loaded in the last of the seventh and no one out. Donovan was the pitcher of record thus far, but it was unlikely he would take the mound to finish, having just thrown seven innings against Montreal. Other ballplayers who were members of the starting lineups on May 20 had since departed their squads, so replacements would be required for their positions, as well.

In International League news: Additional International League All-Star team selectees were: first base, Luke Easter, Buffalo; second base, Mike Goliat, Toronto; third base, Woody Smith, Havana; shortstop, Ed Kasko, Rochester; outfielders, Cal Abrams, Miami; Bill Renna, Richmond; Tom Burgess, Rochester; and Lew Morton, Toronto; catchers, Ray Noble, Columbus, and Dick Rand, Rochester; righthanded pitchers, Larry Donovan, Buffalo; Don Cardwell, Miami; and Ed Blake, Toronto; lefthanded pitchers, Pat Scantlebury, Havana, and Bob Kusava, Columbus. Coaches would be Bruno Betzel of Toronto and Dixie Walker of Rochester and trainer Bill Smith of Toronto.

International League Standings
July 15, 1956

	W	L	Pct.	G.B.
Montreal	54	40	.574	—
Rochester	51	40	.560	1½
Toronto	51*	40	.560	1½
Miami	48	43	.527	4½
Richmond	44	50	.468	10
Columbus	44	51	.463	10½
Havana	42	52	.447	12
Buffalo	37*	55	.402	16

*Not including suspended game of 5/20

Games 28 and 94—Monday, July 16, Toronto, Canada:
Game 28—Toronto 6, Buffalo 5; Game 94—Toronto 1, Buffalo 0

*Game 28 – July 16, 1956 (completion of suspended game of May 20)

Buffalo	200 003 0 – 5	9	1
Toronto	000 010 5 – 6	9	1

WP – Romberger (2-1)   LP – Hahn (4-8)

Game 94 – July 16, 1956

Buffalo	000 000 000 – 0	3	0
Toronto	100 000 00x – 1	5	0

WP – Blake (10-5)   LP – Weiss (2-6)

In the curfew suspended game of May 20, the Bisons led 5-1, but the Leafs had the bases loaded and no outs. Fred Hahn replaced hurler Larry Donovan (who had just pitched on July 15). Manager Cavarretta replaced Joe Caffie in left field, sending Caffie to center field to replace the injured George Bullard. Ed Mierkowicz took Joe Brovia's place in right field and Norm Sherry covered third base for the injured Bill Serena. Pete Castiglione had replaced Billy DeMars at shortstop on May 20. Pat Tomkinson, Luke Easter and Lou Ortiz were the only starters left in the game.

Sam Jethroe was the first batter Hahn faced and he ripped the lefty for a two-run single. When Hahn followed by walking Loren Babe to load the bases again, Cavarretta sent for Joe Coleman. The Bison reliever fanned Archie Wilson, but pinch-hitter Bill Wilson slammed a two-run single of his own to tie the game at 5-5. Lew Morton's base hit scored Babe for the Toronto win.

In the regularly scheduled game, Toronto's Ed Blake made a first-inning run hold up for the full nine-inning game. Loren Babe doubled off the Bisons' John Weiss with two out in the first. Ed Stevens singled him home. That was it. Blake set down the first 12 men to face him and allowed the Bisons only three hits all game, walking but one. Buffalo's best chance came on Luke Easter's 400-foot double to the scoreboard in center field in the seventh. Toronto manager Bruno Betzel responded with a game-saving defensive move. He benched left fielder Archie Wilson, moved Sam Jethroe from center field into left against the pull-hitting Ed Mierkowicz, and put Bill Wilson in center. Mierkowicz's drive to the left-field corner was run down by Jethroe.

Game 95—Tuesday, July 17, Toronto, Canada: Buffalo 9, Toronto 3

Ed Mierkowicz broke up the game with a three-run homer in the fifth and drove in five.
Nicholas fanned nine to offset his four walks.

```
Game 95 – July 17, 1956
Buffalo          002 030 400 – 9  11  1
Toronto          200 000 010 – 3   9  2
WP – Nicholas (3-8)      LP – Hetki (3-4)
```

Harry Nicholas survived a first inning that saw him give up two singles, a walk, and a two-run single to Archie Wilson after two were out. Ed Mierkowicz tied it in the third with a two-run single of his own off Toronto starter John Hetki. Joe Caffie and Lou Ortiz scored the runs. Mierkowicz's bat roared again in the fifth after Caffie had slapped a single off Hetki's glove and Easter was intentionally walked. Ed's sixth home run of the year put the Bisons ahead 5-2.

The Herd put the game out of reach with a four-run seventh off reliever Pete Wojey. Nicholas and Caffie both got base hits. Luke Easter's two-out single scored Nicholas. A walk to Mierkowicz loaded the bases and brought in Dutch Romberger to become the new Leaf hurler. He faced manager Cavarretta, once again stationed out in left field. Phil slugged a double to score Caffie and Easter and, when right fielder Lew Morton's throw went astray, Mierkowicz motored home as well. Buffalo 9, Toronto 2.

Toronto got a third run in the eighth on an Ed Stevens single, a walk to Earl Battey and Walt Derucki's RBI single to score Stevens. The loss knocked Toronto out of first place. Rochester claimed that position with a win over Montreal.

BISON TALES: The victory was Nicholas' third complete game in a row, winning two and losing one. This was his best pitching of the year.

Cavarretta said the 6-5 loss of the suspended game took more out of him than any incident he could recall in his entire career. He had gotten on the phone between games with general manager Stiglmeier to discuss roster needs. Stiglmeier had responded that pitching help was on the way.

Lefthanded hurler Steve Nagy turned up at the Bisons' Toronto hotel following this day's game. The 37-year-old had had brief appearances in the majors with Pittsburgh in 1947 (1-3) and Washington in 1950 (2-5), but had toiled primarily in the Pacific Coast League for the past nine seasons. He refused to sign this year with the American Association Louisville Colonels and had instead been hurling semipro ball, looking for a better offer. Last year, he had been 6-12 with the San Francisco Seals. Nagy's presence was vital since Karl Drews' arm had not been responding.

Position players were impossible to come by and the Buffalo situation had become even worse with the news about Peanuts Lowrey. Sent back to Buffalo for evaluation, Peanuts had been diagnosed with a slipped disk and could be lost for the season. He would need to rest for several days before a more definitive assessment could be made, according to the team's physician, Leonard Berman. He would likely need a back brace if future play this season was even possible. Norm Sherry started the game at catcher but spelled Cavarretta in left field in the eighth due to the manager's aching back. Pat Tomkinson took over behind the plate.

Game 96, Wednesday, July 18, Toronto, Canada: Toronto 8, Buffalo 7

Two unearned runs cost the Bisons the ballgame after a seven-run rally in
the fourth inning had put them in the lead.

Game 96 – July 18, 1956
Buffalo   000 700 000 – 7 9 2
Toronto   130 220 00x – 8 13 1
WP – Jacons (3-4)   LP – Nagy (0-1)

In a battle of lefthanders, Fred Hahn squared off against former Bison Ken Johnson. Hahn gave up a run in the first and was touched for three more in the second. Johnson, who had won 12 games for Buffalo in 1952 and then added 14 in the following year, held the Herd in check until the big fourth.

Ed Mierkowicz, Pat Tomkinson and Billy DeMars strung consecutive singles for one run. Hahn's single made it four in a row and another run across. Pete Castiglione coaxed a walk to load the bases, and Joe Caffie unloaded them with a triple into the left-field corner. So much for Johnson's day. In came Tony Jacobs with two out and Lou Ortiz stepping into the batter's box. One swing of the big second baseman's bat and the sacks were empty again on Lou's 18th of the year. Buffalo had a 7-4 lead.

Naturally, the first pitch to Luke Easter was so high and tight that even the catcher missed it. Bat in hand, the 6-foot, 4-inch, 235-pound Luke started for the mound and his 5-foot, 9 inch, 155-pound opponent, but Cavarretta raced in from his third-base coach's box and bear-hugged Jacobs to pull him out of any danger. Threats came to nothing. The next pitch to Easter went behind him. Easter growled, but as he said after the game, this is baseball. Somebody reaches you for a home run and the next man is likely to go down. Eventually, the Buffalo first baseman collected a walk. Mierko-wicz's ground out ended the inning.

Blessed with a three-run lead, Fred Hahn gave two of the runs right back in the Toronto half of the fourth, both due to his own two errors. Now only a run up, Cavarretta turned to the new lefty, Steve Nagy, to start the fifth. Toronto scored another pair off Nagy to take the lead at 8-7. That was the way the ballgame ended, with Nagy taking the loss in his first appearance as a Bison.

BISON TALES: Norm Sherry again played left field to give Cavarretta's back a day off.

Some good news for a change in the pitching department. Another former major league hurler was joining the staff. Zeb Eaton had pitched briefly for Detroit in 1944 and fashioned a 4-2 record with them in 1945. The Tigers also used him as a pinch-hitter. He hit .250 in 1945 with two home runs. Eaton also pitched for Buffalo in 1944, 1946 and 1949, recording a 7-8 mark overall. He hit five home runs with the 1944 club and six for the Herd in 1946, averaging .290.

Eaton retired after a serious beaning in 1949 playing with the Birmingham Barons in the Southern Association, but desire for the game kept him on the diamond. He had been busy hurling for the Amigones in the Buffalo MUNY Leagues. On Tuesday afternoon, he walked into Offermann Stadium to speak with general manager John C. Stiglmeier and offer his services if they could help. Eaton's vacation from his machinist's job at Curtiss-Wright would begin Friday, when the 36-year-old would once again don a Buffalo uniform.

Game 97, Thursday, July 19, Toronto, Canada: Toronto 3, Buffalo 2

A second effective outing by Buffalo's Bill Froats went for naught
as the Herd suffered a second straight one-run loss.

Game 97 – July 19, 1956

Buffalo	200 000 000 – 2	5	0
Toronto	000 110 01x – 3	6	0

WP – Lovenguth (15-6)   LP – Froats (1-6)

Buffalo got both their runs in the first inning. With Lynn Lovenguth pitching, Pete Castiglione whisked a leadoff double down the right-field line. Joe Caffie was retired on a soft fly to center, but then Lovenguth walked Lou Ortiz and gave up a base hit to Luke Easter for the game's first run. Ed Mierkowicz's single sent Ortiz home with the second tally, but a fine throw from center fielder Bill Wilson nailed Easter at third for out number two. Norm Sherry went down on strikes, and that was going to be it for the Bisons. Lovenguth allowed only them two more hits.

Bill Froats pitched a scoreless three innings for the Herd until Mike Goliat led off the Toronto fourth by slamming a curveball over the left-field wall. It was Goliat's 13th home run of the season. The Maple Leafs tied it in the next inning when Ed Stevens led off with a double and Earl Battey sent him home with a double of his own.

The ballgame remained a tie until the eighth frame, when Sam Jethroe legged out a triple to left center. Hector Rodriguez, the next batter, brought him home with the winning run on a sacrifice fly to left. The Bisons made a comeback try in the ninth as Ortiz walked to lead off but was forced at second on Easter's grounder. Roger Bowman was sent in to run for Easter. After Mierkowicz was retired, Sherry walked to move the tying run to second base. The ballgame ended on Pat Tomkinson's ground out.

BISON TALES: Lovenguth's win was his first against Buffalo this season. His record at home was 12-1, his only loss coming in the Leafs' home opener. The victory moved Toronto back into first place in the league.

Bill Froats was now 0-6 lifetime against Toronto. Catcher Norm Sherry was once again stationed out in left due to the player shortage.

July 19 was Phil Cavarretta's 40th birthday, but rather than celebrating he spent a long time into the evening in the visiting manager's office, conferring with general manager John C. Stiglmeier. The general manager had come up to Toronto to meet with the players and assure them that the ball club was going to stay in operation.

The July issue of Buffalo Business magazine featured an article by Paul Becker entitled "A Baseball Game Is a Bargain at Any Price." In an effort to encourage more attendance at Offermann, Becker recounted an evening he had spent at the ballpark back in June, watching spectacular plays pulled off by Jim Clark at shortstop and George Bullard in center field. Baseball is an "American tradition worth fighting for," Becker wrote, citing the highlight of his evening as watching "father and son sitting together at the ballpark."

"Buffalo has already suffered one black eye this year," Becker added, "in the near-loss of the Erlanger Theater. We'd better prepare for another sock in the eye at Offermann Stadium unless someone wakes up the baseball fans."

Friday, July 20, Buffalo: Rainout

Yet another rainout back home in Buffalo, the season's ninth. With Rochester in town, the Bisons could ordinarily expect to draw a sizable contingent of fans from this nearby rival, especially on a weekend, but this evening there was no ballgame, no attendance, no gate receipts.

In other bad news, Stiglmeier reported that pitcher Ron Mrozinski had been returned to the Philadelphia Phillies. His sore arm would not respond to treatment. The pitching staff was down yet another hurler.

On the plus side, Bill Serena had had the stitches taken out of his hand before the club left Toronto and possibly could return to third on Sunday. If so, Cavarretta would send Pete Castiglione out to left field, where he could cover more ground than Norm Sherry. Pete's arm was still not right, but it would have to do. Cavarretta had to rest his back after his outfield stints on the road trip. The most he might be able to do now was pinch-hit.

Karl Drews reported considerable improvement in his arm. He had not gone on the road trip but had stayed back in Buffalo to rest. He also might be available for the Sunday doubleheader, but likely only in short-term relief.

So new pitcher Zeb Eaton's story was an interesting one to contemplate on this rainy day. The Bisons definitely needed him on the mound, but he might also be a help in the outfield.

A native of Cooleemee, North Carolina, Zeb had a history of overcoming adversity, a fitting tale for the saga of the 1956 Buffalo Bisons. Eaton was only 2-6 with his hometown club in the North Carolina State League in his first year in organized baseball back in 1939, but pitching for Alexandria in the Evangeline League the next year he won 23 games, lost 11 and stymied the hitters with a 1.77 ERA. He also hit .286 and drove out five home runs.

This caught the eye of the Detroit Tigers, who signed him to a contract to pitch for Beaumont in the Texas League. Zeb won 8 and lost 15 for that 1941 club before entering the military. Following two years of service, he was promoted to the Buffalo Bisons in 1944. He won 3 and lost 4, and the Tigers called him up at the end of the season.

Zeb stayed with Detroit during the World Series–winning 1945 campaign, contributing a 4-2 record, two home runs and 10 men driven home. He appeared for one at-bat in the World Series, striking out as a pinch-hitter. He came back to Buffalo for 1946, when the Tiger regulars came home from war duty.

Zeb went 3 and 4 for the Bisons again, but he also appeared in an additonal 41 games as an outfielder/pinch-hitter, batting .290 with five home runs. The Philadelphia Athletics bought his contract in 1947 and converted him into an everyday player to take advantage of his bat.

Now 27 and an outfielder for Birmingham in the Southern Association, Eaton was scorching the league with a .359 average and 73 runs driven home in 98 games, until he was struck in the head by a fastball that put him in the hospital for 18 days. A brain hemorrhage leaked blood into his spinal column, affecting his vision. He lost the entire 1948 season. His attempted comeback in 1949 saw him hitting only .232 when released by Savannah in the Sally League. Detroit signed him once again and sent him to Buffalo once more, and he posted one victory at the end of the season.

Still suffering from the beaning, Eaton was to lose 1950 as well, but desire for the game kept him coming back. For Class B Greenwood in 1951, he registered 13 wins, 16 losses, six home runs and a .254 average. Suiting up for Tri-State B League Gastonia in 1952, he went 16-11. He added four home runs and hit .224.

At 32 years of age, Eaton finally called it quits, returning to his new place of permanent residence in Buffalo to work at an ordinary job. Still, he kept his hand in as a MUNY League competitor. Out of organized baseball for the past four years, Zeb was willing to offer his services for a fourth appearance with Buffalo, if they would have him. The Bisons were happy, only too happy, to oblige.

Game 98, Saturday, July 21, Buffalo: Rochester 12, Buffalo 7
The Red Wings, contending for first place,
scored early and often and sent the Bisons to their third straight defeat.

Game 98 – July 21, 1956
Rochester   420 501 000 – 12 15 1
Buffalo   010 123 000 - 7 17 2
WP – Faszholz (6-9)   LP – Bowman (6-12)

Roger Bowman, the lefty who had taken the measure of the Wings only two weeks ago in the Flower City in a game he had won 5-3, didn't last two innings. The first four men to face him got on base and scored. Cavarretta brought in Steve Nagy after Rochester added two more runs in the second. Nagy got the inning's final out, but the Red Wings caught up with him two innings later.

Rochester's Kelton Russell started just as poorly as had Bowman, but Rochester manager Dixie Walker had more of a bullpen to turn to than did Cavarretta. He brought in Jack Faszholz in the first inning after Russell had loaded the bases with only one out. Faszholz slammed the door shut without the Bisons being able to score a run. It wasn't until Pat Tomkinson hit a solo home run in the bottom of the second that the Herd was able to get on the scoreboard, but by then the Red Wings were ahead 6-1.

And Rochester added five more scores in the top of the fourth, capped by Allie Clark's grand slam home run. That inning finished Nagy. New Bison Zeb Eaton was called in to pitch the fifth, entering a game the first time he suited up, just as had been the case with Nagy in Toronto. The performance he put on made it look like he well could be the answer to a number of Bison woes.

Eaton pitched the final five frames, allowing only three base hits (all in the sixth inning for the only run charged against him), struck out three, walked three, got a single and a double in three at-bats and scored a run. The Bisons kept trying to get back into the game, scoring once in the fourth, two more in the fifth and a triad in the sixth to make it 12-7 in favor of the visitors. They could get no closer. Mel Wright took over for Faszholz in the sixth. The third Red Wing hurler kept the Bisons off the scoreboard in the final three innings, even though they managed five hits against him.

Bison Tales: Bill Serena played third base and went one for five, starting the game's only double play. Pete Castiglione was in left field.

Buffalo outhit the visitors 17 to 15—every position player registered a base hit—but left a dozen men on base. Key hits went missing, starting with the bases-loaded first-inning failure.

The Bisons suffered through a 2-8 road trip in Canada and would start a southern swing on Monday after the upcoming Sunday doubleheader against the Wings. Larry Donovan, who had made a specialty of winning the seven-inning affairs, would likely hurl that contest for Buffalo. Harry Nicholas, who two-hit Rochester back on July 8, would start the nine-inning set-to. The Bisons needed a double victory to take this series.

Not too many fans might read Buffalo Business magazine. Despite the fine article by Paul Becker, attendance registered at the ballpark for this game was only 2271.

Games 99 and 100, Sunday, July 22, Buffalo: Buffalo 9, Rochester 2; Buffalo 7, Rochester 6
*The doubleheader sweep allowed the Bisons to take
the rain-shortened series. Donovan and Drews got the wins.*

Game 99 – July 22, 1956 (first game of doubleheader)

Rochester	000 001 100 – 2	11 0
Buffalo	400 031 10 x – 9	12 0

WP – Donovan (7-4)   LP – Markell (7-5)

Game 100 – July 22, 1956 (second game of doubleheader)

Rochester	100 302 0 – 6	9 2
Buffalo	050 010 1 – 7	10 0

WP – Drews (9-7)   LP – Wright (1-2)

Larry Donovan pitched the scheduled nine-inning afternoon game and turned in his second nine-inning complete game victory this season. He'd beaten Toronto on the road back on May 28, winning 4-3. Counting the three previous seven-inning assignments, Donovan now had four complete-game wins in the month of July.

Duke Markell had had his struggles with Buffalo this season, and the first game was no different. He lasted only one-third of an inning. Pete Castiglione led off with a single and stayed at first as Joe Caffie popped out, but a double by Lou Ortiz put two runners in scoring position for Luke Easter. Markell fell behind in the count and Dixie Walker, the Red Wings manager, ordered Easter intentionally passed. With the bases full, Ed Mierkowicz connected for home run number seven, a grand slammer over the wall in left. Cot Deal entered the game to pitch for Markell.

Donovan allowed the Wings 11 hits, but the defense behind him kept the game under control. Rochester managed a baserunner in each of the first three frames, but three Bison double plays kept the four-run lead intact.

The Herd added three more runs off Deal in the fifth. Bill Serena homered to start the inning, his 11th of the season. Two more men came home when Donovan, Castiglione and Caffie all rapped two-out base hits. Deal finally put the Wings on the board in the sixth inning when he tripled to center leading off and scored on a Joe Cunningham single. Buffalo matched it in the bottom of the inning. Easter pulled a double down the right-field line. Serena's infield base hit got him to third. Pat Tomkinson's long sacrifice fly to center brought him in.

Doubles by Mel Nelson and Deal made for another Rochester run in the seventh, but the Bisons got that back in the home half of the inning. With one away, it was Donovan's turn to boom a triple. Deal got Castiglione on a one-hopper to third, Donovan holding, and then manager Walker, playing the percentages, ordered the lefthanded-hitting Caffie intentionally walked to get to Ortiz. Ortiz, undisturbed by the percentages, clipped Deal for a solid single to left. Donovan came home with the game's final run.

In the nightcap, Bill Serena led off the seventh and final scheduled inning by guessing a first-pitch curveball from reliever Mel Wright. Serena sent it high over the screen in left for the game winner. It was Bill's second home run of the day, making a winner out of Karl Drews and giving Buffalo a sweep of the double bill.

Bases on balls hurt Harry Nicholas, who walked leadoff man Ron Plaza to start the game. Two outs later, Joe Cunningham made him pay for the walk with an RBI double. The Bisons were held scoreless in the first against John Mackinson but erupted for five runs in the bottom of the second.

Following a Serena ground out, Norm Sherry and Billy DeMars both singled. Nicholas moved the runners up with a sacrifice. Pete Castiglione then caught the triple fever from game one and slammed the ball to right center. With the ball skipping between the outfielders and rolling to the wall, the two baserunners scored easily, and Castiglione wound up at third base. Joe Caffie's double to right brought in Castiglione and sent Mackinson out of the game. Lou Ortiz stood in against new pitcher Jack Roberts and lined the ball over the third-base bag for Buffalo's third straight extra-base blow. Caffie scored. Four runs were home, and Luke Easter's single up the middle plated Ortiz to make it five. Roberts finally retired Ed Mierkowicz to end the inning.

Three runs put the Red Wings back in the game in the fourth. Ed Phillips led off with a single and moved to third on a double by Dick Rand. Mel Nelson got the third straight hit, a double that cashed both baserunners. After Jay Van Noy, pinch-hitting for Roberts, made it four base knocks in a row, Cavarretta signaled to the bullpen. Karl Drews would make his first appearance in two weeks.

Drews stopped Rochester cold, allowing no more runs. The Bisons added another run of their own in the fifth, this one off Duke Markell, back again after his one-third of an inning in game one. Mierkowicz singled. DeMars doubled him home with his second hit of the ballgame.

It was a vital run because Rochester reached Drews for a pair in the sixth and knotted the game at six apiece. Nelson drew a walk to start the inning. Cot Deal pinch-hit a single and Sonny Dixon was sent in to run for him. The runners moved up on Plaza's sacrifice and came home on Ed Kasko's single to center.

Drews set the Red Wings down in the top of the seventh. The win was Drews' ninth of the year, his second as a reliever.

Bison Tales: In the dressing room afterward, Serena said he figured Wright's arm was tired from going three-plus innings in last night's showdown and that he would start him with a curve. With his hand still affected by the injury, Serena added, the curve was the only ball he felt he could drive with power to make a difference. Bad hand and all, Serena went five for nine in the twin bill. Easter had been pounding the ball over the last 21 games, batting .428 with four home runs and 21 RBIs. Mierkowicz had belted two homers in the last six games and had knocked in 11 runs, hitting .291 over that period.

Lou Ortiz was named by International League President Frank Shaughnessy to replace the injured Mike Goliat and start at second in the All-Star contest against the Milwaukee Braves.

Peanuts Lowrey made an appearance in the press box during the doubleheader and took a turn behind the mike to call a couple of innings. He could be back on the field, he said, wearing a back brace to cope with the disk problem.

Monday, July 23, Toronto, Canada

International League All-Star Game: Milwaukee Braves 3, International League All-Stars 0

The All-Star event should have been called the Bob Trowbridge show. The 26-year-old rookie righthander who hadn't able to break into the Braves' starting rotation threw a nine-inning one-hitter against the International League's best. After escaping a bases-loaded jam in the first—he had walked the bases full—Trowbridge therafter had allowed only a Clyde Parris fourth-inning leadoff single and two more free passes for the rest of the game.

The National League leaders could muster only six hits against four International League pitchers. Home run sluggers Hank Aaron and Eddie Matthews only played part of the game and collected no big blasts. Aaron drove in the game's first two runs.

Luke Easter, Lou Ortiz and Larry Donovan got caught up in Toronto traffic and arrived late, taking the field only in the last two innings. Easter's 400-foot blast to center was pulled in by the Braves' Billy Bruton. Ortiz did not hit.

Donovan was eager to pitch the ninth and fanned two, but he also allowed two hits, one of them Del Rice's solo shot over the left-field fence.

In major league news: Joe Cronin and Hank Greenberg were elected into the Baseball Hall of Fame in Cooperstown, New York, bringing that august body to a total of 81 men.

Tuesday, July 24, Richmond, Virginia: Rainout

The rained-out game was rescheduled as part of a doubleheader to be played on Wednesday.

With the season two-thirds gone, the Bisons were not where they want to be and not where they had anticipated being: in last place in the league standings with a 40-60, .400 record, and far, far behind at the box office.

The rainouts had been the major culprit in creating the financial problem. Had there not been 11,008 fans on hand to witness the home opener, that too would have been cancelled. Single-game rainouts that were later played as part of makeup doubleheaders could not bring in two games' worth of receipts.

A second factor could be the club's poor record, making the fans less likely to spend their free time and disposable dollars at the ballpark. In response, club officials and community business leaders and organizations had been working overtime to arrange promotional "ball club nights" to increase attendance. In previous years, no such intensively concerted efforts were required because the major league parent club (most recently the Detroit Tigers) would underwrite most of the player salary expense, which was by far the greatest cost of operation.

No one had anticipated the need to build a community promotional network when the proposal to become a community-owned ball club was first approached. The Bisons were playing catchup in this respect, just as on the diamond.

Predicted with some good rationale to be a first-division ball club—including by manager Phil Cavarretta, a man with a reputation of telling it like he saw it—the Bisons found themselves occupying the cellar, two and a half games behind the seventh-place Havana Sugar Kings. The first division was 14 games away, and frontrunner Toronto held a 19-game advantage over the Herd.

Onfield woes were due to injuries and, perhaps most importantly, the lack of a major league affiliate to turn to for replacement players. Injuries were part of the game and were to be expected over the six-month-long, 154-game schedule. Veteran players were even more susceptible to the injury bug, and Buffalo could easily lay claim to being the oldest ball club in the circuit. When starters went out of commission, a fresh supply of talent from a major league farm system was crucial to a team's success.

Buffalo had been flirting with first-division status until the middle of May, the cutdown day for the major league ball clubs. On May 19, the Herd had an 11-15 record, a .423 winning percentage, and was in fifth place, seven games out of first but only a half-game behind the fourth-place Columbus Jets. At that same time, Havana, in eighth place, was only one game worse than the Bisons. It was a very tightly packed competition.

Since that time, the Buffalo club had gone 29-45 (.391) to find themselves fallen into the cellar. Injuries had played the dominant role. Every position player but two had missed time on the field: Tomkinson (catcher), arm and spike wound; Easter (first base), legs; Ortiz (second base), leg; DeMars (shortstop), arm; Serena (third base), thumb and hand; Castiglione (utility), stomach and arm; Caffie (right/center field), collision with fence; Bullard (center field), hand; Lowrey (coach, outfield, infield), concussion; Cavarretta (manager, first base, outfield), back. Only later acquisitions Ed Mierkowicz (outfield) and Norm Sherry (catcher) had remained healthy. Sherry had been called on for emergency duty in the outfield and at third base; Mierkowicz had taken a turn at first. John Blatnik's retirement had been a serious blow.

The pitching staff had also been struck by the injury bug. Donovan's arm had not been ready early in the season. Drews' arm acted up on him in July. Keriazakos was sidelined by illness in June and had never truly recovered. Mrozinski, a June replacement for Mario Picone, turned up with a bad arm. Things had gotten so bad that the manager, before Bill Serena's hand injury and before the arrival of Steve Nagy and Zeb Eaton, had begun discussions with International League president Frank Shaughnessy about reassigning Serena's roster position from infielder to pitcher.

If you talked to Bison trainer Jimmy Mack, he would tell you that the Buffalo injury epidemic was the worst he had seen in his 30 years in the business, and that included stints with a number of hockey teams. Playing injured made matters worse. Had Cavarretta had the luxury of sitting Karl Drews when the hurler first strained the tendon, for instance, it was likely it would not have blown up into a two-week absence. Easter was playing with a chronic ankle injury after the early-season collision in Richmond at first base. This only worsened his chronic leg problems stemming from an automobile accident earlier in his career. Mack worked on him for at least a half-hour before each game, using three yards of athletic tape to get him ready to play.

Other teams in the league with major league ties or with the deep pockets of Jack Kent Cooke, owner of Toronto, and the new ownership in Miami, could find skilled fill-ins when required.

Toronto was in first place (60-42, .588) because owner Cooke had the cash needed to purchase the best and the leverage to demand the best. The Toronto–White Sox arrangement for catcher Carl Sawatski was for the full year.

Second-place Rochester (56-43, .565), was stocked with players from the St. Louis Cardinals extensive farm system. St. Louis had Triple A clubs in both Rochester and Omaha, Nebraska, and could move players back and forth as needed.

Miami's Marlins (56-43, .565) were tied for second, thanks to outstanding young pitching from the Phillies organization and independent wealth that had enabled the purchase of Woody Smith to bring needed power to the mix.

Montreal (56-48, .538), in fourth place, had been hurt by Brooklyn's callup of Rocky Nelson, but the Dodgers had later sent American Association All-Star Jack Spears to replace shortstop Chico Fernandez when he, too, was brought up.

Richmond (48-54, .470) struggled out of the gate until the Yankees sent down Jerry Lumpe to become the International League All-Star shortstop and acquired Kansas City's Bill Renna to terrorize International League hurlers.

Columbus (46-57, .446) had been challenging for the top spot until the Kansas City Athletics recalled the red-hot Al Pilarcik. Without Pilarcik, Columbus had tumbled to sixth place.

Havana (43-58, .425) was in seventh place because the parent Cincinnati Red Legs, fighting Milwaukee for first place in the National League, had not offered the Sugar Kings any new help.

Club Statistics: 100 Games

Pitchers	W	L	ERA	Notes
Drews	9	7	4.02	Arm trouble sidelined him for 3 weeks
Donovan	7	5	3.38	Completed and won last 4 starts
Bowman	6	12	4.66	Has pitched better than record indicates
Hahn	5	7	5.10	ERA jumped by nearly 1 run
Coleman	3	0	4.27	ERA jumped by nearly .5 run
Nicholas	3	8	5.52	Has pitched his best in last 3 weeks
Weiss	2	6	4.85	Inconsistent both starting and relieving
Froats	1	6	7.21	More promise in last 2 starts (both losses)
Eaton	0	0	1.80	One relief appearance
Nagy	0	1	8.09	Battered in 2 relief appearances

Hitters	G	AB	R	H	HR	BI	Avg
Easter	97	330	45	99	20	66	.300
Caffie	76	276	40	82	6	30	.297
Ortiz	98	345	54	97	18	61	.281
Mierkowicz	50	176	27	49	7	30	.278
Castiglione	82	270	23	75	0	18	.277
Lowrey	79	217	28	60	1	20	.273
Bullard*	67	237	34	61	2	10	.257
Cavarretta	27	44	7	11	1	6	.250
DeMars	62	196	17	46	0	12	.234
Sherry	32	93	9	22	0	5	.230
Serena	82	255	33	58	12	39	.227
Tomkinson	60	156	13	35	2	9	.224

*Missed last 29 games due to injury.

Games 101 and 102, Wednesday, July 25, Richmond, Virginia: Richmond 3, Buffalo 2; Richmond 7, Buffalo 1

Ed Lopat outdueled John Weiss in the close seven-inning opener.
The Bisons managed only two hits in game two.

Game 101 – July 25, 1956 (first game of doubleheader)

Buffalo	000 020 0 – 2	5	0
Richmond	020 001 x – 3	5	1
WP – Lopat (8-4)	LP – Weiss (2-7)		

Game 102 – July 25, 1956 (second game of doubleheader)

Buffalo	000 000 100 – 1	2	1
Richmond	000 330 01x – 7	7	1
WP – Cereghino (2-5)	LP – Froats (1-7)		

John Weiss had been inconsistent since his move to a starter role. A poorly pitched game, which he lost, was followed by a well-pitched game for which the Bisons didn't get him enough runs. In this outing, it was hard to decide which was the case. Weiss walked Bill Renna starting off the second inning, gave up a single to Hal Rice and then plunked Dee Phillips to load the bases. Neal Watlington, the next man up, hit into a double play that allowed Renna to score, but no RBI for Watlington. Bobby Kline singled immediately following the twin killing, cashing Rice with run number two.

In the first game, Ed Lopat kept the Buffalo hitters off balance until they were finally able to knot the score in the top of the fifth. Jerry Lumpe had no play on Bill Serena's grounder to deep shortstop, the Buffalo third baseman legging out a hit without a throw being attempted. Pat Tomkinson's sharp single to center gave no one a chance for a play. With two men out and both runners off at the crack of the bat, Billy DeMars' long double into the right-field alley evened the score at 2-2. It stayed that way for only an inning.

Renna scored the winning run in the home half of the sixth. Weiss pitched him tight to keep the power hitter from extending his arms, but the pitch was too close and caught Renna in the shoulder. Weiss was too far out over the plate to the next batter, Rice, who boomed a triple off the center-field fence and brought Renna home with the go-ahead run, his second score of the night. The Vees couldn't get Rice across the plate, but it didn't matter with Lopat on the mound.

It was three up and three down for the Bisons in the seventh and final inning of the first game. In addition to holding the Herd to but five hits, Lopat did not walk a man. Weiss also limited Richmond to five safeties, but the difference turned out to be a walk and two hit batsmen.

Losing one-run games like this was costing Cavarretta some postgame hours wondering what he could have done differently to affect the outcome. Weiss didn't pitch a bad game. Lopat pitched a better one.

The second game wasn't close. Too many bases on balls by Buffalo hurlers and timely hitting by the Richmond club made the difference. A Buffalo error cost a run. At the beginning, though, it was a pitcher's duel between Bill Froats and the Vees' Ed Cereghino.

Each man held the opposition scoreless for three innings until the Virginians broke through for three tallies in the bottom of the fourth. It could have been more. Hal Rice got on base on Serena's muff of his ground ball to third. Bill Renna and Rance Pless singled back to back, with Rice scoring. A walk to Cal Neeman loaded the bases. Jerry Lumpe became a Froats strikeout victim for the first out, but Renna scored the second run after Bobby Kline collected Froats' second walk of the inning. Pless scored on Cereghino's sacrifice fly ball to left.

The score doubled to 6-0 in the next frame. Dee Phillips roped a hit down the left-field line good for two bases. Froats gifted Rice with his sixth walk of the evening. With runners on first and second, Renna hit his 12th home run of the campaign over the center-field fence. Cavarretta let Froats finish out the inning now that the sacks were empty. Roger Bowman was up and throwing in the bullpen.

Unlike their success against him in spring training and battering him from the mound in Offermann Stadium in his only other start against them back on July 1, the Buffalo hitters could do nothing against Cereghino's curveball. His slants were a mystery. Buffalo batsmen swung futilely against the hook or watched it dart over the black at the last minute for a called strike three. The Bisons went hitless until the sixth inning, when Joe Caffie finally spanked a hard ground ball that found its way through the right side for a two-out single. Lou Ortiz couldn't capitalize, grounding out to retire the side.

Bowman pitched a perfect bottom of the sixth, and the Bisons looked like they might get back in the game in the top of the seventh as Cereghino finally weakened in the heat and humidity. He walked the first three men to face him—Luke Easter, Ed Mierkowicz and Bill Serena. Manager Lopat went with his hook and brought in Sonny Dixon to extinguish the threat. Dixon got Norm Sherry, the first man he saw, on a called third strike, but Billy DeMars' sacrifice fly ball was hit deep enough to center to score even Easter from third. That would be it for Buffalo. Manager Cavarretta, pinch-hitting for Bowman, grounded into a force play at second for the third out.

Joe Coleman shut out the Virginians in the bottom of the seventh. Lou Ortiz got a two-out double off Dixon in the top of the eighth but was left hanging. Kline and Dixon both walked to lead off the Richmond eighth, and Coleman and the Bisons were faced with yet another bases loaded and no one out situation following Len Johnston's excuse-me roller down the first-base line that went for an infield hit. Phillips' ground out scored Kline. Coleman got Rice to hit into a 1-6-3 double play, and the inning was over. Dixon set the Bisons down in order in the ninth.

BISON TALES: Although struggling at the plate when he first rejoined the lineup, Billy DeMars had been on a 10-game hit streak that was stopped by Cereghino and Dixon. He was hitting .369 before the horse collar. DeMars drove in all three of the Herd's runs in the doubleheader.

The Bisons suffered from a power outage in their three-four-five hitters. Ortiz got the only hit, a double, in the second game, giving the trio a one-for-17 afternoon. In addition, 12 Bisons went down on strikes in game two. Cereghino fanned nine and Dixon rang up three.

The double victory pushed the Vees' win streak to six games. Game one was played in a quick hour and 33 minutes.

Buffalo residents Dick Switala, his son, Dick, and a friend, Bill Szatowski, were in the stands while in the area on vacation.

Game 103, Thursday, July 26, Richmond, Virginia: Buffalo 7, Richmond 2

Buffalo salvaged the third game of the visit thanks to
Luke Easter's potent bat and one of Fred Hahn's best outings of the year.

```
Game 103 – July 26, 1956
Buffalo          010 220 002 – 7  13  1
Richmond         020 000 000 – 2   3  0
WP – Hahn (5-8)         LP – Nardella (6-7)
```

Buffalo grabbed a one-run lead in the top of the second when Easter led off the inning with a double to left center against Richmond starter Wimpy Nardella. A two-out single from Pat Tomkinson brought him home. The Vees took the lead in their half of the frame. Hahn walked leadoff man Rance Pless to get himself in trouble, and Bobby Kline made him pay for it with a two-out double that scored the baserunner. Nardella followed with a second double that made it 2-1. The Bisons waited an inning before they regained the lead for good in the fourth.

Again, it was Easter to start the action. He poled a Nardella fastball over the wall in right for his 21st home run of the year. And, once again, it was Tomkinson to keep the inning going. The Bison catcher got his second base hit of the night, and Billy DeMars, with his first, moved the runner to third. Hahn punched a single to center that scored Tomkinson with the tiebreaker.

The Bisons added two in the fifth. Joe Caffie lined a double that was followed by a Lou Ortiz single for the first run. Ortiz took second on the throw to the plate and came home himself on Easter's third base knock of the night, a single.

Hahn handcuffed the Virginians on one hit the rest of the way. Buffalo put two insurance runs on the board in the ninth. Caffie scratched an infield single. Ortiz drew a walk. Easter, needing a triple to complete the cycle, settled for a single to plate Caffie and move Ortiz to third. Harry Nicholas ran for Easter. Ortiz scored on Ed Mierkowicz's sacrifice fly. Cavarretta covered first base in the seventh inning.

BISON TALES: Cavarretta had been impressed with Zeb Eaton's still lively fastball and savvy pitching against the Red Wings on Saturday in Buffalo. In that game, he had also proved that he was still a solid hitter. Zeb had come along to Richmond with the team after Cavarretta had asked him to request a leave of absence from his foreman at work.

Cavarretta credited Eaton's hitting with helping his and Peanuts Lowrey's Chicago Cubs to the 1945 National League pennant. On July 15 of that season, Eaton, pinch-hitting for Detroit, slugged a grand slam home run off New York Yankee hurler Hank Borowy that wound up in the third deck of Yankee Stadium.

Shortly thereafter, the Yanks, headed for an undeniable fourth-place finish, sold Borowy to the Cubs for $125,000, even though he had already posted 10 victories for the New Yorkers. Borowy won 11 more games in his half a season with Chicago, helping them make it into the World Series— to face off against Eaton's Tigers. Borowy threw a shutout in winning game one, started and lost game five, won game six in relief, and started and lost game seven. Eaton had one pinch-hit at-bat in the series. Borowy struck him out in the first game. Cavarretta hit .423 against Detroit; Lowrey posted a .310 mark.

THE MINORS VERSUS THE MAJORS: IV
Thursday, July 26, Buffalo

Following several conferences with baseball commissioner Ford C. Frick and a number of baseball executives at the 18th Hall of Fame game in Cooperstown, New York, the previous Monday, general manager John Stiglmeier revealed that the Bisons would drop their claims that the Detroit Tigers had not held up their end of the bargain in the sale of the Bison ball club to the city's local interests.

The sticking point had been the failure of Detroit infielder Mel Hoderlein, outfielder Bill Killinger and catcher Pierce McWhorter to report to Buffalo after their sale to the Triple A club. Frick offered that Detroit had had a "moral obligation" to assist Buffalo when these men retired rather than be transferred to the Buffalo ownership, but he held that in the final analysis it was Buffalo's responsibility to induce them to show up for spring training once they had been placed on the Bisons' roster.

Stiglmeier countered that Detroit had sent the Bisons Fred Hahn as a replacement when one of the nine men to be included in the deal, Dick Rozek, retired over the winter. He further argued that the Tigers were aware of Hoderlein's medical condition and that he would be unable to play at the start of the season. If Detroit could offer another player in place of Rozek, Stiglmeier continued, why were not similar arrangements made for the absence of Hoderlein and McWhorter? Frick's response was that he would speak with the new Detroit ownership to see what they might be able to offer, but that as far as baseball rules went, he was unable to order them to send the Bisons new men.

Speaking to reporters back in Buffalo, Stiglmeier reasserted his belief that the Tigers were obligated to assign men to the transfer agreement wbo were both healthy and willing to continue to play. As it was, of the nine players offered only three were currently with the team—pitchers Hahn and John Weiss and outfielder George Bullard, who was on the disabled list. The remainder of the players who did report had been released outright following spring training.

While in Cooperstown, Stiglmeier also met with general managers Hank Greenberg (Cleveland Indians) and Joe Cronin (Boston Red Sox) and front-office men from Arnold Johnson's Kansas City A's. Stiglmeier returned home with the impression that either the Indians or the A's might be seeking a new Triple A agreement for 1957, but for now he had to keep his focus on completing the 1956 season and encouraging increased fan attendance.

The club needed to average 4000 a game for the rest of the season to hit the 200,000 mark, Stiglmeier said. He offered that that number would ensure the Bisons' existence for 1957. Expenses had been cut to the bone, he added, but the club still needed good weather for the remainder of the year and a positive response from the fans. He hoped the fans would show their loyalty starting with the return home from the road the following Monday.

Stiglmeier also stated that he had for now backed away from any further talk of congressional investigation into baseball's "monopolistic" control of minor league players. He had been told while in Cooperstown of new major league plans to respond to complaints from the minor league ownership.

Also in Cooperstown: 1954 World Series hero Dusty Rhodes slammed two home runs to lead the New York Giants over the Detroit Tigers in the annual Hall of Fame game.

Rhodes' second shot was a two-run walkoff blast in the bottom of the 12th inning to give the

Giants a 12-11 slugfest victory. For the game, Rhodes was four for five with three runs scored and four driven home.

The victory gave the National League the edge in the series, eight games to seven, after American League wins in 1954 and 1955 had tied the classic. The Giants and the Tigers had appeared only once before in Cooperstown, ironically facing off against each other in 1946. The Giants took that game by a score of 9-5. Hall of Famer Mel Ott went two for four with two RBIs.

Downtown Buffalo, Circa 1950s

Game 104, Friday, July 27, Columbus, Ohio: Columbus 3, Buffalo 2

Johnny Lipon's three-run blast in the seventh inning
smashed Red Donovan's bid for a fifth straight win.

Game 104 – July 27, 1956
Buffalo   010 000 100 – 2 6 0
Columbus   000 000 30x – 3 7 3
WP – Herbert (7-5)   LP – Donovan (7-5)

Both hurlers were on the mark in this contest, Donovan for the Bisons and Ray Herbert for the Jets. One bad pitch made Donovan the loser.

Buffalo grabbed a one-run lead in the second after Bill Serena doubled off the Columbus starter and Billy DeMars plunked a single to center. Center fielder Dick Getter overran the ball, and Serena was waved home to score on the misplay. The Herd doubled the lead to make it 2-0 when Pete Castiglione broke a dry spell at the plate and doubled in the seventh. He scampered to third on a wild pitch from Herbert and then scored when Joe Caffie, the next batter, did his job by hitting the ball to the right side. The ground out, second to first, sent Castiglione home and padded the slim Bison lead.

The two runs turned out to be not enough. Columbus finally broke through against Donovan in the home half of the same inning. The Buffalo starter had held the Jets to only four hits through six, but he opened the seventh by surrendering one of his three walks to the leadoff man, Russ Rose. Billy Shantz's single put runners on first and third with no one out. Bearing down, Donovan got the next two men, including a strikeout of Ben Downs, hitting for Bill Kern. He nearly made it out of the inning unscathed, but Johnny Lipon cracked a 2-2 pitch that got too much of the plate and sent it on a line over the left-field wall. It was Lipon's sixth home run of the season and gave the Jets the lead. It was the game-winning blow. The Bisons could do nothing against Herbert in their last two chances in the eighth and ninth.

Luke Easter gave the Bisons some hope when he put the tying run on base in the ninth inning, stinging his second single of the night. Cavarretta sent Harry Nicholas in to run for the big man, but Herbert shut down the rest of the order and left the runner stranded. The Bisons took a tough one-run loss, a defeat that would have Cavarretta up for hours after stranding nine men on the base paths. What more could he do to get those baserunners home?

Bison Tales: Easter's two sharp singles tonight gave him six base hits in his last seven official trips to the plate.

Pete Castiglione had been suffering through a 0-for-12 slump before his double in the seventh.

The three runs scored by the Jets were the most Donovan had allowed in his last five outings. Again, he went the distance as the visiting pitcher, hurling eight innings. The loss broke his string of four straight wins in his last four appearances.

Continuing the appearance of Buffalo fans at away games, Helen Berny, one of the team's directors, was in town to take in the contest.

Game 105, Saturday, July 28, Columbus, Ohio: Buffalo 4, Columbus 3

Luke Easter's 22nd of the season put the Bisons ahead in the first.
A bouncing single by Pete Castiglione in the ninth won it.

Game 105 – July 28, 1956

Buffalo	200 010 001 – 4	7	0
Columbus	000 010 020 – 3	9	2

WP – Bowman (7-12)   LP – Spicer (9-3)

On a night of steady rain with its precarious moments, Buffalo once more took the lead in the opening frame. Columbus starter John Wingo set down the first two Bison batters but made his first mistake when he walked Lou Ortiz. He made his second mistake when Luke Easter connected for home run number 22, giving Roger Bowman an immediate two-run lead. Wingo allowed only one more hit in the five frames he worked, but it led to the Bisons' third run in the fifth. Billy DeMars' infield dribbler up the third-base line was ruled a base hit, and he motored all the way around to third on Wingo's two-base throwing error on the play. Bowman scored the Buffalo shortstop with a sacrifice fly to center.

Bowman found himself in trouble in the home half of the fifth by walking leadoff man Russ Rose and giving up singles to Billy Shantz and pinch-hitter Ray Noble. Noble's hit scored Rose with the Jets' first run. DeMars then turned in a fielding gem when he knocked down center fielder Bill Kern's bouncer in the hole. It was an infield single, but it kept a second run from scoring. The bases were now loaded with no one out. Bowman induced a force play at the plate on John Lipon's grounder to third. Curt Roberts went down swinging. Finally, the pitcher coaxed a fly ball from Russ Sullivan. The lefty's gritty work and DeMars' big play kept the damage to only one run.

Bowman's fortune was not so good in the bottom of the eighth. Sullivan's two-out fly ball was deeper this time and left the ballpark for a solo blast. Rich Getter followed in the order, and he added a second home run. Now the game was tied and would go down to the final inning, where seeing-eye grounders would make the difference.

Pat Tomkinson's bouncer was deep into the shortstop hole. Rose knocked it down but could not make a play. DeMars beat out an infield single of his own, moving Tomkinson to second. Cavarretta, pinch-hitting for Bowman, lined a drive that Lipon, playing first, just was able to knock down and throw on to second to force DeMars, but Tomkinson took third on the play. Pete Castiglione's two-out bouncer through the middle scored Tomkinson with the game winner.

Joe Coleman came on in relief, set the Jets down in order in the bottom of the inning and saved Bowman's seventh victory of the season.

BISON TALES: General manager John Stiglmeier would miss the upcoming Polish-American night event at Offermann. He would instead attend a special meeting of independently owned baseball clubs in Miami on August 8. The invitation was extended by Harold Cooper, general manager of the Columbus Jets, whose team's fortunes took such a sour turn after the recall of the hot-hitting Al Pilarcik by the Kansas City A's.

Games 106 and 107, Sunday, July 29, Columbus, Ohio: Columbus 9, Buffalo 2; Columbus 1, Buffalo 0

*Long balls by Columbus' Russ Sullivan in the opener and lack of
run support for Karl Drews in the second meant a double defeat.*

Game 106 – July 29, 1956 (first game of doubleheader)

| Buffalo | 010 010 000 – 2 8 2 |
| Columbus | 104 100 30x – 9 11 1 |

WP – Duser (5-2)　　　LP – Nicholas (3-9)

Game 107 – July 29, 1956 (second game of doubleheader)

| Buffalo | 000 000 000 – 0 4 0 |
| Columbus | 000 000 001 – 1 5 0 |

WP – Cox (8-10)　　　LP – Drews (9-8)

In the first game, Harry Nicholas was the victim of a windblown infield fly in the first inning. Serena couldn't corral it, and it fell for a two-base hit to the leadoff man, Bill Kern. Jet cleanup hitter Russ Sullivan took advantage of the break and singled Kern home. Buffalo got it back in the second when Serena singled with one out and moved to third on a base hit by Norm Sherry. Billy DeMars' walk loaded the bases, and then Jet hurler Carl Duser lost Nicholas as well for the RBI free pass. Serena scored, but that was all the Bisons could manage. Pete Castiglione hit into an inning-killing double play.

The first three men in the Columbus lineup reached base in the bottom of the third: single, single, walk. Russ Sullivan cleaned up again. His grand slam line drive, his second home run in two games, went over the fence in left at the 360 mark. Nicholas finished the inning, but he was also finished for the day as far as Cavarretta was concerned. Zeb Eaton, in to relieve, started the fourth with the Bisons behind by a score of 5-1.

The Jets made it 6-1 when they tallied an unearned run off Eaton in the bottom of the fourth. Ray Noble singled to left, moved to second on a ground out and scored when Castiglione dropped a fly ball out in left field. Buffalo got that one back in the top of the fifth following a single by Luke Easter, Ed Mierkowicz's ground out and a long double by Serena that allowed Easter to score from second.

The score remained at 6-2 until the bottom of the seventh, when Sullivan again found the range and added to the Columbus lead. Eaton had retired the first two men, but then gave a free pass to Curt Roberts. Sullivan followed by connecting for his second homer of the game, almost to the same spot as the first. Butch McCord, the next hitter, also took Eaton deep and the score stood at 9-2. Steve Nagy was brought in to get the final out of the inning. He stayed in to pitch a perfect eighth, but it was too little, too late in the pitching department for the Herd.

Buffalo bats were again unable to produce in a timely fashion. The Herd managed eight safeties and were gifted with five walks, but they stranded nine runners. Three double plays turned by the Jets killed several chances.

Glenn Cox and Karl Drews locked up in a second-game pitcher's duel decided in extra innings. The game was scoreless at the end of the regulation seven innings, with each man having limited his opponents to four hits. Each had put only two runners on base via walks, and Drews had fanned four. Cox had set down six men on strikes. Each team had claimed a double play. Joe Caffie had the only extra-base hit, a double in the first inning, but was he was unable to advance. Cox didn't allow another Bison to touch second base for the remainder of the game.

Drews survived a scare in the home half of the seventh when he loaded the bases on his first walk of the night, Russ Sullivan's single and a second free pass with two down. The veteran was able to escape by coaxing a Ben Downs grounder to Lou Ortiz at second. Ortiz flipped to Billy De-Mars for the inning ending force out.

The teams played through a scoreless eighth until the contest was decided in the bottom of the ninth. After Bill Kern had rolled out, John Lipon got his second hit of the nightcap, a triple down the line that eluded Ed Mierkowicz's desperate effort in right field. Curt Roberts, the next batter, sent a fly ball to Caffie in center that Joe gathered in, but the throw was late and Lipon scored with the game's only run.

Bill Serena argued adamantly that the runner had left before the catch, but the arbiter wasn't buying it. Cavarretta joined in the protest, but to no avail. The argument was lost, and so was the ballgame and the twin bill.

BISON TALES: Buffalo hit into two more double plays in the second contest, again frustrating opportunities to score. The long season, now two-thirds played, was hard on ancient legs and the Bisons had a number of those out on the basepaths.

Drews crafted a quality performance on the mound and seemed to have bounced back strong from the arm ailment. He faced the minimum of 20 batters over the first six and two-thirds innings in the second game. This was good news for the Herd, who needed his leadership and his stopper role in the pitching corps. Better offensive support would have given him a victory.

Billy DeMars continued with his hot hitting, leading the club with a .380 mark on the road trip. He was followed by Easter at .375 and Joe Caffie with .346, but the rest of the crew was unable to rise to this level. The next highest average was Tomkinson's at .222. Lou Ortiz (.095) and Ed Mierkowicz (.083) were mired in ineffectiveness.

The club had gone 2-5 on this southern swing. Earlier in the month, in Canada, they had won two and dropped eight. The home record for July was six wins and seven losses, but only because of the three-game sweep of Rochester. Returning home on Monday, the club would face the first-place Miami Marlins. The onrushing Marlins had knocked Toronto out of the first station by one percentage point in the standings. Rochester was only a half-game behind those two frontrunners. Montreal, in fourth, was 4 1/2 games off the pace.

In the second division, Richmond was 10 games back of the Marlins, Columbus 12 and the Sugar Kings 13 1/2. Seventh-place Havana had widened the gap between themselves and the last-place Bisons to 5 1/2 games.

Russ Sullivan's three for three in the first game with the two home runs gave him seven RBIs, easily his best such outing of the campaign.

In major league news: The pennant races were not so tight as in the International League. In the American League, the New York Yankees were ahead of second-place Cleveland by 9 games. Kansas City, in the basement, was 31 1/2 games back. The National League was a tighter affair. Milwaukee, at the top of the standings, was 2 1/2 games in front of Cincinnati. The Dodgers were another game and a half back. The last-place Giants were 23 1/2 out.

Game 108, Monday, July 30, Buffalo: Miami 6, Buffalo 5

A five-run first-inning deficit and the craftiest relief pitcher
on the planet sent the Bisons to a third straight defeat.

Game 108 – July 30, 1956

Miami	500 010 000 – 6	11	0
Buffalo	003 000 101 – 5	13	1
WP – Farrell (7-3)	LP – Weiss (2-8)		

Buffalo returned home overnight to face the red-hot Miami Marlins, 21 and 4 in their last 25 contests. John Weiss started and couldn't get a man out. Cal Abrams led off the game with a home run over the screen in left field, followed by base hits by Yo Yo Davalillo and Ed Bouchee. Weiss next walked Bob Bowman, loading the bases for new Marlin third baseman Woody Smith, purchased from Havana just six games ago and an offensive key to Miami's recent climb in the standings. Smith whacked a triple to the scoreboard that cleaned the sacks and sent Weiss to the showers. Bill Froats came in to relieve, gave up a sacrifice fly ball to Larry Novak for run number five, and pitched one-run ball for the next six innings.

Buffalo rebounded with three in the third. Miami starter Turk Farrell walked Froats with one out. With two gone, Joe Caffie singled him to third. Lou Ortiz plunked a single for the first run, Luke Easter doubled for a second and Bill Serena, now batting in the fifth slot, added his own single to score Easter. The Bisons were back in the ballgame.

Smith pushed it to a three-run advantage for Miami when he solved Froats for a bases-empty long ball in the fifth. Smith had been pounding the ball at a .560 clip since donning a Marlins uniform. The homer off Froats was his 16th.

Buffalo managed a fourth run in the seventh when Joe Caffie came home on a Serena ground out. Then, with two down in the ninth, Serena made it a one-run ballgame by lofting his 13th home run of the year over the left-field screen. After Ed Mierkowicz followed with a single, manager Don Osborn went to the bullpen to call on the oldest player in the league to face one of the youngest.

No one really knew how old Satchel Paige was, but Norm Sherry, the Buffalo batter, was 24 years old and the second youngest man on the Bisons. (Larry Donovan was 22.) Sherry was looking for Paige's famed heat; the ageless wonder threw the Buffalo catcher three tantalizingly slow curves, each one slower than the last and all with a mysterious darting action at the end. Sherry took three swings and the ballgame was over.

BISON TALES: The win promoted Miami into sole possession of first place and dropped the Bisons 20 games behind them. The Bisons had really wanted this game. Cavarretta had used 17 players to try to pull out a victory.

Peanuts Lowrey, wearing the back brace he had mentioned, pinch-ran for Mierkowicz in the ninth. It was Lowrey's first appearance in a game since the pinched nerve suffered back on July 14.

Paige's season record was 8 wins and 3 losses. He had made 22 relief appearances. His ERA was 1.50.

Games 109 and 110, Tuesday, July 31, Buffalo: Buffalo 6, Miami 5; Miami 6, Buffalo 4
Luke Easter's monster walkoff home run to center field captured game one.
A four-run Bison rally in the second contest fell just short.

Game 109 – July 31, 1956 (first game of doubleheader)

Miami	110 003 0 – 5	7	0
Buffalo	000 200 4 – 6	10	2

WP – Coleman (4-0)   LP – LiPetri (3-2)

Game 110 – July 31, 1956 (second game of doubleheader)

Miami	000 040 101 – 6	9	2
Buffalo	000 000 400 – 4	3	0

WP – Snyder (6-2)   LP – Hahn (5-9)

Harry Nicholas took the hill for Buffalo and gave up a first-inning home run to Ed Bouchee to start the Marlins on their way in the seven-inning opener. Catcher Gus Niarhos just missed a homer and doubled off the left-field screen in the second. He moved to third on Mickey Micelotta's ground out and came home on Miami starter Don Cardwell's long sacrifice fly to right.

The Buffalo bats got rolling in the home half of the fourth when Bill Serena and then Ed Miereko-wicz slammed back-to-back homers. Serena's ball flew over the wall in left and Mierkowicz's drive went out in right center. It was a tie ballgame, but not for long.

Miami's relentless offense added three more runs in the sixth on a walk, a single, a double, a sacrifice fly and an error by Lou Ortiz. Nicholas was relieved after closing out the sixth. Joe Coleman came in to hurl the seventh and brought the necessary magic with him, setting the Marlin hitters down in order. Cardwell tried to close out the win in the bottom of the seventh, but the Bisons had other plans.

Billy DeMars popped up to lead off the inning, but manager Phil Cavarretta, inserting himself as a pinch-hitter for Coleman, delivered a line drive single. Pete Castiglione, hitless thus far, lifted a short fly into left that both third baseman Woody Smith and left fielder Larry Novak thought the other would go for. It fell for a base hit. Rattled, Cardwell hung a pitch that Joe Caffie drove to the wall in right center and legged out for a triple. Manager Don Osborn turned to the bullpen and called for Angelo LiPetri.

Lou Ortiz's short fly ball to left made it two outs with the runner holding. LiPetri went to a quick two strikes and then a ball to Easter but then failed with a low outside fastball on the next effort. Easter's swing sent the ball an estimated 475 feet to straightaway center field, just to the left of the scoreboard. The ball struck the red roof of the house behind the fence on the fly and then bounced over the roof of the house behind it and out of sight. A dramatic ending to game one to snap the ball club's three-game losing streak. Coleman got the win; LiPetri was tagged with the loss.

Game two was a pitchers' duel for four innings until Miami broke on top in the fifth. The Bisons' lefty Fred Hahn was matched against the Marlins' Gene Snyder, another southpaw. Each man went the first four innings without surrendering a hit, giving the lie to the myth about the hazards of sending lefthanders to the mound in Offermann.

Hahn lost his no-hitter in the fifth when Woody Smith blasted a home run to left center field.

Next up, left fielder Glen Gorbous walked and catcher Ray Holton, following in the order, hit the second Miami home run of the frame. His cleared the screen in left. The fourth Miami score came as the result of a Mickey Micelotta single and a double by Cal Abrams. That ended Hahn's night and brought in John Weiss to get the side out. The Marlins notched a tally off Weiss in the top of the seventh after Gene Snyder singled and came home on Bob Bowman's bases-loaded fielder's choice. Although it was the only run the Marlins could manage from the situation, it turned out to be the game winner.

Snyder's no-hit mastery of the Bisons extended until the bottom of the seventh, when Buffalo finally struck back for all of their runs. An error helped. Norm Sherry walked to lead off the inning, and Billy DeMars followed with a surefire double-play ground ball to short, but Miami second baseman Yo Yo Davalillo dropped the throw from Micelotta and all runners were safe.

Ed Mierkowicz had been injured when he fouled a ball off his foot batting in the sixth, so Zeb Eaton had gone out to play right field in his place starting the seventh. Eaton flew out to short right against Snyder, but Pete Castiglione singled cleanly to left for the Bisons' first hit and their first run. Joe Caffie was retired on a short fly ball to make it two out, leaving it up to Lou Ortiz. Lou slammed his 19th of the year far over the well-used left-field screen, and suddenly the Bisons were only down by a run. Tony Ponce was brought in to pitch for Miami to make sure it stayed that way.

Ponce got Easter for the third out to end the seventh. He gave up a harmless single to Zeb Eaton in the ninth but was otherwise untouchable. Cal Abrams added a final Marlin tally by slugging a ninth-inning home run to right off Joe Coleman.

BISON TALES: Mierkowicz's foot was seriously swollen and Cavarretta announced after the game that Zeb Eaton would be starting in right for the remainder of the Miami series.

Buffalo bats were good for 10 hits in the first game but were limited to a paltry three in the second.

When asked about the previous night's cool weather (65 degrees), Satchel Paige reported that he had worn four light woolen sweatshirts under the long-sleeved rubber shirt that he had also worn under his uniform, just to keep himself warm. Buffalo was not yet the Miami of the North, at least according to Mr. Paige.

Several scouts were on hand to take in the proceedings. Gene Martin, farm director of the Philadelphia Phillies, was there, as were Steve O'Neill, the ex-Bison manager who was now affiliated with Cleveland. Hugh Poland of the New York Giants was also in attendance. Larry Donovan's name came up in discussions.

The league learned that coach Rinaldo Cordero of the Havana Sugar Kings had been suspended for the rest of the season. He was charged with "misconduct" for spitting at umpire Frank Guzzetta during a July 20 argument in a game played in Miami—three times!

Game 111, Wednesday, August 1, Buffalo: Miami 7, Buffalo 1

Larry Donovan had a no-hitter and a 1-0 lead through four
when an injury and Woody Smith's hot bat put him in the loss column.

Game 111 – August 1, 1956
Miami	000 020 302 – 7	9	1
Buffalo	010 000 000 – 1	6	1

WP – Morehead (7-7)   LP – Donovan (7-6)

Bill Serena gave Buffalo a 1-0 lead in the second inning with a solo home run off Miami's Seth Morehead, but that was to be it against the young (21) lefthander. He allowed only five more hits and no more runs and fanned 10 with a hard forkball. Only Joe Caffie had any real luck after Serena's blast. Joe picked up a triple and two singles but stayed anchored on the basepaths.

Another Bison injury factored in the game's outcome. Zeb Eaton, starting in right for the injured Ed Mierkowicz, was himself disabled in the fourth inning after he crashed into the right-field concrete wall running down Ed Bouchee's fly ball. Peanuts Lowrey, bad back and all, had to come in to cover right field.

Bob Bowman drew a walk off Donovan in the fifth, and Woody Smith broke up the no-hitter with a triple into the right-field corner that Peanuts had no chance on. Bowman scored easily. Smith came home on Glen Gorbous' sacrifice fly to give the Marlins the lead. Miami added three more in the seventh. Bouchee led off with a solo home run. Bowman notched a single and so did Smith, hitting a rocket that Billy DeMars could only knock down into short left but on which he had no play. Gorbous' long single to right center brought in both runners.

Miami added two more in the ninth when Smith singled and Donovan walked Mickey Micelotta with two outs. Morehead and Cal Abrams each stroked RBI singles.

BISON TALES: Red Donovan did not pitch poorly, and Cavarretta let him stay on the mound for the entire game to see if the Bison bats could catch up. Donovan handled seven chances in the field and picked Smith off first base in the third inning with a tricky move. Abrams was caught leaning in the sixth by that same move.

Smith's price tag was reportedly $15,000, but Miami's millionaire owners could easily afford it. Buffalo, on the other hand, was struggling just to make payroll and afford bandages and liniment.

Joe Caffie had taken over team leadership in hitting, now batting .302 to Luke Easter's even .300. Joe had put together an eight-game hit streak, 14 for 33, for a torrid .424 mark.

International League Standings
August 1, 1956

	W	L	Pct	GB
Toronto	64	46	.581	—
Miami	63	46	.577	½
Rochester	59	48	.551	3½
Montreal	58	54	.517	7
Columbus	52	59	.468	12½
Richmond	51	60	.459	13½
Havana	50	59	458	13½
Buffalo	43	68	.387	21½

Game 112, Thursday, August 2, Buffalo: Buffalo 3, Miami 1

Karl Drews, the Bisons' stopper, was back on form.
His five-hitter gave the Herd the victory in the final game of the series.

Game 112 – August 2, 1956
Miami   010 000 000 – 1   5   1
Buffalo   000 101 01x – 3   7   1
WP – Drews (10-8)   LP – Owens (3-2)

Matched against the Bisons' nemesis Jim Owens, Drews had to be on his toes.

Leadoff man Cal Abrams liked to look for walks. It was imperative, therefore, that the pitcher get two fast strikes on him to force him to swing at the hurler's selection, not give him an opportunity to be choosy. The same strategy held for the number two man in the lineup, Ben Tompkins. As for the power hitters, Drews' strategy was to keep the ball up and away from Ed Bouchee. The young first baseman hadn't yet learned to pull the ball, so he would have to furnish his own power.

Bob Bowman, author of three home runs against Buffalo back on June 15, needed to be fed pitches low and outside to get him to reach. This would diminish his ability to pull. As for Woody Smith, Drews had noted his tendency to lunge at the ball. So the big righthander planned to throw him sinkers in on the wrists, move him back at the plate and then follow with low breaking balls outside. About the new outfielder, Glen Gorbous, Drews wasn't quite so sure. He hadn't seen him before, and this would take some working out during the course of the game.

Owens was a tough opponent, and the Marlins staked him to a one-run lead in the second. Billy DeMars booted Bowman's ground ball leading off. Drews nicked Smith with an inside pitch and both runners advanced on a ground out. Ray Holton scored Bowman with a sacrifice fly.

The Bisons finally tied it in the fourth with an unearned run of their own. Luke Easter and Bill Serena opened the frame with singles, and then Bouchee mishandled Peanuts Lowrey's ground ball, allowing Easter to come home. A second Herd run came in the sixth. Easter smote a hot single to right to begin and later scored as DeMars waited out a bases-loaded walk.

Drews pitched out of threats in the fourth and the sixth and got only stronger as the game progressed. A double play helped as he set down the last 12 men to face him.

Buffalo created an insurance run in the eighth. Easter walked for the second time, and Steve

Nagy was sent in to run. With the bases loaded, Cavarretta pinch-hit for the righthanded-hitting Norm Sherry and ripped a single to plate Nagy.

BISON TALES: Billy DeMars was hitless in his previous 16 at-bats before his bases-loaded walk in the sixth drove home the winning run.

Cavarretta had pinch-hit four times in this series. He collected three hits, scored once and drove in the insurance run in this game.

In International League news: Clyde Parris of Montreal was leading the league in hitting at .334. Luke Easter topped the circuit in home runs (23) and RBIs (73). Toronto's Lynn Lovenguth had registered 17 victories versus eight defeats to lead in the win column.

Offerman Stadium, Circa 1956

Games 113 and 114, Friday, August 3, Buffalo: Havana 5, Buffalo 2; Buffalo 9, Havana 8

Havana managed five runs on four hits in taking game one.
Joe Caffie's bases-loaded single in the eighth won the second.

Game 113 – August 3, 1956 (first game of doubleheader)

Havana   100 100 3 – 5   4   0

Buffalo   011 000 0 – 2   8   0

WP – Cueche (3-1)   LP – Nagy (0-2)

Game 114 – August 3, 1956 (second game of doubleheader)

Havana   002 200 022 – 8   9   1

Buffalo   300 040 11x – 9   11   1

WP – Froats (2-7)   LP – Minarcin (12-7)

Steve Nagy started his first game as a Bison and suffered a tough loss as Havana ran its winning streak to eight games. Nap Reyes' Sugar Kings squad had been getting all the breaks, and the hits had been coming at just the right time. You saw this in the first inning.

Don Nicholas doubled to open the first match, and number-three hitter Hal Bevan followed with a one-out single that gave the visitors the lead. Buffalo evened it in the second behind Norm Sherry's first home run of the season off Cuban starter Joe Hatten. It was the Herd's turn to take the lead in the third. Singles by Lou Ortiz and Luke Easter and a two-out double by Peanuts Lowrey produced a go-ahead run. Easter held at third and the Bisons couldn't bring him home.

The Bison lead lasted for no longer than Ultus Alvarez could pick up a bat in the fourth. The Sugar King first baseman hit a prodigious drive over the left-field wall, and the teams went into the seventh and final inning of the short first game knotted at 2-2.

Alvarez drew a one-out walk. Pablo Bernard's perfect double play grounder to Billy DeMars was flipped to Lou Ortiz at second for the first out, but the usually surehanded second baseman flubbed the throw to first and Bernard was safe. Nagy compounded the matter by plunking Nino Escalera to put two runners aboard. Third baseman Owen Friend made the Bisons pay. His three-run blast to left field made it 5-2 in favor of Havana.

Emilio Cueche had taken over for Hatten to hold the Bisons scoreless from the third inning on, but Buffalo made a vigorous attempt to come back in the bottom half of the seventh. With one gone, Easter slammed a double and Bill Serena's bloop single to center moved him to third. A walk to Peanuts Lowrey loaded the bases. Cavarretta then announced himself to pinch-hit for Sherry, going lefty against righty. Reyes countered with lefthander Jay Heard and Cavarretta replaced himself with the righthanded-swinging Ed Mierkowicz. Mierkowicz fouled out to Friend near the visitor dugout. DeMars struck out with the bases loaded to end the ballgame.

Game two also went down to the final innings. Bill Froats snuffed out a last-ditch effort by Havana. It was Buffalo's turn to grab the first-inning lead, and Luke Easter did it in style, rocketing homer number 24 off the Sugar Kings' ace righthander, ex-Bison Rudy Minarcin. Joe Caffie and Lou Ortiz scored ahead of him to put the Herd up 3-0.

Roger Bowman, pitching for Buffalo, had two tainted runs marked against him in the Havana third. DeMars made an outstanding stop of Friend's chopper up the middle but threw wildly to first to put the runner aboard. Friend scored moments later when catcher Dutch Dotterer doubled into the left-field screen. Dotterer himself came home on a passed ball that eluded Tomkinson.

The Sugar Kings took a 4-3 lead in the fourth after Nino Escalera singled and Owen Friend blasted his second home run of the day. Bowman finished out the inning, but Cavarretta sent Bill Froats to the mound to pitch the fifth and give the Herd a fresh arm to rally behind.

Rally they did. Joe Caffie got it going in the bottom of the fifth with a single. Lou Ortiz doubled him in with the tying run. Minarcin walked Easter rather than giving him anything good to hit and to set up the double play. Bill Serena, who had struck out twice with men in scoring position in game one, spoiled the strategy, sending a screaming drive over Angel Scull's head in center that struck the base of the scoreboard and went for a triple. The Bisons had a two-run lead. Pat Tomkinson plated Serena on a sacrifice fly to right center.

The Bisons padded the lead to four with Serena's 16th home run of the year in the seventh. Jay Heard, relieving Minarcin, was the victim. It was a needed tally because the never-say-die Cubans got to Froats for a pair of markers in the eighth. Scull singled and Alvarez's ground ball through the right side moved him over to third. Pablo Bernard rolled out to Easter at first base for out number two, but Scull came home on the play while Alvarez moved on to second. A looping base hit to right by Nino Escalera brought in Alvarez.

They didn't know it at the time, but the Bisons picked up the winning run in the bottom of the eighth. Billy DeMars punched a single up the middle. Froats tried to sacrifice him to second but Heard wound up walking him instead. Pete Castiglione sent a topper down the third-base line that nobody could make a play on. It went for an infield hit to load the bases. Joe Caffie then scorched a single to right to drive in DeMars.

Froats took his three-run lead into the top of the ninth and was fortunate to make it to the victory circle. Dutch Dotterer scraped a leadoff single to right. Froats retired the next two men with ease, but not so Angel Scull. The diminutive center fielder popped a high fly ball down the short right-field line that just made it over the fence, and it was back to a one-run ballgame. Froats fanned Hal Bevan and the Bisons gained the split.

BISON TALES: In game one, Nagy did not strike out a batter nor did he walk a batter. The Sugar Kings did not leave a man on base.

Joe Caffie pilfered two bases in the second game and Cavarretta was credited with a steal after subbing for Ed Mierkowicz in the seventh and drawing a walk. Heard forgot all about holding him on as he was pitching to Tomkinson. It was Cavarretta's first of the year, and perhaps the most unanticipated theft of a base this season.

An ailing Ed Mierkowicz was able to go only six innings in the second game. Peanuts Lowrey had to sit out the second contest because of his back. The battered Bisons' efforts epitomized the term "professional."

THE MINORS VERSUS THE MAJORS: V
Friday, August 3, Buffalo

A joint committee of major league owners and general managers, appointed by baseball commissioner Ford C. Frick, issued a statement today recommending financial support for minor league operations in 1957. The committee consisted of Joe Cronin, Boston Red Sox; Gabe Paul, Cincinnati Reds; George Medinger, Cleveland Indians; Arnold Johnson, Kansas City Athletics; Horace Stoneham, New York Giants; and Bob Carpenter, Philadelphia Phillies. The group called for the American and National Leagues to make available the sum of $500,000 for this purpose.

National League club owners and other officials endorsed the proposal but asked that it be tabled until the exact needs of the minor leagues could be made known. A "definitive report" was requested so that the major leagues could respond "as promptly as possible." American League officials adjourned their meeting without comment on the report.

George Trautman, the president of the minor leagues, endorsed the committee's proposal. "There have been very profitable meetings for all concerned," he said, "and there is some evidence that the majors are making a sympathetic approach to the problems of the minor leagues."

"I do not feel, however," he was quick to add, "that the minors should exist just to produce talent for the majors. The primary function of the minor leagues has always been and always will be to provide entertainment for the spectators."

Commenting in the Buffalo Evening News, general manager Stiglmeier offered, "[It is a]t least a step in the right direction. The major league proposition shows the big magnates are gradually recognizing our problems and are likely to be receptive to any ideas that may be culled from the [upcoming] Miami session [of independently owned minor league teams]."

Or would they?

Saturday, August 4, Buffalo: Rainout

Fred Hahn warmed up in the right-field bullpen until the regulation starting time arrived, then retired to the dugout as the drizzle turned into a heavier downfall. At 9:10 p.m., the stadium's loud-speaker announced to the 500 remaining faithful that it was "time to go home."

Rainouts cost the home team money and also played havoc with pitching staffs. Hence, the delay in deciding to cancel the game. This series with the Sugar Kings had already been scheduled for a wrapup doubleheader on Sunday, so this Saturday postponement would now have to be shifted to Havana on the Herd's next trip to the Cuban capital. It would be played as part of a twin bill in that final southern series. The Bisons lost not only their home field advantage but also their home team receipts. They would have to settle for the visitors' purse in Havana.

Attendance for the week to come was deemed critical to the club's success. Starting with the Sunday doubleheader and running throughout the week, the Bisons were hoping to draw 45,000 fans through the turnstiles to stave off the threat of bankruptcy. Sloan Night was on tap for Monday evening to honor general manager Stiglmeier at the opening of a four-game series with Rochester. Stiglmeier had been the mayor of Sloan for many years. Current mayor John Jablonski reported that 1600 residents of the 5000-member community were expected to be on hand to witness the presentation of a plaque to the Buffalo general manager. Stiglmeier would then leave on Tuesday for Miami and the equally critical meeting of independent minor league teams.

Groups from Lancaster, Depew and the East Lovejoy section of Buffalo were expected to join in the Monday night tribute. Selections by the Lancaster Moose drum corps and the Sloan recreation department band were scheduled to highlight the tribute. Could more communities get on board in a similar fashion?

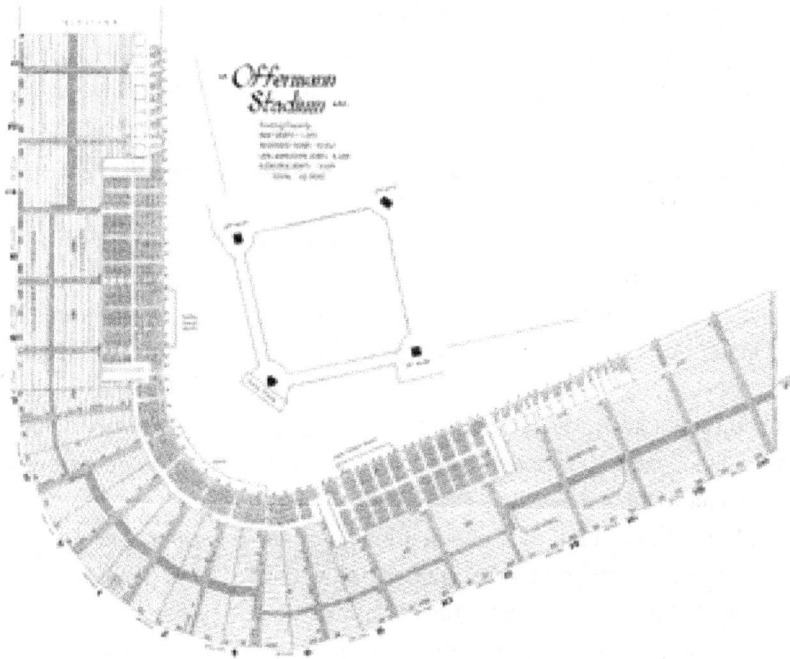

Stadium Seating Chart
Courtesy of Bruce Barber

Games 115 and 116, Sunday, August 5, Buffalo: Buffalo 3, Havana 2; Havana 5, Buffalo 3

Luke Easter's titanic three-run homer won the opener for Fred Hahn.
Two extra-inning runs beat Red Donovan in game two.

Game 115 – August 5, 1956 (first game of doubleheader)

Havana	000 000 110 – 2 8 0
Buffalo	000 003 00x – 3 6 0

WP – Hahn (6-9)   LP – Lane (7-8)

Game 116 – August 5, 1956 (second game of doubleheader)

Havana	000 012 02 – 5 9 0
Buffalo	300 000 00 – 3 6 0

WP – Hatten (4-5)   LP – Donovan (7-7)

The weather did allow the ballgames to be played, but the threatening skies held attendance to 3434. The absentees missed Easter's mighty blow that sailed over the right-field light tower, over a two-story house across Woodlawn Street and onto the roof of a home in Emerson Place before bounding down onto the street. The distance for homer number 25 was estimated at 500 feet. Easter said the pitch was a slider. He thought that the one he had hit a week ago in Columbus might have gone farther.

Fred Hahn had been scheduled to pitch on Saturday night and had put in his time warming up in the bullpen in a light rain until the weather worsened and the game was finally called off. He was limbered up for this evening.

In game one, Hahn managed the Sugar Kings handily through six frames, scattering five hits and using his curve effectively to register six strikeouts. A fifth-inning Bill Serena to Lou Ortiz to Luke Easter double play also helped. Havana starter Jerry Lane matched Hahn shutout inning for shut-out inning, allowing only two hits until the momentous sixth. Joe Caffie led off with a scratch base hit. Lou Ortiz helped out with a single to left. Easter turned on a slider. The pitch left the ballpark immediately and Lane's departure came right behind it.

Emilio Cueche entered with no one out and retired the next three men. Cueche gave the Bisons only one more hit the rest of the way.

Hahn struggled through the seventh as Havana got one back on Ultus Alvarez's leadoff smash over the wall in left. Alvarez was the culprit again when he singled home Angel Scull in the eighth with one man gone.

This last action sent Cavarretta out to the mound and brought Joe Coleman in from the bullpen. Coleman's stuff, like Cueche's, was working tonight. He shut down the Cubans over the last two innings without a hit. Hahn got a well-deserved win.

Buffalo grabbed a three-run lead in the first inning of game two for Larry Donovan, a pitcher who specialized in winning the seven-inning affairs. New Cuban hurler Sandalio (Sandy) Consuegra, a 1954 American League All-Star with the Chicago White Sox, just sent down to Havana by the Baltimore Orioles, gave up singles to Joe Caffie and Lou Ortiz, but he fooled Luke Easter, who went down swinging. No game changer for Luke in this at-bat. Bill Serena waited out a walk to fill the bases with two gone. Ed Mierkowicz, foot still hurting, platooning now with Peanuts Lowrey, who had played right field in game one, emptied the sacks with a blow into right center to the scoreboard. Mierkowicz was left at second, but the Bisons had a three-run lead and that was usually money in the bank with Donovan pitching a short-inning affair.

Red scattered several hits until Pablo Bernard reached him for a home run over the right-field wall in the fifth. The tying runs came home the next inning. Amado Ibañez, pinch-hitting for Consuegra, dropped a single into right in front of the charging Mierkowicz. Angel Scull slashed a double to left to put both men in scoring position. Ibañez came home on Hal Bevan's ground out. A single by Alvarez sent Scull home from third.

Joe Hatten had taken over for Consuegra in the sixth and the Bisons could not figure him out. He walked but one man in the three innings he toiled. Donovan retired the side in the seventh, but the Cubans won the game in the extra inning. Speedy leadoff man Don Nicholas singled. Scull connected for his second double of the night, Nicholas scoring on the play with Scull racing to third on the relay to the plate. A sacrifice fly to center by Hal Bevan brought Scull home with an insurance run. Cavarretta brought Joe Coleman in to deal with the pesky Alvarez and he retired the Cuban cleanup hitter on a grounder to DeMars.

Buffalo had no success against Hatten in the bottom of the eighth. The club was frustrated with the loss.

BISON TALES: The patrons were treated to an afternoon of excellent defense. Joe Caffie made a spectacular running grab of Dutch Dotterer's fly ball in game one to save a certain run that would have tied up the ballgame. The hot corner was blistering tonight with Bill Serena and Havana's Owen Friend turning in a number of fielding gems at third.

Havana manager Nap Reyes, speaking with Buffalo Evening News reporters on the way out of town, paid the Bisons a number of compliments. "The best last place team in baseball," he called them. As for Luke Easter, Reyes commented, "[He] never hit the ball any further, and I've known him for a long time." And Joe Caffie? "He's the fastest man in the game. His speed wrecks an infield."

Reyes pitched around Easter when he could. The Bison first baseman was walked twice in each game of the doubleheader on Friday and three times in this evening's first game. Luke had only one official at-bat in the opener, but it made all the difference to the outcome.

Cavarretta spelled Luke in the last inning of the first game to rest the big man's legs. Sherry caught a foul tip off his meat hand in Friday's first game and now he was out of action for a time. Pat Tomkinson had to catch this day's doubleheader and would be the man behind the plate until Sherry's injury subsided.

The fan turnout was disappointing, of course, but club and community representatives were working to develop still other attendance events for the remainder of the season. A Citizens' Appreciation Night was being bandied about for the final home game on August 31. Organizers planned to meet for a Monday luncheon at the Buffalo Athletic Club to discuss the particulars. Among the sponsors of the event would be Buffalo Mayor Steven Pankow, Patrick J. McGroder, A.T. O'Neill and former Yankee mastermind Joe McCarthy.

Game 117, Monday, August 6, Buffalo: Buffalo 4, Rochester 1

Peanuts Lowrey's second-inning grand slam gave
Roger Bowman all the runs he needed for a well-deserved victory.

Game 117 – August 6, 1956
Rochester 000 010 000 – 1 6 0
Buffalo 040 000 00x – 4 5 0
WP – Bowman (8-12)   **LP – Russell (6-4)**

Inclement weather again kept the crowd low, but the village of Sloan turned out more than 25% of its residents and the Bisons registered a count of 2178 through the turnstiles. The victory was a happy result for the Sloan attendees and the additional 250 non-paying guests from the Catholic Guild for the Blind. Buffalo city recreation director Vince McNamara provided a vivid play by play description for those visitors, à la Bill Mazer upstairs in the radio booth. Many later said they were able to follow the sound of bat on ball to know when a good hit was being made.

Rochester starter Kelton Russell lasted only an inning and two-thirds, giving up three hits, two of them to Lowrey. Cavarretta had sent his player-coach into the leadoff spot in order to rest the weary Pete Castiglione in left field, and Peanuts had responded with a double in the first inning and a grand slam home run in the second.

Russell had had no trouble with the next five men in the order after Lowrey's opening base knock, but suddenly his control went. Maybe it was the chill of the evening. Pat Tomkinson drew a walk with two down in the second frame. Billy DeMars chipped a single to right. Russell's problems deepened when he walked Bowman to fill the sacks. Back in the batter's box for the second time, Lowrey picked out a second Russell delivery to his liking and sent it on a high arc over the left-field screen for a four-run lead.

That was all for Russell for the night. The Herd managed only two more safeties off relievers Gary Geiger and Cot Deal, but Bowman's stylish pitching made the early offense stand up.

Using a sinker, screwball and a low sweeping curve, Bowman scattered six hits in going the distance, fanning seven and allowing only two fly balls to leave the infield. One was pulled in by Joe Caffie in center field. The other was Ed Phillips' solo shot in the fifth. Again, the left-field screen proved no deterrent.

Easter recorded 14 putouts at first base. The infield had 16 ground ball assists.

BISON TALES: Prior to the start of the game, John C. Stiglmeier was presented with a plaque of appreciation for his service to the Village of Sloan and his service to the Western New York community for his past and current efforts on behalf of the Buffalo Bisons. Sloan mayor John Jablonski co-chaired the event along with Sloan police chief John A. Piekarski. Police captain Henry Herman, the original chair, had had to give way to due to a major surgical procedure. He was recovering at Millard Fillmore Hospital.

Last-place Buffalo was 19½ games behind first-place Toronto, but over in the American League the Kansas City A's were 31 games behind the Yankees. The tail-end New York Giants trailed Milwaukee by 22½ in the National League.

Buffalo had out-homered the Red Wings by 21 to 14 in their meetings and had a three-game victory edge in the series between the two clubs.

Game 118, Tuesday, August 7, Buffalo: Buffalo 1, Rochester 0

For the second night in a row, a Bison home run made the difference.
Karl Drews gutted out a 10-hit shutout.

Game 118 – August 7, 1956
Rochester   000 000 000 – 0 10 0
Buffalo   000 000 10x – 1   6 1
WP – Drews (11-8)   LP – Markell (8-7)

Neither pitcher could have been called sharp on a wet evening that brought out 2414 fans for Eden Night. The town in question provided a group of 400 patrons, complete with a marching band, horns, bells and other noisemakers.

Rochester's Duke Markell held the Herd to six hits in the seven innings he worked, but he walked five. Drews was touched for 10 safeties but conceded only one free pass. Wet basepaths meant station-to-station baseball for baserunners.

The Red Wings threatened in the sixth after Joe Cunningham and Gene Green opened with singles, but Drews collared Allie Clark on a fastball down and in, and Peanuts Lowrey saved the day with a sliding catch down the left-field line off Jay Van Noy's bat. Dick Rand bounced out.

Drews slipped in the muddy footing on a pitch to Markell leading off the seventh, and the opposition hurler jumped on it, driving the ball into the screen in left for a double, just missing a four-bagger. Ron Plaza banged an infield hit off Drews' glove as the Bison pitcher again slipped coming off the mound, Markell taking third. The Buffalo veterans stepped up to the challenge.

Bill Serena cleanly fielded Eddie Kasko's hit to third, took a step toward second to open up the throwing lane and fired a strike to Pat Tomkinson to catch Markell at the plate. Tom Burgess lined to Easter for two down. Drews got behind Cunningham and then walked him intentionally to load the bases. Green bounced into a fielder's choice, DeMars to Ortiz. Inning over.

Joe Caffie led off for Buffalo in the home half of the seventh and sent a 3-2 changeup over the right-field wall near the flagpole for his seventh home run and the only run of the game. Markell had fooled him three times earlier on that same pitch but had gone to the well once too often.

BISON TALES: Caffie had been hitting .350 in spring training and had expected to be on the Cleveland Indians' opening-day big-league roster. Instead, he was sent out to San Diego in the Pacific Coast League and used only intermittently by the Padres, struggling to hit .250. When the Indians loaned him to Buffalo, it took Joe a couple of weeks in the everyday lineup to get his confidence back and begin the road back to .300.

George Bullard had been reactivated. To make room for him, Zeb Eaton was placed on the inactive list due to his knee injury. Cavarretta was apt to leave Caffie in center and station Bullard either in right or in left, resting Lowrey and Mierkowicz as needed.

Pete Castiglione's emergency left-field play had allowed the club to compete, but the team would be much stronger with a fleet ball hawk with a stronger arm patrolling out there. Cavarretta could now sit Ortiz or DeMars part time and use Pete as a more than adequate infield replacement.

Norm Sherry today had the little finger on his right hand X-rayed to see if it had been broken. Pat Tomkinson had caught the last five games and gone 0 for 14.

MAKING THE TURNSTILES GO 'ROUND
Monday, August 6, Buffalo

Club hopes were raised with a rousing turnout at Monday's August 6 noon luncheon at the Buffalo Athletic Club. Fourteen thousand dollars in ticket sales were pledged within 10 minutes' time for the August 31 final home game of the season against the Montreal Royals. Dubbed "Citizens Appreciation Night," the evening was to be held as another honor to Bison general manager Stiglmeier.

Patrick J. McGroder, chairman of the board of Municipal Auditorium-Civic Stadium, was the luncheon's host and the chairman for Citizens Appreciation Night. Following a brief round of speeches, Mr. McGroder called on Harry Altman of the Towne Casino to get the ball rolling. According to the Buffalo Evening News, Altman responded, "Now is the time to start this ticket sale. We won't be together again. Put me down for $300 worth of tickets." The mood was infectious.

Bankers Lewis G. Harriman from M&T Trust and John M. Glavin from Marine Trust agreed to take a similar amount, as did Mrs. Bernard King, Chester A. Gorski, Max Gross and Kenneth Kelly, the manager of the Hotel Lafayette and president of the Buffalo Hotel Association.

Cheektowaga supervisor Benedict T. Holtz committed the Town of Cheektowaga to 1000 tickets, while John Grysinski, leading an East Side group, pledged 1000 more for his members. Peter J. Crotty, Chairman of the Erie County Democratic Committee, stated that his organization would buy out the entire bleachers and give the tickets away to orphanages and "other worthy youngsters of the city."

Mayor Steven Pankow, heading a contingent of a dozen city officials, pledged his administration would take and sell 5000 seats. Charles J. Wick of Niagara Hudson took $500 worth of tickets, as did L. M. Jacobs. Ed Don George committed to $50.

McGroder took another $300 himself, making it a near sellout of the ballpark. Invited dignitaries who were sure to be in attendance, he said, were Joe DiMaggio, the Yankee Clipper; baseball commissioner Ford C. Frick; Minor League commissioner George M. Trautman; and International League president Frank Shaughnessy.

In International League news: A new minor league game attendance record was established when Miami hosted Columbus in a game at the Orange Bowl. A crowd of 57,713 came out to watch Satchel Paige down the Jets by a score of 6-2. The old attendance record had been set back on October 9, 1944, when 52,833 had attended in Baltimore to watch the minor league Orioles drop a 5-4 decision to the American Association Louisville Colonels in the fourth game of the Junior World Series. That game had been played at Baltimore's Municipal Stadium, a horseshoe-shaped structure built in 1922 as a football venue. The minor league Orioles had moved there in midseason 1944 after their original baseball home, Oriole Stadium (previously named Terrapin Park), burned down. An infield was laid at one end of the grounds, resulting in a very deep outfield.

Most football stadia are not configured for baseball. The Marlins threw up a screen fence partway along the short right-field wall only 216 feet from the plate. Balls dumped over the screen went for ground rule doubles. The left field distance was only marginally greater at 250 feet. Seven ground-rule doubles were struck during the contest and only one home run.

Although the turnout was less than the 80,000 Miami owner Sid Salomon had hoped for, he made up the difference in gate receipts and made good on his vow of a $20,000 donation to Miami charities.

A major league owner with a small ballpark up in Brooklyn was paying close attention to the fan turnout at the Orange Bowl game. The major league Baltimore Orioles currently played at Municipal Stadium, rebuilt in 1949/1950 and with the addition of a second deck to attract a major league franchise. A losing club like Baltimore could put more than 47,000 fans in the seats. A winner in Ebbets Field could shoehorn only about 35,000 fans into its tiny confines, if you didn't mind standing.

THE MINORS VERSUS THE MAJORS: VI
Tuesday, August 7, Buffalo

General manager John C. Stiglmeier, before boarding his flight for the meeting of independent clubs in Miami, offered the major leagues a four-point plan to assist minor league baseball, especially the independent clubs such as the Bisons. Cy Kritzer of the Buffalo Evening News quoted him as saying, "If some drastic legislation is not passed this year, there will be no minor leagues in ten years and mediocrity will engulf the majors."

Stiglmeier's plan proposed the following:
1. Abolish the bonus rule.
2. Establish territorial rights for all minor league clubs and give them first chance to sign and develop players.
3. Bind the International League, the American Association and the Pacific Coast League to the same waiver rule.
4. Establish a pension fund for minor leaguers.

Stiglmeier went on to say that baseball commissioner Ford C. Frick had called for a show of hands recently at a meeting of major league farm club directors and the majority were in favor of doing away with the bonus rule. The bonus rule gave away large sums of money to untried talent and prevented that money from being invested in minor league development. The major league clubs, he added, actually wanted to do away with the program but did not trust each other not to continue the process under the table.

Instead, Stiglmeier suggested that minor league clubs should be assigned defined geographic areas in their location and then be allowed to sign young ballplayers who emerged from those regions. That, or that the commissioner of baseball should establish a universal scouting and draft system, as was the case with professional football, and then allow the minors to share in the information obtained as well as the drafting opportunities.

The plan would additionally prevent the sending down or transfer of players from or between the Pacific Coast League, American Association and International League without these players being subject to waivers from all the teams in each of the three leagues. This would prevent the current practice, for example, of the Brooklyn and St. Louis clubs shifting their players from the International League to American Association, or vice versa, and then back again without allowing other teams in their respective leagues to claim their services. It would prevent players from being sent to a lower classification within the major club's farm system without giving the other teams in the league a chance to bid for their services.

Major league clubs with strong farm systems had been able to keep Triple A players in lower classifications for years because of the strength of their major league rosters and the binding nature of the reserve clause that every ballplayer had to sign. While this had helped the major clubs, it frustrated the talents of the ballplayers and prevented the minor league clubs from offering appropriate playing opportunities.

Paul Richards, current skipper of the Baltimore Orioles, had tried to establish a universal draft when he was the manager of the Bisons back in 1948. Stiglmeier believed that commissioner Frick and executives of several baseball teams such as Richards, Joe Cronin of the Boston Red Sox and Gene Martin of the Philadelphia Phillies would support his proposals. It remained to be seen what the meeting of the independent clubs would come up with and how the majors would then respond.

Had Stiglmeier's recommendations been in effect in 1956, the Bisons would not have suffered the dearth of effective replacements they had struggled against throughout the season. It would have been a vastly different campaign. The team could have been at least the first-division club that Cavarretta had spoken of at the outset of the year.

Lou Ortiz belts a grand slam
Photo courtesy of SUNY Buffalo State Courier-Express Collection

Game 119, Wednesday, August 8, Buffalo: Rochester 9, Buffalo 4

Polish-American Night saw 6008 paying customers
witness 29 base hits, 18 walks, and a 9-4 Rochester victory.

Game 119 – August 8, 1956
Rochester   003 221 100 – 9 21 1
Buffalo   103 000 000 – 4 8 1
WP – Wright (2-3)   LP – Froats (2-8)

As promised, a stellar crowd turned out to support Ed Mierkowicz and the Bisons. Under the leadership of chairman Ray Wasielewski, there were festivities aplenty and noisemakers and bells and horns galore. George Feusl's band opened the evening, followed by the Polish-American Club orchestra. Ed Mierkowicz, the man of the hour, was gifted with a portable television set and a radio. Patrons, including more than 100 members of the Knights of St. John, were then treated to a precision marching display by the Adam Plewacki Post drill team, the raising of the flag and the National Anthem.

Lou Ortiz got the ballgame started the right way, sending a two-out John Mackinson fastball into the left-field screen and winding up on third with a triple. Did the crowd noise bother Mackinson? Ortiz scored moments later as the pitcher heaved one into the dirt for a wild pitch.

Mierkowicz helped the ball club stay in front with a fine running catch of Jay Van Noy's sinking liner in the second, but the Red Wings broke through in the third and took the lead for the first time in the series. Three runs drove Harry Nicholas from the hill, and Bill Froats had to corral the third out. Then Buffalo came back with three of their own in the bottom of the frame.

Ortiz doubled to the wall in left, and Luke Easter hit number 26 of the season, a dead center-field shot, and the game was tied. Arm trouble sent Mackinson out of the game after he walked Bill Serena and got Mierkowicz to hit into a fielder's choice. His replacement, Jack Roberts, had little time to warm up. Maybe the crowd got to him, too. Pat Tomkinson got a free pass, Billy DeMars singled and the notoriously poor-hitting Froats walked to put the Bisons back out in front by one. Reliever Mel Wright collared Peanuts Lowrey for the final out of the inning.

Froats didn't make it through the fourth. Ron Plaza, with three hits in this game (he had four the night before) knotted it up with a home run. Eddie Kasko tripled, and Gene Green singled him home to give the lead back to the Wings. Joe Coleman stopped the rally there, but then he, too, was pummeled for four more runs in the next two frames. Mierkowicz made another fine play to gun down left fielder Allie Clark at the plate and prevent a 10th Rochester tally.

Buffalo could do nothing with Wright despite four hits and seven walks. He also fanned seven.

Bison Tales: Frank (Beauty) McGowan, an outstanding Bison center fielder from the 1930s, was in the seats as a Baltimore scout. Steve O'Neill was in town from the Cleveland Indians. They were looking at Caffie. George Bullard pinch-hit unsuccessfully for John Weiss in the eighth. It was his first appearance in the lineup since he broke his hand in batting practice back on June 27.

Thursday, August 9, Buffalo: Rainout

Rains cancelled the ballgame. The West Seneca Night festivities in honor of Lou Ortiz were re-scheduled for August 20.

A new special night was in the works to honor Luke Easter and Joe Caffie on August 24. The effort was being spearheaded by businessman Marshall Davis Miles, a partner with his brothers in the Miles Brothers Dairy, as well as real estate investments in Buffalo and out west. He was prominently known as a patron of the boxing scene and in his role as Joe Louis' manager from 1946 through the Champion's retirement in 1949.

Game 120, Friday, August 10, Buffalo: Buffalo 4, Toronto 3

Larry Donovan was moved up in the rotation to face
league-leading Toronto and won the game with both his arm and his bat.

Game 120 – August 10, 1956

Toronto	101 010 000 – 3	9	1
Buffalo	000 102 01x – 4	10	0

WP – Donovan (8-7)   LP – Blake (13-8)

Al Schacht, the Clown Prince of Baseball, appearing as a personal favor to John Stiglmeier, got the night started with a hilarious 25-minute comedy program. His best routine was an interpretation of Babe Ruth's "called shot" against the Chicago Cubs in the 1933 World Series. The Bell Aire singers from the Bell Aircraft Corporation opened the evening with a medley at 7:00 p.m. Schacht tore out onto the field from the home team first-base dugout shortly thereafter. The club had hoped to land the comedian on the diamond via helicopter, but the Civil Aeronautics Association nixed those plans, citing the danger of the maneuver in such a tight space. Bell employees helped swell the turnout to 3980.

Toronto's Archie Wilson drove in the first two runs of the game with sacrifice flies in the first and third innings. Bill Serena's infield ground out scored Lou Ortiz from third base in the fourth. Sam Jethroe's third-straight base hit and Wilson's single in the fifth restored the two-run Toronto lead.

Buffalo tied it in the sixth. Peanuts Lowrey rapped a two-out single to right and Donovan drew a walk from Leaf starter Ed Blake. Pete Castiglione's line drive base hit scored Lowrey. Donovan came home on a Joe Caffie ground ball that scooted into center field for a base hit.

Cavarretta again proved his managerial wisdom. First, he sent Donovan out to contain the Toronto bats. Then, three key decisions came in the eighth. Ed Mierkowicz singled and George Bullard was sent in to run. Norm Sherry pinch-hit for Pat Tomkinson and laid down a sacrifice bunt as ordered. Finally, Donovan was allowed to hit for himself. Toronto manager Bruno Betzel waved his outfield in to cut off any potential hit and stop Bullard from scoring, but Donovan crossed the Leafs up, and his fly ball to the left center field gap fell just out of Jethroe's reach and rolled to the wall. Bullard scored the winner.

Donovan had retired 11 in a row until walking Loren Babe and hitting Jethroe with two gone in the ninth. Cavarretta called on lefthanded Steve Nagy to face lefthanded Lew Morton. Morton grounded to first for the final out.

Game 121, Saturday, August 11, Buffalo: Buffalo 11, Toronto 4

Lou Ortiz's grand slam home run and six RBIs led
the Herd to a second straight win over the league leaders.

Game 121 – August 11, 1956

Toronto	000 011 110 – 4	10	0
Buffalo	130 001 60x – 11	13	0
WP – Hahn (7-9)	LP – Lovenguth (18-10)		

A crowd of 2373 turned out to watch the Bisons continue the Offermann jinx against the league's leading hurler, Lynn Lovenguth. The 18-game winner walked six and gave up four runs in less than two innings. A double by Joe Caffie and a bases-loaded walk to Bill Serena accounted for the first-inning score. Two more walks, a run-scoring double by Pete Castiglione, another free pass and a two-run double by Lou Ortiz brought home George Bullard, Fred Hahn and Castiglione in the second. New Toronto pitchers Ross Grimsley and Pete Wojey got the final two outs.

Hahn kept the Leafs off the scoreboard until Earl Battey clubbed one of his offerings over the left-field wall in the fifth. Bill Wilson cut the score to 4-2 when he also tagged Hahn for a four-bagger in the sixth. Luke Easter gave Hahn his cushion back by singling home Joe Caffie in the bottom half of that inning off Wojey.

Battey led off the seventh by hitting his second homer of the night over the friendly left-field barrier. When Ed Blake got a pinch-hit and Sam Jethroe added a single, manager Cavarretta went to his hot reliever, Steve Nagy. Nagy retired the side on a double-play ball.

The Bisons sealed the victory in the home half of the inning. Ten men went to the plate against Tony Jacobs and Dutch Romberger in the seventh. The culminating blow was Lou Ortiz's grand slam home run to left center.

Nagy allowed the game's last run, an Archie Wilson solo homer in the eighth over the popular left-field barrier. Archie now had 12 home runs on the year, eight of them against Buffalo.

BISON TALES: Ortiz now had 20 home runs, a new season high for him. George Bullard started his first game in over a month, playing right field and picking up a single, a stolen base, two walks and two scores. Donovan's win yesterday was his third against Toronto with no losses.

Pete Castiglione was back at shortstop in this series due to Billy DeMars' ongoing arm ailment. Pete was five for nine in the two games played. Pat Tomkinson's slump had reached 0 for 24 before Cavarretta pinch-hit Norm Sherry for him on Friday. Sherry, still with a bad hand, had had to take over behind the plate for the remainder of that game and allowed a passed ball. Sherry was behind the plate in this game, going 0 for five.

Lefthanded starter Roger Bowman (8-12) was sold to the Minneapolis Millers of the American Association. The move was made because Steve Nagy had now worked himself into starting shape and Cavarretta believed he could take over Bowman's role in the rotation. Finances were also a factor. Purchased for $7500 at the start of the year, Bowman's contract was sold at a profit that provided critically needed liquid assets.

Game 122, Sunday, August 12, Buffalo: Toronto 10, Buffalo 8

This game was a homerfest. The wind was blowing out,
the pitches were up, the batters took advantage.

Game 122 – August 12, 1956

Toronto	023 003 002 – 10	12	0
Buffalo	000 220 040 – 8	10	1

WP – Grimsley (2-1)   LP – Coleman (4-1)

A crowd of 3813 was on hand to witness seven home runs for the Leafs, three for the Bisons and a valiant comeback effort that went for naught. Karl Drews didn't last three innings. The Leafs' Mike Goliat led off the second with a blast over the left center field fence. An unearned run came home on Ed Stevens' single and Drews' throwing error.

Archie Wilson singled in the third and Carl Sawatski hooked a Drews pitch over the right-field wall for two more runs. Goliat again went deep, this time over the screen in left with two out. Harry Nicholas came in to relieve.

Toronto hurler Don Johnson made a mistake to Luke Easter in the bottom of the fourth, and the Bison first baseman belted number 27 into Woodlawn Avenue behind the right-field wall. Bill Serena singled after Easter's drive and eventually scored on George Bullard's one-baser in the same inning. Buffalo cut the deficit to one after Lou Ortiz took Johnson deep (number 21) in the next inning with Joe Caffie aboard.

Nicholas watched Stevens' 18th home run soar over the right-field wall to start the visitor sixth and then, two outs later, with a man on base thanks to a walk, he watched Lou Morton's drive do the same thing. Steve Nagy got the third out and doused the Leafs' fire for two innings more.

Buffalo fought back to a tie with four runs in the home half of the eighth. Lou Ortiz's double started it. Bill Serena's 17th home run of the season, a mighty blow to left center, cut the deficit in half. A Peanuts Lowrey single led to a pitching change followed by a walk to George Bullard. Cavarretta batted for Norm Sherry and got his club-leading fourth pinch-hit of the season, plating Lowrey. Ed Mierkowicz failed in a pinch-hit assignment for Nagy, but Bullard came home with the tying run when Pete Castiglione rapped a clean single to right.

Joe Coleman couldn't hold the Leafs in the ninth. Lou Morton parked his second drive of the night over the right-field wall, a solo shot, and one out later Carl Sawatski also swatted his second homer, also to right. Bill Froats got the last out.

Buffalo thought they had a chance after Ross Grimsley walked Lou Ortiz to open the ninth, but Easter hit into a fielder's choice and Lynn Lovenguth, of all people, came in to get the save.

BISON TALES: There were 15 home runs in the last two games, 11 by the Maple Leafs and four for the Bisons. Luke Easter might lead the league in long distance blows (27), but the Toronto club had the team lead—122 homers in 120 contests. Seven pitchers saw duty for the Herd in the last two games, nine for Toronto. It was Coleman's first loss of the year. He had won four.

Game 123, Monday, August 13, Havana, Cuba: Havana 4, Buffalo 1

The Sugar Kings broke open a close game with a three-run
winning outburst in the eighth against starter John Weiss.

Game 123 – August 13, 1956

Buffalo	000 000 001 – 1	10	1
Havana	010 000 03x – 4	10	2
WP – Marrero (2-1)		LP – Weiss (2-9)	

Buffalo left by airplane in the early hours of the morning to arrive in Havana for the start of a five-game series to be played in four days. Four more games would follow in Miami over the following three days. This was the aftermath of the early season rainouts and would be a difficult stretch for an older team assailed by injury.

Despite their weariness from the flight and the high temperatures, Buffalo kept it a one-run game and had their chances until the fatal inning. Weiss gave up a second-inning single to Nino Escalera and a two-out double to Don Nicholas to put the Cubans on the board with a run. He scattered four more hits and three walks over his seven innings of work before the heat did him in.

Meanwhile, the Sugar Kings' Connie Marrero was keeping the Herd at bay, distributing seven base knocks and two free passes through seven but doubling down when he needed to. Joe Caffie and Lou Ortiz were each 0 for five in the game and Luke Easter 0 for three. Marerro saved his two walks for Easter and Serena to take the bat out of their hands at critical times. A double play also helped to keep the Bisons off the scoreboard.

Weiss suddenly hit the wall in the eighth. Angel Scull opened with a bunt single. Hal Bevan walked. Ultus Alvarez hit a ball up the middle that Castiglione knocked down but had no play on, a hit that filled the bases. On a 2-2 offering, Pablo Bernard plunked a ball into short left that Lowrey just could not reach and Scull came in to score. With the bases still loaded and Bill Froats hurriedly warming up in the bullpen, Escalera ripped Weiss with a blow to right center that plated two more. Froats finally took over and got three in a row, but the damage was done.

Buffalo tried to make a comeback in their last at-bat. Jay Heard had come on for Marrero in the eighth and Ed Mierkowicz opened the ninth with a single. Pinch-hitter Billy DeMars singled with one down. Pete Castiglione's base hit scored Mierkowicz and brought the tying run to the plate. Heard rose to the challenge, striking out both Joe Caffie and Lou Ortiz to save the win.

BISON TALES: Yet more injuries. George Bullard was scratched from the lineup after pinching a nerve in his neck making an awkward catch at the wall in the seesaw game on Sunday. Trainer Jimmy Mack had gone to work on him right away, but the bumpy plane flight had kept the condition from healing.

Luke Easter and Bill Serena erupted with power surges in the 15-game homestand just concluded. Luke went 15 for 49 for a .303 average, with five home runs, eight runs scored and 13 driven home. Serena hit .244, but seven of his 12 safe blows were for extra bases: a double, a triple and five home runs. He accounted for eight runs scored and 12 men batted in.

In International League news: Forty-eight-year-old Satchel Paige (or is he 56? or is he 106?) threw a seven-inning, 4-0 one-hitter this day against the Rochester Red Wings.

Games 124 and 125, Tuesday, August 14, Havana, Cuba: Havana 5, Buffalo 4; Havana 3, Buffalo 0

The Sugar Kings grabbed two from the Herd on a costly
throwing error in game one and a crafty pitching display in the second.

Game 124 – August 14, 1956 (first game of doubleheader)

Buffalo	002 002 0 – 4 8 1
Havana	000 113 x – 5 9 2

WP – Cueche (5-1)   LP – Drews (11-9)

Game 125 – August 14, 1956 (second game of doubleheader)

Buffalo	000 000 000 – 0 7 2
Havana	000 000 03x – 3 12 1

WP – Consuegra (2-1)   LP – Donovan (8-8)

Buffalo gave Steve Nagy a two-run lead in the third frame of the seven-inning first game on a Joe Caffie single off Cuban starter Jerry Lane and a Lou Ortiz RBI double. Lane carefully walked Luke Easter, but Bill Serena crossed up that strategy with a clean single to plate Ortiz. Raul Sanchez was brought in to close out the inning.

Nagy was stung for six hits and the two tying runs in the fourth and fifth innings. Hal Bevan banged a double in the fourth and was singled home by Ultus Alvarez. In the fifth, it was a Don Nicholas single that was followed by an Angel Scull triple to right center.

Sanchez exited in the fifth for a pinch-hitter and Emilio Cueche became the third Havana hurler of the night. Buffalo got to work on him right away, thanks to a pair of errors and a clutch single by Ortiz. Ed Mierkowicz's grounder was bobbled by Bevan to open the sixth. Manager Cavarretta sent George Bullard in to run and take over right field. Billy DeMars, pinch-hitting for Norm Sherry, forced Bullard at second. Pinch hitter Cavarretta then appeared in the batter's box and drew a walk. A popup to short by Pete Castiglione made it two out, but Buffalo caught a break on the play. Short-stop Pablo Bernard threw wildly trying to double DeMars off second, and both runners moved up a base into scoring position. With first base now open, the Sugar Kings decided to intentionally walk the lefty-swinging Joe Caffie and take their chances with righty Lou Ortiz. Ortiz sliced a two-run single to right and the Bisons were up by two. Both runs were unearned.

Three runs in the bottom of that inning won it for Havana. Cavarretta called on Joe Coleman to hold the lead, but Joe walked Alvarez leading off. Bernard was retired on a popup, but Nino Escalera reached Coleman for a base hit and the manager decided he didn't like what he was seeing. Buffalo's stopper, Karl Drews, was called on. Drews fooled Amado Ibañez on a swinging strike three in the dirt, but both runners took off on the pitch and Pat Tomkinson wildly overthrew third trying to catch Alvarez. Alvarez scored easily and Escalera, never stopping, raced home with the tying run. Two unearned runs.

The winning run in the same inning was hard to swallow. Drews and the plate umpire, Harry Schwarts, couldn't agree on a strike zone. Dutch Dotterer wound up with a single off Drews to left field and moved into scoring position when ball four was called on Cueche. Don Nicholas' base hit scored Dotterer with the game winner.

Bullard got a last-gasp two-out single off Cueche in the seventh but was stranded at first.

Red Donovan escaped jam after jam in game two until his luck ran out in the eighth inning. Donovan and Cuban starter Sandy Consuegra had matched zeros until that point. The Herd made a threat in the top of the eighth, loading the bases behind singles by Pete Castiglione and Joe Caffie and a walk to Luke Easter, but Consuegra got Bill Serena on strikes and Peanuts Lowrey tapped meekly back to the mound for the easy putout at first.

In the home half of the inning, Ultus Alvarez led off with a double that might have gone for a triple, save for a fine play by Bullard to cut the ball off in the gap. Owen Friend flew out to Joe Caffie, and manager Cavarretta called for an intentional pass to the lefthanded-swinging Nino Escalera, pitting the righthanded Donovan against the righthanded-swinging Amado Ibañez.

Ibañez was already three for three against Donovan and perhaps the Bison manager thought he had by now used up his quota of success against the Bison hurler, but such was not the case. Or perhaps Ibañez was as insulted as had been Lou Ortiz in the first game under the same circumstances. A sharp single sent home Alvarez with the game's first tally. Dutch Dotterer then blooped a Donovan offering into short right field behind Easter at first base and Escalera came around to score. The fleet Ibañez scored right behind him, all the way from first, when Bullard's off-balance throw to third sailed wide to Serena's left and into the left-field foul territory.

Consuegra shut the Bisons down in the ninth, foiling both Ed Mierkowicz and Cavarretta in pinch-hit efforts.

BISON TALES: The Cubans managed only one extra-base hit off Donovan, who gutted out the game even while his stuff was off. The losing streak was now up to four.

Buffalo stranded 10 men in each contest. Havana manager Nap Reyes was taking the bat out of Luke Easter's hands by showering him with walks. Luke collected two in each game, plus being hit by a pitch in the opener.

Following the outcome of the game one, Drews and Cavarretta had a five-minute conversation with plate umpire Schwarts out at home plate. It was not a pleasant chat. The Bison manager and hurler made their views known to ensure that they were getting a fair shake from the arbiter.

A number of International League teams fighting for playoff position had been asking about the availability of Karl Drews, Luke Easter, Lou Ortiz and Bill Serena. General manager John Stiglmeier replied said these men were going nowhere. The Bisons were committed to putting a quality team on the field and these men were the nucleus of making that effort happen.

Lou Ortiz had been the target of a good many boos. The Havana fans remembered his time with Cienfuegos a few years back in winter ball, when he had gotten off to a terrible start at the plate.

Game 126, Wednesday, August 15, Havana, Cuba: Buffalo 4, Havana 3
Fred Hahn's six-hitter snapped the four-game losing streak.
George Bullard got the winning hit and Joe Caffie made a key throw.

Game 126 – August 15, 1956
Buffalo	030 000 010 – 4	9	0
Havana	000 030 000 – 3	6	3
WP – Hahn (8-9)	**LP – Hatten (3-7)**		

Following a scoreless first, it was strength against strength to lead off the second inning with the Bisons coming to bat. Rudy Minarcin, on the hill for the Sugar Kings, was a lowball pitcher and Luke Easter a lowball hitter. Easter opened the scoring with a mammoth shot over the right-field wall at the 400-foot mark in Havana's Gran Stadium. It was Luke's 28th. The Herd quickly added two more.

Fuming at the home run, Minarcin walked Bill Serena. Billy DeMars reached him for a one-out base hit. The next batter, Norm Sherry, topped the ball down the first-base line and Sugar King first baseman Nino Escalera scooped it up and fired to third in an attempt to catch Serena. When the heave went wild, Cavarretta, coaching at third, sent Serena home, and when he saw that left fielder Juan Delis was late getting to the ball, he windmilled DeMars on as well. The throw from Delis was not even close. Billy scored and Buffalo had a three-run lead.

Hahn made the lead hold up until the Sugar Kings tied it in the fifth. Owen Friend drew a walk and the pitcher, Joe Hatten, who had relieved Minarcin in the fourth, slugged a triple just out of Joe Caffie's reach in center. Delis' ground out to second scored Hatten to cut the deficit to one. Angel Scull took a high curve that didn't break and sent it on a line over the left-field wall at the foul pole. Game tied.

Hatten, the ex-Dodger, was stuck with the loss after he walked Easter with one gone in the eighth and Serena followed with a solid single. Cuban manager Nap Reyes turned to his bullpen for Emilio Cueche to take on George Bullard, but Bullard crossed up the strategy with a single of his own to plate Easter with what turned out to be the winning run. One single later, Raul Sanchez came on to get the third out.

Hahn tired in the ninth. Nino Escalera led off with a hit to right center that he tried to stretch into a double, but an on-the-money throw from Joe Caffie to DeMars caught him at second for the putout. Cavarretta called on Harry Nicholas to finish up. Amado Ibañez, first-ball hitting, flew out to Bullard. Friend went down on strikes. Buffalo had taken their first game of the series.

BISON TALES: It had been a long and wearying season, but the travel and the Havana heat, and maybe the food, too, led Cavarretta to keep both Ortiz and Peanuts Lowrey out of the starting lineup. Lowrey took a turn pinch-hitting in the sixth. Ortiz was a defensive entry in the ninth. Cavarretta also planned to keep them on the bench for the Thursday game. They needed to regain their strength for the upcoming series in Miami.

Cuban Night saw a noisy, enthusiastic crowd of 17,000-plus in the stands. The rooting didn't help the Sugar Kings, but the visitors' share of the gate was critical for the Bisons' bottom line.

Game 127, Thursday, August 16, Havana, Cuba: Buffalo 7, Havana 3

*Karl Drews went nine strong innings to give the Bisons the win
in the finale of the five-game set. Buffalo pounded out 11 hits.*

Game 127 – August 16, 1956
Buffalo   100 012 300 – 7 11 0
Havana   000 200 100 – 3   8 2
WP – Drews (12-9)   LP – Heard (2-2)

Drews was back on the mound and umpire Harry Schwarts was again working the plate. This time the two men were in agreement where the strike zone was. Drews fanned five batters in this game and walked only one.

Buffalo got the first run of the ballgame in the first inning on a Joe Caffie triple to left center and a misplay on the throw from the Sugar Kings' left fielder Juan Delis. As the ball got away from Amado Ibañez at third and skittered into the dugout, Caffie was waved home with an unearned tally.

The Sugar Kings were hitless against Drews until they strung together four straight singles in the bottom of the fourth. Delis, Nino Escalera, Ibañez and Dutch Dotterer gave Havana starter Jay Heard a 2-1 lead. Heard gave it back in the fifth. Pat Tomkinson drew a walk, took second on Drews' ground out and tied the game up by scoring on Pete Castiglione's crisp single to left.

Drews drove in the winning runs himself in the next inning. Bill Serena reached first on Ibañez's second error of the evening. George Bullard beat out a sacrifice bunt for a base hit. Billy DeMars' bid for a base hit was knocked down by Hal Bevan in the hole between first and second and DeMars was thrown out at first base, but the runners moved into scoring position. Manager Nap Reyes had Pat Tomkinson intentionally walked to set up the double play with the bases full, but Drews crossed him up by ripping a Heard pitch into center field to score Serena and Bullard.

The Herd put it away with three more in the seventh. Mierkowicz started with a one-baser. Easter was retired on a fly ball, but Serena drew a walk and Bullard again beat out an infield roller to fill the sacks. Billy DeMars was not to be denied this time. His double into the gap in right center chased home all three baserunners and gave Drews a five-run cushion.

The Cubans notched one final run in the bottom of the seventh. Ibañez tripled over Caffie's head in center field and came home on a sacrifice fly off the bat of relief pitcher Raul Sanchez. The final two innings were scoreless for each team.

BISON TALES: This was the Herd's final appearance against Havana for the year. The Cubans took the season series, 13 games to nine.

As planned, Lou Ortiz and Peanuts Lowrey again sat out the heat. Their replacements, Castiglione at second and Bullard in left field, amassed a total of three hits in nine at-bats. Bullard scored twice and Castiglione drove in a run. This was the difference it made having a healthy bench.

Tomkinson's woeful slump was now 0 for 31. He walked twice in this game. Bullard had gotten hot since rejoining the lineup and had a six-game hit streak, eight for 19 for a .421 average.

MAYOR'S PROCLAMATION HONORS EASTER, CAFFIE
Friday, August 17, Buffalo

The Buffalo Courier-Express photo on August 17 showed Luke Easter, Dick Fischer and Joe Caffie surrounding Acting Mayor King W. Peterson of the City of Buffalo, with smiles all around. The accompanying article read:

Acting Mayor King W. Peterson yesterday proclaimed August 24 as Luke Easter-Joe Caffie night to help honor the two stars of the Buffalo Bisons at a special night in their honor. Co-chairmen for the affair are Marshall Davis Miles and Fred Perry. Dick Fischer is honorary chairman.

> *Whereas, Luke Easter and Joe Caffie, two of Buffalo's outstanding baseball players and members of Buffalo's community owned baseball club, who have shown great ability and fine sportsmanship in their chosen profession; and Whereas, the Buffalonians' booster committee, a group of prominent civic, sports and fraternal leaders is co-operating in the observance of a Luke Easter-Joe Caffie night at Offermann Stadium on August 24th; and Whereas the citizens of Western New York wish to show their appreciation of the efforts of these outstanding players and the entire team; Now, therefore, I King W. Peterson, Acting Mayor of the City of Buffalo, do hereby proclaim Friday, August 24, 1956 as 'Luke Easter-Joe Caffie night' and call upon all our citizens, sportsmen and lovers of fair play to join with the committee in paying tribute to our team by attending the game that night.*
>
> *Signed:*
> *KING W. PETERSON*
> *Acting Mayor of Buffalo*

The picture for next season was still very cloudy, but attendance promotions such as had been held recently, and such as were planned for the future—including the Easter-Caffie night—were making a strong impact on the thinking of the front office and the board of directors.

Attendance was on the upswing, and, while not yet all that had been hoped for in recent games, a revised estimate of season attendance saw the final tally as coming close to 180,000. According to general manager Stiglmeier, this could allow the team to come close to breaking even. The club had sliced overhead and front-office expenses to the bone. The commitment was to making payroll for the ballplayers.

The Bisons were again playing competitive ball. First, veterans such as the Bisons had on the roster did not throw in the towel. Second, the team had benefitted from newcomers to the pitching staff. Third, the return of others from injury status had allowed manager Cavarretta some room to maneuver in his game plans.

The ballplayers themselves were committed to the idea of the team. Most of the veterans had said they would like to see the community-owned experiment work, and they would like to return to Buffalo next year if that was possible. They believed in Cavarretta and Stiglmeier. They had also been impressed with the fans, their loyalty and their acceptance of the team's struggles.

What everyone agreed was necessary, however, was that a major league tie-up was a must. The team had to have player personnel resources to draw upon when the injury bug struck. And strike it would, to young and old.

The second critical need was an influx of more funds to support the operation. A stockholders' meeting would have to directly address this issue and find solid commitments if the future was to be bright. Buffalo had a long and storied baseball history and had survived previous challenges. This year had been one of the most difficult, but things were looking up.

Joe Caffie slides home
Photo courtesy of SUNY Buffalo State Courier-Express Collection

Game 128, Friday, August 17, Miami, Florida: Miami 3, Buffalo 2

Two unearned runs cost John Weiss a tough loss,
and the ancient Satchel Paige was again proved the Marlins' salvation in relief.

Game 128 – August 17, 1956
Buffalo   002 000 000 – 2 9 2
Miami   110 010 00x – 3 9 1
WP – Farrell (9-5)   **LP – Weiss (3-10)**

Buffalo errors led to two Miami runs in the first two innings. Cal Abrams, leading off for the Marlins, got a life when Luke Easter mishandled his ground ball. A ground out and a passed ball moved the runner to third. Woody Smith's sacrifice fly brought him home.

In the second, Ben Tompkins and Ray Holton singled to put runners on first and third. Bill Serena booted a slow roller from the pitcher, Turk Farrell, and the error allowed Tompkins to score.

The Bisons tied it in the top of the third with three straight hits off Farrell. Joe Caffie slashed a double down the left field line to lead off. Ed Mierkowicz singled Caffie home and took second on the throw to the plate. Easter brought Mierkowicz home with a single of his own. The next three men went down in order.

The winning run came in the Miami fifth when Pompeyo (Yo Yo) Davalillo, all of 5 feet, 3 inches, and 140 pounds, scalded a double to right center. Only a fine cutoff play and throw by George Bullard held him to second. Two outs later, Larry Novak singled to left and Davalillo scored the go-ahead.

An odd 2-3-5 double play and Satchel Paige frustrated the Bisons in the eighth. Joe Caffie caught the Miami defense napping, leading off and turning on the jets to turn a single to left into a double. Ed Mierkowicz's dribbler in front of the plate was pounced on by catcher Holton, who fired to first baseman Ed Bouchee for the out on the batter. Caffie, hesitating until Holton's throw, took off for third. Bouchee threw a strike to Woody Smith, who nabbed Joe at the bag. Luke Easter's 400-foot double off the center-field wall was wasted with no one on base. Paige was called to the hill to fan Bill Serena for the inning's third out.

Buffalo made a last-gasp attempt in the ninth. Peanuts Lowrey pinch-hit a single for Billy DeMars with one gone. Lou Ortiz, batting for Pat Tomkinson, popped up for out number two. Manager Cavarretta pinch-hit himself for Weiss and ripped a single to send the tying run to third. Paige fanned Pete Castiglione to end the game.

BISON TALES: Tomkinson collected his first base hit since July 30. He singled in the top of the fourth to break a 0-for-34 dry spell. The slump had plummeted his average to .193.

Cavarretta planned to continue to sit Lowrey and Ortiz in the southern heat as long as he felt his starting lineup had a chance to win.

National Airlines had halted almost all of its flights due to a labor dispute, affecting the Bisons' efforts to get home after the Miami series. The team had been scheduled to fly National on Monday morning, bringing them home via Washington, D.C. Now the club would fly Eastern Airlines through New York City.

Game 129, Saturday, August 18, Miami, Florida: Buffalo 3, Miami 2

The Bisons were the victors thanks to two gift runs.
Harry Nicholas got the win in relief of a well-pitched game by Steve Nagy.

Game 129 – August 18, 1956

Buffalo	100 000 002 –	3	6	1
Miami	001 000 100 –	2	7	3

WP – Nicholas (4-9)   LP – Qualters (4-5)

Jack Spring started for Miami and gave up the only run he would allow when Pete Castiglione scorched a leadoff double over the third-base bag. Joe Caffie's short single moved the baserunner to third. Castiglione scored as Lou Ortiz rapped into into a rally-killing 5-4-3 double play.

Steve Nagy held the Marlins at bay until the third inning, when a well-stroked single by Miami's Ed Bouchee, a ground out by Woody Smith and another single by Bob Bowman made it a tie ball-game. Miami took the lead in the seventh. Ben Tompkins led off with a single, moved to second on a ground out and scored as Spring connected with a base hit to center.

Managerial maneuvering took over in the last two innings. Cavarretta sent Norm Sherry up to pinch-hit for Pat Tomkinson in the eighth. Spring issued his first walk of the game. Peanuts Lowrey pinch-hit for Nagy, and he, too, drew a free pass. Miami's Don Osborn went to the bullpen and brought in Tom Qualters. Cavarretta ordered a successful sacrifice bunt from Castiglione that put the runners into scoring position. Caffie, coming to the plate with three hits on Friday and already three more in this contest, was given an intentional walk. With the bases full, Qualters set down Lou Ortiz and then Luke Easter on strikes.

Harry Nicholas pitched the eighth for Buffalo, and the Herd won it for him with two unearned runs in the top of the ninth. Mierkowicz led off and reached safely when Smith threw into the dirt at first for an error. A second error was charged to Smith when he couldn't find the handle on a ball hit by George Bullard. Billy DeMars' sacrifice bunt (scored a fielder's choice) loaded the bases when Qualters' throw to third was too late to catch Mierkowicz. Sherry hit to the right side of the infield and was retired at first but brought Mierkowicz home with the tying run. Bill Serena came up to pinch-hit for Nicholas, and Osborn countered with Angelo LiPetri for Qualters. LiPetri walked Serena to load the bases. Pete Castiglione finally drove a fly ball to center, and the fleet Bullard tagged and brought home the go-ahead run. Caffie walked for a second time, loading the bases once more. Ortiz bounced into a fielder's choice, short to second. Joe Coleman was Cavarretta's choice to get the save, and he set the Marlins down in order.

Bison Tales: It was Men's Night in Miami. Of the 3235 in attendance, only the 1100 women in the stands had to pay admission.

The National Airlines labor problem had been resolved and thus Rochester would be able to make it back from Havana and be in Buffalo on Monday night for the makeup of the August 9 rain-out. The Bisons would stick with their rearranged plans to fly Eastern. Both clubs would arrive in the Queen City on Monday morning.

Game 130, Sunday, August 19, Miami, Florida: Miami 5, Buffalo 4

It was age versus youth in the first game of a scheduled doubleheader.
Satchel Paige's arm and bat bested Larry Donovan.

Game 130 – August 19, 1956
Buffalo   200 001 001 – 4 8 2
Miami   210 002 00x – 5 8 2
WP – Paige (11-3)   LP – Donovan (8-9)

In game one, three former Negro League stars faced off against each other in the top of the first. Satchel Paige walked the red-hot Joe Caffie, who collected his third straight base on balls going back to the previous contest. Luke Easter timed a Paige delivery and sent it 420 feet over the wall in left center for his 29th homer of the season and a two-run lead.

The Marlins tied it in their half of the first. Gus Niarhos walked, Ed Bouchee singled and Woody Smith singled to score Niarhos and move Bouchee on to third. Larry Novak's sacrifice fly to right field brought Bouchee home. In the Miami second, Yo Yo Davalillo scratched an infield hit. Ben Tompkins' single sent him to third. Cal Abrams' sacrifice fly put Miami ahead.

The Bisons evened it in the top of the sixth. Caffie roped a base hit to center field. A one-out walk to Easter moved him into scoring position, and a pinch-hit double to left center by Peanuts Lowrey brought him home. Easter had to be held at third. An intentional walk to George Bullard loaded the bases. The strategy paid off as Billy DeMars hit into an inning-ending double play.

A walk to Novak led off the bottom of the sixth. Bob Bowman sacrificed him to second. DeMars fielded Davalillo's grounder to short, held the runner at second and got the putout at first, and then Cavarretta called for an intentional walk to Tompkins to bring Paige to the plate. Ever the competitor, Paige won the ballgame for himself with a soft liner to center that just skipped past the drawn-in Caffie. The blow went for a double, two runs scored, and the ballgame.

A series of rain squalls blew up, suspending play for an hour and ten minutes. When the game resumed, Harry Nicholas took over on the mound for Buffalo. Paige lasted until the ninth, when the Bisons struck for one more. A dropped toss to first base put Peanuts Lowrey on base to start the inning. Paige fooled George Bullard on a swinging strike three and got a popup from DeMars for two quick outs, but Bill Serena walked in a pinch-hitting role and moved Lowrey to second. Cavarretta again called his own number to pinch-hit for Nicholas and came through yet again. His single to right plated Lowrey and put the tying run on second. Fireballing Turk Farrell replaced Paige on the mound. Castiglione bounced to Tompkins at second, and this time Bouchee held the throw. Game over.

Game two was called in the second inning due to rain. Buffalo had taken a 1-0 lead in the first on singles by Lou Ortiz, Luke Easter and Bill Serena. Fred Hahn had held Miami scoreless in their half. The rains returned with George Bullard at bat in the second. This game was lost and would not be rescheduled. The Marlins won the season series, 13 games to eight.

Game 131, Monday, August 20, Buffalo: Buffalo 12, Rochester 2

The rescheduled Lou Ortiz Night saw Lou collect two hits,
two runs and two RBIs, but Fred Hahn and Luke Easter also shone in the Bison win.

Game 131 – August 20, 1956
Rochester   011 000 000 – 2 5 1
Buffalo   012 500 40x – 12 18 1
WP – Hahn (9-9)   LP – Markell (9-9)

Rochester's Gene Green opened the scoring with a solo blast off Hahn in the top of the second. In the bottom of the inning, Bill Serena got a life after Red Wing catcher Dick Rand muffed his foul pop for an error. He drove the next pitch from Rochester's Duke Markell off the left-field wall for a triple. Two men were down and Serena still on third when Markell intentionally walked Billy De-Mars to put Hahn in the batter's box. Hahn rapped a single to make it a tie ballgame.

The Red Wings went back in front on their next trip to the plate. Mel Nelson wheedled a walk out of Hahn, took second on Markell's perfect sacrifice bunt and scooted home on a bloop single by Eddie Kasko. The Bisons answered again in the home half. Lou Ortiz slugged a one-out single. Bill Serena's two-out drive to left cleared the wall for his 18th homer of the year. Buffalo had the lead for the first time.

Three straight Bison base hits to open the fourth chased Markell. Peanuts Lowrey singled, Joe Caffie followed him with another and Ortiz's double to right center sent both men home. Jack Roberts came in to pitch for the Red Wings. Luke Easter's greeting was home run number 30 high over the left center field wall. Bill Serena's single made it five hits in a row before Roberts could finally retire Bullard and Sherry, but an unintentional walk to DeMars and a second single by Hahn brought in Serena. Nineteen-year-old Gary Geiger took over the pitching duties and held the Bisons at bay for the next two frames.

A 5-4-3 double play, the Herd's 125th of the season, got Hahn out of a two-on, no-out fifth inning. The last 11 Red Wings went out in order.

Buffalo added four runs in the seventh on singles by DeMars, Lowrey, Caffie (DeMars scored) and Easter's second home run of the night, this one to right field. Number 31.

Bison Tales: Vincent C. Bowhers, the master of ceremonies, and Carlton H. Doster co-chaired the West Seneca night. Milford S. Smith presented Ortiz with an engraved watch. Edward Doerfel, president of the West Seneca Junior Chamber of Commerce, praised the second baseman as a "fine neighbor, whom we all hope to have with us for many years." Town Board Councilman Clarence H. Hopper was there, too.

The Vigilant Fire Company Band and Winchester Hose Company Drum Corps were present to serenade Ortiz on the occasion. They broke out with "Happy Days Are Here Again" on each of Easter's blasts.

A group of Little Leaguers from Tonawanda, who actually held stock in the team, made up part of the crowd of 2223, as did the Ontario Midget League champions from St. Catharines, Ontario.

Games 132 and 133, Tuesday, August 21, Buffalo: Richmond 5, Buffalo 1; Buffalo 12, Richmond 3

Richmond manager Ed Lopat tossed a two-hitter to win the seven-inning opener.
Buffalo struck for seven first-inning runs in game two.

Game 132 – August 21, 1956 (first game of doubleheader)
Richmond   010 002 2 – 5 11 1
Buffalo   010 000 0 – 1 2 2
WP – Lopat (10-6)   LP – Drews (12-10)

Game 133 – August 21, 1956 (second game of doubleheader)
Richmond   000 001 002 – 3 11 1
Buffalo   700 002 03x – 12 11 2
WP – Weiss (3-9)   LP – Coates (12-11)

Over 3100 fans came out to watch a well-pitched game between two savvy veterans.

In the seven-inning opener, Buffalo ace Karl Drews, a 12-game winner who could still call on an overpowering heater, faced off against the junk man Ed Lopat, the Richmond manager, seeking his 10th win of the season.

Fans in the stands made their presence known throughout the game. The faithful Eden 400 were out once again, aided and abetted today by a contingent of 900 strong from Cheektowaga's volunteer fireman corps. The firemen showed up accompanied by a drum corps, sirens and fire bells. The noise produced had no effect on the veteran starters.

Richmond plated an unearned run off Drews in the second inning. Rance Pless singled cleanly off the righthander and moved into scoring position when Luke Easter misplayed Hal Rice's grounder for an error. Tom Hamilton's single scored Pless from second. The Bisons tied it in the bottom of the inning. Bill Serena banged a leadoff double off the wall in left in the corner. Two outs later, Billy DeMars doubled to right center to bring him home.

Lopat shut the door tight after the DeMars blow. The Bisons didn't get a hit for the remainder of the game. The team didn't get another baserunner until Lopat walked Lou Ortiz in the sixth with two out.

A pair of Richmond runs in the sixth inning and another brace in the seventh made the final score Richmond 5, Buffalo 1. Pless singled again to lead off the visitor sixth. Drews collared the next two batters, but the lefthanded-swinging Neal Watlington doubled down the right-field line and Pless made it all the way around to score the go-ahead run. Watlington crossed the plate moments later. Lopat took Drews the other way and sliced a ball that landed just inside the left-field line. Lopat pulled up at second with the double. In the seventh, Jerry Lumpe bounced an infield single. Pless, who had been giving Drews fits all afternoon, drove his third hit of the game over the left-field screen for the final two runs.

George Bullard got the Bisons' hopes up with a one-out walk in the home half of the seventh. Lopat stranded him there to pick up the win.

The Cheektowaga firemen surely hosed down Richmond's Jim Coates' spirits in the second game. The merrymakers paraded up and down the stands between the games and opened up raucously as game two got under way. Buffalo dodged a bullet in the opening half-inning, thanks to a leaping catch by George Bullard on Jerry Lumpe's slicing liner with the first two men on base and no one out. John Weiss then fanned the cleanup hitter, Bill Renna, and retired third baseman Rance Pless on a popup.

When it came Buffalo's turn to bat, they made the most of the opportunity. Pete Castiglione got the Bisons rolling with a leadoff double to left. Coates walked Joe Caffie. Lou Ortiz's Texas Leaguer to center loaded the bases. Luke Easter's screaming line drive to right center cashed Castiglione and Caffie and sent Ortiz on to third. First-base coach Peanuts Lowrey windmilled Easter on to second on the play when he saw Richmond catcher Cal Neeman throwing to the hot corner to try to nail Ortiz. Both men were safe. Ed Lopat, serving solely in his role as manager in this game, ordered the hot-hitting Bill Serena intentionally walked to set up the double play, but by now Coates was rattled. He also walked George Bullard and that forced in a run. Ed Mierkowicz became the first out after going fishing for an outside fastball that became strike three, but Pat Tomkinson took that same pitch for ball four and another run was home.

Dick Starr took over the mound as the bells and the whistles and the Bisons continued to make big noise. John Weiss fanned for the second out, but Starr fell behind Castiglione and wound up walking him. Another Bison run was in. Caffie's double off the left-field wall drove home Bullard and Tomkinson. Seven runs.

The fans kept up the commotion, but the players calmed down until the sixth when Weiss lost his shutout. Renna singled and Cal Neeman later singled him home. Buffalo added a pair in the bottom of the frame. Ed Cereghino, now pitching for the Vees, walked Easter. Serena crashed home run number 19 to deep left field.

The last three Bison runs came in the eighth. Castiglione rapped his third hit of the day, and he and Caffie were both safe when shortstop Jerry Lumpe threw away Caffie's sure double-play ground ball. A line drive single by Ortiz sent Castiglione home. Caffie scored on Easter's base hit. Serena's third hit of the night plated Ortiz.

Singles by Richmond's Bobby Kline and Len Johnston were followed by Lumpe's two-run double in the ninth to complete the scoring.

BISON TALES: Bill Serena had gone seven for 10 in the three games played since returning to Buffalo. He had hit and scored in all three contests, collecting a double, a triple and two home runs, plus six runs scored and five runs driven home.

Richmond's Len Johnston, who was leading the league in stolen bases with 33, made several sensational catches in center field that took Bison hits away. George Bullard's leaping stab of Lumpe's liner in the first inning changed the complexion of game two.

Easter now led the International League in home runs (31) and RBIs (95). Ortiz was in third place in homers (21) and fourth in RBIs (77). Serena was tied for fourth in home runs with Bob Bowman of Miami and Carl Sawatski of Toronto (19). Joe Caffie (.320) was right behind Montreal's Clyde Parrish.

Fred Hahn, last night's victor, had won his last four decisions. In his last five trips to the hill, one of those in relief, he had fanned 21, walked 14 and held the opposition to a 2.84 ERA. Ed Lopat had now beaten Buffalo four times with no defeats. His ERA against the Bisons was 2.16.

Four patients from the University of Buffalo Chronic Disease Research Institute (Respirator Center) were guests of the Bisons, seated behind home plate while fitted out with breathing equipment: Richard Flanders from Watertown, Nancy Lee of Avon, Edyth Faust of Binghamton and Michael Harrity of Baltimore.

Game 134, Wednesday, August 22, Buffalo: Buffalo 6, Richmond 4

Steve Nagy picked up his first win of the season, and Serena and Easter
each made it three homers apiece in the last four games.

Game 134 – August 22, 1956
Richmond   102 000 010 – 4 8 1
Buffalo   300 100 20x – 6 11 0
WP – Nagy (1-2)   LP – Jordan (9-8)

Nagy retired the first two men he saw but then grooved one to Jerry Lumpe for a sharply hit single. A walk to Bill Renna moved Lumpe into scoring position and a single by Rance Pless brought him home. Niles Jordan, starting for Richmond, also retired the first two men he saw, but then he walked Lou Ortiz and gave up a single to Luke Easter. Bill Serena, on a tear, sent home run number 20 high over the left center field wall and Nagy had a two-run lead.

Four straight base hits tied it for the Vees in the third: a Lumpe double, a single by Renna, another base hit by Pless, a single by Cal Neeman. After consultation with Cavarretta at the mound, Nagy knocked over the next 14 men in a row.

Buffalo went ahead to stay in the fourth inning. Nagy drew a walk and came home on base hits by Pete Castiglione and Joe Caffie. They added to the total in the seventh at the expense of Jim Coates, now pitching for Jordan.

Easter led off with home run number 32 to left field near the light standard. A steaming Coates hit Serena in the head on his very next pitch, the ball spinning the batting helmet around on his head and sending the Buffalo third baseman sprawling to the ground. A last-minute shove by catcher Neeman may have pushed Serena out of more serious harm's way. Serena tore out to the mound only to be pushed down by Coates. Back on his feet, Serena went for the hurler again. Both benches emptied, each side trying to restrain their combatant.

No one got ejected, and Serena was awarded first base for being hit by the pitch. The Bisons then loaded the bases on a walk and an infield single, and Pete Castiglione came through with a short, two-out single to right that scored Serena.

Coates lasted two-thirds of an inning. Reliever Jim Post got the third out and kept the Bisons off the scoreboard in the eighth. Nagy gave up a walk and singles to Renna and Tom Hamilton for a fourth Richmond run in the eighth.

BISON TALES: A catcher's job is to back up first base on an infield hit. Norm Sherry did just that as an attempted double-play throw from Castiglione bounced wide of Easter. The Herd got the force at second, and Sherry's hustle kept the batter from moving into scoring position.

Edgar Moeller had been added to the pitching staff. The 28-year-old righthander from North Tonawanda had been out of organized ball since 1955 due to a contract dispute with the Eastern League Albany Senators. Moeller had last appeared with Charlotte (Sally League) and with Southern Association Chattanooga in 1954, compiling a 4-6 record with the two teams. Buffalo purchased his contract from Albany.

Employees from Worthington Company and Sylvania Corporation were in the crowd, as were 1500 Boy Scouts who were guests of the Bisons.

Thursday, August 23, Buffalo: Rainout

The Bisons suffered their 11th home rainout of the season, frustrating plans for a large Ladies' Night attendance and also the presence of an organized group of fans from the Lake View community south of the city. This was to have been the final meeting between Buffalo and Richmond for the year. As with the lost game in Miami on the road trip, this game would not be rescheduled. It was another lost opportunity for gate receipts.

Richmond won the season series, capturing 12 victories while Buffalo took nine. Luke Easter, with 32 home runs to date, was on a pace to become one of the Bisons' all-time season home run leaders. Ollie Carnegie, who patrolled left field for the club back in the 1930s, had the single-season record of 45 home runs struck back in 1938. Second place belonged to first baseman Billy Kelly, who drove out 44 in 1926. Carnegie also held third place with 37 long balls in 1935, as well as connecting for 36 in 1932. Two other Bisons had also finished a season with 36 home runs. George (Showboat) Fisher did it in 1929 and, more recently, so had Jack Wallaesa in 1953. Wallaesa had started his year with the Springfield Cubs and was then acquired by the Bisons partway into the season. Once he reached Offermann Stadium, Wallaesa's long fly balls easily turned into home runs. Luke had 19 games left to bash his way into that top tier in the Buffalo home run record book.

Luke had already surpassed the 30 he struck the previous year with Charleston in the American Association. His greatest home run year in organized baseball came in 1952, when he bashed six home runs at American Association Indianapolis in 14 contests and then hit an additional 31 in 127 more games with the Cleveland Indians. Back in 1949, in only 80 games with the San Diego Padres of the Pacific Coast League, he had clubbed 25 roundtrippers before being called up to the Indians. He was also whaling the ball at a .362 clip at that time and had driven home 97 baserunners. Obviously, he belonged in the big time. (Easter can lay claim to 76 home runs in one year while playing first base with the Pittsburgh Homestead Grays in the Negro Leagues.)

Joe Caffie's average of .314 was not unexpected, either. Joe recorded a .342 mark with Duluth in 1952 to lead the Northern League in batting and in base hits (171). Joe was now vying for the International League batting championship but would have to stay hot to have a chance at overtaking a nine-percentage point lead held by Montreal's Clyde Parris. The last Bison to win the International League batting title was Frank Carswell, hitting a sizzling .344 in 1952. Both Luke and Joe were slated to be honored at the Friday evening ballgame.

The Columbus Jets would provide the opposition on Friday and for the next three games following. The Jets had stumbled once more after the second recall of center fielder Al Pilarcik. Pilarcik had been hitting .325 with 18 home runs in 91 games and was a legitimate MVP candidate. Pitcher Jose Santiago, with a won-1 and lost-2 record with the major league A's, was sent down to replace him. The Jets had fallen to seventh place, only three and a half games ahead of Buffalo. The Pilarcik business had made it almost certain that Columbus would not renew its ties with Kansas City for next year.

A four-game sweep of the series would move the Herd out of the cellar. To date, the Jets had taken 12 of the 18 contests between the two squads. Some notable baseball dignitaries were scheduled to be on hand for the Citizens' Appreciation Night at the close of the season that would honor general manager John Stiglmeier. Charles Sagar, the chief aide to baseball commissioner Ford C. Frick, was slated to be in attendance. George Trautman, President of the National Association of Baseball Leagues, would also be present, as would Frank J. Shaughnessy, President of the International League.

Game 135, Friday, August 24, Buffalo: Buffalo 2, Columbus 1

The second largest fan turnout of the year, 7063 paid admissions,
came out to honor Luke Easter and Joe Caffie and see a thrilling win.

Game 135 – August 24, 1956
Columbus   000 000 001 – 1   4   0
Buffalo   100 000 001 – 2   8   0
WP – Donovan (9-9)   **LP – Wooldridge (5-8)**

It was a pitchers' duel with plenty of fine fielding efforts on both sides, Red Donovan throwing for Buffalo and Bob Kusava for the Jets. Kusava made one bad pitch to Lou Ortiz in the first inning and Ortiz made him pay for it. Lou rocketed a solo home run, number 22 of the year. Donovan, yielding only three singles, made the run stand up until fans were heading for the aisles in the top of the ninth with two gone.

Ben Downs' solo home run over the left center field wall stopped them in their tracks. The Bisons would have to win it in the ninth. Fortunately, they had Cavarretta calling the shots.

Floyd Wooldridge had taken over for Kusava in the eighth. Ortiz led off the ninth and drew a walk. Luke Easter, hitless until now, rifled a hard single to right field that sent Ortiz on to third. Strategy time for Columbus manager Nick Cullop. First, an intentional walk to Bill Serena. Second, he brought the infield and outfield in.

Strategy time for Cavarretta. Billy DeMars was sent in to run for Ortiz. Peanuts Lowrey's bouncer to Wooldridge became a force play at the plate. One down. Cavarretta stepped in himself to pinch-hit for George Bullard. Cullop went out to the mound, stalling to give time for his lefthander, Carl Duser, to warm up in the bullpen. Plate umpire Smith finally called for the game to move along. Only then did Wooldridge throw his first pitch to Cavarretta. Low, ball one. Now, Cullop brought in Duser. Cavarretta replied by sending Steve Nagy in to run for Easter and then called on Ed Mierkowicz to finish his own at-bat. Righty versus lefty once again, and Duser had to throw at least one pitch. When he did so, Mierkowicz slashed it past the drawn-in Jet first baseman for the Bison win. Cavarretta puffed very contentedly on a cigar after the game.

BISON TALES: Pregame ceremonies lasted 45 minutes, starting with a band and a parade at 7:15 pm. Several Elks lodges sent marchers, who were joined by baton twirlers, dancing girls, a Military Police unit, two drum corps and women's auxiliaries. A convoy truck rolled out over home plate provided a stage for two nightclub acts, The Eagle and Man trumpet duo and The Moonglows, with Lenny Page as emcee.

Gifts were presented by assistant district attorney Robert Burrell. Easter and Caffie each received new baseball gloves from Dick Fischer, movie cameras, silver cuff links, wrist watches, leatherbound copies of the Sports Encyclopedia, gift vouchers for various stores, cigars, cases of beer, clothing, and checks for a sizable amount of cash. And finally, Pat Tomkinson's mother had made them a two-tier cake with a diamond in icing for after the game.

Marshall Davis Miles and Fred Perry co-chaired the night. Afterwards, Easter commented on the "wonderful, wonderful" outpouring of affection, and added gratefully that neither he nor Caffie had had to make a speech.

Game 136, Saturday, August 25, Buffalo: Buffalo 6, Columbus 3
*A fourth straight win moved the Herd to within one and
a half games of seventh place. Harry Nicholas was superb in relief.*

Game 136 – August 25, 1956
Columbus   000 300 000 – 3 9 0
Buffalo   300 011 10x – 6 9 0
WP – Nicholas (5-9)   LP – Santiago (0-4)

Jet starter Mike Kume didn't last an inning. Wildness led him to walk the first three men in the batting order, Pete Castiglione, Joe Caffie and Lou Ortiz. Luke Easter stepped in with the bases loaded and sent a hard ground ball toward the hole between first and second. Butch McCord, Jet first baseman, made a lunging stab to knock the ball down before throwing to Kume for the out at first, but Castiglione scored on the play. Caffie scored moments later on Bill Serena's single to left field. Kume's night was over.

Jose Santiago was rushed to the mound for Columbus with only his eight warmup pitches to prepare him to face the Bison batsmen. Peanuts Lowrey singled to right, and Ortiz's run put the Bisons ahead 3-0. Santiago got George Bullard on a fly out to short center. He then pitched around Norm Sherry, walking him, and struck out Fred Hahn for the inning's final out.

Hahn continued his excellent run of pitching, holding Columbus to an infield single through three until he lost his edge in the fourth. Russ Sullivan's double reached the wall in left center with one out. Ray Noble singled in front of Lowrey in left field, Sullivan holding at third. Dick Getter took a Hahn fastball on the hip, and the bases were loaded. Jerry Carter's high fly ball to left found the wall halfway up and went for a double, scoring two. Cavarretta went out to the mound to tell Hahn his night was finished. Harry Nicholas was called in to take over.

McCord, the first batter Nicholas faced, promptly lined the ball over Ortiz's head to make it a tie ballgame. Nicholas got Santiago swinging for the second out. Now it was Lowrey's time to make the play of the game. Bill Kern's twisting fly ball into the left-field corner might have scored McCord with the go-ahead run had it fallen, but Lowrey got there just in time to make a leaping stab of the ball and keep the score at 3-3.

Buffalo took the lead once more in the fifth, thanks to Santiago's wildness. Lowrey drew a free pass and Bullard doubled him to third. A walk to Sherry loaded the bases. Another walk, this one to Nicholas, sent home the go-ahead run. Ortiz made it a two-run lead in the next inning with his 23rd home run. The final Bison tally came on Bullard's walk in the seventh, Sherry's infield base hit and a line single by Castiglione.

BISON TALES: Lowrey added a pair of nice running catches to his game-saver in the fourth. Columbus hurlers surrendered 10 bases on balls, three in a row to Sherry until his seventh-inning scratch hit.

Pat McGroder, chairman of the committee planning Fan Appreciation Night on August 31 to honor general manager John Stiglmeier, called for a luncheon meeting at the Buffalo Athletic Club before Sunday's doubleheader with the Jets.

A twin win for the Herd would raise them out of the cellar and ahead of Columbus.

Games 137 and 138, Sunday, August 26, Buffalo: Columbus 6, Buffalo 3; Columbus 7, Buffalo 3

Seventh-place dreams woke up to a grim reality.

The Bisons fell hard in a double defeat at the hands of the determined Jets.

Game 137 – August 26, 1956 (first game of doubleheader)

Columbus	103 200 000 – 6	12	2
Buffalo	100 100 100 – 3	4	2

WP – Theis (4-9)   LP – Drews (12-11)

Game 138 – August 26, 1956 (second game of doubleheader)

Columbus	102 130 0 – 7	16	0
Buffalo	100 000 2 – 3	12	1

WP – Cox (11-10)   LP – Weiss (3-11)

The crowd of 5460 fans was frustrated by the afternoon's outcome. Columbus was in no mood to concede seventh place to the Bisons.

It was a matchup of Karl Drews and submariner Jake Theis for the Jets in game one. Theis was on his game and Drews was not. Columbus manufactured a run in the first on three straight singles from Curt Roberts, Russ Sullivan and Ben Downs. Joe Caffie got the Bisons even in the bottom of the frame, slamming his eighth four-bagger of the year over the right-field wall.

The winning blow for the Jets came in the third inning. Roberts and Sullivan had singled, and Ray Noble turned around a Drews fastball and sent it on a line over the left center field fence for a two-out, three-run blast. Drews got the inning's third out but departed for pinch-hitter Zeb Eaton when the Bisons took their turn at the plate in the home half. Bill Froats came on in relief to make his first appearance in 14 games.

Columbus added two unearned runs in the top of the fourth. Russ Rose reached on a base hit, and a two-out error by Pete Castiglione on Roberts' ground ball put two men on. Sullivan's looper to left filled the bases. Rose and Roberts scored when Caffie dropped Downs' fly to center.

Bill Serena made it a 6-2 ballgame in the bottom of the fourth, touching Theis for a second Buffalo solo home run. It was Bill's 21st. Joe Coleman rescued Froats in the seventh with two down and the sacks crammed and stopped the Jets without a run.

The Bisons third and final tally came in the seventh. Norm Sherry got a life when third baseman Jerry Carter booted his ground ball. A walk to Coleman, one of the six Theis allowed, moved the runner into scoring position. Pete Castiglione hit a flare behind second base that fell safely and brought Sherry home.

Luke Easter managed a single off Theis in the eighth frame but the Bisons couldn't turn it into a threat. Two Columbus double plays helped seal the outcome for the Jets.

Game two was more of the same misery for the home crowd. Bill Kern singled off John Weiss to start the game. Russ Sullivan, 4 for 4 in the opener, plus a hit-by-pitch, doubled and Kern scored the game's first run. The Bisons got the run back immediately against Columbus' Glenn Cox. Pete Castiglione doubled to lead off for the Bisons, and Joe Caffie followed with a run-scoring single to make it 1-1.

Buffalo had managed only four hits off Theis in the first game. In the second, they rapped out an even dozen, but Cox worked his way out of a number of jams and kept the Herd run total to three. Two Jet double plays helped offset the 12 hits and three walks.

Columbus, erupting for 16 hits in the second game, chased Weiss in the third. Sullivan—him again! —slashed a single and was sent home on a double by Ben Downs. Sullivan's hit was his sixth straight in six official plate appearances. Butch McCord's double plated Downs and brought Zeb Eaton in to get the last two outs. The Jets added an unearned run off Eaton in the fourth when Pat Tomkinson's pickoff throw to third sailed into left field and let Russ Rose come in. Zeb was sent packing in the fifth. The first five men he faced got base hits—Downs, McCord, Ray Noble, Leon Carter and Rose—good for three more runs. New hurler Edgar Moeller, given a chance to show what he could do, stopped the Jets without a run for two innings. Joe Coleman threw a scoreless seventh.

Buffalo got their final two runs when Lou Ortiz singled in the seventh and Luke Easter hit home run number 32 out of the park in right.

BISON TALES: A dramatic shift by the Jet infield put four infielders between first base and second when Luke Easter came to bat with the bases empty. Luke still managed four hits in six official trips to the plate in the twin bill.

Columbus decided not to renew its working relationship with Kansas City for 1957. But Buffalo needed a major league tie-up, and the A's would now need a Triple A partner. Thus, Bernie Guest, Kansas City farm director, was in town to watch not only the Columbus club but possibly the next year's affiliate, too—the Bisons. He and John Stiglmeier were observed in lengthy talks.

Buffalo was almost certain to wind up in the cellar and much discussion was under way concerning the fate of both the club and the personnel. Stiglmeier had said that what would happen next year had to wait until the 1956 season's bottom line was determined. Healthy attendance in the final home stand would help keep the club in the black and the team in the city.

Luke Easter, speaking for the players, voiced support for manager Phil Cavarretta when asked about next year. The fine season he was personally having, Easter said, was because Cavarretta had gotten him into the best shape of his life in spring training. Cavarretta had instilled his fighting spirit in the players such that the Bisons had never given up. Even when pitching fell apart early in the year and the club often found itself down four or five runs almost from the start of a game, the men had always bounced back to make the score competitive.

Cavarretta was a man the players wanted to play for. They felt the club was jelling now and a successful 1957 was easily within reach. With the addition of some pitching and some key personnel changes, the nucleus of this Bison club could honestly make a run for the pennant. Even the prediction of a first-division finish for 1956 had been reasonable. The club had been fighting for fourth place until the major league cutdown came, and then the slew of injuries had hit. The players were most grateful to the Buffalo fans who had stuck by them and continued to offer their support even in the darkest of days.

The Jets took the season series, 14 games to eight, as the Herd remained mired in last place.

Game 139, Monday, August 27, Rochester, New York: Rochester 3, Buffalo 2

The bus ride to Rochester in the morning was uneventful,
but all hell broke loose at the ballgame that evening after a blown call.

Game 139 – August 27, 1956
Buffalo	000 000 110 – 2	4	0
Rochester	001 100 001 – 3	9	0

WP – Wright (5-4)   LP – Coleman (4-2)

It had been a tightly pitched duel through seven innings for the Bisons' Steve Nagy and the Red Wings' Duke Markell. Rochester had drawn first blood, picking up a run in the third on three short singles by Ron Plaza, Sherry Dixon and Eddie Kasko and a bases-loaded sacrifice fly by Joe Cunningham. Bob Rand made it 2-0 in the fourth with his 11th home run of the year.

Markell had stymied Buffalo on two hits for six innings. In the seventh, he issued his fourth walk of the game, this one to Lou Ortiz, and the Bisons took advantage. Bill Serena's long double to left center brought Ortiz around to snap the Markell shutout bid. In the eighth the Red Wing pitcher lost his control. George Bullard drew a leadoff walk. Cavarretta, pinch-hitting for Norm Sherry, also walked. Mel Wright came in to the mound to relieve Markell.

Billy DeMars, hitting for Nagy, laid down a sacrifice bunt to move the runners up. Wright got Pete Castiglione on a strikeout, but Joe Caffie's bouncer to the mound flicked off Wright's glove and wound up unplayable, going for an infield hit. Bullard scored to tie it up. Joe Coleman relieved for Nagy in the bottom of the eighth.

With the game tied at 2-2 in the bottom of the ninth, Cot Deal led off for the Wings with a pinch-hit single. Peanuts Lowrey, now directing the Herd as Cavarretta had had to retire from the game after pinch-hitting, brought in Harry Nicholas for Coleman. A wild pitch into the dirt let Deal take second. A sacrifice bunt moved him to third. Lowrey pulled the infield in and Kasko bounced straight to Castiglione at short, who threw to the plate to catch Deal, only that wasn't the way plate umpire Augie Guglielmo saw it. The throw was too late, the runner was safe and Rochester had won the ballgame. The Bisons were livid!

No way could he have scored, they argued, with Pat Tomkinson effectively blocking the plate and Castiglione's throw having beaten Deal by a mile. After five minutes of the uproar from the Bisons, Guglielmo asked for police protection and escort from the grounds. Cavarretta vowed he would appeal to league headquarters. Guglielmo would post his own report of the game.

BISON TALES: The Bisons were frustrated at losing the game in this fashion following Sunday's disheartening double defeat.

Bill Serena extended his hitting streak to nine games. He was hitting .500 for that stretch, with 14 hits in 28 at-bats, including four home runs, nine runs scored and 11 runs driven home.

In International League news: Columbus' Curt Roberts belted four home runs, one of them inside the park, in a seven-inning game against the visiting Havana Sugar Kings. He had six RBIs in the Jets' 10-7 victory. Roberts was the first International Leaguer to hit four homers in a seven-inning contest. He had doubled his season total from four homers to eight in one game.

Tuesday, August 28, Rochester, New York: Rainout

Yet again, rain intervened in the schedule and made the grounds too wet to play. The teams would make up this lost game in a doubleheader on Wednesday.

Games 140 and 141, Wednesday, August 29, Rochester, New York: Buffalo 2, Rochester 0; Rochester 4, Buffalo 0

The clubs played a twilight doubleheader to make up for Tuesday's lost game.
Buffalo won the opener and dropped the nightcap.

Game 140 – August 29, 1956 (first game of doubleheader)
Buffalo   000 101 0 – 2 5 0
Rochester   000 000 0 – 0 4 0
WP – Donovan (10-9)   LP – Deal (13-7)

Game 141 – August 29, 1956 (second game of doubleheader)
Buffalo   000 000 000 – 0 7 2
Rochester   001 003 00x – 4 11 0
WP – Blaylock (8-4)   LP – Hahn (9-10)

Red Donovan had been making a habit of winning the seven-inning contests and didn't disappoint. Although holding the Red Wings to only four hits, the shutout was a struggle, as he also dealt out four walks and hit three batters. His wildness made few of the Rochester players look comfortable digging in against him.

Defense also played a major part in the win. Pete Castiglione stole at least two hits from his shortstop position and converted the first one into a double play. The Bisons pulled off three double plays in all.

Donovan's major threat came in the third inning when his mound opponent, Cot Deal, singled to lead it off. The Rochester hurler was then victimized by the Donovan pickoff move. That was most fortunate for the Bisons because the next man up, Sherry Dixon, walked and promptly stole second base. Donovan fell behind on Eddie Kasko and walked him, too. Tom Burgess was at the plate with two strikes on him when Dixon pressed his luck trying to pilfer third. Burgess fanned on the pitch, and Norm Sherry's perfect throw to Bill Serena caught Dixon for the inning-ending double play.

Deal, always tough on Buffalo, was steadier on the hill than Donovan but made two mistake pitches, one coming in the fourth inning and the other in the sixth. Luke Easter connected for his 34th home run in the fourth. Lou Ortiz gave Donovan an insurance run to work with in the sixth by belting his 24th of the year off his old Red Wing teammate.

The Herd was gratified by the win coming against Deal, whose slide home into Pat Tomkinson two nights earlier had cost them a hard-fought ballgame. There was still a bitter taste in the mouth about that outcome and the subsequent stance taken by league president Frank Shaughnessy. Essentially, all of the blame for the argument about the decision had been placed on Cavarretta. The Bisons maintained that Deal was out and that plate umpire Guglielmo had blown the call.

Buffalo had been held to five hits in the opener but had scored twice and won. In game two, they collected seven but were shut out by the Red Wings' Bob Blaylock. Ed Kasko's stick work tagged Fred Hahn with the 4-0 loss.

Kasko went 5 for 5 in the second contest, scoring one run and driving home two. The first Rochester score came in the bottom of the third when Kasko lined a two-out double and came home on a single by Joe Cunningham. That was the only run until the sixth inning.

Singles by Pete Castiglione and Joe Caffie put runners on first and third with only one down in the visitor half of the sixth, but both Lou Ortiz and Luke Easter were retired on infield popups. In the Rochester half of the inning, Ed Phillips singled to lead off and was sent on home when Tom Burgess scalded a triple to right center. With a run home and a man on third, Hahn pitched carefully. He walked Ron Plaza. Blaylock was a strikeout victim, but Sherry Dixon also walked to load the bases. The stage was set for a force at home or a double play, but Kasko would not oblige. His single to right scored the Red Wings' third and fourth runs.

Hahn left for a pinch-hitter in the eighth, bringing John Weiss to the hill. Weiss was touched for two base hits but kept Rochester scoreless for his inning of work. In the top of the ninth the Bisons knocked Blaylock out of the box. Literally.

Easter led off with a walk. Bill Serena, the next hitter, sent a line shot back to the box that smacked off Blaylock's shin for a single. The Rochester pitcher could not continue and had to limp off the field. Mel Wright was called in to relieve. He got George Bullard to bounce into a force play and fanned the next two men.

BISON TALES: Club president Reginald B. Taylor watched the game from behind the Bisons' dugout. Also in the stands were Mr. and Mrs. Francis State, relatives of general manager John Stiglmeier. Charles Topping, a Buffalonian who attended most of the home games, motored down from the Queen City to watch the doubleheader.

Buffalo would win the season series with Rochester no matter the outcome of Thursday's final meeting of the two clubs. Buffalo had already won 12 contests while the Red Wings had taken nine. Rochester was the only club against which Buffalo would accomplish this feat.

Luke Easter and Lou Ortiz each had hit six home runs against Rochester. Bill Serena's nine-game hit streak was stopped by Deal in the first game. He was two for four against Blaylock.

The whitewash in game one was Donovan's second shutout of the year, both coming by 2-0 margins, both of them in seven-inning contests. The complete game was also his 12th of the season, including those scheduled abbreviated affairs.

Rochester picked up two wounded this day. In addition to Blaylock's sore shin, Allie Clark was forced out of the first game after being hit in the elbow by a Donovan fastball.

In International League news: As of August 29, Montreal's Clyde Parris (.318) was holding off Columbus' John Lipon (.314) and Joe Caffie (.312) for the batting crown. Luke Easter was far in front in the home run race with 34. Lynn Lovenguth of Toronto had a 22-10 record and was seven wins ahead of his teammate, Ed Blake, who boasted a 15-11 mark.

Satchel Paige would not pitch enough innings to qualify for the league's ERA title, but his current numbers were 1.57 runs per game. There was nothing you could say about Paige that wasn't believable.

Thursday, August 30, Rochester, New York: Rainout

Another downpour cancelled the final game of a season series between the Bisons and an International League foe. More lost revenue.

The rain on the diamond was old news. The big question of the day was the future of baseball in Buffalo. Could the club, the players and the fans weather the news that general manager Stiglmeier had finally accepted the appointment to the New York State Liquor Authority?

The offer had come from Governor Averill Harriman more than three months previously, but Stiglmeier had delayed his decision about the position in order to place his full energies at the disposal of the Buffalo ball club. Toiling all year long at no salary in order to minimize the financial costs to the team, Stiglmeier had finally had to say yes to the offer and the $15,000 salary.

He planned to drive to Albany first thing Friday morning to be sworn in to his new duties, then return that afternoon to be on time for the opening game of the doubleheader Citizens' Appreciation Night that was being held in his honor.

A TRIBUTE TO JOHN C. STIGLMEIER AND THE BISONS
Friday, August 31, Buffalo

The fans, 15,063 strong, left no doubt in anyone's mind that Stiglmeier was their man and the Bisons were their team. Baseball would be staying in Buffalo and no question about it. Quoting the Buffalo general manager in the following day's Buffalo Evening News, "[T]his tremendous outpouring of loyalty will insure baseball for Buffalo...Frank J. Shaughnessy, President of the International League, asked me, 'How are you going to field a team without a working agreement? It's impossible.' I say here tonight that we fielded a fine ball club...that for fighting spirit, it is the best in the International League. This team gave us everything. We're mighty proud of it!"

Festivities began early with the color guard of the Adam Plewacki Post of the American Legion leading the Vigilant Hose Company No. 1 band from Ebenezer through the right-field gates. Chairman of the Citizens' Appreciation Night, Patrick J. McGroder, presented watches to Stiglmeier, business manager Harry Bisgeier and their wives. Each of the players and each of the club directors received cuff links and tie bars inscribed "Bisons, 1956."

There were gifts galore. Four youngsters under the age of seven accompanied McGroder to home plate for the ceremonies: Irene Curo and Theresa Kiplar, and Dennis and Terrence McConnell, the sons of George McConnell, who was the auditor general for McGroder's business. Each of the youngsters carried a wicker basket full of presents. Among the items Stiglmeier received were a pen and pencil set presented by the ex-Cornell football star Al Dekdebrun, representing the Greater Buffalo Advertising Club. Cheektowaga supervisor Ben Holtz presented a check on behalf of the Buffalo Bowlers Association. Phil Cavarretta, Peanuts Lowrey and the Bison squad presented the Stiglmeiers with a 96-piece silver service.

International League president Frank (Shag) Shaughnessy, at home due to illness, sent his accolades to Stiglmeier and the ball club for their accomplishments. George Trautman, president of the National Association of Professional Baseball Leagues, was quoted as saying, "I can't ever remember anything like this, for a capacity house to salute a last place team. I feel certain that for next season, the Bisons won't have to shop long for a major league tieup." This crowd was certain to "secure the Bisons' future."

Baseball friends such as Joe McCarthy, ex-Bison player and World Series–winning manager of the New York Yankees, and former Bisons manager Steve O'Neill (1938–1940) paid their respects. Hall of Famer Ray Schalk, the Bisons manager from 1932–1937, was quoted as saying, "I'd crawl on my hands and knees to be here to honor John."

Club president Taylor addressed Stiglmeier's devotion to baseball and his leadership in overcoming the financial crises the club had endured. The turnout swelled the season attendance to 178,000, remarkable for a last-place club suffering the terrible spring weather that caused so many games to be rained out. Taylor asserted that the team would finish the season in the black. Buffalo baseball would be back in business the next year, he assured the writers covering the affair, but the team would need both a major league connection and at least $50,000 to start the year. The bad spring weather probably cost the team at least that much. The roster would need a catcher, an outfielder and a couple of pitchers. If these players could be found, the price tag would be around that amount.

As Charley Young of the Buffalo Evening News reported it in his column on September 1, 1956, Taylor offered this assessment of the team's future: "The fans have been splendid. I think we should go ahead for next year. But we'll have to decide that at a meeting of directors after the season closes. It'll be next week before we're able to survey the books and see just where we stand...The outlook right now is optimistic. Certainly a crowd like this indicates there's real interest in baseball in Buffalo."

Looking ahead to 1957, there was speculation about the changes that would be forthcoming. Stiglmeier would have to surrender his post as general manager, given his new State Liquor Authority post. "But that doesn't mean I will not be able to continue as a director and adviser, providing they want me," he commented. Taylor's response was, "John's heart is in baseball and it will be until the day he dies...we are gratified to know that he will be with us..." Asked about his own return as president of the club, Taylor was noncommittal. That was a decision that would have to be made by the stockholders, he said, and allowed that this had been a very difficult year.

Charley Bailey, sports director of radio station WEBR, broadcast the ceremonies direct from the field, calling Stiglmeier "the man who kept Buffalo in baseball and baseball in Buffalo."

Games 142 and 143, Friday, August 31, Buffalo: Buffalo 6, Montreal 3; Buffalo 7, Montreal 3

An overflow crowd of 15,063, the largest single-game attendance since 1949,
came out to honor John C. Stiglmeier and watch the hometown
Bisons sweep the doubleheader.

Game 142 – August 31, 1956 (first game of doubleheader)

Montreal	000 021 0 – 3	12	1
Buffalo	105 000 x – 6	10	1
WP – Nagy (2-2)	LP – Cole (4-5)		

Game 143 – August 31, 1956 (second game of doubleheader)

Montreal	010 101 000 – 3	7	3
Buffalo	000 103 03x – 7	9	1
WP – Drews (13-11)	LP – Harris (7-8)		

Steve Nagy went the distance in the seven-inning opener, despite giving up 12 hits. His saving grace was that he did not walk a man and was able to strand nine Royals baserunners. Buffalo put the game away with a five-run third.

Dave Cole started for the fourth-place Montreal club and allowed the Bisons a run in the first. Joe Caffie's drive off the wall in left center went for a double. Lou Ortiz was credited with a ground rule double and an RBI when his fly ball went into the temporary bleachers behind the outfield ropes that had been installed in center.

Caffie started it again in the third inning, beating out a bunt. Ortiz doubled for a second time with Caffie holding at third. Then, manager Greg Mulleavy of the Royals ordered Luke Easter intentionally passed, loading the bases and looking for the double play. Instead, Bill Serena's bouncer wide of first skipped off first baseman Bob Hale's glove and was ruled a hit. Caffie scored and the sacks remained filled. On to relieve came Glenn Mickens.

Peanuts Lowrey slapped a Mickens offering to right field, sending Ortiz home and keeping the bases full. George Bullard's single brought in Easter and Serena. Norm Sherry's grounder to shortstop led to a force on Bullard at second, but the relay on to first was into the dirt and Lowrey scored the fifth run as Sherry was called safe.

Montreal got two back in the fifth when Jack Spears and Bob Wilson hit back-to-back ground rule doubles. Wilson moved to third on a passed ball by Sherry and scored as Clyde Parris bounced out, Ortiz to Easter. The last Montreal run came on George Shuba's sacrifice fly in the sixth following singles by John Roseboro and Sparky Anderson.

A come-from-behind win in game two made Karl Drews a 13-game winner. Montreal had taken the lead with single runs in the second and fourth frames. Bob Hale singled in the second, moved to third on a John Roseboro ground rule double and scored on a Clyde Parris sacrifice fly. In the fourth Bob Wilson singled, George Shuba singled him to third and Hale's ground out produced another tally. The Herd got one of those back in the bottom half of the fourth off Royals starter Bill Harris. Joe Caffie sliced a triple past a diving Bob Williams in center. Easter rifled a single to right for the RBI.

The Royals scored a third time in the sixth on Jack Spears' single, a ground out and George Shuba's one-base knock. Buffalo answered and took the lead in the home half of the inning. Lou Ortiz drew a walk and came all the way home on Easter's long double. Bill Serena's 22nd home run of the season, high over the left-field screen, scored Easter ahead of him and put the Herd in front by a run.

Three more scores wrapped it up in the eighth. Bob Walz, the new Montreal pitcher, walked Easter, the first man he faced. The second man, Serena, singled to put runners on first and second. Pete Castiglione went in to pinch-run for Easter. Peanuts Lowrey's sacrifice bunt was misplayed by Walz, who threw the ball over Parris' head at third base trying to catch Castiglione. Pete scored, Serena moved to third and Lowrey took second. A sacrifice fly from George Bullard scored Serena. A line single by Pat Tomkinson to right field brought in Lowrey.

Ortiz's defense in the ninth sealed the win. With two Royals on base, Lou knocked down a shot from Hale that was headed toward right field, scrambled to his feet and threw on to first for the final out.

BISON TALES: This was the Herd's fourth doubleheader sweep of the season, with two of those twin killings coming against the Royals.

John C. Stiglmeier Night attendees
Back row: George Trautman, Mary G. (Dougherty) Stiglmeier, John Stiglmeier, Ray Schalk, Steve O'Neill
Front row: Dennis O'Connell, Irene Curro, Theresa Kiplar
Photo courtesy of SUNY Buffalo State Courier-Express Collection

Game 144, Saturday, September 1, Buffalo: Montreal 2, Buffalo 1

John Weiss took a tough 2-1 loss to a Montreal team
determined to stay in the hunt for first place.

Game 144 – September 1, 1956

Montreal	010 000 100 – 2	5	0
Buffalo	000 001 000 – 1	7	1

WP – Milliken (2-1)   LP – Weiss (3-11)

Montreal catcher John Roseboro started the scoring with a two-out, line drive solo home run over the right-field wall in the top of the second inning. John Weiss' mound opponent, Bob Milliken, was being tough on the Bisons. It took until the sixth frame for the Herd to tie it up. Norm Sherry stroked a leadoff single to center field, followed by a perfect sacrifice bunt by Weiss to put him in scoring position. Billy DeMars, who had returned to shortstop Friday evening, singled to right center.

Royals center fielder Chuck Diering cut the ball off in the gap but then had to check his momentum, pivot and make his throw back to the infield. Cavarretta waved baserunner Sherry around third and on home. Not the fastest of runners, Sherry nonetheless made a long slide to the third-base side of the plate and snuck in under the tag. DeMars took second.

The Royals reclaimed the lead in their next at-bat in the top of the seventh. Bob Wilson sent a screamer down the left-field line for a double. George Shuba did his job at the plate by bouncing to Lou Ortiz. The ground out moved Wilson to third base. The next batter, Bob Hale, did the same thing as Shuba. His bouncer to Ortiz scored Wilson while he was being thrown out at first. With Wilson's speed there was no chance of catching him at the plate.

The Bisons could not counter as Milliken continued his mastery. He allowed a leadoff single to George Bullard in the eighth but stopped him there. Sherry failed at two sacrifice attempts before going down swinging. Cavarretta, pinch-hitting for Weiss, could only manage a fly out to right. DeMars was the third out on a fly ball.

Joe Caffie scratched a hit to start the ninth and moved to second base on Ortiz's sacrifice, but Joe couldn't get any farther. Luke Easter grounded to short and was thrown out at first as Caffie held the bag at second. The Bisons' last gasp, a thrill to the crowd of 2937 when it started out, was Bill Serena's line drive to the wall in left field. Shuba backed up to the fence and pulled it in for the final out. The thrill turned to dismay.

BISON TALES: Luke Easter complained of a sore neck following the game. He struck out in his first three at-bats and could manage only a weak grounder to short in his final appearance.

Weiss allowed only four hits in his eight innings of work. Milliken yielded seven in a route-going performance but did not walk a man.

Attendance was now over 180,000. Fans were encouraged to turn out in numbers for the final home game on Sunday. Any unused tickets that had been purchased with stock certificates would be honored at the contest. On Sunday, the Bisons would also be selling tickets to the Monday doubleheader that was to be played in Toronto, and also to the single game that was scheduled for Tuesday in that same city. The Maple Leafs had graciously consented to allow all such sales by the Bisons to be credited to the Buffalo coffers.

Game 145, Sunday, September 2, Buffalo: Montreal 14, Buffalo 4

*Montreal made it an unhappy ending to the home season by pummeling four
Buffalo pitchers for 15 hits and 14 runs before 3795.*

Game 145 – September 2, 1956
Montreal   010 500 701 – 14 15 0
Buffalo   000 201 001 – 4 7 3
WP – Kipp (20-7)   LP – Donovan (10-10)

Montreal's 19-game winner, Fred Kipp, faced the Herd's 10-game victor, Red Donovan.
As in the previous game, the Royals took the lead in the second frame when John Roseboro once again slugged a solo home run.

Unlike that contest, however, Montreal erupted for five more scores in the fourth inning. Donovan faced six men in that frame but only retired one of them. The other five scored, the first on
Peanuts Lowrey's dropped fly ball and the rest on a bases-loaded double by Kipp and a subsequent
single by Jimmy Williams. Ed Moeller replaced Donovan on the hill. He gave up the Williams single
but then retired the side.

Buffalo got two back in the home half of the fourth when Bill Serena, batting third today, followed Joe Caffie's single with his 23rd home run. The ball screamed over the wall in left center. Two
innings later, Peanuts Lowrey sent his third home run of the season over the left-field screen and
pulled the Herd within three. The blow must have woken up the sleeping Montreal bats. The Royals
put a 7-spot on the scoreboard in their next turn at the plate.

Moeller had been in control for two innings, but after retiring shortstop Jack Spears to start the
seventh the roof fell in. He gave up five hits in a row, the last two being a three-run home run by
Roseboro (his second of the game and third in two nights) and a solo shot by Clyde Parris. Bill Froats
was called in but he, too, found trouble. He retired Sparky Anderson but then walked the next
three men. Wilson's second double of the inning brought Zeb Eaton to the mound to get George
Shuba for the third out.

The Royals added an unearned run in the top of the ninth, a bad inning for Norm Sherry. Harry
Schwegman had taken over at third base for Parris, and Sherry, the Buffalo catcher, dropped his
infield popup, allowing Schwegman to get on base. Sherry's pickoff throw to first went wild for his
second error of the inning, and Schwegman moved down to second. Williams' base knock sent him
home from there. Peanuts Lowrey created the Bisons' final tally with a solo home run in the ninth,
his second of the day.

BISON TALES: For the second game in a row, a Montreal pitcher did not walk a batter. Luke Easter
was missing from the lineup, complaining of weakness and a headache and stiff neck. Cavarretta
moved Serena to the third spot in the order, batted Lou Ortiz in the cleanup role and sent Ed Mierkowicz in to play first base.

Total fan attendance for the year had reached 184,003, almost 53,000 more than came out for
last year's sixth-place club. general manager Stiglmeier estimated that the season losses would
be less than $10,000, not counting the income still to come from the ticket sales in Buffalo for the
three games yet to be played in Toronto. Cy Kritzer quoted Cavarretta in the Buffalo Evening News:
"We received loyal support from the fans. They were wonderful to me and the players."

Games 146 and 147, Monday, September 3, Toronto, Canada: Buffalo 2, Toronto 1; Toronto 3, Buffalo 0

Pete Castiglione bested his old teammates in game one.
The Herd was horse-collared in game two.

Game 146 – September 3, 1956 (first game of doubleheader)
Buffalo   000 020 000 – 2   7   0
Toronto   001 000 000 – 1   6   0
WP – Hahn (10-10)   LP – Johnson (15-8)

Game 147 – September 3, 1956 (second game of doubleheader)
Buffalo   000 000 0 – 0   6   0
Toronto   000 012 x – 3   5   0
WP – Lovenguth (23-11)   LP – Nicholas (5-10)

Fred Hahn started for Buffalo in the first contest and was wild, walking 10 men in his seven-plus innings. He also gave up six hits, but the only Toronto tally came in the third after Archie Wilson reached him for a single. A base on balls to Mike Goliat moved Wilson to second. Bill Wilson's clean line shot to center field brought Archie Wilson home.

Despite the walks, key strikeouts had saved Hahn until Cavarretta had to call Red Donovan in to retire Hector Rodriguez with the bases loaded in the eighth.

Buffalo rallied off Toronto's Don Johnson in the fifth. George Bullard's bloop single to left was followed by a Billy DeMars' bouncer into center field and Norm Sherry's sacrifice. Hahn fanned, but Castiglione became the hero by sending a 1-1 pitch on a line over Goliat's head into right center for the winning runs.

Caffie had overslept from an afternoon nap and was late to the ballpark. Cavarretta sent him up to hit for Castiglione in the seventh and take over defensively. Donovan stopped the Leafs in the ninth.

Lynn Lovenguth won his 23rd game of the season in the nightcap. Harry Nicholas had matched him zero for zero through four innings, but the Leafs got a run in the fifth after Nicholas hit Lovenguth with a pitch to start his troubles. A walk to Sam Jethroe compounded them. With runners on first and second, Lew Morton singled to center and Lovenguth scored.

The Leafs scored two more in the sixth on a Mike Goliat double, an RBI single by Loren Babe and a ground ball from Hector Rodriguez that was just out of Lou Ortiz's reach for the RBI base hit to right field.

BISON TALES: Luke Easter had remained home in Buffalo with a mysterious stomach ailment. Cavarretta and Ed Mierkowicz split the first-base duties.

Game 148, Tuesday, September 4, Toronto, Canada: Toronto 8, Buffalo 3

Ed Blake won his 17th game of the season and put his club within one win of the pennant. Lou Ortiz homered in the losing cause.

Game 148 – September 4, 1956
Buffalo   100 000 020 – 3 8 1
Toronto   010 003 40x – 8 13 0
WP – Blake (17-11)   LP – Nagy (2-3)

Buffalo scored first on first-inning doubles by Pete Castiglione and Lou Ortiz. With Steve Nagy on the mound for the Herd, Toronto tied it in the second. Bill Wilson stung a single to left. Carl Sawatski's infield hit moved him to second. Walt Derucki's bloop hit to right brought him home.

Nagy scattered hits and dodged more trouble until Toronto battered him in the sixth. Sawatski singled again, as did Derucki. Ed Stevens' first hit of the night was a three-run drive over the right-field fence to make it 4-1. The Leafs salted the game away in the seventh with four more. Sam Jethroe singled leading off and was sacrificed to second. Archie Wilson rifled a shot to left center to drive in Jethroe and took second on the throw to the plate. Mike Goliat singled in his turn at bat, and Wilson came home. Cavarretta decided, unwisely, to let Nagy pitch to one more batter. Bill Wilson sent his 13th home run ball out of the park to left to make the score 8-1. Joe Coleman relieved to get the last two outs.

Buffalo tried to get back in the game in the top half of the eighth. Pete Castiglione got a one-out single. With two out, Lou Ortiz delivered his 25th home run over the left-field wall, almost in the same spot where Wilson's had disappeared.

Blake, like Johnson and Lovenguth in the Monday doubleheader, was working on two days' rest. Toronto skipper Bruno Betzel called in Ross Grimsley to face Luke Easter. Luke sliced a single to left, and Bill Serena followed him with a walk. That sent Betzel back out to the mound with a gesture to the bullpen for John Hetki. Peanuts Lowrey's hot shot to third was knocked down and went for a single, but Easter could not score and the bases were loaded. Hetki stopped the comeback there. Billy DeMars flew out to Archie Wilson in left for the third out.

John Weiss held Toronto scoreless in the eighth. Hetki did the same to the Bisons in the ninth.

BISON TALES: Betzel was shooting for his third International League pennant. He had won the crown previously with Montreal (1945) and Jersey City (1947). This day's win, coupled with a Rochester loss, put the Leafs' magic number at one. Rochester would visit Toronto next for a series that would determine who would claim first place.

Cavarretta favored the Leafs to win the playoffs, calling them the "best balanced" team in the circuit. Miami had better pitching due to the depth of their rotation and bullpen, but every Maple Leaf in the lineup was dangerous. Eighth-spot hitter Ed Stevens, supposedly having an "off year," had hit 17 home runs and had 70 RBIs.

Easter played tonight though still weak. The Herd would come home for two days of rest before leaving on Friday to finish the year in Montreal. Toronto won the season series, 12 games to 10.

Wednesday and Thursday, September 5-6, Buffalo: Scheduled Days Off

The league schedule had created two bye dates at the tail end of the season in an effort to allow for makeup games. The Bisons would rest before travelling to Montreal for the season-closing series. It would be too costly to travel elsewhere to make up lost contests.

A TRIBUTE TO HARRY BISGEIER

Newspaperman Frank Lillich of the Buffalo Evening News sat down with the Bisons' business manager, Harry Bisgeier, during the Sunday, September 2, home game against Montreal. In Lillich's "Second Guessing" column, Bisgeier was quoted as saying,

"Last spring I said building a team for Buffalo was a three-year, not a one-year job. I still believe that. I had hoped and expected a season's attendance of from 225,000 to 250,000, but I think the bad weather in the spring cost us 50,000 in admissions. The team was going well then, and the fans were enthusiastic. That first Sunday postponement alone, I think, cost us 10,000 fans.

"But, the big thing, as far as I am concerned, has been the steady interest for the last month in an eighth-place club. Attendance even picked up in August. We had an interesting club, sure, but even so you'll usually only find the fans patronizing a winner.

"When we started to put together this club a year ago, we had nothing in the way of players. Now we have a solid nucleus. As a matter of fact, it is likely we could dispose of some of our players now and show a profit for the season. As it is, the loss won't be too great, and we now have some trading material to help fill the gaps in our lineups.

"Yes, I think we've accomplished the first third of our three-year goal."

For 1957, Bisgeier stated,

"We need catching help, at least two—make that three—front line pitchers, an infielder and one or two outfielders. That's enough to make us contenders. Remember, the sixth-place Bisons of 1955 finished 30 games out of first place. Right now, in eighth place, we're about 22 games back. That's evidence of something else, too—this is a stronger league, top to bottom, than it has been in some time.

"We also need some tieup with a major league club, even if only on a friendly basis or a partial working agreement.

"I firmly believe we did all baseball a service with our method of operation and with our appeal to commissioner Ford Frick. Now, for the first time, the major leagues are coming to the aid of the minors. Incidentally, I think the $500,000 the majors have earmarked for minor league aid should go to the lower minors – the Triple-A clubs should be able to stand on their own feet."

Lillich noted that Bisgeier had served without pay, as had club president Reginald B. Taylor and general manager John C. Stiglmeier.

"I did the best job I could," Bisgeier offered.

"And an excellent job it was, too, Harry," Lillich concluded.

Game 149, Friday, September 7, Montreal, Canada: Buffalo 10, Montreal 6

It was a cold night in Montreal but not if you had a bat in your hands.
The two teams amassed 30 hits. Steve Nagy got the relief win.

Game 149 – September 7, 1956			
Buffalo	211 012 102 – 10	17	0
Montreal	004 101 000 – 6	13	2
WP – Nagy (3-3)	LP – Mickens (8-7)		

Fred Kipp was on the mound for the Royals and seeking his 21st victory, but the Bisons got to him early. Lou Ortiz slammed a double with two out in the first and Luke Easter crashed home run number 35 to right field to make it 2-0. Drews' single plated another run in the second after one-basers by Billy DeMars and Norm Sherry. The Herd added a fourth run in the third on singles by Easter, Bill Serena and Peanuts Lowrey.

Karl Drews, going for his 14th win, lost his magic in the Montreal half of the third. He got the first two men to face him, but then Bob Wilson singled. Wilson was replaced by George Shuba after twisting his ankle retreating to the bag on the play. Oscar Sardinas doubled to right center to put runners on second and third. Bob Hale lined a single to right to score both men and cut the lead to 4-2. John Roseboro's drive over the high scoreboard in right center made it a tie ballgame. That was all for Drews. Apparently, the two-day restup in Buffalo hadn't been all that helpful for his timing. Steve Nagy came in to get Clyde Parris and end the onslaught.

Montreal went ahead in the next inning after Sparky Anderson singled and Nagy suddenly lost control, walking the next two men and loading the bases. The Herd was lucky to escape with only Anderson scoring on a Shuba ground out. The Bisons knotted the ballgame with a run in the fifth. Ortiz led off with a single, Easter walked and Bill Serena drove Ortiz home with a single of his own. Serena's blow also meant Kipp's departure. Glenn Mickens set down three in a row to put out the fire in this frame, but the Bison bats started up again in the very next inning.

Buffalo added two runs in the sixth to take back the lead. Pete Castiglione led off with a double over Hale's head at first. Joe Caffie drew a walk. Ortiz cashed both runners, lining his second double of the night down the left-field line, Caffie's speed bringing him all the way around from first base. Montreal cut the lead to one by scoring again in the bottom of the frame. Shuba doubled. Sardinas singled him home.

The Herd countered with run number eight in the seventh inning. Castiglione picked up his second hit of the night, moved to third on two groundouts and scored when first baseman Hale dropped the throw on Easter's grounder. Two more runs in the ninth put it away. Four Bisons reached base safely against hurler Bob Walz. Sherry collected his second hit. Nagy got a base on balls. Castiglione's third hit sent Sherry home. Joe Caffie's second single scored Nagy with the team's 10th run.

BISON TALES: Every Bison starter got at least one hit. Nagy, who came on in relief, was the only Bison to go without, but he scored a run.

The loss knocked Montreal out of a chance for a second-place finish.

Game 150, Saturday, September 8, Montreal, Canada: Buffalo 3, Montreal 2

Bill Serena's 24th home run of the year,
an eighth-inning three-run blast, gave Red Donovan his 11th victory.

Game 150 – September 8, 1956

Buffalo	000 000 030 – 3	5	0
Montreal	000 001 100 – 2	9	2

WP – Donovan (11-10)   LP – Harris (11-11)

Buffalo managed only five hits off the Montreal starter, Bill Harris, but three of them came in the eighth inning, along with one of Harris' six walks. Bison hurler Donovan was reached for nine safeties but allowed only one free pass and turned back all but two of the threats against him.

A hanging curve to George Shuba opened the scoring in the bottom of the sixth. Shuba crushed it high over the right-field scoreboard. The Royals picked up a second run in the next inning. Clyde Parris belted a leadoff single and moved to second on Sparky Anderson's sacrifice. Jim Williams' single gave Harris a two-run lead.

Joe Caffie dragged a bunt single to open the Buffalo eighth. Lou Ortiz's grounder forced Caffie at second, but the Buffalo second baseman beat the relay to keep one man aboard. Harris pitched carefully to Luke Easter and walked him. A fastball up over the outer half of the plate was turned around by Bill Serena to put the Bisons ahead, 3-2. Serena's blow, like Shuba's, also cleared the scoreboard in right. Peanuts Lowrey struck for another hit but was left stranded.

Donovan pitched scoreless ball over the last two frames. Earl York, pinch-hitting for Harris in the last of the ninth, went down swinging for the final out. It was Donovan's only strikeout.

BISON TALES: The Montreal loss meant that the Royals would finish in fourth place. Toronto's win against Rochester in 11 innings had given them the pennant. The Red Wings would end up in second place, Miami in third, Richmond in fifth, Havana in sixth, Columbus in seventh and the Bisons in the cellar.

Joe Caffie had been "sold back" to the Cleveland Indians and would report to that club after Sunday's final International League contest. Steve O'Neill, former Buffalo skipper and current scout for the Cleveland ball club, recommended the purchase. Joe's contract had been purchased by the Bisons from Cleveland with the understanding that, if Joe had a good year in Buffalo, the club would sell him back at the end of the campaign. Joe's outstanding speed and his ability to drag a bunt for a hit boosted him to over .300. He was fourth in the league in average and had also amassed 19 steals. He would have likely added more thefts had Cavarretta not held him back once the Buffalo power hitters had found their home run swings.

General manager John Stiglmeier said that the money involved in the Caffie sale was not the primary consideration. Finances had been a factor in the sale of Roger Bowman, but in this case it was the first step in establishing a mutually helpful relationship between the Bisons and the Cleveland club. Stiglmeier was looking for more such arrangements with other big-league teams. To his way of thinking, a close, primary agreement with only one organization could work to the Herd's disadvantage. With an exclusive major league tie-up, the big club might suddenly decide that it needed a hot bat or a strong arm in a particular circumstance, and such a recall could be very inopportune for the Bisons.

Game 151, Sunday, September 9, Montreal, Canada: Montreal 5, Buffalo 2

Buffalo was held to five hits for the second night in a row and
dropped the season finale. Fred Hahn took the loss.

Game 151 – September 9, 1956

Buffalo	020 000 000 – 2	5	1
Montreal	100 202 00x – 5	6	3

WP – Cristante (9-8)   LP – Hahn (10-11)

Montreal leadoff man Jim Williams opened the game for the Royals by drawing a walk in the home half of the first inning. Jack Spears, the second batter to face Hahn, put the Bisons down 1-0 with a slicing drive past Pete Castiglione in right field that went for a run-scoring double. Hahn got the next three men in order.

Buffalo took the lead in the second inning without the benefit of a hit. Luke Easter worked a leadoff walk from Montreal starter Bob Milliken. Bill Serena fouled out for one away, but then Milliken walked Peanuts Lowrey to put runners on first and second. Easter reached third and Lowrey the keystone sack on a wild throw by Montreal catcher John Roseboro trying to pick Peanuts off first base. Billy DeMars' ground ball to second sent Easter home, Lowrey moving on to third. Peanuts scored when a Milliken curveball to Norm Sherry broke into the dirt and away from Roseboro for a wild pitch.

Greg Mulleavy, Royals manager, worked his pitchers three innings at a time in this final game of the year. Leo Cristante replaced Milliken to start the fourth inning. Montreal took the lead for good in the bottom half of that frame. Clyde Parris roped a leadoff single that was followed by a walk to Sparky Anderson to put the first two men on base. Cristante's sacrifice moved both runners into scoring position. Hahn got Williams swinging for the second out, but Spears came through again, this time with a single to center that cashed both men. Montreal 3, Buffalo 2.

The Royals got their last two in the sixth. Hahn's fifth walk of the night put leadoff hitter Roseboro on first base. Parris' stinging double to right center made it men on second and third. Roseboro scored on Anderson's sacrifice fly. Williams hit a two-out double to plate Parris.

Ed Moeller finished up for the Herd. Dave Cole hurled the last three innings for the Royals. Neither man allowed a hit.

BISON TALES: And so came the end of a long and challenging season. The Bisons finished in the cellar, but, as had been said of them earlier, "they are the best cellar-dwelling team in baseball." The Herd took the final series by two games to one, but Montreal prevailed over the season, 14 games to eight.

Luke Easter's home run total ended at 35, leading the league in that category. Lou Ortiz had 25 and finished in second place. John Roseboro of Montreal tied him at 25. Bill Serena smashed 24.

Phil Cavarretta flew out after the game to wrap up business affairs in his former hometown of Dallas, Texas. He would winter in his new year-round residence in Ft. Lauderdale, Florida.

George Bullard, Joe Coleman and Steve Nagy also left by air for their home destinations. The remainder of the team took the train back to Buffalo with coach Lowrey. Joe Caffie would report to Cleveland. Larry Donovan was anticipating that he might be getting a call from Detroit.

Player	G	AB	R	H	2B	3B	HR	RBI	SB	AVG
Caffie, Joe	128	482	84	150	16	6	8	46	19	.311
Eaton, Zeb	11	13	2	4	2	0	0	0	0	.308
Easter, Luke	145	483	75	148	20	3	35	106	0	.306
Blatnik, John	22	51	5	15	6	0	0	2	0	.306
Lowrey, Peanuts	117	352	41	97	12	1	4	33	0	.276
Castiglione, Pete	128	445	39	122	20	4	0	33	2	.274
Ortiz, Lou	148	518	89	140	39	1	25	88	3	.270
Cavarretta, Phil	57	69	10	18	2	0	1	10	1	.261
Serena, Bill	134	419	62	106	16	5	24	73	1	.253
Bullard, George	96	322	46	80	12	2	2	17	15	.248
DeMars, Billy	104	320	26	78	9	0	1	22	2	.244
Brovia, Joe	46	122	12	28	7	0	6	28	0	.230
Mierkowicz, Ed*	87	281	33	64	10	1	8	37	3	.228
Sherry, Norm	64	181	14	39	5	0	2	7	0	.215
Tomkinson, Pat	91	229	21	45	8	0	2	13	0	.191
Vollmer, Clyde	14	43	4	7	1	0	1	4	0	.163
Heyman, Lou	36	90	7	14	5	0	4	12	0	.156
Clark, Jim	10	21	3	1	0	0	0	2	0	.048

Player	W	L	PCT	ERA	G	IP	H	R-ER	SO	BB	CG	SHO
Stryska, Vic	1	0	1.000	1.50	6	6	5	1-1	2	2	0	0
Donovan, Larry	11	10	.524	3.67	31	174	172	77-71	70	64	12	2
Drews, Karl	13	11	.542	3.84	29	171	186	79-73	88	49	11	3
Eaton, Zeb	0	0	.000	4.05	5	14	10	10-6	8	7	0	0
Coleman, Joe	4	2	.667	4.22	46	79	78	47-37	34	52	0	0
Bowman, Roger	8	12	.400	4.29	23	128	69	69-61	66	57	8	2
Nagy, Steve	3	3	.500	4.37	16	68	74	35-33	18	21	3	0
Weiss, John	3	12	.200	4.37	45	136	156	73-66	58	56	6	0
Hahn, Fred	10	11	.476	4.47	36	163	166	93-81	104	101	6	0
Walsh, Jim	0	1	.000	4.50	2	4	4	2-2	0	1	0	0
Keriazakos, Gus	3	5	.375	4.77	14	66	71	41-35	32	35	4	0
Nicholas, Harry	5	10	.333	5.52	28	119	120	75-73	94	61	5	0
Moeller, Edgar	0	0	.000	6.42	3	7	6	5-5	5	3	0	0
Froats, Bill	2	8	.200	7.02	37	109	133	92-85	93	63	2	1
Mrozinski, Ron	1	1	.500	8.43	3	11	11	10-10	7	7	1	0
Jordan, Milt	0	0	.000	8.52	2	6	9	6-6	0	4	0	0
Schultz, Bob	0	1	.000	16.20	2	2	4	3-3	1	3	0	0
Picone, Mario*	0	0	.000	0.00	5	0	0	0	0	0	0	0

Chapter 7: Postseason Results

International League Standings
Final Results, 1956 Season

	W	L	Pct	GB
Toronto	86	66	.566	—
Rochester	83	67	.553	2
Miami	80	71	.530	5½
Montreal	80	72	.526	6
Richmond	74	79	.484	12½
Havana	72	82	.468	15
Columbus	69	84	.451	17½
Buffalo	64	87	.424	21½

POSTSEASON PLAY

The Bisons and the rest of the second-division finishers—the Jets, the Sugar Kings and the Virginians—were out of it. These men would clean out their lockers and "wait 'til next year." Some would not be back, winning promotion to the big club. Some would be farmed out to a lower classification in need of more experience, and others would continue the yo-yo between classifications: too good for a lower tier but still not capable of satisfying the demands of Triple A. Others, the former big-leaguers, would continue their descent to even lower levels of play, their skills declining but their hearts holding fast to the hope of making it back up one more time. The game might be willing to let them go, but they were not yet ready to let go of it.

Some men would leave the game altogether, having realized that the dream was over. Others would find new meaning in the role of coach, manager, scout, perhaps even taking the field from time to time as the circumstances demanded and the body was still capable. Anything to stay attached to the game.

For the Buffalo men, home was the first stop; then a number were headed out to winter ball following a few weeks of rest. Luke Easter picked up a bonus check for $1000 from the team upon his return to Buffalo. It was his reward for hitting more than 30 homers. Luke was returning to his home in Cleveland, where he planned to have some discussions with Hank Greenberg, general manager of the Indians, about a possible working relationship with the Bisons. Luke was then headed south of the border to play in the Puerto Rico League. Both he and Karl Drews were signed to play for the Caguas-Guayama entry.

Joe Caffie would also stop off in Cleveland, following a very brief visit to his hometown of Warren, Ohio, because Joe would be continuing his season by suiting up with the Indians. He planned to make his presence felt in such a manner as to justify sticking with the big club on opening day 1957. At the end of major league play, Joe would be found in the Pampero outfield in the Venezuela Association.

Bill Serena was set to take on a managerial role for the Navajoa Mayos in the Mexican Pacific Coast League. He had starred as a third baseman for that club during the 1955-1956 winter campaign. Pete Castiglione might also be looking for a Mexican League hookup.

Larry Donovan did not receive the hoped-for call to join Detroit. On his way home to Cedar Rapids, he would be stopping in the Motor City to inquire about his options.

The Governors' Cup Playoffs

The top four clubs continued 1956 postseason play to determine who would face the winner of the American Association playoffs in the Junior World Series. Fourth-place Montreal visited first-place Toronto on Tuesday, September 11, while third-place Miami squared off in Rochester against the second-place Red Wings on that same day. Each series was scheduled to follow a best-of-seven format, with the winners of the initial round meeting one another in the finals. The American Association top four—Indianapolis, Denver, Omaha and Minneapolis—would enact a similar ritual in the Midwest. The Maple Leafs disposed of the Royals by four games to one. The Red Wings clipped the Marlins by the same result. In the finals, Rochester edged past Montreal, four games to three, and won the right to meet the Indianapolis Indians in the Little World Series.

It was the Red Wings' second consecutive trip to this playoff for bragging rights of supremacy in Triple A baseball. In 1955 the Rochester contingent had lost four games to three to the American Association pennant winner and playoff victors, the Minneapolis Millers. That Millers squad had featured a second baseman named Lou Ortiz. In 1956 Rochester would again go up against an opponent that had taken both the American Association pennant and the playoffs. This year the New Yorkers would fare even worse.

The Little World Series

Indianapolis swept the series four games to none. The Red Wings were trampled, 24 runs to 6. A Triple A rookie outfielder destined for greater things, Roger Maris by name, threw out the tying run in the first game to preserve the Indianapolis victory. He powered two home runs and drove home seven in the 12-4 second game win. The Indians took the next two games handily. The man behind the bench leading his club to their second pennant in three years, including this year's Triple Crown achievement—pennant, playoffs and Junior World Series—was two-time Minor League Manager of the Year Kerby Farrell.

INTERNATIONAL LEAGUE 1956 SEASON LEADERS
- Final Statistics as Compiled at Season End
- Batting Leaders: Average
- Clyde Parris, Montreal, .321; Joe Cunningham, Rochester, .320; Joe Caffie, Buffalo, .311; John Lipon, Columbus, .310; Luke Easter, Buffalo, .306; Bob Wilson, Montreal, .306; Eddie Kasko, Rochester, .303; Hal Bevan, Havana, .302; Archie Wilson, Toronto, .301; Gene Green, Rochester, .300.
- These men were the league's only .300 hitters.
- Batting Leaders: Home Runs
- Luke Easter, Buffalo, 35; Lou Ortiz, Buffalo, 25; John Roseboro, Montreal, 25; Bill Serena, Buffalo, 24; Mike Goliat, Toronto, 23; Gene Green, Rochester, 23.
- Batting Leaders: Runs Batted In
- Luke Easter, Buffalo, 106; Gene Green, Rochester, 96; Ed Bouchee, Miami, 94; Bob Wilson, Montreal, 90; Lou Ortiz, Buffalo, 88.
- Other Offensive Leaders: Runs Scored

- Sam Jethroe, Toronto, 105; Cal Abrams, Miami, 100; Jim Williams, Montreal, 96; Clyde Parris, Montreal, 92; Russ Sullivan, Columbus, 91.
- Other Offensive Leaders: Stolen Bases
- Len Johnston, Miami, 40; Sam Jethroe, Toronto, 22; Don Nicholas, Havana, 22; Joe Caffie, Buffalo, 19; Angel Scull, Havana, 17.
- Pitching Leaders: Percentage
- Bob Spicer, Columbus, 12-4, .750; Fred Kipp, Montreal, 20-7, .741; Satchel Paige, Miami, 11-4, .733; Don Cardwell, Miami, 15-7, .682; Cot Deal, Rochester, 15-7, .682.
- Pitching Leaders: Earned Run Average
- Ed Blake, Toronto, 2.61; Lynn Lovenguth, Toronto, 2.68; Joe Hatten, Havana, 2.68; Don Cardwell, Miami, 2.85; Seth Moorhead, Miami, 2.87. (Satchel Paige, who did not pitch sufficient innings to qualify for the earned run title, finished with a mark of 1.86.)
- Pitching Leaders: Wins
- Lynn Lovenguth, Toronto, 24-12; Fred Kipp, Montreal, 20-7; Ed Blake, Toronto, 17-11; five with 15 wins.
- Pitching Leaders: Strikeouts
- Seth Moorhead, Miami, 168; Lynn Lovenguth, Toronto, 153; Don Cardwell, Miami, 139; Don Johnson, Toronto, 132; Al Cicotte, Richmond, 129.

POSTSEASON HONORS

Manager of the Year: Miami's Don Osborn. Osborn had taken a floundering, second-division Marlin ball club and, with the timely infusion of both pitching and hitting, made a strong run at the pennant. His squad cooled off only in the season's final days.

International League All-Star Team: First base: Ed Bouchee, Miami (Luke Easter was third in the voting); second base: Mike Goliat, Toronto (Lou Ortiz was second); third base: Clyde Parris, Montreal; shortstop: Eddie Kasko, Rochester; outfielders: Archie Wilson, Toronto; Cal Abrams, Miami; Bob Wilson, Montreal (Joe Caffie was fifth); catcher: Carl Sawatski, Toronto; righthanded pitcher: Lynn Lovenguth, Toronto (Larry Donovan was third); lefthanded pitcher: Fred Kipp, Montreal.

- Most Valuable Player: Mike Goliat, the Maple Leaf second baseman. He was followed by Eddie Kasko of Rochester, Ed Bouchee of Miami, Clyde Parris of Montreal and, in fifth place, Luke Easter of the Bisons.
- Most Valuable Pitcher: Lynn Lovenguth of Toronto. He was trailed by Fred Kipp, Montreal, and Satchel Paige, Miami. Larry Donovan finished in eighth place in the tabulations.
- Outstanding Players (as ranked by the league managers)
- Pitcher most ready for the big leagues: Lynn Lovenguth, Toronto
- Best pitching prospect: Don Cardwell, Miami
- Best fastball: Don Cardwell, Miami
- Best curveball: Ken Johnson, Toronto
- Best hitting prospect: Ed Bouchee, Miami
- Most dangerous hitter (tie): Luke Easter, Buffalo; Clyde Parris, Montreal
- Best defensive infielder: Eddie Kasko, Rochester
- Best infield arm: Eddie Kasko, Rochester
- Best defensive outfielder: Ben Nelson, Rochester

- Best outfield arm: Bob Bowman, Miami
- Best throwing catcher: John Roseboro, Montreal
- Fastest runner (tie): Joe Caffie, Buffalo; Sam Jethroe, Montreal; Ben Nelson, Rochester
- Best baserunner: Len Johnston, Richmond

JOE CAFFIE'S MAJOR LEAGUE NUMBERS—1956

Joe Caffie made his major league debut on September 13, 1956, leading off for the second-place Cleveland Indians in a home game against the sixth-place Baltimore Orioles and singling in his second at-bat against Oriole starter Connie Johnson. Joe finished one for four on the day, although the Indians lost, 4 to 1. Caffie appeared in 11 more contests for the Indians before the season closed. He posted a notable .342 batting average, rapping out 13 hits in 38 plate appearances, scoring seven times and driving in one baserunner. He also swiped three bases and was caught twice.

His numbers gave him a good argument for making the major league roster when the Indians broke camp at the end of the 1957 spring training ritual. But if the Tribe couldn't use a fleet .300 hitter in their outfield, surely some other big-league club could benefit from his talents.

Speed was a potent weapon in baseball, and Joe Caffie had plenty to offer.

Chapter 8: Not Waiting 'til Next Year

SEPTEMBER 1956

"The Bisons hustled. They were a fighting club. They never quit." This from Cy Kritzer in his September 11 column in the Buffalo Evening News. And Kritzer had it right.

The club's spirit and hustle were the direct result of their on-field and off-field leadership. When team president Reginald B. Taylor, general manager John C. Stiglmeier and treasurer Harry Bisgeier were looking for a manager, they sought a man who had had big-league experience as both a player and a manager. They found those qualities in abundance in Phil Cavarretta, but also something more, something that had likely been in their minds, if not yet put into words: a competitor. In Cavarretta they had a competitor par excellence, a man who hated to lose. And he powerfully communicated that drive to the men who made up his squad. Above all and throughout the season, Cavarretta wanted to win. His team wanted to win. Everyone played to win.

What cost the team severely and caused the tailspin into last place were a number of factors, but perhaps most critical of these was the lack of a major league affiliation. Injuries shook the Bisons hard, but injuries are always a part of the game and even more so with a veteran club such as the Bisons had. What made the disabled list so difficult to endure was the lack of any backup resources to carry the load when the front-liners went down. Only John Stiglmeier's assertive challenge to major league baseball operations brought the Herd some measure of player assistance that allowed the club to finish the season with at least a degree of competitiveness.

The loss of catcher Carl Sawatski to Toronto was a major blow to Stiglmeier's efforts to field a first-division ball club. Sawatski was sold to the Maple Leafs by Chicago for a sum of $10,000, Stiglmeier found out. At the time, the Bisons thought that they had won his contract rights with an offer $5000 higher. No wonder Stiglmeier expressed his bitterness at the turn baseball operations had taken since he was last in the game back in the 1940s.

The Bisons showed a distressing record of 30 won and 46 lost for the first half of the season, a winning percentage of less than .400, occupying the cellar and standing 15 1/2 games out of first place. They ended the year at 64-87, still in last position but with an overall percentage of .424. They finished behind the pennant-winning Maple Leafs by a 21 1/2-game margin.

Having Joe Caffie at the start of the year would have certainly made a considerable difference. He would have had regular playing time from the start and would have found his hitting stroke much sooner, quite likely soaring above the .311 mark he eventually posted for the year. Had Easter donned his new eyeglasses at an earlier point in the year, his output may also have been even more impressive. He turned a first-half average of .265 with 17 home runs and 45 RBIs into final totals of .306, 35 and 106. Lou Ortiz was Mr. Consistency, with first-half statistics of 12 home runs and 45 RBIs to go along with a second-half production of 13 long balls leaving the park and an additional 43 runs chased across. Bill Serena's healed hand and new specs also led to a dramatic season turnaround. Hitting only .223 with eight homers and 31 RBIs in the first half, Bill finished up with .257, 24 and 73. Lowrey, Cavarretta and DeMars, once the latter was healthier, all picked up their offense as the season wore on.

Despite having three of the league's top four home run hitters—Easter (35), Ortiz (25) and Serena (24)—Cavarretta's prediction of a 150-homer year for the squad did not materialize. The club wound up with 123, while the opposition slugged Herd hurlers for 140. The losses of Blatnik and

Brovia (his defensive liability was too great to overcome) probably helped to keep the Bison total down. Buffalo was second to the pennant-winning Maple Leafs' total of 155. Carl Sawatski contributed 22 of that number.

Signing Ed Mierkowicz was a boost for a time until his bat tailed off significantly at the end. Pete Castiglione was an unsung hero, rarely flashy but always dependable. His versatility was a valuable asset to a team that had men going down at every station. He suited up in 128 contests and played three infield and two outfield positions for the club. Lou Ortiz anchored the team's double-play defense as well as providing the club with the greatest offensive output of his long career.

The Bisons tried to save money by shortening the spring training season, and this did have the desired effect of keeping expenses to a minimum, but the limited conditioning may have cost the club in player performance more than had been anticipated. Cavarretta and player-coach Peanuts Lowrey whipped the men into better shape than a number of them had seen in years, but the big guns in the lineup were slow to get going for the first month of play. Still, Buffalo was flirting with the first division until the major league cutdown time arrived. The competition surged with this new influx of talent while the Bisons stood pat.

The pitching staff, even with a full month to get into shape before the start of league play, struggled with inconsistency. Karl Drews' arm ailment reduced his season from an 8-won, 6-lost start to a final record of 13-11. Red Donovan picked up the slack, as did Fred Hahn. Donovan was 3-4 in the first half, but 8-6 in the second. He deserved an end of season callup by the Tigers that didn't come. Fred Hahn went 7-5 after July 2 to finish with a final won-lost total of 10-11. And Harry Nicholas, woeful at 1-7 in the first half, won four and lost only three in the remainder of the season. Roger Bowman was 3-3 in the second half before his sale to Minnesota. His replacement, Steve Nagy, also recorded a 3-3 mark.

The receiving corps suffered from injury and a lack of offensive production after a brief, explosive start to the year. Pat Tomkinson's foot injuries likely affected his plate production all season long, as well as his ability to cut down baserunners. Norm Sherry was acquired only after much arm twisting by John Stiglmeier and the baseball commissioner, but even he was coming off an injury and was limited in what he could manage. Management and the manager were unable to correct or substitute for these deficiencies.

A plethora of injuries to other men, particularly Billy DeMars' arm woes, hurt the team defensively. The club as a whole combined for a total of 146 double plays, far short of the wished-for number of 165 that DeMars had thought in spring training he and Lou Ortiz might turn together. This shortfall certainly affected the work of the pitching staff, playing a role in prolonging innings and calling for extra mound effort. For their part, the hurlers did not always keep the ball low, as witness the 140 home runs allowed.

Nor did Herd home run prowess compensate for the slowness of foot on the base paths. Offensive output was stifled by hitting into 153 twin killings. Only George Bullard and Joe Caffie had any speed to offer to pressure the opposition pitchers and fielders, but injuries limited Bullard to 96 appearances and Caffie got a late start on the season and wound up playing in only 128 contests.

In sixth position on June 11, the Herd was in arrears of the league-leading Montreal Royals by 13 1/2 games but still had a two-game lead over seventh-place Richmond and led the last-place Cubans by a half-game more. A disastrous seven-game losing streak that started on June 12 plunged the Bisons into the cellar. The team climbed into seventh place on June 19 and held that position for one more day. Dropping the next three out of four to the last-place Virginians put them back in the basement to stay. By midseason, on July 2, the ball club was solidly in the cellar. They had one last chance to overtake the seventh-place Jets in late August, but it would have meant sweeping the four-game series. The Bisons won the first two. The Jets took the next pair. Buffalo had by then run out of chances. They would finish in last place, but they would continue to fight for every game yet to be played. In fact, they won the final series against Montreal, on the road, two games to one.

The difficult year on the field was made even more uncertain because of financial insecurities off of it. Rainy weather cost the club many dates at home and perhaps at least $20,000 in revenue. At one time it seemed as though the Bisons would be unable to make payroll, but that danger was temporarily overcome, and then the fan base rallied in the late going to help fill the coffers. The special nights for the players, and especially the turnout for John Stiglmeier, gave both a financial and an emotional boost to all involved. Thus the season, no matter how many problems the club had faced, ended on a positive note that boded well for the future.

The future was what club president Reginald Taylor had in mind when he called a board of directors meeting for September 14. Club secretary J. Eugene McMahon sent out notices to the board's 14 members for a meeting at 4:30 pm at Offermann Stadium. Matters for discussion would be the anticipated deficit of $18,000, how to raise an additional $50,000 to get next year's operations off on positive footing, Stiglmeier's status as the team's general manager and the status of Phil Cavarretta as the field manager.

Stiglmeier, in meetings in New York City to clarify his new appointment to the State Liquor Authority, would be at the September 14 gathering to let the board know what connection he would be allowed to have with the club. Cavarretta, meanwhile, had let it be known prior to leaving for his home at the close of the season that he would be interested in returning to Buffalo, but only if there was a major league tie-up of some nature that could be arranged. Otherwise, he had at least two other offers to consider.

There was good news aplenty to report at the September 14 meeting. President Taylor, in his earlier estimations about the team's likely deficit, had overlooked the as-yet unreceived checks from the Bisons' road games in Columbus, Miami and Havana. According to the unofficial audit in hand, these monies would virtually wipe out the anticipated loss, said secretary McMahon. At worst, the club would face a nominal shortfall. President Taylor shared encouraging words about raising the $50,000 that would be needed to start 1957. Commenting that the "little fellows" would first be approached to purchase more shares in the ball club, he hinted that other interests had been impressed with the organization's 1956 efforts. There was the strong likelihood of additional deep-pocketed sources to call upon if and when the time came.

General manager Stiglmeier brought the heartening news that he would be able to continue to serve the board in an unpaid vice-presidential capacity in 1957. He could serve out the remainder of this year as the club's general manager. The board would look for someone to replace him in the general manager role for 1957.

Board members also received the good news that promising discussions with at least two major league teams were in the works for affiliation. Stiglmeier was headed shortly for Cleveland where he would meet with Luke Easter, he said, but the impression was strong that a confab with Indians general manager Hank Greenberg was also forthcoming. Easter had already been bending Greenberg's ear. It was revealed that Cleveland was in the process of ending its relationship with its top minor league affiliate, the Indianapolis Indians, in addition to the Kansas City A's and the Columbus Jets having already parted ways. The major league Indians and the Kansas City American Leaguers were now both in need of a new Triple A partner.

The directors expressed their gratitude to Taylor, Stiglmeier and business manager Harry Bisgeier for their "untiring efforts" throughout the year. They praised the work of those who had arranged the special attendance nights, especially Pat McGroder's efforts on the tribute to Stiglmeier. President Taylor also called the attendees' attention to the work of the Bisons' office manager, Joe McShane. "[McShane] shouldered a big job this summer, and he did it smoothly," Taylor was quoted in the News. "Joe worked tremendous hours and handled a heavy amount of paperwork on players and tickets, without a hitch. He is a big man in our ball club."

Board members John C. Montana and Edwin F. Jaekle were excused from the meeting due to prior commitments. Present were Thomas W. Ryan, Frank F. Cannon, Dick Fischer, John J. Krysinski, Ed M. Kelly, Helen A. Berny, Roxie Gian and Wade Stevenson. Another directors' meeting would be arranged once the final audit was completed. An annual stockholders' meeting was scheduled for the second Saturday in March 1957 as dictated in the bylaws. Last-minute speculations were raised about the possibility of the city purchasing Offermann Stadium from Sportservice and constructing parking surrounding the ballpark. This idea would bear further conversation.

In major league news: Sal Maglie pitched the Dodgers' second no-hitter of the year on September 25, a 5-0 victory over the Philadelphia Phillies. Roy Campanella hit a two-run second inning homer. The Dodgers also won their second consecutive National League crown under manager Walt Alston's guidance. Dodger pitcher Don Newcombe dominated his league with a 27-7 record and was selected as the circuit's MVP. He also took home the very first Cy Young Award accorded by major league baseball. At its outset, only one Cy Young Award was given annually to the best major league pitcher in both the National and American Leagues combined.

In the junior circuit, the New York Yankees won their second pennant in a row and seventh in eight years under manager Casey Stengel. Mickey Mantle, Yankee center fielder, was the unanimous choice for the league's MVP after a Triple Crown season: .353, 56, 130. With 132 runs scored, Mantle's offensive output surpassed all players in both leagues in all four categories.

The Dodgers and Yankees would square off for the second straight year in the World Series. The Dodgers had taken the previous year's classic, four games to three, with a stunning 2-0 Johnny Podres shutout in game seven. Brooklyn left fielder Sandy Amoros had made a crucial, sixth-inning, one-handed grab of a twisting fly ball off the bat of Yogi Berra to save the game. It was the first World Series victory ever by a Brooklyn nine. In Flatbush, next year had finally arrived! Could lightning strike a second time?

OCTOBER 1956

The Bisons let no grass grow under their feet in making preparations for 1957. General manager Stiglmeier announced on October 2 that the club had purchased outright from the Kansas City A's the contracts of catcher Ray Noble, pitcher Ray Herbert, first baseman Joe Golden and shortstop Arthur Ehlers. In one go, Buffalo had shored up team deficiencies at four positions.

Cuban-born Rafael Miguel Noble, now 37, had spent the 1956 campaign with the Columbus Jets, batting .230 with 13 home runs. A former Negro Leaguer playing with the New York Cubans, Noble had spent parts of three seasons with the New York Giants (1951–1953), hitting for a .218

mark and nine home runs in that span. Noble was a member of the pennant-winning 1951 Giant club that lost to the Yankees in the World Series. He had been an International Leaguer since 1954 and was possessed of a strong arm, something the Bisons lacked in 1956 due to injuries to both Tomkinson and Sherry. A squat 5 foot, 11 inches, and 240 pounds, Noble had a powerful bat and had already demonstrated its potency against Offermann's short left-field barrier.

Ray Herbert, turning 27 in December, had already had five years in the majors with Detroit and Kansas City, going 13-22 over that span. A disastrous 1-8 campaign with the A's in 1955 sent him down to Columbus for 1956. Primarily a relief specialist, he had registered a 9-9 record for the 1956 Jets. His acquisition would help shore up the Herd's off-and-on bullpen.

Golden, 24, was a lefty swinger who last played in 1954 when he hit .290 for Class A Savannah in the Sally League. He was currently in the Army but would be discharged the coming winter. Adding another first baseman was a must. Luke Easter's aging legs needed rest for the late innings and manager Cavarretta's back would no longer allow him to function in that role.

Ehlers was also in military service at the time of this purchase. The 23-year-old had played only 17 games in his organized baseball career, hitting .235 in 1955 for the same Savannah club where Golden had performed. Billy DeMars' arm injury had severely limited his playing time and his per-formance in the past season. Both Golden and Ehlers would be long shots, but the front office was proving itself hard at work mending the cracks in the team's makeup.

Could this deal be a forerunner of a relationship with Kansas City? Stiglmeier wasn't saying more than that the parties were in the negotiation phase. Critical to the Bisons was the right of rejection of players who would not fit into the Buffalo scheme, as well as the ability to turn to other major league clubs for player assistance when needed.

The news of the player purchase from Kansas City also raised speculation on a potential 1957 role for Buffalo's own Danny Carnevale. Canisius College grad Carnevale, who had played for the Bisons in 1938 and again in 1940, had most recently skippered the 1955 club to a 65-89 sixth-place International League finish. When Phil Cavarretta was chosen to manage Buffalo for the 1956 sea-son, Carnevale signed on to a Kansas City scouting role. Perhaps the A's would suggest consider-ation of Carnevale as a general manager candidate when Stiglmeier resigned at the end of the year. Carnevale's work in 1956 had made him familiar with the Kansas City farm personnel.

The evening of October 6 brought the news that Buffalo and Kansas City had indeed inked a par-tial working agreement. The pact as arranged between John C. Stiglmeier for the Buffalo Baseball Club, Inc. and Parke Carroll, business manager for the Kansas City A's, as well as Hank Peters, A's director of player personnel, had been given the official stamp of approval by baseball commission-er Ford C. Frick.

Under the agreement, the A's committed to provide Buffalo with Triple A caliber players on option to the club. Buffalo would not have to accept players that did not satisfy that condition. Moreover, Kansas City would pay part of the salaries for players with major league contracts who were sent down to the Herd. This would be a significant help in reducing Buffalo's payroll costs.

Players would be sent to the Bisons for an agreed-upon specified period of time and could not be recalled by the A's until that time period had been satisfied. Buffalo would also accept a player under the 24-hour recall option if there was a desperate need for that man's contribution to the Bisons. But the Herd also agreed to return the player within the 24-hour time period if the Kansas City fortunes suddenly deteriorated and they desperately needed that man back.

Players purchased by Buffalo from the big-league club would be resold to the A's at the same price for which their contracts were purchased. Kansas City would have no financial stake in the Bisons. They would have no say in selecting a manager.

The original pact as agreed to by the parties had been for a period of two years. This was modified by commissioner Frick to make it a one-year arrangement.

Stiglmeier advised that Kansas City would immediately begin to assign their top minor league prospects to the Buffalo roster. According to Parke Caroll, "The A's are not in a position to supply a Triple A club with all of its playing talent, but...I believe that if you picked the best players from the present Buffalo club, and added the best of the Columbus team, you would have a first-division outfit." These words, appearing in Bill Coughlin's Courier-Express column on October 1, would turn out to be prophetic.

In other news on October 6, the Bisons reported the sale of catcher Norm Sherry to the St. Paul Saints of the American Association. Sherry was being returned to the Brooklyn Dodger organization.

October 13 found the Bisons purchasing three more A's pitchers: righthanders Al (Dutch) Romberger, Bill Bradford and Jose Santiago, all relievers. Romberger, a 29-year-old, had appeared in 23 games for this season's pennant-winning Toronto club, winning two and losing one. His ERA was 6.75. In 1955 he had authored a 7-4 record and a 2.28 ERA with the Columbus club, but a fight that year that involved Toronto first baseman Lou Limmer, as well as his own Columbus manager, Nick Cullop, left him with a broken hand that was still affecting him in the past season. In the majors, Romberger had posted a 1-1 mark with the (then) 1954 Philadelphia A's. (The A's relocated to Kansas City as of 1955.)

Jose Santiago, a Negro League New York Cuban hurler at the age of 18 back in 1947, had been used sparingly in Cleveland and Kansas City over the past two years before being sent down to the Jets in the middle of 1956. His Cleveland record in 1955 was 2-0 with a sparkling 2.48 ERA despite limited innings. For 1956, he was 1-2 with the A's before being sent down to the Jets to get more work. In Columbus the 27-year-old struggled at 1-4 in 10 games.

Bradford, the oldest of the trio at 34, had had a number of good years for the San Francisco Seals in the Pacific Coast League before being picked up by the New York Giants. He pitched for Minneapolis in the American Association in 1956, where he put together a 5-7 record in relief. Kansas City purchased his contract at the end of the year. He was limited to one game for the A's.

Joe Astroth, one of the game's top-rated receivers, was purchased from San Diego of the Pacific Coast League on October 15. Astroth was a 10-year major league veteran, primarily with the Philadelphia Athletics/Kansas City A's and came with a lifetime batting average of .254. On June 8, 1950, he had tied a major league record with six RBIs in one inning. He was sent to San Diego early in 1956 and posted a .246 mark at the plate. He and Noble gave the 1957 Bisons a formidable catcher corps, Noble with power and Astroth with his defense.

The addition of the two new catchers raised the question of Pat Tomkinson's status. Might the Bisons sell or trade him? Club president Taylor was quick to respond to that line of questioning. On October 18, he told the News' Cy Kritzer, "Never again will this club be so desperate for catching as we were before the season opened last April. Then we had only Pat and he had a bad hand. It was the worst fix of the season...You can't have too many experienced catchers to start the season. They are always in demand." Answer: Pat Tomkinson is staying in Buffalo!

October 18 brought four more players to the Bisons preseason roster as a result of the Kansas City pact. Rudy Mayling, an outfielder, 26 years of age, had spent the previous year with the Abilene Blue Sox in the Class B Big State League, slugging 32 home runs and driving home 103 with a .277 average. Fleming (Buddy) Reedy Jr., also 26 and also an outfielder, registered a .295 mark with Columbia in the Class A Sally League. He was a lefthanded swinger. Third baseman Joe Fahr, 28, Reedy's teammate at Columbia, had rapped the ball at a .315 clip. Shortstop Gilberto Valentin, 25, a native of Mayagüez, Puerto Rico, also from the Columbia squad, had hit .263.

A day later, and from the Cleveland organization, the Bisons picked up the promise of two more men. Outfielder Rod Graber, 26, spent 1956 with the Double A Mobile Bears of the Southern Association, where he rang up an impressive .312 mark. He also hit .270 in 22 games when promoted to the Little World Series–winning Indianapolis Indians. Fayetteville Highlander outfielder Ed Cook was sent on option to Buffalo from the Indians. Playing in the Class B Carolina League, the 25-year-old Cook fashioned a .272 average. The day ended with yet another Abilene Blue Soxer added to the squad—shortstop George Wegerek, 23, who hit .260 for the season just ended.

With such an abundance of new players to add to the men already under contract to the team, president Taylor noted that the Bisons might be able to assist other minor league clubs that were seeking personnel. In this manner, Buffalo could bargain for reciprocal assistance from those clubs' parent organizations. The Herd was also anticipating more help from Detroit now that Buffalo friends Jack Tighe and John McHale had been elevated to Tiger manager and director of player personnel, respectively.

Nor had the postseason front office work been focused solely on stocking the roster. New stockholders were required, too. Taylor had a goal of raising $50,000 to start the year right and get the team off on a stable footing. Larger spring training expenses were anticipated. More men would be in camp and the training would start earlier than the present year's experiment. Letters had gone out to current shareholders and a pitch would be made at the March 1957 annual meeting for each one to recruit one new shareholder who would purchase at least 100 shares in the community-owned venture.

Bob Bonebrake, a 22-year-old righthander from the New York Yankee system, was added to the Bison fold on October 24. Bonebrake had gone 15-14 in four previous seasons, reaching as high as Class A Binghamton in 1953 and 1954. He was currently at college and would report to the Bisons at the close of the 1957 spring academic calendar.

The final player moves that took place in October concerned two of the Detroit pitchers who toiled for the Herd during the past season. Righthander Larry Donovan was officially placed on the 1957 Bisons roster. Lefty Bill Froats was optioned to Birmingham, Alabama, in the Double A Southern Association.

In other International League news: Syracuse interests were feeling the economic loss of their International League franchise. The Salt City patrons had not turned out to watch the Class A Eastern League replacement. Chiefs owner Joe Reardon, with assistance from advertising executive Bud Coollcan and Post-Standard sports editor Bill Reddy, was spearheading a drive to raise $50,000 in one night, with fans purchasing stock in the team for $1 per share. A citizens' committee supported by business owners would eventually take over running the club. The long-range goal was to return an International League team to the city and revive the instate rivalry with Buffalo and Rochester.

Speaking of Rochester, the Red Wings reported significant financial losses in 1956 despite the postseason playoffs and the Little World Series receipts. The parent St. Louis Cardinals announced on October 30 that they would no longer operate the Rochester franchise. General manager Frank (Trader) Lane announced that it was "no longer practical" to maintain three top minor league teams for the purposes of player development. In addition to Triple A Rochester, St. Louis operated the Triple A American Association Omaha Cardinals and the Double A Houston Buffs. Lane hoped that local Rochester interests would take over running the team, promising "some sort of working agreement with the Cardinals, if desired," according to the News.

In major league news: The Yankees reversed the 1955 World Series outcome by beating Brooklyn by four games to three. Don Larsen started for the Yankees on October 8 and won game five of the series, 2-0, pitching the only perfect game in World Series history. Mickey Mantle homered deep down the right-field line in the bottom of the fourth for the first run. Hank Bauer singled home Andy Carey in the sixth. Sal Maglie took the loss.

NOVEMBER 1956

It was an upbeat board of directors that left Offermann Stadium on Friday afternoon, November 16. The financial message they had received from club secretary J. Eugene McMahon was more than satisfactory. McMahon reported that the 1956 Bisons had finished the season with a loss of only $62.30. He cautioned that this figure did not include player depreciation, usually rated at 20% per season for tax purposes, although in some instances minor league players had been known to have been depreciated as much as 33.3%. Nor did the accounting include the expenses incurred for the promotions the club had staged to bring out the fans over the last weeks of the season. Still, it was a remarkable outcome that only a couple of months earlier had been unthinkable. The directors dedicated themselves to raising the additional $50,000 that Taylor had said was necessary to begin 1957 on a solid financial footing.

The directors accepted John C. Stiglmeier's resignation as general manager. As previously indicated, Stiglmeier said he would continue his efforts on the team's behalf as a member of the board and as the team's unpaid executive vice president. Harry Bisgeier was also named to the board of directors, after he had announced that he would have to leave the post of business manager to return to private business. Like Stiglmeier, he had foregone a salary in 1956 to help the club stay solvent. Unlike Stiglmeier, however, he had not received a new $15,000 position from New York State to sustain him for the year to come.

Ratification of the working arrangement with Kansas City passed without objection. Stiglmeier noted that a year previous, at this date on the calendar, the Bisons had only nine men on the roster, three of whom never put on a uniform in 1956. Currently the roster already stood at 31 and was growing.

Still to be resolved were the critical issues of field leadership, hiring a new general manager and deciding on a Florida spring training site. Despite some criticism of the last-place finish, the directors voted their intention to bring Cavarretta back for a second year. Perhaps their thinking was swayed in part by comments from the players. It was rumored that Luke Easter, Lou Ortiz, Bill Serena and Karl Drews, among others, had expressed a desire to be traded if Cavarretta was not coming back. Now the decision would be up to Cavarretta.

The Bison field manager had flown immediately from Montreal to Dallas following the ball club's final game of the season in order to finalize matters related to the sale of his home. He had then flown on to his new residence in Ft. Lauderdale, Florida. Prior to leaving, the skipper had announced his interest in returning for 1957, but only if the Bisons were able to arrange a satisfactory working agreement with a major league program. The Kansas City-Buffalo pact was satisfactory to the Bisons' head office and directorate. Would it be sufficient for Cavarretta?

Stiglmeier and club president Taylor would be heading to the minor league baseball club convention in Jacksonville, Florida, on December 2. At that time, if not sooner, they would sit down with Cavarretta to discuss terms for the year to come. Also to be decided was the fate of the general manager position. Once more, Danny Carnevale's name had surfaced.

The general manager/Danny Carnevale question brought forth an answer on November 21. Carnevale was offered and agreed to take the post. As manager of the Herd in 1955 and as a scout for Kansas City the past season, much of that time being spent in Offermann, Carnevale had had an excellent seat from which to continue his knowledge of International League personnel as well as deepen his understanding of the Kansas City farm talent. He had also had the year to observe from the outside how the new community ownership program had worked for the Bisons.

(Carnevale's name had been raised as a Buffalo manager candidate for 1956, but it had been widely believed that he had wished to remain with the Detroit organization and was in line to fill the managerial post for the Charleston, West Virginia, ball club. In fact, his losing season with the Bisons was the only time in his eight-year managerial career when he had failed to make the first division. Previously, he had led five clubs to championship seasons and had taken three others into the playoffs. When the Tigers and Carnevale eventually changed course on the Charleston job, it was too late for Carnevale to apply to return to the Herd. The directorate had already decided that they wanted a man with major league player credentials, and managerial experience, too, if available. Phil Cavarretta fit that description exactly.)

President Taylor outlined the new general manager's duties: promotions and ticket sales; negotiating most player contracts; keeping a close eye on the waiver list and setting up player deals. He was also to set up and manage the spring training base, overseeing arrangements for travel and road trips. Former general manager John C. Stiglmeier would provide his direct supervision.

On November 27, with his first week under his belt, Carnevale revealed that he would be going to the December 2 minor league meetings in Jacksonville along with Taylor and Stiglmeier in the search for player help. Discussions with the A's and at least two other big-league operations had focused on getting a proven Triple A shortstop and at least two outfielders. Pitching, of course, was always wanted. Phil Cavarretta was expected to join the three front-office men at the meetings and sign his field manager contract for 1957 at that time.

Taylor, Stiglmeier and Carnevale departed for Florida on Friday, November 30. The club's first objective was to build an outfield with righthanded power. This would take advantage of the short left-field fence in Offermann and would also discourage opponents from throwing lefties at the Bisons in an effort to neutralize Luke Easter. There was also talk of trading reliever Joe Coleman to a Pacific Coast League squad. Coleman had expressed a preference to be out on the coast and at least one Pacific Coast League team had already put in a feeler bid for him. With the number of hurlers now on the roster, Buffalo might be able to let go of a pitcher in order to shore up some other deficiencies. Outfielder Rod Graber's name was also mentioned for potential trade to several Southern Association clubs. Graber was a lefthanded center fielder who had accounted for only six home runs last season. His .270 average after his promotion to Triple A was just short of Cavarretta's desired production for that position—.275. Graber might help the Bisons through a player exchange.

Consultation was scheduled to take place on December 1 in Jacksonville with Kansas City general manager Parke Carroll and farm director Bill Peters. The men would review potential selections for the December 3 draft, when the minor league teams would participate in a draft of players from lower classifications. The Bisons now had the benefit of reviewing the A's minor league scouting reports before making their decisions.

The three critical issues to be resolved once the front office reached Jacksonville were the signing of the field manager, determination of spring training headquarters and selection of a new trainer for the 1957 season. Phil Cavarretta was the club's choice to return as skipper of the Bisons, but would Cavarretta be agreeable to the terms the club would set forth? The arrangement with Kansas City should satisfy Phil's proviso that the Bisons have a working agreement with a major league club, but what was uncertain was the matter of Peanuts Lowrey's status and Cavarretta's reaction to it.

Phil had taken the job in 1956 on the condition that Peanuts would be his player-coach. Lowrey got into more games than anyone had anticipated and the Bisons were fortunate to have had his veteran skills both in the lineup and in the first-base coach's box. His .276 average was third-high on the team and his ability to play both infield and outfield positions had helped immeasurably when the squad encountered its multitude of injuries. Yet his own injury had slowed him down near the season's end and it was a serious question how long his 38-year-old legs could continue to carry him on the field. Looking at his considerable salary, the directors wanted to use that money to sign a younger, power-hitting outfielder who might also double as player-coach. They wondered if Cavarretta would go along with such a plan.

Trainer Jimmy Mack's status was uncertain. His age had been raised as a concern. He had not responded well to the rigors of the team's travel. The directorate had also questioned his methods and the length of time it had taken players to heal from their injuries under his ministrations. The younger Frank Christie's name had been raised as an alternative. Christie, the current trainer for the Buffalo hockey Bisons, had strong backing from some of the Bison directorate.

Lastly, where the Bisons would be spending spring training was now dependent upon the new schedule of spring training games that would be forthcoming under the Kansas City tie-up. Kansas City affiliates would replace Detroit farm clubs for those contests. Would the team be better off returning to Bartow, or even Plant City, both locations in the interior of the state? What about returning to Dunedin on the west coast? Phil Cavarretta, who now had a home on the east coast in Ft. Lauderdale, had been scouting a number of possibilities in his vicinity.

DECEMBER 1956

Meeting with president Taylor, vice president Stiglmeier and new general manager Dan Carnevale on Sunday, December 2, at the outset of the annual convention of the National Association of Professional Baseball Leagues, Phil Cavarretta inked a second one-year contract to manage the Herd for 1957. The terms would remain the same. Cavarretta insisted, and the front office thereupon agreed, that Harry (Peanuts) Lowrey was to return as the Bisons' player-coach. Now the men could turn their attention to the spring training site.

Cavarretta had scouted four locations on the Florida east coast and had wound up recommending Pompano Beach. Conveniently for the Bison manager, this site was only 11 miles north of his new home in Ft. Lauderdale. A meeting with the city officials would take place December 3.

In other International League action on the same day, league directors extended for two more years the contracts of league president Frank J. Shaughnessy and secretary-treasurer Harry Simmons. Jack Kent Cooke, owner-president of the Toronto Maple Leafs, was elected vice president of the league. John Stiglmeier's proposal that the International League become an "open classification" operation, in the same manner as the Pacific Coast League, was defeated. Open classification would have provided the league with a number of advantages: teams would be able to extend the contracts of their players from four years to five before they could be drafted; draft player purchase prices would rise from $10,000 to $15,000; open classification clubs would be on a par with the Pacific Coast League when it came time for the minor league draft.

Buffalo's opening game of the season was designated to take place on April 17, 1957, a road outing against the Columbus Jets. Havana was slated to open the season at home against Montreal on April 15, two days earlier than the rest of the league due to Holy Week festivities. The other openers on April 17 would see Rochester visiting Richmond and Toronto at Miami. Still to be decided was the date for the northern clubs to hold their home openers. Owner Harold Cooper of Columbus proposed that the date be April 24. Northern clubs were holding out for May 1.

Buffalo and Montreal both submitted bids for the All-Star game to be held in their cities. It seemed likely that the New York Yankees would provide the opposition. Seven Montreal "home games" were scheduled to take place in Quebec City, Quebec, 175 miles from Montreal. Each of the other clubs would visit there once.

Rochester's "save the Red Wings" campaign to purchase the ball club from the St. Louis Cardinals had proven successful. Businessman Morris Silver was elected permanent chairman of the new Rochester Community Baseball Inc. Buffalo's success in 1956 had inspired the Flower City residents to duplicate the Bisons' efforts. The benefits to the city of having a Triple A organization could be easily seen by looking only 90 miles east toward Syracuse.

Agreement with Pompano Beach as the Bisons' spring training site took place in an early evening gathering on December 3 in that city. Pompano Beach was charged with building a new field and clubhouse in time for the early March 1957 reporting of pitchers and catchers. Later, the Buffalo four of Taylor, Stiglmeier, Carnevale and Cavarretta were hosted at dinner by Kansas City owner Arnold Johnson. A's manager Lou Boudreau and other team officials were also present and assured the Herd front office that the Bisons would have first crack at any Kansas City ballplayer that could be deemed helpful to the Buffalo cause.

The Bisons did not participate in the first round of the minor league draft on the advice of KC personnel. The latter were convinced that Rod Graber and Ed Cook from the Cleveland chain would provide the outfield help the Bisons needed. Cleveland farm director Mike McNally reinforced the pledge on these two men and even hinted that Joe Caffie might return. The Cleveland outfield was fully stocked with the addition of the young power hitters from the Junior World Series winning Indianapolis club. The A's also thought highly enough of shortstop Gilberto Valentin to suggest that he could make the Bisons' roster and answer the question at that position. Cavarretta would have the final say after his look-see in spring training.

As the league meetings progressed, the northern clubs' home opening date was decided as May

1. Team rosters would be cut from 21 men to 20, but with the addition of a coach who could also be a player. All hitters would now wear protective helmets when batting. And in good news for all minor league teams, a new rule was proposed making it mandatory for all major league squads to cut down from 40 to 28 players as of the April 16 major league opening day. This would make more than 100 players available to the minor league squads a month earlier than had been the case in the past. This talent would first be available to the Pacific Coast League and the Triple A circuits and then filter down as far as the Class D level.

Of course, implementation of this final plan depended upon agreement by the majors. The big-league clubs were meeting in Chicago the week of December 10, but this amendment had already won the approval of baseball commissioner Ford C. Frick and was thus considered almost a foregone conclusion. It was yet another manner in which the majors, already committed to a $500,000 fund to assist struggling minor league programs, could help the minor teams stay afloat in an increasingly community-owned world.

The minor league gathering ended on December 6, and the Bison front office and manager Cavarretta split up to follow separate paths. President Taylor and vice president Stiglmeier headed north. General manager Carnevale and manager Cavarretta headed south. The latter pair would finalize discussions in Pompano Beach as to spring training housing and meals for the players and team personnel. They would also continue the vital search for front line pitching.

The Buffalo Evening News reported on December 8 that Carnevale and Cavarretta had signed an agreement with Pompano Beach city manager James S. Hughes, calling for the Bisons to spend spring training at the city's Kester Field from March 15 through April 15, 1957. The city council had approved the deal by a vote of three to two. The city promised to spend $25,000 on improvements to the ballpark and its facilities. An additional $31,000 contribution was to be forthcoming from the Chamber of Commerce to assist with training costs.

The two nay votes were cast by councilmembers Albert Smoak and W.W. Cheshire, who object-ed on the grounds that the Buffalo club had five "Negroes" on its roster and their presence would go counter to the city's segregation policies. The African American ballplayers would undoubtedly attract African American spectators, the two men argued, and since the ballpark was situated in a white neighborhood this would certainly bring about "racial integration in the city's parks." In a move to deflect this concern, Lyle Weaver, the manager of the Chamber of Commerce, responded that the black players would be housed separately from the others in an African American section of the city. He suggested, further, that the ballplayers should be regarded simply as "employees" when playing at the field, and thus working in the same manner as domestic help or laborers who were to be found in all sectors of the city. Not persuaded, Smoak added that he considered the $25,000 expenditure "a waste of the taxpayers' money."

On December 13, the St. Louis Cardinals agreed to sell the Rochester Red Wings to Rochester Community Baseball, Inc. for $525,000. The deal included the International League franchise, the stadium, the contracts of 12 players and a working agreement with the Cardinals. Approximate-ly 7200 fans had agreed to purchase more than $330,000 worth of stock in the new communi-ty-owned ball club.

Dan Carnevale concluded his first trade in his new general manager role on December 17, send-ing pitcher Harry Nicholas to Detroit's Charleston club in return for outfielders Bill Stewart and Gil Daley. The deal had been agreed to by Bisons president Taylor and vice president Stiglmeier at the minor leagues convention. It was sealed on this day by Carnevale and Detroit director of personnel, John McHale. With the promise of at least five hurlers from the tie-up with Kansas City, the righthanded Nicholas was considered expendable. His record for the season just concluded had been 5-10, with an ERA of 5.52.

The key man for the Bisons was Stewart. Stewart had managed only .158 in a brief try with Kansas City in 1955 but had batted .296 and .299 at Triple A Ottawa (1954) and Columbus (1955). A broken shoulder suffered while diving for a line drive late in 1955 ended that season prematurely. The past year he and manager Nick Cullop could not get along, and he was traded to Charleston, West Virginia, in the American Association where, after hitting over .320 in his first 10 games, another effort at a diving catch led to a broken wrist. He wound up the season hitting .250. The 28-year-old righthanded batter was a double-digit home run slugger who had amassed a personal high of 32 with Class A Lincoln back in 1952. His swing was meant to see action in Offermann Stadium.

Daley, a 29-year-old portside hitter, had shown speed and a good arm, according to Carnevale, but had struggled at the plate over the past two seasons as he moved up in classification. A .365 hitter in Class A ball prior to two years of military service, he was finding it hard to adapt to Triple A pitching. In 1956 he toiled for three different franchises. He finally did manage a .385 mark in six games for the Columbus Jets at the end of the year.

A new starting time for evening ballgames at Offermann was set in an effort to draw more patrons. Evening games were now to begin at 7:30 p.m. instead of the past year's 8:15. Twilight doubleheaders would still start at 6:30. Sunday games would continue at 2:00. The season opener against Columbus was scheduled to begin at 3:00 to allow for opening-day ceremonies.

The Bisons wanted to emulate the black-ink success of the Columbus Jets' Harold Cooper, who had shown a profit at the gate in each of the last two seasons. His Jets team drew 207,000 in 1955, but in 1956 the Columbus club had drawn less than the Bisons—only 167,000—and still Cooper had managed to pay off the mortgage on the ballpark. The key was the sale of box seats, with the directors of the Columbus team acting as advance ticket sellers on a goal of 1000 boxes sold before the start of the season. Vice president Stiglmeier reported that many Bison box seat holders had renewed for 1957, but the push was on to increase that response by a significant number.

To help in that regard, the Bisons rolled out a pricing schedule that listed a box seat at $100 for the year and $78 for a reserved seat. Fans without that much disposable cash would now be able to buy as many individual game seats as they might want at the beginning of the season. It would also be possible to make the purchase on a time payment plan, general manager Carnevale announced. Ticket offices at the stadium, at 1515 Michigan Avenue, were being held open from 9 to 5 daily, and fans were being encouraged during the month of December to think of tickets and even shares of stock as worthy Christmas presents. Club president Taylor noted that in the days leading up to Christmas, a good number of shares of stock had already been sold for that purpose.

With plans under way for additional stockholders in 1957, directors and community owners of the Buffalo Baseball Club Inc. could look back on a difficult but ultimately successful season with both a sense of relief and a sense of pride. No one, not even John C. Stiglmeier, had anticipated the difficulties the club would face in simply fielding a healthy lineup, much less a winning team, for 1956. Baseball times had changed since Stiglmeier's previous direct involvement with the International League back in the 1940s, and to the detriment of the minor leagues, he would assert.

Still, the drive for community ownership, which had started late in 1955, had been a success. The committed front office leadership of Stiglmeier, Bisgeier and Taylor; manager Cavarretta; coach Lowrey; and the players had met the challenges of fielding a ball club that had fought through injury, lack of adequate reserves and a huge payroll scare to keep International League baseball in Buffalo. The fans, more than 2700 of whom had opened their wallets to purchase stock in the team at the outset, had also come through at the end, rallying with large turnouts for the final home games and sending a clear message to organized baseball: Buffalo would not go the way of the 1953 Springfield Cubs or the 1954 Ottawa A's or 1955's Syracuse Chiefs.

Buffalo was in the International League to stay!

"Play ball!"
Photo courtesy of SUNY Buffalo State Courier-Express Collection

Chapter 9: From Worst to Nearly First—1957 and Beyond

Kansas City A's general manager Parke Caroll had said it first, suggesting back when the clubs were negotiating the working agreement, that combining the "best" of the 1956 Bisons with the "best" of the Columbus Jets roster would result in a "first-division outfit" in 1957. In fact, the two tail-enders from the year before (Buffalo wound up in eighth place, the Jets seventh) nearly pulled off a worst-to-first reversal of fortunes, losing out to the repeat pennant-winning champion Toronto Maple Leafs by one half-game.

Buffalo and Toronto each posted 88 victories. The Leafs' margin of success came as a result of the Canadian city's Sunday curfew laws. One Sunday game in the Canadian city had been postponed as a result of this restriction, and the Leafs were not forced by the league officials to make it up. The Bisons protested to no avail. Toronto owner Jack Kent Cooke's millionaire persuasiveness was as influential in this matter as it had been in his quest for catcher Carl Sawatski the year before. The Bisons had to settle for second.

But this was a different Buffalo ball club than the year before. President Taylor and vice president Stiglmeier were back, of course, still heading up the front office, and now with the help of new general manager Danny Carnevale and a new business manager, Joseph V. McShane, who had replaced Harry Bisgeier. Phil Cavarretta was back, too, and the field manager and his drive to win led the Herd to an 88-68 reversal of fortunes. Luke Easter slammed 40 home runs and led the league in that category for the second year in a row. Luke's achievement made him only the third Bison belter to reach the 40-home run plateau. (International League home run king Ollie Carnegie had terrorized the league with 45 back in 1938; first baseman Billy Kelly had rocked 44 out of the park in 1924.) One of Luke's mighty blasts even cleared the imposing 60-foot-high center-field scoreboard on the evening of June 14. The Columbus Jets' Bob Kusava was the unfortunate victim in an 11-4 Buffalo win. Just to show it wasn't a fluke and he wasn't playing favorites, Luke did it again on August 15, this time picking on Willard Parsons of the Richmond Virginians. Score: Buffalo 9, Richmond 3. Easter also topped the league in RBIs for a second time with 128.

Although Luke's batting average fell off to .279, Joe Caffie was back, and he bumped his up to a league-best .330. Lou Ortiz replaced Peanuts Lowrey as the team's "captain" while Lowrey moved on to become the manager of the New Orleans Pelicans in the Southern Association. Ortiz continued his long-ball contribution with 22 homers and again topped all league second basemen in double plays. Bill Serena suffered through a year-long slump, winding up at .211 and only 11 homers. Pete Castiglione was again the valuable utility man, suiting up in an even 100 contests.

On the mound, only Karl Drews, the previous year's ace, lefty Fred Hahn and the late 1956 signee Steve Nagy survived cuts to the squad that Cavarretta brought north. Drews fashioned an 8-8 record in 1957 with a 3.91 ERA. Hahn went 9-10 and 3.26. Nagy compiled a 10-6 mark and lowered his ERA to 3.71. All of the hurlers benefitted from the club's improved defense. New trainer Joe Carroll, replacing Jimmy Mack, had a hand in keeping arms limber.

A core of the 1956 Jets made a significant contribution to the Bison pitching staff. Ray Herbert, 9-9 the year before as a starter, went 13-8 for Buffalo. Glenn Cox put together a 12-5 record and slammed seven home runs, five of them coming in three consecutive starts on the hill in Offermann Stadium. Mike Kume became Cavarretta's go-to reliever and won six games, dropping only one decision. Walter (Rip) Coleman, a 1956 Yankee, recorded a 7-5 record in the latter half of the season after being sent down by the A's. He spun a club-best ERA of 2.76.

The most valuable pitcher on the staff turned out to be rookie lefthander Walter Craddock. Only 8-9 the season before, mostly spent with Double A Shreveport in the Texas League, Craddock posted an 18-8 won-lost record, hurled 15 complete games and fanned 154 batters in 217 innings. He easily copped International League Rookie of the Year honors.

As for position players, Ray Noble and Joe Astroth gave the Bisons the power, defense and durability behind the plate so lacking in 1956. Noble had shown that he had liked Offermann's short left-field fence as a visitor. He responded with 21 home runs in 1957 when he could call Offermann his home ballpark. Astroth, a highly regarded defensive standout as a 10-year major leaguer, brought out the best in the mound corps. Russ Sullivan in the outfield upped his average to .314 and contributed 13 home runs. Dave Melton made a solid outfield contribution and batted .259. Rod Graber, coming over from the Indians organization, played a secure center field and satisfied Cavarretta's expectations by hitting .277.

The league's MVP replaced Billy DeMars at shortstop. Mike Baxes had struggled at Kansas City in 1956 after a .323 season with the 1955 Pacific Coast League's San Francisco Seals. Sent down to Buffalo, Baxes stabilized the infield by appearing in all 154 games and hitting .303. More than that, the 26-year-old led the league in runs scored with 101, was third on the Bisons in RBIs with 76 and slammed 13 home runs. On August 4 in Offermann, with Havana providing the opposition, Baxes drilled two grand-slam home runs, a double and a single in six trips to the plate, driving home 10 runners and leading the Bisons to a 20-1 drubbing of the Sugar Kings. He was a shoo-in for the league's MVP.

Denied a share of the league crown, Buffalo drove through the postseason playoffs with a vengeance, beating third-place Richmond four games to two in the first round, and polishing off Miami, victors over the Maple Leafs, by a four-to-one margin in the finals. Taking the Governors' Cup won the Herd the right to face the American Association's powerful Denver Bears in the Little World Series, but manager Ralph Houk's sluggers made it no contest. Batting .333 as a team and scoring 47 runs, the Bears overwhelmed the Bisons, coming out the victors by a margin of four games to one.

John Blanchard (.429), Norm Siebern and Marv Throneberry were the hitting stars. Buffalo managed an anemic .227 as a team (Graber hit .368) and counted only 18 tallies, four of them coming on a Lou Ortiz grand slam in a losing cause in the series opener. Glenn Cox pitched the only Buffalo win, a nifty 2-1 victory at Offermann, in game four to prevent a sweep.

As tribute to the Bisons' success, vice president John C. Stiglmeier was chosen The Sporting News' Minor League Executive of the Year for 1957. Buffalo's attendance topped every other minor league club: 386,071. This figure was up almost 200,000 from 1956.

In March 1958, on the strength of the team's 1957 run, treasurer Frank Cannon informed the stockholders at the annual meeting that the ball club was now worth $500,000. The board of directors thereupon voted a 10 cents per share dividend, the only dividend that would ever be paid out.

The club tumbled to seventh position in 1958, the final year of Cavarretta's managerial run. Attendance fell to 286,480. The figure was still more than any other International League entry, but it was nearly 100,000 less than in 1957. The Bisons' front office, Cavarretta and Kansas City all looked for a change in 1959.

And major changes did take place. A new major league relationship was established with the Philadelphia Phillies. A new manager was ushered in. A community hero was released.

Major Kerby Farrell, who had led the Cleveland Indians to a sixth-place finish in 1957, was let go and joined the Philadelphia Phillies organization the following year. In 1958, he had skippered the International League Miami club to seventh place. He now came to Buffalo as part of the new Philadelphia tie-up. It was to pay off in a positive way.

Community hero Luke Easter had gotten off to an atrocious start in 1959 and was replaced at first base by Francisco (Panchón) Herrera, a hot young Philadelphia prospect. On May 14, Easter was given his release! It was perhaps the hardest baseball decision he had ever had to make, said John Stiglmeier.

To salve the fans' dismay at seeing Luke depart, Herrera responded by leading the league in batting average (.329), home runs (37) and RBIs (128), becoming the only Bison to ever win the league's Triple Crown. Easter, to everyone's delight, was signed as a player-coach with Thruway rival Rochester. He would continue to make Buffalo appearances whenever the Red Wings came to town.

The Farrell-led 1959 Bisons won the pennant, performing before a club record 413,263 fans. The attendance was the best in all of minor league ball. The joy was short lived. The club lost to Richmond in the first round of the Governors' Cup playoffs.

In 1960, the club tumbled to fourth place. It was the last Bison team to play at Offermann Stadium, as the ballpark was razed at the close of the season to make way for a new public high school. The final game at Offermann took place on a chill September 17 evening, the Toronto Maple Leafs winning 5-3, and again the Bisons were knocked out of the playoffs in the first round.

The team relocated to War Memorial Stadium at the corner of Jefferson Avenue and Best Street in 1961 and improved to a third-place finish for the season, followed by victory in the Governors' Cup playoffs and then the club's first Little World Series championship since 1906. Rookie center fielder Ted Savage led the league in both hitting (.324) and daring on the base paths and easily took home the MVP award. In the playoffs, Buffalo beat Charleston four games to none in round one and then took Rochester by a four-to-one margin to advance to the Little World Series. The American Association entry, the Louisville Colonels, had no chance. The Bisons swept to the title. Fan turnout for the year was 259,724.

Still under Kerby Farrell's managerial oversight, the team slumped to sixth place in the 1962 standings. Francisco Herrera came back to slam 32 homers and drive in 108 runners, leading the league in the first category and tying in the second. A young Canadian named Ferguson Jenkins took the mound in six games and posted a less than Hall of Fame 1-1 record with a 5.54 ERA, but he would do better in the rest of his career. Attendance continued its slide in 1962, with only 214,134 passing through the turnstiles. Community ownership, it appeared, was losing its appeal.

The Bisons turned to the New York Mets for a new working relationship in 1963, hoping this affiliation might turn around the club's fortunes. With a National League–worst record of 40-120 in 1962, the big-league club had little to offer to their Triple A affiliate. Eighth place was the best the 1963 Bisons could manage in a 10-team circuit, and attendance fell right along with the ball club, plummeting to barely over 136,000. Not even Marvelous Marv Throneberry (16 home runs in 88 games, but only a .176 average) could induce people to come out to the ballpark. Pumpsie Green, the first African American player to take the field with the Boston Red Sox back in 1959, led the Herd in hitting with a .308 mark.

Community ownership lasted until the annual Buffalo Baseball Club, Inc. meeting of November 1963, when club president John Stiglmeier was voted out of office by a new stockholder group.

Kerby Farrell had also been fired at the end of the season. Thus it was that not one of the players, managers, coaches, front office personnel or directors from 1956 now remained with the ball club. These men—and several women, too—had done their job. They had saved baseball in Buffalo for another day. That other day had arrived.

Would later generations look back at this time to recognize this effort and be grateful?

Triple A baseball lasted in Buffalo until 1970. Deteriorated attendance and a deteriorating stadium led to the forfeiture of the franchise on June 4 to the Montreal Expos, at that time the Buffalo club's major league parent. The team was moved to Winnipeg, Manitoba, Canada, leaving the Queen City of the Lakes without a professional baseball team for the first time since 1877.

Professional ball returned to town in 1979 in the form of a relocated Double A Eastern League entry, the Jersey City A's. Ninety Buffalo citizens, led by Mayor Jimmy Griffin and his friend, Don Colpoys, plunked down $1000 apiece to purchase the Jersey City club. John Sikorski, a Broadway Market candy dealer, fronted the money to pay for the franchise and the league and National Association fees. The Bisons signed a working agreement with the Pittsburgh Pirates, Colpoys became general manager, and Steve Demeter, the Bisons' 1955 third baseman, was hired to manage. Most certainly the parties involved had hearkened back to the 1956 experience and the lesson that the community could step up and make baseball work in Buffalo. And all were of the same mind: Buffalo needed baseball, and baseball needed Buffalo.

Save that Buffalo is not a Double A city. Attendance declined so much that the team was once again in jeopardy of being lost until Robert E. Rich, Jr., of the Rich Products Corporation purchased the debt-ridden club in 1983 and turned it into a money maker. Rich soon announced the purchase of the Triple A Wichita franchise in the American Association and relocated that club to Buffalo in 1985. It was renamed the Bisons, of course. In 1991 a new downtown stadium was built, and because it was built the people came. The new Buffalo Bisons set records for minor league attendance for a decade.

In 1998 the Bisons finally returned to the International League, where they belonged, the goal of so many people—big and small—who made the hope of community baseball work way back in 1956.

Chapter 10: What Happened to Our Heroes

What happened to those men who saved baseball for the city of Buffalo in 1956? Here are thumbnail descriptions of the lives of those in the front office and on the field who responded to the call.

THE FRONT OFFICE
Reginald B. Taylor

This patrician polo player and John C. Stiglmeier, the rough-and-tumble blacksmith who shoed the horses, had made an awkward pair from the start, but they persevered in their relationship through the 1956 and 1957 seasons for the good of the team. Once the new community-owned ball club was on its feet and thriving, Taylor departed the scene, turning the presidency over to Stiglmeier in 1958 and eventually leaving the board of directors. He continued to serve in leadership positions with local banks, cultural and social service organizations and social groups (Saturn Club) and was part of the assemblage that eventually brought the National Hockey League Buffalo Sabres to the city. Taylor received an Honorary Doctorate from Norwich University on June 13, 1965. He died at home on August 2, 1984.

John C. Stiglmeier

The veteran of the honorable baseball wars of the 1940s and the stalwart challenger of the changing baseball world of the mid-1950s was named the 1957 Minor League Executive of the Year by The Sporting News. He assumed the presidency of the Buffalo Baseball Club, Inc. in 1958 and continued in that capacity until ousted by a new stockholder group in 1963. During his tenure as Bison president, he was also elected an International League vice president on three occasions. The Buffalo Athletic Club named him one of their "Sportsmen of the Year" in 1959; he was also chosen as the "Outstanding Sportsman 1959-1960" by the Buffalo Jaycees. In 1969, the Bisons' board of directors brought Stiglmeier back to the club as general manager in hopes that he might resuscitate fan interest in the team. Instead, club operations folded in mid-1970 and the team was relocated to Winnipeg, Manitoba, Canada. John C. Stiglmeier became a member of the Buffalo [Bisons] Baseball Hall of Fame. A Fourth Degree Knight of Columbus and a member of the Blackthorn Club of Buffalo, he remained active well into his 80s, dying on February 11, 1980.

Harry Bisgeier

Harry Bisgeier made a significant personal financial sacrifice in 1956 to keep the Bisons on the base paths and the fans in the seats to watch them, but he could not continue to serve as the team's business manager for 1957. Bisgeier needed to make a living. His association with the club continued in an associate vice-presidential capacity and as a member of the board of directors for a number of years. The Bisons held a Harry Bisgeier Night in 1957, following which Bisgeier asked that the receipts from the turnout of 6901 be used for baseball scholarships for ballplayers from the University of Buffalo and Canisius College. Owner of a sign-painting business, as well as a wholesale paint store and a retail liquor store, he was appointed the chairman of the Buffalo Urban Renewal Board in 1963 by mayor Chester A. Kowal. Harry Bisgeier died on December 20, 1967.

THE COACHING STAFF

Phil Cavarretta

Phil Cavarretta delivered a major league impact for the 1956 season despite a last-place finish from his undermanned but determined crew of major league and Triple A veterans, plus a few who were still searching for the ladder of success. Cavarretta was a man who wanted to win and a manager for whom men wanted to win. The 1956 season would be his last to swing the bat and take the field. He returned to manage the Bisons to a second-place finish in 1957 and an unsuccessful trip to the Junior World Series. His 1958 squad plummeted to seventh place, and his contract was not renewed. Post-Bison employment saw him take on major league coaching responsibilities for the Detroit Tigers from 1961 through 1963, later serving in a scouting capacity. He also piloted minor clubs in the Eastern, California and Southern Leagues in 1960 and again from 1965 through 1972. In 1973 he became the New York Mets' full-time hitting instructor for minor league personnel. He finished with the big club in 1978. A four-time National League All-Star, National League batting champion and MVP in 1945, a 22-year major league veteran with a final average of .293 and a life-long Cub fan in retirement, Philip Cavarretta died on December 18, 2010.

Harry (Peanuts) Lowrey

Peanuts Lowrey had been slated to return as manager Cavarretta's player-coach in 1957 but instead assumed the manager-player role for the 1957 New Orleans Pelicans in the Double A Southern Association. As a manager, Lowrey saw his squad go 60-94, a .390 winning percentage. Lowrey himself hit .361. He managed in the Texas and Pioneer Leagues in 1958 and 1960, respectively, finishing up with a three-year managerial winning percentage of .499. His last season swinging a bat came as a player-coach with the 1959 Triple A Seattle Rainiers (.177). Lowrey began a 17-year major league coaching career in 1960 with the Philadelphia Phillies, San Francisco Giants, Montreal Expos, California Angels and Chicago Cubs, retiring in 1981. Harry Lee (Peanuts) Lowrey, a U.S. Army veteran, died on July 2, 1986.

Jimmy Mack

Jimmy Mack's contract was not renewed for 1957.

THE BALLPLAYERS

John Blatnik

John Blatnik retired from professional baseball at age 35 after 22 games with the 1956 Bisons. His average at the time was .306. He had accepted the offer to become the deputy director of the Bureau of Workers Compensation of the State of Ohio. Blatnik continued an active role in sports, refereeing high school, college and semipro baseball and football games. An active supporter of youth, he was also a cofounder of the Colt and PONY league baseball operations in the Ohio Valley and served a number of times as tournament director for the eastern half of the United States, Canada and Cuba. In 1998, John Blatnik was named the Ohio Baseball Hall of Fame's Man of the Year as he was inducted into that organization. John Louis Blatnik, a U.S. Army veteran, died on January 21, 2004.

Roger Bowman

Roger Bowman's sale to the Minneapolis Millers in the last part of the 1956 season helped the Bisons' bottom line and helped the Millers gain a fourth-place postseason playoff slot. They lost to the Indianapolis Indians in the first round. Bowman lost game two of the playoffs, 4-0, surrendering a two-run home run to Roger Maris. Bowman continued pitching from 1957 through 1961, hurling for the Louisville Colonels (American Association) and the Sacramento Solons, Portland Beavers and Hawaiian Islanders of the Pacific Coast League. Off-season and post career, Bowman owned the Roger Bowman Custom Upholstery in Los Angeles until his retirement in 1997 after 45 years in business. Bowman earned a bachelor's degree from Colgate and later an education degree from UCLA. He was a private pilot and gave aviation lessons and was the past president of both the Westwood Exchange Club and AirSpacers, both of Los Angeles. Roger Bowman, a U.S. Navy veteran, died on July 21, 1997.

Joe Brovia

Joe Brovia finished out 1956 with the Class C San Jose, California, JoSox, hitting .361 with 22 home runs and 90 RBIs in 72 games. He played briefly with Vera Cruz in the Mexican League in 1957 before retiring. Post-baseball activities saw him coaching in the Santa Cruz, California, Little League and working at a number of different jobs in that city. Health problems led to four back surgeries in the 1970s and eventual replacement of both hips. Later he suffered from cancer. Joseph John Brovia died on August 15, 1994. He was inducted into the Pacific Coast League Hall of Fame in 2004.

George Bullard

Unable to produce the .275 average Cavarretta wanted from him as the starting center fielder for the Buffalo Bisons, George Bullard suited up for the Double A Austin Senators in 1957, hitting .268. Again, injuries plagued his production. His final year in professional baseball found him with Class A Topeka in the Western League in 1958, where he batted .280. Post baseball, Bullard returned to Buffalo and secured a civil service position as a housing project maintenance engineer. In retirement, Bullard returned to his home state of Massachusetts and was an avid golfer. George Bullard died on December 23, 2002.

Joe Caffie

Joe Caffie hit .342 in 12 games for the Cleveland Indians at the end of the 1956 campaign. In 1957, despite his speed and a good showing in spring training, Caffie was unable to compete with the power displays of Indian outfielders Roger Maris and Rocky Colavito. He returned to the Bisons for 108 games, led the International League in hitting (.330) and made the All-Star Team. He was called up to the Tribe in early August and managed .270 in 32 contests. In 1958 he was back with the Bisons once more, this time for the full year. He batted .295 and led the team in hits. He tied with Luke Easter for most runs scored in the club. Caffie continued at the Triple A level in 1959 (Buffalo/St. Paul Saints) and 1960 (Montreal/Miami), but his hitting declined. His final season was 1961, when he appeared in 43 games with the Class A Charlotte Hornets (.226) and 31 games with Class B Wilson of the Carolina League (.267). Joe Caffie returned to his hometown of Warren, Ohio, and spent the next 37 years as a laborer for the Thomas Steel Company before retiring. He is a member of the Buffalo [Bisons] Baseball Hall of Fame.

Pete Castiglione

Pete Castiglione took another turn as the Herd's go-to utility man in 1957, batting .255 in an even 100 appearances. The 1958 campaign was his last year in baseball; he played 19 games for Buffalo, 53 games for Double A Little Rock and 12 games for Class A Binghamton of the Eastern League. Moving to Pompano Beach, Florida, Castiglione worked as a letter carrier for the U.S. Postal Service while keeping active in sports. He coached high school and American Legion baseball clubs, refereed and umpired sports contests, scouted for the Pittsburgh Pirates, wrote a column for the Pompano Town News and won a number of local tennis tournaments. Peter Paul Castiglione was a U.S. Navy veteran who died on April 10, 2010.

Jim Clark

Jim Clark, born James Petrosky, saw service with San Antonio and Fort Worth of the Texas League in 1956, as well as his stint of 10 games with the Bisons. He stayed at the Triple A level in 1957, getting into 19 games with Montreal and five with St. Paul of the American Association. His last professional appearance came in 1960, when he got into six contests with Class C Bakersfield in the California League. Clark owned and operated an apartment building in Santa Monica, California, following his baseball career. He died on October 24, 1990.

Joe Coleman

Joseph Patrick Coleman retired from the professional baseball player ranks following the 1956 season but then served as a batting practice pitcher for the Boston Red Sox. He operated a chain of sporting goods stores in the Boston area before relocating to Fort Myers, Florida. His son, Joseph Howard Coleman, pitched for 15 years in the major leagues, winning 142 games against 135 losses. Twice a 20-game winner with the Detroit Tigers, son Joseph Howard was named to the 1972 American League All-Star Team. He has since served baseball as a minor league manager and minor league and major league pitching coach. Joseph Howard's son, Joseph Casey Coleman, grandson of Joseph Patrick, reached the major leagues in 2010 with the Chicago Cubs. He has pitched in parts of four major league seasons. Joseph Patrick Coleman, a U.S. Navy veteran, died on April 9, 1997.

Billy DeMars

Billy DeMars was sold by the Bisons to the Pacific Coast League Portland Beavers in February 1957. He played the 1957 campaign for Portland, hitting .242. In 1958 he suited up for Portland and the Vancouver Mounties of the Pacific Coast League before taking over managing the Class C Aberdeen Pheasants of the Northern League in late May. He managed in the Baltimore Orioles minor league system for 11 years, winning the Midwest League with the Appleton Foxes in 1964. From 1969 through 1981, DeMars was a coach for the major league Philadelphia Phillies, moving as a coach to the Montreal Expos from 1982 to 1984 and to the Cincinnati Reds from 1985 to 1987. DeMars was a highly regarded hitting instructor and served the Phillies minor league system in that capacity in the 1990s. William Lester DeMars served honorably in the U.S. Navy.

Larry Donovan

According to The Sporting News of February 27, 1957, Larry Donovan and his 11-10 record at Buffalo were being counted on to help the Detroit pitching staff for the upcoming season. He was named to the major league roster in spring training. Instead, a sore arm led to his option to Toronto in the International League. Donovan suffered through a losing season with four teams in 1957—being sent from Toronto (1-3) to Charleston in the American Association (1-3) and on to Double A Binghamton (1-1) before being placed on the disabled list in late July. He returned at the end of the year to pitch for Augusta in Class A (1-1). A losing record at Binghamton (0-1) and no decisions with the Eastern League Lancaster Red Roses (0-0) marked Donovan's last stop in professional baseball in 1958. He returned to his hometown in Ionia, Michigan, where he worked a number of jobs while studying part-time at Western Michigan University. Upon earning his bachelor's and master's degrees, he assumed a managerial role for the Michigan Department of Corrections until retirement. Hobbies included an interest in gold, poker, hunting and fishing, following the Tigers and time spent with his family and his dogs. Lawrence William Donovan died April 3, 2016.

Karl Drews

Karl Drews, the mainstay of the 1956 mound crew, returned to Buffalo in 1957 and fashioned an 8-8 record with a 3.91 ERA. Buffalo released him after six games in 1958 (0-0), after which he caught on briefly with Double A Nashville (0-1) and then American Association Indianapolis (1-1). He was released by both Indianapolis and the Miami Marlins at the start of 1959, but moved on to the Mexico City Reds, for whom he compiled a 16-8 record. He pitched again for the Reds in 1960, winning 10 and losing eight. Karl August Drews was a sales representative for a sporting goods company when he was hit and killed by a drunk driver in Dania Beach, Florida, on August 15, 1963.

Luke Easter

Luke Easter, after leading the league in home runs (35) and RBIs (106) in 1956, went on to even greater heights with the second-place 1957 Bisons. Despite a dip in batting average to .279, home run production increased to 40 and RBIs to 128. Luke clobbered that ball at a .307 pace in 1958, adding 38 homers and 109 teammates chased across the plate. Returning for 1959, Luke's limited mobility was a defensive liability to the club, nor was he hitting. In what he described as the most difficult decision he had ever had to make in baseball, Buffalo president John C. Stiglmeier notified Easter of his release from the club on May 14, 1959. Easter was gracious in his acceptance of the realities of baseball. He signed shortly thereafter with the Rochester Red Wings and for the year hit 22 home runs with 76 RBIs. Playing part-time for the Red Wings over the next four seasons, Luke averaged better than .280 at the plate, plus 11 home runs and 50 RBIs per year. He was as popular in Rochester as he had been in Buffalo. Luke hung up his spikes after appearing in 10 games in 1964 but stayed on in Rochester to coach until 1966. He then returned to Cleveland and began work at TRW Inc. in Euclid. As chief steward for the Aircraft Workers Alliance at his place of business, Luke Easter had just cashed paychecks for the company employees on March 29, 1979, when he was accosted by two armed robbers and shot to death. The men were caught and prosecuted for their crime. Myth, legend and superstar are words that have been used to describe Luscious Luke Easter, and all of them are true. He is both a member of the Buffalo [Bisons] Baseball Hall of Fame and a charter member of the Rochester Red Wings Hall of Fame.

Zeb Eaton

Zeb Eaton's professional baseball career ended with his service to the 1956 Buffalo Bisons. Although he had retired from organized baseball in 1952, he stepped back up from Buffalo-area MUNY ball to help the Bisons out in a pinch, and he had given a good account of himself prior to being injured. Following the season, Eaton resumed his employment with the Town of Tonawanda Parks Department. He was a 20-year exempt member of the Elwood Volunteer Fire Department. Zebulon Vance Eaton died on December 17, 1989, in West Palm Beach, Florida.

Bill Froats

Bill Froats never did get the hang of control to pair with his unhittable curve ball. Arm problems limited his 1957 season with the Louisville Colonels of the American Association to three games with no decisions. He pitched and lost one game with Double A Corpus Christi in the Texas League in 1958 (0-1) and retired from baseball. William John Froats died on February 9, 1998.

Fred Hahn

Fred Hahn contributed nine victories to the 1957 Bisons' run to that year's Little World Series against Denver. He was charged with 10 defeats but had the fourth-best ERA on the team (3.26), down more than a run per game from the year before. Arm trouble in 1958 led to his option in May to the Little Rock Travelers (Southern Association), where he won three and lost three. Recalled to Buffalo in July, his record for the Bisons for the year was 8-5 with a sparkling 2.86 ERA. The arm trouble resurfaced in 1959. Hahn lost one game for the Herd and was released in May. Post baseball, he worked in the Public Works Department for the New York State Highway Division. Frederick Aloys Hahn died on August 16, 1984.

Lou Heyman

Lou Heyman finished the 1956 campaign catching for the Little Rock Travelers in the Southern Association, where his bat woes continued (.181 in 59 games, but with seven homers). He hit .231 in a part-time role for Little Rock in 1957 and finished his career with the same club in 1958, batting .215. Louis William Heyman died on December 24, 2000.

Milt Jordan

Milt Jordan ended his baseball career with the 1956 Buffalo Bisons. He was then employed as a miner for the Cayuga Rock Salt Mine in Lansing, New York. A veteran of the U.S. Army Air Corps, Milton Mignot Jordan died on May 13, 1993.

Gus Keriazakos

Gus Keriazakos pitched in tough luck with the 1956 Bisons. On the mound, he lacked run support, after which he was struck down by the ailment that led to his release back to the New York Yankee organization. Later in the year he was sent to the Columbia Gems of the Class A Sally League, where he finished the season with a record of 2-0. This was his final year in organized baseball. He retired as the general manager of sales for the Essex Chemical Corporation of Clifton, New Jersey. Constantine Nicholas Keriazakos died on May 4, 1996.

Ed Mierkowicz

Ed Mierkowicz played 99 games for the 1957 Texas League San Antonio Missions, hitting .262 with 12 home runs. He also saw duty that season with the Mexican League Nuevo Laredo Tecolotes before hanging up his spikes. Post baseball, Mierkowicz worked for the waste treatment plant in his hometown of Wyandotte, Michigan. He became the oldest living member of the 1945 World Series-winning Detroit Tigers. He died on May 19, 2017.

Ed Moeller

Ed Moeller had come out of retirement (he was pitching MUNY ball in the Buffalo area) for a brief whirl with the 1956 Herd. He returned to the squad in 1957 but retired for good after pitching in three games and learning that he was to be sent down to the Little Rock Travelers in the Southern Association. He resumed his lifelong career as a carpenter and house builder with Balling Construction in Buffalo. Following retirement from The Carpenters Union in Buffalo, he relocated to Virginia Beach, Virginia, and took on the role of construction supervisor for the Marquis Construction Company of Portsmouth. A Lifetime Member of the Rescue Volunteer Fire Department Benevolent Association of North Tonawanda, and a Navy veteran, Edgar J. Moeller died on January 6, 2017.

Ron Mrozinski

Torn shoulder tendons ended Ron Mrozinski's 1956 season with Buffalo after a record of 1-1. He pitched for Tulsa in the Texas League in 1957 (11-13) and again in 1958, making the All-Star team (15-13, 3.27 ERA). Twelve games in Buffalo in 1959 resulted in no decisions, but he finished that year with a 12-8 record for Birmingham in the Southern Association and led the league in ERA (1.86). His 1960 record with Birmingham was 10-10. In 1961 he contributed seven wins to the league-champion Chattanooga club of the Southern Association. His final season of professional baseball was 1962, when he split the year with Charlotte (South Atlantic League) and Williamsport (Eastern). His record was 7-7. Post baseball, Mrozinski worked as a production mechanic for the American Can Company in Washington, New Jersey. He loved the times he was in Buffalo, whether as a Bison or as a visiting opponent, because of the city's Polish culture. Ronald Frank Mrozinski died on October 19, 2005.

Steve Nagy

Steve Nagy was picked up by the Bisons toward the end of the 1956 year and recorded a 3-3 record for the basement dwellers. He was back for spring training and the full season in 1957 and rewarded the team with a 10-6 mark to help the club to the Little World Series. Nagy completed his professional baseball career with the 1958 Bisons, pitching to a 1-5 record for a seventh-place club. He became a buyer for a Seattle, Washington, department store. Steven Nagy died on July 24, 2016.

Harry Nicholas

Harry Nicholas concluded his professional baseball career with the 1956 Bisons but went on to acclaim in his role as a private citizen. As a businessman, he retired as a First Citizens Bank (Charlotte, North Carolina) executive and an active community contributor. He became one of the top senior golfers in North Carolina and organized the Senior PGA Tour Event held in Charlotte. In 1980 he was named the Charlotte area "Sportsman of the Year." Wake Forest University inducted him into its Hall of Fame in 1993. Harry Justin Nicholas died on August 15, 2005.

Lou Ortiz

Lou Ortiz had found his power stroke in 1955 and went on to slug his career high in homers (25) for the 1956 Bisons, tying for second place in the league behind Luke Easter. Once again, he led all International League second basemen in fielding percentage. Named the team's captain for 1957—assuming some of the coaching responsibility in the absence of Peanuts Lowrey—Ortiz topped the league again in fielding percentage, plus putouts, assists and, for the fifth time in his Triple A career, double plays. In addition to 22 regular-season homers, he connected for a grand slam in the team's losing Junior World Series effort. Lou's final season was 1959, when his legs started to fail him. A 30-game experiment in left field was tried in order to let a younger man patrol second base, but the results left the club hurting for offense and Ortiz was restored to his infield position at the close of the campaign. It was the final year of his baseball career. With 19 more home runs added to his total in this 1958 season, Ortiz became the Buffalo Bisons' all-time career home run leader at that position (64 of 66 home runs struck while playing second base). Post baseball, Ortiz became the general manager for the San Diego office of the Lindberg (truck) Leasing firm. He was elected to the Rochester Red Wing Hall of Fame in 2007. U.S. Army veteran Louis Peter Ortiz died on October 3, 2010.

Mario Picone

Mario Picone's last appearance in a professional baseball uniform was with the 1956 Buffalo Bisons. He returned home to Brooklyn, New York, where he owned an aluminum siding business. Mario Peter Picone died on October 23, 2013.

Bob Schultz

Bob Schultz finished his professional baseball career in 1956. After his release by the Bisons (0-1), he pitched for both Chattanooga and Nashville in the Double A Southern Association, compiling a 7-7 record with those two clubs. Robert Duffy Schultz was a U.S. Marine Corps veteran. Working as a house painter, he was shot to death at a VFW post in Nashville, Tennessee, on March 31, 1979. His assailant was charged with first-degree murder.

Bill Serena

Bill Serena took advantage of Offermann Stadium's short left-field porch in 1956 to claim fourth place in the International League with 24 home runs. In contrast, the 1957 campaign was a nightmare as the Buffalo third baseman struggled in a slump all year. His batting average plummeted to .211 and his home runs fell off to 11. Serena retired from the game following the 1957 season and took up residence in his home state of California. He stayed connected with baseball as a scout for the Cleveland Indians, Milwaukee Braves, Atlanta Braves, Texas Rangers, Detroit Tigers and Miami Marlins. He was also a teamster for Lucky Stores supermarkets. William Robert Serena died on April 17, 1996.

Norm Sherry

Twenty-five-year old Norm Sherry had had back surgery in December 1955 and had played only nine innings with the Texas League Ft. Worth club before being sent to the Bisons. Three more years followed in Triple A before making his major league debut with the Los Angeles Dodgers in late 1959. Sherry spent three years with the Dodgers (1960-1962) and one year (1963) with the New York Mets, all as a part-time receiver, batting a career .215. He returned to Buffalo in 1964, hitting .232 in 100 games with seven home runs. Sherry became a minor league manager for the Dodgers for three years, served as a scout for the New York Yankees and the California Angels and joined the Angels' coaching staff in 1969. He stayed there until 1971, then managed in the Texas League and the Pacific Coast League before rejoining the Angels in 1976 as a coach under a new manager, Dick Williams. Sherry was promoted to manager of the Angels for the last part of the season when Williams was fired. Sherry was fired himself in 1977 as the Angels fell into fifth place. Sherry signed on to coach the Montreal Expos under Williams from 1978 through 1981 and then followed Williams to the San Diego Padres in 1982 and coached there through 1984. From 1986 through 1991, he was a coach for the San Francisco Giants, following which he managed the Everett Giants in the Northwest League in 1992 and 1993. Larry Sherry, Norm's brother, pitched in the majors from 1958 to 1968, primarily for the Dodgers, winning 53, losing 44 and saving 82 games.

Vic Stryska

Victor J. Stryska's last year in professional baseball was his appearance with the 1956 Buffalo Bisons. He went out a winner with a 1-0 record.

Pat Tomkinson

Troubled by injuries, Pat Tomkinson's 1956 year was his last in baseball. He wished that he had been able to play in Offermann earlier in his career when he was more physically capable. The Buffalo-born catcher went to work for Sears, installing aluminum doors and windows before starting employment in the Coke Ovens at the Bethlehem Steel Plant in Lackawanna, New York. He also co-owned the Quakerfield Horse Stable in Orchard Park, New York, with his wife, and from there supplied horse manure to the steel plant to prevent inground pipes from freezing in the winter. Promoted to foreman at the Buffalo plant, he transferred to the Burns Harbor, Indiana, plant and retired from there as general plant foreman in the Coke Ovens division. Phillip A. (Pat) Tomkinson served honorably in the U.S. Army.

Clyde Vollmer

Clyde Vollmer ended his 1956 season with Little Rock/Montgomery in the Southern Association (the ball club moved during the season). With the Travelers/Rebels he hit .284 and 12 home runs in 59 games. This was Vollmer's last year in professional baseball. Post baseball, he owned the Lark Lounge in Florence, Kentucky, and was a member of the American Legion and a number of social organizations. Clyde Frederick Vollmer, a U.S. Army veteran, died on October 2, 2006.

Jim Walsh

Jim Walsh's last season in professional baseball was with Buffalo in 1956. Post baseball, he worked for a trucking company. James Gerald Walsh died on November 12, 1990.

John Weiss

John Weiss pitched his final season in professional ball in 1957, putting in four games with Birmingham in the Southern Association. His record was 1-1. After hanging up his spikes, Weiss worked as a supervisor with the Los Angeles, California, Probation Department. John Alphonse Walsh died on December 16, 2002.

BUFFALO'S BOYS OF BASEBALL

Whatever happened to the Western New York high schoolers with their dreams of major league success, the athletes we met in the preseason and spring training? Here is a brief rundown on a few of them mentioned in this book.

Werner (Babe) Birrer. Not a high schooler, Babe Birrer was a 25-year-old, first-year major leaguer in spring 1956, having the year before compiled a pitching record of 4-3 with the Detroit Tigers. Following his elevation from the Buffalo Bisons' roster in 1955, his auspicious major league debut came on July 19 and saw him strike a pair of three-run home runs in two at-bats, plus earning a save. He was unable to stick with the Tigers and was claimed off waivers in April 1956 by the Baltimore Orioles. He appeared in four games with Baltimore with no decisions and was sent down to the Double A San Antonio Missions, where he recorded a 13-8 record. Back in Triple A in 1957, he pitched for the Los Angeles and Vancouver clubs in the Pacific Coast League. A 12-5 record with Montreal saw him again elevated in midseason 1958 to the Los Angeles Dodgers. He appeared in 16 games but again had no decisions. He spent 1959 and part of 1960 back with Montreal before rejoining the Buffalo Bisons in late 1960. He and Wally Seward were the Bisons' winningest pitchers (11 victories) in 1961, the season that saw the Bisons win the Junior World Series. Birrer finished his career with the Bisons, retiring after the 1966 season.

In 18 seasons of professional play, Birrer won 143 games and lost 148. He had a lifetime batting average of .223. Following baseball, he earned a degree in education from the State University of New York at Buffalo and a master's degree from Niagara University. He then taught for more than 20 years in the Buffalo school system and later was a member of the Williamsville Board of Education. He was a founding member of the North Forest Civic Association and was active as a coach for high school and youth sports, including baseball, football, basketball and cross country. He also directed summer baseball camps. A standout athlete at Kensington High School, a member of the Army 101st Airborne Division during the Korean War and a member of the North Carolina National Guard, as well as a 1995 inductee into the Buffalo [Bisons] Baseball Hall of Fame, Werner Joseph

(Babe) Birrer died November 19, 2013.

Art Buczkowski. He had played in 1955 with Bristol in the Appalachian League and Lakeland in the Florida League, both Class D. His final year in professional baseball was 1956, also a split season with Erie and Bradford in the Class D PONY League.

Allen Chester. He had started pitching for Tampa in the Class B Florida International League in 1953, working his way up to a fine 16-10 record in 1955 in a season divided between Class C and Class A. His final year in professional baseball was 1956, when he logged an 8-8 record in another season split between Class C and Class B.

Alan Dwyer. A 20-year-old rookie with Jamestown in the Class D PONY League in 1955, where he put together an 8-8 record, he went on to play for Idaho Falls and Terre Haute in 1956, managing a 9-10 record with these two Class C and B clubs. He pitched two more years of professional baseball, fluctuating between Class D and Class A. He compiled an overall record of 31-38 in his four seasons of play.

Al Henningham. A baseball and basketball star at Tonawanda High School and a member of the school's Wall of Fame, he played two years at Erie Community College, pitched a two-hitter against a strong Simon Pures team and signed a professional contract with the Detroit Tigers, going 4-9 for Jamestown in the Class D PONY League in 1955. He played two more seasons, going 5-10 for Jamestown in 1956 and 2-2 for Erie (Class D) in 1957. He was the player-coach of the Eldridge Club AAA MUNY League Baseball Team that won championships from 1972 to 1975, also winning the National Amateur Baseball Federation Championship in 1974. Additionally, he was a high school basketball referee and a lifelong member and past treasurer of the Eldridge Bicycle Club. He was inducted into the Western New York Baseball Hall of Fame in 1998. Al Henningham died on November 28, 2011.

Nick Koleff. Buffalo's Cy Williams had signed Koleff to a Detroit Tigers contract after a starring career at Lackawanna High School and a brief period with the MUNY League Kicks team. He had won 15 and lost 11 in 1954 and had managed a 15-14 record in 1955, making the jump to Class B Durham at the end of the season, where he had gone 1-2. He struggled to a 4-8 record in 1956, pitching for Durham, Class C Idaho Falls in the Pioneer League and back to Class B with Terre Haute in the Three-I League. His last year in professional baseball was in 1957 with Durham, going 3-1.

Dan Lewandowski. He made his major league debut with the St. Louis Cardinals on September 22, 1951, pitching in two games with a 0-1 record. A standout in the lower minors, notching a 24-6 record at Allentown, Pennsylvania, in 1951, he later kept his hand in the game by playing semipro ball in Galt, Ontario. Dan Lewandowski died July 19, 1996, in Hamilton, Ontario, Canada.

Jimmy Ludka. He played a total of seven minor league seasons, starting at age 18 with Amsterdam in the Canadian-American League. An infielder, he managed a .224 average in 1956 with Eastern League Binghamton. His final year in professional baseball was 1957, split between Nashville and New Orleans in the Double A Southern Association. He hit .257.

James Lumadue. He finished up his three-year professional baseball career in 1956, playing 119 games for Jamestown in the PONY League (Class D) and Idaho Falls in the Pioneer League (Class C), hitting .278. He was named to the Riverside High School Hall of Fame and set a then-record of 60 points scored in Harvard Cup competition during his high-school years. He was a member of the Simon Pures MUNY League team that won 15 league titles. A .340 lifetime MUNY hitter, he was chosen as Player of the Year in 1960. He was an assistant coach at Canisius College and a member of the Western New York Baseball Hall of Fame. James Lumadue died on September 21, 2016.

Don McAndrews. He finished his professional baseball career in 1956, getting into 12 games with the Eastern League (Class A) Syracuse Chiefs. He was a member of the Matthew Glab Post, past president and cofounder of the Southtowns Club High School Hockey League, and a veteran of the Korean Conflict. Daniel William Lewandowski died on October 18, 2000.

Hank Nasternak. After a seven-year professional baseball career from which he had already retired, he was unable to make a comeback with the 1956 Bisons, but he did keep active in sports, overseeing baseball, basketball and bowling teams for his local Catholic Youth Organization. He retired in 1988 as a salesman for Universal McKinley Liquors in Buffalo. A Marine who saw service on Okinawa during World War II, Hank Nasternak died on January 31, 2012.

Herb Neibergall. Once a player for the Washington Market Team in MUNY baseball, he coached and managed the Cheektowaga Travelers for 48 years. The Travelers were the winningest team in Cheektowaga Classic history. The Town of Cheektowaga named the town park after him, calling it the Herb Neibergall Memorial Park, installing a plaque at the park entrance. He was also a scout for the Cleveland Indians, Los Angeles Dodgers and Philadelphia Phillies.

Tom Van Remmen. He won 6 and lost 8 in 1956, hurling for three ball clubs (Class B Terre Haute, Class A Augusta and Class A Syracuse). In his final year, 1957, Van Remmen won 5 and lost 6, pitching for Class A Augusta and Class AA Birmingham. His overall record for four years of professional baseball was 38-28. He went on to pitch 12 years of MUNY baseball, throwing a no-hitter in league play and a perfect game in an exhibition. He was both an insurance agent and an assembly line worker for General Motors. He coached in Little League, in AAABA, and as an assistant to his son Kevin on the 1993 St. Francis High School team that won the Georgetown Cup. He was inducted into the Bishop Timon Hall of Fame in 1987 and as an inaugural class member of the Western New York Baseball Hall of Fame in 1997. Thomas E. Van Remmen died on February 24, 2014.

Bobby Williams. All-Catholic at shortstop at Timon/St. Jude in 1954 and All-Catholic as a pitcher at St. Francis in 1955, he played two years of professional baseball (1956-1957) in the Georgia State, Georgia-Florida and Alabama-Florida Leagues, winning 10 games and losing 10. He then played 14 years of MUNY baseball in Buffalo. A 33-year member of the Buffalo police force, he received the VFW Medal of Honor Award for Bravery in 1978. He coordinated all activities of the Police Athletic League from 1978 until his retirement in 2001. The two diamonds in Cazenovia Park are named for him and his father, Cy Williams. Cy Williams was a super scout for the Detroit Tigers for 29 years, plus an additional 13 years as a member of the Major League Scouting Bureau. Both Bobby Williams and his father, Cy, are members of the Western New York Baseball Hall of Fame. Robert J. Williams died on June 27, 2012. Edwin (Cy) Williams died on May 8, 2006.

Phil Cavarretta, manager and player

Harry "Peanuts" Lowrey,
coach and player

Image of Phil Cavarretta courtesy of Bruce Barber; image of Harry Lowrey courtesy of 1956 Buffalo Bisons Scorebook

Karl Drews, pitcher

Fred Hahn, pitcher

Gus Keriazakos, pitcher

Images of Karl Drews and Gus Keriazakos courtesy of SUNY Buffalo State Courier-Express Collection; image of Fred Hahn courtesy of 1956 Buffalo Bisons Scorebook

Follwing page: Both images courtesy of SUNY Buffalo State Courier-Express Collection

Harry Nicholas, Karl Drews, Roger Bowman, pitchers

John Weiss, pitcher

Don McAndrews, catcher

Pat Tomkinson, catcher

Image of Don McAndrews courtesy of SUNY Buffalo State Courier-Express Collection; image of Pat Tomkinson courtesy of 1956 Buffalo Bisons Scorebook

Luke Easter, first base

Joe Caffie, outfield (left); Luke Easter (Luke Easter and Joe Caffie Night, August 24, 1956)

Billy DeMars, shortstop (left);
Lou Ortiz, second base

Images of Luke Easter and Billy DeMars and Lou Ortiz courtesy of 1956 Buffalo Bisons Scorebook; image of Joe Caffie and Luke Easter courtesy of SUNY Buffalo State Courier-Express Collection

Lou Ortiz, Luke Easter, Ed Mierkowicz, outfield

George Bullard, outfield

Image of Lou Ortiz, Luke Easter, and Ed Mierkowicz courtesy of SUNY Buffalo State Courier-Express Collection; image of George Bullard courtesy of 1956 Buffalo Bisons Scorebook

John Blatnik, outfield

Joe Brovia, outfield

Both images courtesy of 1956 Buffalo Bisons Scorebook

Clyde Vollmer, outfield

Pete Castiglione, utility

Both images courtesy of 1956 Buffalo Bisons Scorebook

Appendix A: Final Bison Averages—1956 Season

A word about statistics. "The things that you're liable to read in the box score it ain't necessarily so." In my reading through the Buffalo Evening News and Buffalo Courier-Express newspaper accounts of the 1956 Buffalo Bisons season, I discovered that the game reports and the written records in the box scores did not always jibe with one another. There were, at times, inconsistencies between the reporters' descriptions when they were reporting on the same games. There were also times of inconsistency between their written accounts and what the box scores of the games revealed. I tried to check these inconsistencies against one another and went primarily to The Sporting News in an effort to reconcile differences. I also accessed other newspapers online or asked for help from SABR (Society for American Baseball Research) contacts to clarify the game accounts. My efforts weren't always successful.

As an example of the difficulties I had finding statistics in the newspapers, the reporting of stolen bases in a game was inconsistent or nonexistent. Sometimes they were there; sometimes they were not. I had a particularly difficult time confirming doubles that may or may not have been struck. At times, I recorded a double in my game box score when it had been mentioned in the newspaper game report but not in the newspaper box score. On one occasion, one newspaper's box score reported no doubles for the game in question. The other newspaper noted six for that contest! I came to another box score and said to myself, "Where's the center fielder in this lineup? There are only eight men listed here. The box score figure for total at-bats by the team shows four extra at-bats than those listed for the men above. Where's Joe Caffie?" I found him in the other newspaper's account and again in The Sporting News, just to be sure. There were similar struggles for triples and pitcher statistics. Sometimes no strikeouts or walks were listed for a game. Was that true, or had the numbers just been omitted or overlooked? Or was there not enough space in the newspaper column to include this information when it came time to set the type?

As a final case in point, in my own research of the box scores I had available to me I could not locate one of the two doubles with which Phil Cavarretta is credited for the year. To make up for that, I found one more double for Pete Castiglione than is listed in his end of season statistics. Cavarretta or Castiglione? Close or confusion? I don't know which is correct. I left the double with Cavarretta. The same goes for an RBI credited to Easter that I thought belonged to Mierkowicz; I left it with Easter.

I have used Baseball-Reference.com statistics in much of the writing of this book. The statistics provided by Baseball-Reference.com are close to but not identical with the end-of-the-year provisional accounts that are to be found in the December 27 and 28, 1956, editions of the Buffalo Courier-Express. Joseph M. Overfield's statistics (The 100 Seasons of Buffalo Baseball) for the 1956 season are almost identical to those found at Baseball-Reference.com. I have used my own research numbers for those ballplayer statistics categories that are missing from the Baseball-Reference.com and Overfield resources. I have credited Joe Caffie with nine home runs and Bill Serena with 134 games played. I used only my own statistics for Ed Mierkowicz, and only for his time spent with the Bisons.

Statistics are important and help to describe the game, but errors in recording details are obviously a part of the game, too.

You can measure hits and stolen bases and innings pitched and earned run average, but it's another thing altogether to try to measure the little things that don't show up in the box score and that win ballgames. It's also hard to measure the heart of a ballplayer or a team. Whatever the final statistics, this team had heart, and plenty of it, and it won the hearts of its fans both then and now.

INTERNATIONAL LEAGUE 1956 SEASON
BUFFALO BISONS INDIVIDUAL BATTING STATISTICS

Player	G	AB	R	H	2B	3B	HR	RBI	SB	AVG
Caffie, Joe	128	482	84	150	16	6	8	46	19	.311
Eaton, Zeb	11	13	2	4	2	0	0	0	0	.308
Easter, Luke	145	483	75	148	20	3	35	106	0	.306
Blatnik, John	22	51	5	15	6	0	0	2	0	.306
Lowrey, Peanuts	117	352	41	97	12	1	4	33	0	.276
Castiglione, Pete	128	445	39	122	20	4	0	33	2	.274
Ortiz, Lou	148	518	89	140	39	1	25	88	3	.270
Cavarretta, Phil	57	69	10	18	2	0	1	10	1	.261
Serena, Bill	134	419	62	106	16	5	24	73	1	.253
Bullard, George	96	322	46	80	12	2	2	17	15	.248
DeMars, Billy	104	320	26	78	9	0	1	22	2	.244
Brovia, Joe	46	122	12	28	7	0	6	28	0	.230
Mierkowicz, Ed*	87	281	33	64	10	1	8	37	3	.228
Sherry, Norm	64	181	14	39	5	0	2	7	0	.215
Tomkinson, Pat	91	229	21	45	8	0	2	13	0	.191
Vollmer, Clyde	14	43	4	7	1	0	1	4	0	.163
Heyman, Lou	36	90	7	14	5	0	4	12	0	.156
Clark, Jim	10	21	3	1	0	0	0	2	0	.048

*Mierkowicz's statistics are only for his games as a Bison (compiled by the author).

All other statistics are from Sports Reference LLC. 1956 Buffalo Bisons. Baseball-Reference.com – Major League Statistics. https://www.baseball-Reference.com/register/team.cgi?id=bc7b27c4.

INTERNATIONAL LEAGUE 1956 SEASON
BUFFALO BISONS INDIVIDUAL PITCHING STATISTICS

INTERNATIONAL LEAGUE 1956 SEASON
BUFFALO BISONS INDIVIDUAL PITCHING STATISTICS

Player	W	L	PCT	ERA	G	IP	H	R-ER	SO	BB	CG	SHO
Stryska, Vic	1	0	1.000	1.50	6	6	5	1-1	2	2	0	0
Donovan, Larry	11	10	.524	3.67	31	174	172	77-71	70	64	12	2
Drews, Karl	13	11	.542	3.84	29	171	186	79-73	88	49	11	3
Eaton, Zeb	0	0	.000	4.05	5	14	10	10-6	8	7	0	0
Coleman, Joe	4	2	.667	4.22	46	79	78	47-37	34	52	0	0
Bowman, Roger	8	12	.400	4.29	23	128	69	69-61	66	57	8	2
Nagy, Steve	3	3	.500	4.37	16	68	74	35-33	18	21	3	0
Weiss, John	3	12	.200	4.37	45	136	156	73-66	58	56	6	0
Hahn, Fred	10	11	.476	4.47	36	163	166	93-81	104	101	6	0
Walsh, Jim	0	1	.000	4.50	2	4	4	2-2	0	1	0	0
Keriazakos, Gus	3	5	.375	4.77	14	66	71	41-35	32	35	4	0
Nicholas, Harry	5	10	.333	5.52	28	119	120	75-73	94	61	5	0
Moeller, Edgar	0	0	.000	6.42	3	7	6	5-5	5	3	0	0
Froats, Bill	2	8	.200	7.02	37	109	133	92-85	93	63	2	1
Mrozinski, Ron	1	1	.500	8.43	3	11	11	10-10	7	7	1	0
Jordan, Milt	0	0	.000	8.52	2	6	9	6-6	0	4	0	0
Schultz, Bob	0	1	.000	16.20	2	2	4	3-3	1	3	0	0
Picone, Mario*	0	0	.000	0.00	5	0	0	0	0	0	0	0

*Did not pitch; was a pinch-runner only.

Statistics are from the author's own compilation from box scores reviewed as well as Sports Reference LLC. 1956 Buffalo Bisons. Baseball-Reference.com – Major League Statistics. https://www.baseball-Reference.com/register/team.cgi?id=bc7b27c4.

Appendix B : Club and City Leaders

BUFFALO BISONS BASEBALL CLUB, INC.
  A stock certificate of incorporation for the Buffalo Bisons Baseball Club, Inc., was filed in Albany, New York, on October 14, 1955.

Incorporators
Harry Bisgeier
J. Eugene McMahon
Thomas W. Ryan
John C. Stiglmeier

Named Incorporator Associates
Frank H. Cannon
Dick Fischer
Edwin F. Jaeckle
John Krysinski
John C. Montante
Wade Stevenson
Reginald B. Taylor
Herbert J. Vogelsang

  A meeting of the major stockholders took place on Monday, October 17, 1955, to select "temporary" officers who would surrender their seats as more shares were sold, increasing the stockholder base to the desired 10,000. These men served without pay.

Temporary Officers, 1955
Reginald B. Taylor, president
John Stiglmeier, first vice president and general manager
Harry Bisgeier, second vice president and business manager
J. Eugene McMahon, secretary and also to provide attorney services for the corporation
Herbert J. Vogelsang, treasurer

Additional Steering Committee Directors
Helen Berny
Roxie Gian
Lewis G. Harriman
Edwin F. Jaeckle, attorney
Edward F. Kelly
J. Eugene McMahon, attorney
John C. Montana
A. T. O'Neill, committee chairman
Reginald B. Taylor

Staff: 1956 Season
Phil Cavarretta, manager/player
Harry (Peanuts) Lowrey, coach/player
Leonard Berman, MD, team physician
Jimmy Mack, trainer

CITY LEADERS

400 Member Citizens Committee
Frank Cannon, co-chair
Ray Nabor, co-chair

Local business leaders who assisted with the team-saving loan in 1955
Peter T. Allen
Edward A. Atwill
Howard W. Clother
Charles R. Diefendorf
Roy W. Doolittle
Leston P. Faneuf
Dick Fischer
Paul E. Fitzpatrick
James Kennedy
Cy King
William I. Marcy
Albert H. Meyer
Robert L. Millonzi
Joe McCarthy
Patrick J. McGroder
Tony Naples
George O'Neill
Ralph F. Peo
P.O. Rial
Dan Roblin
Dexter P. Rumsey
Leonard Simon
Wade Stevenson, "Buffalo's No. 1 fan," chairman, executive committee, Buffalo Chamber of
    Commerce
Charles Turner
C. Taylor Wettlaufer
Walter A. Yates

CITY OFFICE HOLDERS
Steven Pankow, Mayor of Buffalo

King W. Peterson, Acting Mayor of the City of Buffalo
John Kane, secretary to the Mayor

COUNCILMEMBERS

Elmer F. Lux, president of the Council
Thaddeus J. Dulski, majority leader, Walden District
Leeland N. Jones, Jr., president pro tempore, Ellicott District
Anthony R. Lombardo, Republican minority leader, Councilman-at-large
Vincent P. Masterson, South District
Joseph S. Swartz, Masten District
Anthony F. Tauriello, Niagara District
Alfonso V. Bellanca, city assessor
Frank N. Felicetta, police captain
Chester Kowal, city comptroller
Patrick J. McGroder, chairman of the Board of Civic Stadium and Memorial Auditorium
Thomas W. Ryan, former New York State commissioner of Public Safety

Appendix C: Buffalo Fans and Organizations

The names of Buffalonians and Western New York organizations listed in this appendix are mentioned in this book. Please refer to the "Attendees at Specific Events" section for a guide to the chapters in which they appear.

FANS
Abelson, Sam
Allen, Peter T.
Altman, Harry
Atwill, Edward A.

Bailey, Charley
Baker, Roger
Barron, Stan
Becker, Paul
Bellanca, Alfonso V.
Bernicki, Dan
Berny, Helen
Bisgeier, Harry
Black, Kathleen
Black, Margaret
Black, Maurice
Black, Noreen
Black, Patrick
Black, Jr., Patrick
Borowicz, Chester
Bowhers, Vincent C.
Brun, Mr. and Mrs. Vincent
Buffalo Bob Smith (Howdy Doody)

Cannon, Frank H.
Carallo, Sal
Carnevale, Dan
Castine, Maureen
Chapman, Arthur L.
Cierlicki, Frances
Cierlicki, Mary
Clother, Howard W.
Collins, William L.
Colpoys, Don
Conley, Mr. and Mrs. Harold

Cooke, Jack Kent (Toronto Maple Leafs)
Coughlin, Bill
Crimi, Bud
Crotty, Peter J.
Curo, Irene

Davis, Mr. and Mrs. William
Delahunt, Thomas E.
Del Negro, Mr. and Mrs. John
DePoe, Lou
Devine, Robert B.
Diefendorf, Charles R.
Dilger, Franklin (Westbury, Connecticut)
Doerfel, Edward
Doolittle, Roy W.
Doster, Carlton H.
Duch, Henry
Dulski, Thaddeus J.

Ellis, Mike

Faneuf, Leston P.
Faust, Edith (Binghamton, NY; August 21, 1956)
Felicetta, Frank N.
Feusl, George
Fineberg, Michael
Fischer, Dick
Fitzpatrick, Paul E.
Flanders, Richard (Watertown, NY; August 21, 1956)
Flickinger, Jr., Burt P.
Flickinger, S.M.
Flynn, Bernie
Fuerschbach, George H.

Gabbey, Dr. John

Gallagher, Gerry

Ganson, John

Gentile, Harry E.

George, Ed Don

Gerspach, Albert

Gian, Roxie

Gigante, Mike

Glaser, Joe

Glavin, John M.

Gorski, Chester A.

Gregory, Terry

Griffin, Jimmy

Gross, Max

Grysinski, John

Gunnison, Mr. and Mrs. Howard

Hall, Charley

Harriman, Lewis G.

Harrity, Michael (Baltimore, MD; August 21, 1956)

Hausbeck, Al

Heerdt, Allie

Henry, Howard W.

Herman, Mr. and Mrs. Henry

Hochreiter, George H.

Holcomb, William

Holtz, Benedict T.

Hopper, Clarence H.

Horvath, Elizabeth

Howdy Doody (Buffalo Bob Smith)

Hudson, Larry

Hughitt, Mr. and Mrs. Tommy

Hull, Mr. and Mrs. William

Idzik, Dan

Jablonski, John

Jacobs, L.M.

Jaeckle, Edwin F.

Jasper, Richard W.

Jones, Jr., Leeland N.

Kane, John

Kasmier, B.B.

Kean, Dr. Frank

Kelly, Charles

Kelly, Edward F.

Kelly, Kenneth

Kennedy, James

King, Cy

Kiplar, Theresa

Kowal, Chester

Krestic, John

Kritzer, Cy

Krysinski, John

Labelle, Mr. and Mrs. Ed

Lasker, Marge

Latham, Mr. and Mrs. Carl L.

Lee, Mr. and Mrs. Martin

Lee, Nancy (Avon, NY; August 21, 1956)

Lepper, Mr. and Mrs. Barney

Levy, Dr. Dexter F. and son

Lillich, Frank

Logan, Joseph

Lombardo, Anthony R.

Loomis, Mr. and Mrs. Clarence

Luhman, Carl G.

Lux, Elmer F.

Lyons, Hillman

MacLeod, Duncan A.

Marcy, William I.

Martinek, Mike

Masterson, Vincent P.

Maxwell, Clayton G.

Mazer, Bill

McCarthy, Joe

McConnell, Dennis

McConnell, George

McConnell, Terrence

McGroder, Patrick J.

McMahon, J. Eugene

McNamara, Vince

Meyer, Albert H.

Meyers, Barbara

Meys, Eddie
Milch, David
Miles, Marshall Davis
Millonzi, Robert L.
Montana, John C.
Montante, John C.
Munzel, Clara

Nabor, Ray
Naples, Tony
Neibert, Mr. and Mrs. Joe
Nesslin, Florence
Neureiter, Harry

Obernauer, George
O'Connor, Harold
Olson, Andy
O'Neill, A.T.
O'Neill, George E.
O'Shea, Ted

Pack, Stanley A.
Page, Lenny
Pankow, Steven
Parker, George
Peo, Ralph F.
Perry, Fred
Peterson, King W. (August 17, 1956)
Phillips, Harry
Piekarski, Mr. and Mrs. John A. and their three daughters
Porzella, Mr. and Mrs. Frank and son

Quinn, Jimmy

Radice, Joe
Rausch, Mr. and Mrs. Frank
Reiman, Torchy
Rial, P.O.
Rich, Jr., Robert E.
Roblin, Dan
Rumsey, Dexter P.
Ryan, Thomas W.

Saft, Ralph
Sams, Dodie
Sawtelle, Betty
Schillinger, George
Schimmer, Mr. and Mrs. Frank
Schinstock, Joe
Schmitt, Howard
Schriber, Albert
Schrouth, William
Schultz, Dr. and Mrs. Joseph A.
Sexton, Jr., James
Siegel, Roy
Sikorski, John
Simon, Leonard
Smith, Buffalo Bob (Howdy Doody)
Smith, Gloria
Smith, Milford S.
Springer, Joe
Stedler, Bob
Steinhelper, Bob
Steivater, Dorothy
Stevenson, Wade
Stiglmeier John C.
Stiglmeier, Rose
Strzelczyk, Lucy
Sullivan, Jerry and Marge
Swanz, Charley
Swartz, Joseph S.
Switala, Dick, and his son, Dick (July 25, 1956)
Szatkowski, Frank
Szatkowski, Edward
Szatowski, Bill (July 25, 1956)

Tafelski, Dick
Tauriello, Anthony F.
Taylor, Reginald B.
Tomkinson, Wayne
Trimper, George J.
Turner, Charles

Vogelsang, Herbert J.

Warzel, Ed
Wasielewski, Ray
Wettlaufer, C. Taylor
Whiting, Herbert
Wick, Charles J.
Wright, Bill
Williams, Cy

Yates, Walter A.
Young, Charley

LOCAL BALLPLAYERS
Birrer, Werner (Babe), pitcher
Buczkowski, Art, pitcher
Chester, Allen, pitcher
Dabek, Ray, catcher
Dwyer, Al, pitcher (Geneva, NY)
Eaton, Zeb, pitcher/outfielder
Godfrey, Jack, Buffalo Bisons batboy
Henningham, Al, infielder
Koleff, Nick, pitcher
Lewandowski, Dan, pitcher
Lumadue, Jimmy, shortstop
Ludka, Jimmy, shortstop
Moeller, Edgar, pitcher
McAndrews, Don, catcher
Nasternak, Hank, shortstop
Tomkinson, Pat, catcher
Van Remmen, Tommy, pitcher
Williams, Bobby, pitcher/infielder

LOCAL TEAM STAFF
Berman, Leonard, MD, team physician
Mack, Jimmy, trainer

ATTENDEES AT SPECIFIC EVENTS

The Buffalo fan and organization names mentioned below are listed for particular events that took place during the time of team purchase in 1955, events of 1956 and subsequent years. Some names may also appear elsewhere in the text.

BALL CLUB OFFICIALS, SHAREHOLDERS, PRESEASON TICKET BUYERS AND COMMUNITY SUPPORTERS (CHAPTERS 2 THROUGH 5)

Allen, Peter T.

Atwill, Edward A.

Bailey, Charley, radio station WEBR

Baker, Roger, WGRZ, radio broadcaster

Barron, Stan, WKBK, radio station sports director

Bellanca, Alfonso V.

Bernicki, Dan, Erie County Technical Institute, student body president

Berny, Helen

Bisgeier, Harry

Black, Patrick J., purchased shares and tickets for his children—Maurice, 16; Patrick, Jr., 15; Margaret, 12; Noreen, 10; and Kathleen, 8

Buffalo Bob Smith (Howdy Doody)

Borowicz, Chester, Peter Schmitt Co.

Cannon, Frank H.

Carallo, Sal, University of Buffalo, student body president

Carnevale, Dan, Bison player (1938, 1940), manager (1955), general manager (1957)

Castine, Maureen, Rosary Hill, student body president

Chapman, Arthur L., vice president, Radio and Television Division, Sylvania Electric Products Inc.

Cierlicki, Frances

Cierlicki, Mary, Buffalonian who bought shares for herself and her sisters, Frances Cierlicki and Dodie Sams of Rochester

Clother, Howard W.

Cooke, Jack Kent, owner of the International League Toronto Maple Leafs

Coughlin, Bill, Buffalo Courier-Express, sports reporter

DePoe, Lou

Devine, Robert B., purchased for his five godsons

Diefendorf, Charles R.

Dilger, Franklin, of Westbury, CT

Doolittle, Roy W.

Dulski, Thaddeus J.

Ellis, Mike

Faneuf, Leston P.

Felicetta, Frank N.

Fineberg, Michael, 11-year-old stockholder of 80 Traymore Ave.

Fischer, Dick

Flickinger, Jr., Burt P., Buffalo Manager, S.M. Flickinger Co., Inc.

Flickinger, S.M.

Gigante, Mike, Peter Schmitt Co.

Henry, Howard W.

Holcomb, William, Canisius College, student body president

Horvath, Elizabeth

Howdy Doody (Buffalo Bob Smith)

Idzik, Dan, State Teachers College, student body president

Jaeckle, Edwin F.

Jasper, Richard W., S.M. Flickinger Co., Inc

Jones, Jr., Leeland N.

Kane, John

Kelly, Charles, Niagara University, student body president

Kelly, Edward F.

Kennedy, James

King, Cy

Kowal, Chester

Kritzer, Cy, Buffalo Evening News, sports reporter

Krysinski, John, East Side tavern owner

Lombardo, Anthony R.

Luhman, Carl G., president, Cladco Distributors Inc.

Lyons, Hillman, Bisons general manager (1955)

MacLeod, Duncan A.

Marcy, William I.

Martinek, Mike, veteran pro baseball player living in Riverside

Masterson, Vincent P.

Maxwell, Clayton G.

Mazer, Bill, WGRZ, radio broadcaster

McCarthy, Joe

McMahon, J. Eugene

Meyer, Albert H.

Meyers, Barbara, D'Youville College, student body president

Milch, David, 10-year-old stockholder of 44 Hallam Road

Millonzi, Robert L.

Montana, John C.

Montante, John C.

Nabor, Ray

Naples, Tony

Neureiter, Harry, Hasselbeck Cheese Division of Borden Company

O'Neill, A.T., retired chairman of board, Niagara-Mohawk Power Corp.

O'Neill, George E.

O'Shea, Ted, Niagara Frontier Transit bus driver

Pack, Stanley A., Kensington Kiwanis Club

Peo, Ralph F.

Reiman, Torchy

Rial, P.O.

Roblin, Dan

Rumsey, Dexter P.

Ryan, Thomas W.

Saft, Ralph, attorney

Sams, Dodie

Schmitt, Howard, Hasselbeck Cheese Division of Borden Company

Schrouth, William, St. Bonaventure, student body president

Simon, Leonard

Stedler, Bob, Buffalo Evening News, sports reporter

Steinhelper, Bob, Bisons business manager (1955)

Steivater, Dorothy

Stevenson, Wade

Stiglmeier John C.

Strzelczyk, Lucy

Swartz, Joseph S.

Szatkowski, Frank, 80-year-old fan who remembered the Bisons playing in Franklin Park on Buffalo's East Side in the 1890s

Szatkowski, Edward, son of Frank

Tauriello, Anthony F.

Taylor, Reginald B.

Trimper, George J., president, American Power Boat Assn.

Turner, Charles

Vogelsang, Herbert J.

Warzel, Ed, East Side tavern owner

Wettlaufer, C. Taylor

Williams, Cy, Detroit Tigers scout

Yates, Walter A.

Young, Charley, Buffalo Evening News, sports editor

SPRING TRAINING VISITORS (CHAPTER 5)

Collins, William L.

Conley, Mr. and Mrs. Harold

Crimi, Bud

Delahunt, Thomas E.

Del Negro, Mr. and Mrs. John

Fitzpatrick, Paul E.

Gunnison, Mr. and Mrs. Howard

Herman, Mr. and Mrs. Henry

Hughitt, Mr. and Mrs. Tommy

Hull, Mr. and Mrs. William

Latham, Mr. and Mrs. Carl L.

Loomis, Mr. and Mrs. Clarence

Neibert, Mr. and Mrs. Joe

Piekarski, John A. and his three daughters

Schimmer, Mr. and Mrs. Frank

Schultz, Dr. and Mrs. Joseph A.

ATTENDEES AT SEASON OPENING GAME, APRIL 18, 1956, MIAMI, FLORIDA (CHAPTER 6)

Abelson, Sam

Brun, Mr. and Mrs. Vincent

Davis, Mr. and Mrs. William

Duch, Henry

Flynn, Bernie

Gabbey, Dr. John

Gallagher, Gerry

Ganson, John

Gerspach, Albert

Gian, Roxie

Glaser, Joe

Gregory, Terry

Hall, Charley

Kean, Dr. Frank

Labelle, Mr. and Mrs. Ed

Lasker, Marge

Lee, Mr. and Mrs. Martin

Lepper, Mr. and Mrs. Barney

Levy, Dr. Dexter F. and son

Lillich, Frank

Meys, Eddie

Munzel, Clara

Nesslin, Florence

O'Connor, Harold

Olson, Andy

Parker, George

Piekarski, Mr. and Mrs. John and their three daughters

Porzella, Mr. and Mrs. Frank and son

Quinn, Jimmy

Radice, Joe

Sawtelle, Betty

Schillinger, George

Schinstock, Joe

Schutz, Mrs. Joseph A.

Sexton, Jr., James

Siegel, Roy

Smith, Gloria

Springer, Joe

Stiglmeier, Rose

Sullivan, Jerry and Marge

Whiting, Herbert

Wright, Bill

ATTENDEES AT HOME OPENING GAME, MAY 2, 1956, BUFFALO, NEW YORK (CHAPTER 6)

Fuerschbach, George H., 90 years old, at his 68th consecutive home opener

Gentile, Harry E.

Heerdt, Allie, a star on the old Buffalo Germans basketball team

Hochreiter, George H., Greater Buffalo Ad Club, who brought children from the German Roman
Catholic Orphan Home and the Protestant Home for Unprotected Children

Hudson, Larry, 14 years old, Amherst Central Junior High

Kasmier, B.B.

Logan, Joseph

Obernauer, George, secretary of the Buffalo Bowling Association

Phillips, Harry, 87 years old, peanut vendor at the corner of East Ferry Street and Michigan

Rausch, Mr. and Mrs. Frank

Schriber, Albert, 12 years old, Amherst Central Junior High

Swanz, Charley, at his 29th consecutive home opener

Tafelski, Dick

Tomkinson, Wayne, 16 years old, brother of Pat Tomkinson, working behind the scoreboard

ATTENDEES AT SPECIAL EVENTS DURING THE REGULAR SEASON (CHAPTER 6)

Citizens Appreciation Night honoring John C. Stiglmeier

Harry Altman, Towne Casino

Peter J. Crotty, Erie County Democratic Committee

Irene Curo

Ed Don George

Chester A. Gorski

John M. Glavin, Marine Trust

Max Gross

John Grysinski, East Side

Lewis G. Harriman, M&T Trust

Benedict T. Holtz, Cheektowaga Supervisor

L.M. Jacobs

Kenneth Kelly, Hotel Lafayette, president of Buffalo Hotel Association

Theresa Kiplar

Dennis McConnell

George McConnell

Terrence McConnell

Patrick J. McGroder, chair
Steven Pankow, mayor
Charles J. Wick, Niagara Hudson
Luke Easter and Joe Caffie Night
Marshall Davis Miles, chair
Lenny Page
Fred Perry
Polish-American Night honoring Ed Mierkowicz
Ray Wasielewski, chair
George Feusl's Band
Polish-American Club orchestra
R & W Supermarkets (bought out Offermann Stadium seating for June 25)
Al Hausbeck, chair
Sloan Night honoring John C. Stiglmeier
John Jablonski, mayor
John A. Piekarski, police chief
West Seneca Night honoring Lou Ortiz
Vincent C. Bowhers
Edward Doerfel, president, West Seneca JCCs
Carlton H. Doster
Clarence H. Hopper, Town Board Councilman
Milford S. Smith

Organizations and Fan Groups Attending During the Regular Season (Chapter 6)
Adam Plewacki Post band of the American Legion
American Power Boat Association
Amherst Central High School Band
John Krestic, band leader
Amherst Central Junior High School
Amherst Kiwanis Club

Boy Scouts of America
Buffalo Bowling Association
Buffalo Business magazine
Paul Becker
Buffalo, City of
Buffalo, Common Council
Buffalo Courier Express
Buffalo Evening News
Buffalo Hotel Association
Buffalo State Teachers College

Canisius College

Catholic Guild for the Blind
Vince McNamara, Buffalo city recreation director, provided a vivid play-by-play description
Cheektowaga Volunteer Fireman Corps
Civil Service Employees, Inc.
Cladco Distributors

Depew group
D'Youville College

Eagle and Man trumpet duo
East Lovejoy section of Buffalo
Eden 400
Elks lodges
Erie County Democratic Committee
Erie County Technical Institute

George Feusl's Band
German Roman Catholic Orphan Home
Greater Buffalo Ad Club

Hasselbeck Cheese Division of Borden Co.
Hotel Lafayette

Kensington Kiwanis Club

Lake View group
Lancaster Moose drum corps
Lincoln Park Village Club, Town Tonawanda
Little Leaguers from Tonawanda

M&T Trust
Marine Trust
Masonic Night
Military Police unit
The Moonglows

Niagara Mohawk Power Corp.
Niagara Hudson
Niagara University

Ontario Midget League champions, St. Catharines, Ontario

Peter Schmitt Co.

BIBLIOGRAPHY & RESOURCES

BOOKS

Bak, Richard. Cobb Would Have Caught It: The Golden Age of Baseball in Detroit. Detroit: University Press, 1991. (online)

Benson, Michael. Ballparks of North America. Jefferson, NC: McFarland & Co., Publishers, 1989.

Hubbell, Ralph. Come Walk with Me. Englewood Cliffs, NJ: Prentice-Hall, 1975.

Hubbell, Ralph. Three Strikes and You're In. Kenmore, NY: Partners Press, 1988.

Kritzer, Cy. Luck of the Game. Buffalo, NY: Artcraft Printers, 1973.

Lowry, Philip J. Green Cathedrals. New York, NY: Walker & Company (SABR Special Edition), 2006.

Marazzi, Rich and Len Fiorito. Baseball Players of the 1950s: A Biographical Dictionary of All 1,560 Major League Players. Jefferson, NC: McFarland & Co., Publishers, 2004. (online)

Overfield, Joseph M. The 100 Seasons of Buffalo Baseball. Kenmore, NY: Partners Press, 1985.

Ritter, Lawrence S. Lost Ballparks: A Celebration of Baseball's Legendary Fields. New York, NY: Viking Studio Books, 1992.

Snelling, Dennis. A Glimpse of Fame. Jefferson, NC: McFarland & Co., Publishers, 1993.

WBFO News of the Year: Buffalo's 150 Years of History. Buffalo, NY: University Press, 1982.

MAGAZINES

Buffalo Fan Magazine, May/June 1975, Vol. 1, No. 3.

Business First of Buffalo, July 10, 2000, Vol. 16, Issue 42.

NEWSPAPERS

Buffalo Evening News (The Buffalo News since 1982), 1955 to 1998

Charlotte Observer (online)

Courier-Express, 1955 to 1982

Democrat & Chronicle, Rochester, NY, 1956

The Detroit News, February 17, 2015. "Tigers 1945 World Series: One Play, One Ring." by Tom Gage (online)

Ithaca Journal (online)

Pompano Beach Sun-Sentinel (online)

The Sporting News (online)

Tennessean (online)

WEBSITES

Baseball Almanac (www.baseball-almanac.com)

Baseball Happenings (www.baseballhappenings.net/)

Baseball Library (www.baseballlibrary.com)

Baseball Reference (www.baseball-reference.com)

Bill Lee—The Baseball Undertaker (www.baseballundertaker.com)

The Deadball Era (http://thedeadballera.com)

Express Times Obituaries (www.legacy.com/obituaries/etpa/browse)

Find a Grave (www.findagrave.com)

Gary Bedingfield's Baseball in Wartime (http://baseballinwartime.com/player_biographies/player_biographies.htm)
Historic Baseball (http://historicbaseball.com)
The Oakland Oaks of the 1950's (http://oaklandoaks.tripod.com)

SOCIETY FOR AMERICAN BASEBALL RESEARCH (SABR) BIOPROJECT ARTICLES
(http://sabr.org/bioproject)
Johnny Blatnik by John Wickline
Joe Brovia by Jim Sargent
Phil Cavarretta by Ron Jackson
Karl Drews by Peter Mancuso
Luke Easter by Justin Murphy
Norm Sherry by David E. Skelton
Clyde Vollmer by Nelson "Chip" Greene

GUIDES/NEWSLETTERS
The Buffalo Bisons Baseball Club Inc. Roster, 1956 Home and Training Schedule
Buffalo Bisons Baseball Club, Inc. Stockholder Letter, November 3, 1961
Buffalo Bisons Official Spring Training Roster and Schedule, 1957
Buffalo Bisons Sketch Book for Press, Radio, TV, 1958, 1959 and 1960
Pacific Coast League Potpourri, Richard Beverage, ed., June 1996, Vol.9, No. 6
The Phillies 1981 Media Guide (online)
Wake Forest Hall of Fame (online)

PERSONAL CORRESPONDENCE*
Ruben Amaro, June 7, 2002 (written correspondence)
Babe Birrer, June 2002 (written correspondence)
John Blatnik, June 7, 2002 (written correspondence)
Bob Borkowski, November 29, 2002 (written correspondence)
Danny Carnevale, June 20, 2002 (personal interview)
Pete Castiglione, May 28, 2002 (written correspondence)
George Dadderio, May 5, 2002 (personal interview)
Billy DeMars, June 27, 2002 (written correspondence)
Carolyn Donovan (wife of **Larry Donovan**), April 2016 (written correspondence)
Don Erickson, May 31, 2002 (written correspondence)
Bernadette Graff (wife of Milt Graff), June 2002 (written correspondence)
Dallas Green, June 2002 (written correspondence)
Ray Herbert, June 2002 (written correspondence)
Ken Johnson, June 2002 (written correspondence)
Lou Kretlow, August 2002 (written correspondence)
Don Landrum, July 12, 2002 (written correspondence)
Joe Lonnett, July 2002 (written correspondence)
Dave Melton, February 6, 2002 (written correspondence)

Bob Miller, August 10, 2002 (written correspondence)

Edgar Moeller, June 16, 2016 (personal interview)

Bobby Morgan, July 6, 2002 (written correspondence)

Ron Mrozinski, July 2, 2002 (written correspondence)

Steve Nagy, July 6, 2002 (written correspondence)

Cal Neeman, August 24, 2002 (written correspondence)

Al Neiger, July 2002 (written correspondence)

Frank Offermann, Jr., October 19, 2002, and August 5, 2004 (written correspondence); October 4, 2002 (personal interview)

Lorraine Ortiz (daughter of **Lou Ortiz**), September 24, 2005, onward (written correspondence)

Lou Ortiz, May 25, 2002, through October 2010 (extensive written correspondence and personal interviews)

(William) Taylor Phillips, 2002 (written correspondence)

Ted Savage, 2002 (written correspondence)

Norm Sherry, September 17, 2002 (written correspondence)

Russ Sullivan, September 13, 2002 (written correspondence)

Dick Teed, January 14, 2003 (written correspondence)

Pat Tomkinson, January 6, 2011 (written correspondence); January 16, 2011 (personal interview)

Babs Weiss (widow of **John Weiss**), July 2016 (written correspondence)

Cy Williams, May 7, 2003 (personal interview)

Bobby Wine, September 20, 2002 (written correspondence)

* Bison players from 1956 team are in bold.

www.ingramcontent.com/pod-product-compliance
Lightning Source LLC
Chambersburg PA
CBHW080454110426
42742CB00017B/2887